CULTURAL
SEMIOSIS

Editor
Hugh J. Silverman

Managing Editor
Norman Bussiere

Associate Editors
James R. Watson
Stephen H. Watson
Forrest Williams
Wilhelm S. Wurzer

Assistant Editors
Gary E. Aylesworth
James Barry Jr.
James Clarke
James Hatley
James G. Keller
Lajla Lund
Norah Martin
Michael L. Sanders
Brian Seitz

Bibliographer
Hélène Volat

Advisory Board
David B. Allison
Hazel Barnes
Robert Bernasconi
Edward S. Casey
Jacques Derrida
M. C. Dillon
Thomas R. Flynn
Michel Haar
Irene E. Harvey
Patrick A. Heelan
Dominique Janicaud
Dalia Judovitz
John Llewelyn
J. N. Mohanty
Graeme Nicholson
Tony O'Connor
Adriaan Peperzak
William J. Richardson
John Sallis
Charles E. Scott
Jacques Taminiaux
Gianni Vattimo
Bernhard Waldenfels
David Wood

CONTINENTAL PHILOSOPHY VI

CULTURAL SEMIOSIS

Tracing the Signifier

Edited with an Introduction by
Hugh J. Silverman

ROUTLEDGE
New York • London

Published in 1998 by
Routledge
29 West 35 Street
New York, NY 10001

Published in Great Britain by

Routledge
11 New Fetter Lane
London EC4P 4EE

Copyright © 1998 by Routledge

Printed in the United States of America

All rights reserved. No part of this book may be reprinted or reproduced or utilized in any form or by any electronic, mechanical, or other means, now known or hereafter invented, including photocopying and recording, or in any information storage or retrieval system without permission in writing from the publishers.

Library of Congress Cataloging-in-Publication Data
Cultural semiosis : tracing the signifier / edited with an introduction
  by Hugh J. Silverman.
      p. cm. — (Continental philosophy ; 6)
   Includes bibliographical references and index.
   ISBN 0-415-91954-1. — ISBN 0-415-91955-x (pb)
   1. Semiotics. 2. Semantics (Philosophy). 3. Cultural—Semiotic
models. I. Silverman, Hugh J. II. Series
B840.C85 1998
149'.94—dc21   97-21459
                                                 CIP

To the Memory
of
LAJLA LUND

Previously published in the series *Continental Philosophy*
Hugh J. Silverman, editor:

I. Philosophy and Non-Philosophy Since Merleau-Ponty

II. Derrida and Deconstruction

III. Postmodernism
    Philosophy and the Arts

IV. Gadamer and Hermeneutics

V. Questioning Foundations
    Truth/Subjectivity/Culture

CONTENTS

Introduction

Hugh J. Silverman

I. Theorizing the Sign

1. *Peter Carravetta*
THE REASONS OF THE CODE:
READING ECO'S
A THEORY OF SEMIOTICS   23

2. *Alessandro Carrera*
CONSEQUENCES OF UNLIMITED SEMIOSIS:
CARLO SINI'S METAPHYSICS
OF THE SIGN AND
SEMIOTICAL HERMENEUTICS   48

3. *François Raffoul*
LACAN AND THE EVENT OF THE SUBJECT   63

4. *Kelly Oliver*
TRACING THE SIGNIFIER
BEHIND THE SCENES OF DESIRE:
KRISTEVA'S CHALLENGE
TO LACAN'S ANALYSIS   83

II. Cultural Signifiers

5. *Stephanie John Sage*
ELIMINATING THE DISTANCE:
FROM BARTHES' *ÉCRITURE-LECTURE*
TO *ÉCRITURE-VUE* 105

6. *Mark Roberts*
THE END(S) OF PICTORIAL REPRESENTATION:
MERLEAU-PONTY AND LYOTARD 129

7. *Debra B. Bergoffen*
MOURNING, WOMAN, AND THE PHALLUS:
LACAN'S *HAMLET* 140

8. *M. Alison Arnett*
A METAPHOR OF THE UNSPOKEN:
KRISTEVA'S SEMIOTIC *CHORA* 154

9. *Hugh J. Silverman*
THE SIGN OF THE ROSE:
FILMING ECO 167

III. The Limits of Semiosis

10. *Julia Kristeva*
PSYCHOANALYSIS AND THE IMAGINARY 181

11. *John Llewelyn*
APPROACHES TO SEMIOETHICS 196

12. *Michael Naas*
STUMPING THE SUN:
TOWARD A POSTMETAPHORICS 219

13. *Adi Ophir*
THE CARTOGRAPHY OF KNOWLEDGE AND POWER:
FOUCAULT RECONSIDERED 239

CONTENTS

Notes

Selective Bibliography

Notes on Contributors

INTRODUCTION

Hugh J. Silverman

Cultural Studies has come of age, and its reach is wide. The study of the humanities can no longer divide itself into philosophy, literature, history, and social theory, expecting all the while to maintain intellectual and disciplinary autonomy. Cultural studies provides links for the philosophical, the literary, the historical, the social theoretical, and much more. The study of culture and cultures can be taken as the object of a philosophical inquiry—like the philosophy of art, the philosophy of literature, or the philosophy of history. However, understood semiotically, cultural signs and signifiers inscribe themselves in the very fabric of cultural practices. As inscribed in these cultural practices, sign production can be effectively studied and investigated philosophically and theoretically.

We have entitled this volume of *Continental Philosophy*, *Cultural Semiosis* not because we are interested simply in the signs that are produced but even more in the producing of the signs themselves—semiosis rather than semiotics. This volume was to be entitled something like *Eco and Semiotics* or *Barthes and Semiology*—to parallel previous volumes such as *Derrida and Deconstruction* or *Gadamer and Hermeneutics*. But we decided that semiotics is sufficiently polyvalent that we should focus on the semiosis rather than the semiotics (the theory of semiosis). Semiosis is the process or activity of sign production—the signing rather than the signs themselves, the indicating rather than the indications, the inscribing rather than the inscriptions. Sign production involves the adventures of the sign or signs—signs in the semiotic or semiological tradition. The key element to any semiotics or semiology is the signifier—and so we have elected to trace the signifier in the continental traditions through its theoretical itineraries from Barthes, Lacan, Eco, and on.

I. Itinerary of the Signifier

What is the signifier? From the time of de Saussure, the signifier (*le signifiant, der Signifikant*) has been understood as a correlate of the signified (*le signifié, das Signifikat*). Together these two terms constitute the elements of the binary pair known as the "sign." The signifier is the word or the acoustical image, and in the strict sense it invokes a concept which corresponds to it. That a particular signifier corresponds to a particular signified is entirely "arbitrary." There is no necessity that a given signifier will have a particular signified. Hence when one employs different languages, a given signified will most likely have a different signifier in each language, and a particular signifier in a particular language will have one or more signifieds within the context of that language. However, the correspondence between a given signified and a given signifier is (once again) arbitrary.

For example, the word "rose" in English corresponds to a variety of signifieds: a flower, a Medieval stained glass window, a woman, and so forth. In French, the signifier *"une rose"* will also correspond to a flower, a Medieval stained glass window, etc. But *"rosé"* will invoke a color or a kind of wine, while in English it lacks the color signified *per se*.

Signifiers plus signifieds make up signs within a determinate language system. A sign obtains its signification (its meaning) only by its difference from other signs in the same language system. A rose is a rose because it is not a tulip, a house, or a mountain. When a rose is a woman or a window or symbol, it is so as a cultural signifier in a cultural language (*langage*) which could cross over the boundaries set by a language of natural signs. A picture of a rose could be a signifier whose signified would not be dependent upon a particular natural language. And that signified could be pronounced in English as "rose," in French as *"une rose,"* in German as *"eine Rose,"* in Italian as "una rosa," etc.

When the picture is pronounced as "a beautiful rose" or a "red rose"—as *"une belle rose," "eine schöne Rose," "una bella rosa,"* etc.— a further specification to the signified is offered, but as different signifiers from different verbal languages. Hence the transfer from a visual signifier to its signified and then on to various verbal signifiers in various languages accounts for a transfer from language to language—visual to verbal ones through the signified(s) in question. The picture of a rose is also distinguishable in that it is different from other pictures. And should it be painted in certain ways, there are various options: it could be read as something else; it could signify something else; it could have another signification than that of a "rose" or a "beautiful rose." It could for instance signify a face, a woman's genitals, a labyrinth, or a variety of other signifieds. When more than one signified is operative in a given signifier, it is said to be polysemous or polyvalent, which is another way of saying that a given signifier has a multiplicity of corresponding signifieds. When one signified is substituted for another and an equivalence between the two is indicated, it is said to be metaphorical or figurative.

Signification arises out of the relating of a signifier to one or more signifieds in a context of other signifiers which are present either in a sentence, discourse, language, or cultural context. Signification is the crucial element in the activity of the sign as it arises out of the relating of signifiers and signifieds. What is complicated in the history of semiology and semiotics is how signification arises and the role the signifier plays in this effect. Two different traditions are given place in this volume: on the one hand, the Saussurian understanding of semiosis; on the other, that arising out of Charles Sanders Peirce's semiotics. Saussurian semiology lies in the background of the kind of formulation one finds in Lévi-Strauss, Lacan, Barthes, Kristeva, and others, while Umberto Eco as a semiotician and Carlo Sini as a semiotic phenomenologist rely heavily on Peirce and his triadic model of semiosis. The very notion of the signifier is derived primarily from Ferdinand de Saussure, and for that reason I focus this introductory sketch on the Saussurian tradition, which has a certain primacy in the essays offered in this volume.

The signifier as formulated by Saussure has undergone some significant transformations in the semiological tradition. From the strict requirement that the signifier be completed by a corresponding—albeit arbitrary—signified, certain structuralists relying on this tradition place more emphasis on the concept of structure. Lévi-Strauss, for instance, is less concerned with the signifier *per se* than he is with the production of cultural structures which are reproduced and reproducible in many different contexts. According to Lévi-Strauss, a structure is made up of signs. Each sign is a piece of a structure. Structures are neither empirical (located in reality) nor transcendental (generating an account or position with respect to the empirical). Each structure is located somewhere between the empirical and the transcendental. Thus a structure is not part of a particular cultural situation, but rather is identifiable in many different cultural situations. Hence the elements of a myth, for instance, constitute a basic plot or story. Once the particularities of the situation are abstracted from the reading, the basic structure can be found to be repeatable in many different cultural contexts. Lévi-Strauss has shown in *Structural Anthropology I* ("Structural Study of Myths") that myths in very different parts of the world have the same structure even though the particular features of each story might be quite different. What makes up the structure is the specific relationship between key elements. These elements are not the same from one myth to another. What is the same is the structure itself. Hence the signifiers will be quite different from one myth to another, but the relationships among the signifiers in a given myth might be identical with the relationships among the signifiers in another myth from another cultural context. Signifiers then are based in a cultural context, but through their function in the structure they are abstractable from that context.

Lacan's structural psychoanalysis is imbued with semiosis. Like Lévi-Strauss, Lacan found connections with semiology in the 1940s and 1950s and reanimated the semiological model in the 1960s. The essays in Lacan's *Écrits* (1966) are filled with the language of semiology. Most notably, Lacan places special emphasis on the signifier rather than on the relation between the signifier and the signified. Lacan, however, does not focus on the sign, for the given relationship between the signifier and the signified is too fixed to allow for the appropriate Freudian reading that he offers. Lacan finds meaning in reading the "chain of signifiers." Signifiers, words, and images, strung along in a sequence reported by the patient after a dream, or in a Joyce novel, or in a Poe short story, for example, provide a syntagmatic line, but often the presumed connection between signifier and the evident signified is misleading at best. The account that "the unconscious is structured like a language" is another way of saying that what is said operates in a structured way, but what is of interest is not what is said but what is not said, what is negated, what is placed in abeyance.

For Lacan, what prevails is the chain of signifiers, and what it signifies is often imbedded in the chain rather than in the one-to-one correspondence of signifier and signified. Hence what is said adjacent to a given signifier might provide more evidence of what it means than what it denotatively states. The sliding of the signification from one signifier to another is what Lacan calls metonymy, while the overdetermination of the signifier in terms of a multiplicity of signifieds is what he calls metaphor.

When "a rose is a rose," that is one thing, but when "a rose is a rose is a rose," that is another. The juxtaposition of the description of "rose" once might be a case of determination and emphasis, but when "a rose is a rose is a rose," there is something obsessive about the claim. Are these three types of "rose"? Are "roses" said to be something more than what they are? When one says that "a rose is a rose," the claim may be one of matter-of-factness, a shunning of anything special about the rose, a reduction of its amorous, magical, charming qualities. But when Gertrude Stein says "a rose is a rose is a rose," the added sense provides intrigue, uniqueness, something unusual. Is "a rose is a rose" like "love is a pebble laughing in the sunlight"? The latter is a Lacanian example of metaphor—a signifier "love" corresponding to a chain of signifiers: "a pebble laughing in the sunlight." But is the sentence "a rose is a rose" of the same order? Logicians would call it a tautology. But the claim itself suggests something more. To say that it is a metaphor is perhaps too much, but to say that it is a tautology is too little. These are not just two signifiers conjoined by the verb to be. How it is said would help to clarify what is signified. Where it is said would help to clarify what is signified. What conjoins what is said would help to clarify what is signified.

And further, when it is "a rose is a rose is a rose," something even more is operative. As a chain of signifiers, it could just be a case of metonymy—a series of signifiers. The unconscious may be at work in a statement of this sort. But how? Is "a rose is a rose" like "a pebble laughing in the sunlight?" If it is, then the chain of signifiers itself indicates that "a rose" is simply a commonplace for something ordinary, or is it just the opposite: something very important, something special. What is crucial here is that the operations of "a rose is a rose is a rose" are multiple and open to a structural analysis of the processes of semiosis. . . .

For Lacan, the Other is always inscribed in the signifying chain in one way or another. One might ask to whom is the statement "a rose is a rose is a rose" addressed? If it is a poem, then is there a reader who is invoked in a special way? Is this a song, a repetition designed to go deeper and deeper into passion and emotion? Or again is it just the opposite, indicating indifference and boredom? The Other may be imaginary, or real, or symbolic. Whichever, the Other is present as an absence. These differences are inscribed in the signifying chain and the task is to bring out the alternatives through the analytic practice of reading.

Roland Barthes was also attracted to alternative readings (and understandings of what writing is) as early as 1953 when he published *Writing Degree Zero*. However, not until 1964, when *Elements of Semiology* appeared, did he begin to address directly the modes of semiosis—the binary pairs of signifier and signified, denotation and connotation, metaphor and metonymy, and so on. Barthes offered clarifications of the traditional Saussurian binary pairs in terms of many of the different semiotic formulations available up to that time. His principal contribution was to show that the relating of the signifier and the signified is an "act or process" which he called "signification." How signification operates in the reading of texts is developed in terms of the signifier/signified relation and its possibilities of ramification.

In 1973, Barthes published his careful reading of Balzac's short story *Sarrasine* entitled *S/Z*. In the introduction, he offers his famous account of "five codes": the semic, the symbolic, the hermeneutic, the proairetic, and the cultural. These provided access to the text through a kind of classification of each lexeme or lexical unit. In effect, the lexemes are signifiers or groups of signifiers which operate in a particular way in the text. Barthes examined each of these and assessed them in terms of the five codes.

The signifier takes a new turn in the deconstructive writings of Jacques Derrida. In 1967, his *Speech and Phenomena* addressed the question of the "sign," but, oddly, through a reading of Husserl rather than Saussure. Yet by showing that the sign in Husserl is divided between the sign as expression and the sign as indication, Derrida invokes a key semiological problem as a way of accessing Husserl's account in the *Logical Investigations*. For Derrida, the Husserlian sign is indecidable: the sign irretrievably caught between the sign as expression of a content and as indication of something other than the sign itself. The sign as *noesis*, as meaning-giving act, expresses a content—a *noema*, an essence, an idea—which is expressive; the sign as *noema*, as content, as the meaning-given, indicates something other than what it itself is: a thing, an object, a thought, etc. The signifier is clearly embedded in this indecidability since what is signified could be either the meaning-giving act, or the meaning-given, or both. In *Of Grammatology*, which Derrida published in the same year (1967), he takes up the question of the signifier in relation to the semiological (by contrast to the phenomenological) tradition. In *Of Grammatology*, the task is to outline the role and status of writing (*écriture*) in relation to language (*langue*). He writes:

> it seems as though the concept of writing—no longer indicating a particular, derivative, auxiliary form of language in general (whether understood as communication, relation, expression, signification, constitution of meaning or thought, etc.), no longer designating the exterior surface, the insubstantial double of a major signifier, *the signifier of the signifier*—is beginning to go beyond the extension of language. In all senses of the word, writing thus *comprehends* language. . . . "Signifier of the signifier" describes . . . the movement of language: in its origin, to be sure, but one can already suspect that an origin whose structure can be expressed as "signifier of the signifier" conceals and erases itself in its own production. There the signified always already functions as a signifier. The secondarity that it seemed possible to ascribe to writing alone affects all signifieds in general, affects them always already, the moment *they enter the game*. There is not a single signified that escapes, even if recaptured, the play of signifying references that constitute language. The advent of writing is the advent of this play; today such a play is coming into its own effacing the limit starting from which one had thought to regulate the circulation of signs, drawing along with it all the reassuring signifieds, reducing all the strongholds, all the out-of-bounds shelters that watched over the field of language. This, strictly speaking, amounts to destroying the concept of "sign" and its entire logic.[1]

With Derrida the whole concept of the sign is placed in question, if not "destroyed." And the sign in question is unquestionably the Saussurian sign. The Saussurian sign allows for the constitution of language as in some way enclosing and encircling the sign and its components. For Saussure, language is made up of signs, and no signs stand outside a language. They can of course partake of another language but that does not in any way minimize their placement within a language (*une langue*). What Derrida is saying in this opening passage to *Of Grammatology* is that "writing," insofar as it is "the signifier of the signifier" and that which signifies a language, indicates that writing is somehow outside the language which it signifies. But by definition nothing that signifies can be outside the signifying language. This means that writing as the signifier of the signifier is both inside language and outside language: inside, as part of the language system which signifies and outside, as the language system which it signifies. And this unusual status which writing occupies in relation to language—as signifier of the signifier—is precisely what places the whole concept of the sign in question.

Julia Kristeva reinvokes the question of the sign and semiology in her groundbreaking study *Revolution in Poetic Language* (1974). Kristeva distinguishes between the symbolic and the semiotic. For her, the symbolic involves thetic language—postulates, affirmations, assertions—as in Frege's theory of reference, Husserl's theory of intentionality, and Freud's psychoanalytic postulates about functions of the ego. Symbolic language makes claims about reality, affirms by positing what is, and asserts truths about the natural, social, and cultural worlds in which we live. By contrast, the semiotic provides an alternative to the male affirmative postulates of the symbolic. The semiotic is described as a *chora*— the Platonic receptacle, but also the origin of the idea of the chorus—a field of nondeterminate flow and flux. Here semiosis is given its fullest sense of activity and motility. The semiotic is the space of emotion, feeling, drives, waves of energy, bodily rhythms, poetic language.

Hence in Kristeva's work, the signifier takes a significant turn. When part of symbolic formation, the signifier thetically indicates objects and aspects of natural and cultural reality. However, when part of the differential movements of semiosis, the signifier becomes part of a flow of language. In this case, determinations of the speaking subject are placed in suspension in favor of extremes of sense, feeling, expectation, and mood. The signifier is no longer an instrument of scientific knowledge production but rather part of the flow of language—as expressed in poetry, horror, melancholy, love, faith, and estrangement (each of which have served as topics of books by Kristeva). And it is not irrelevant that she has elected to write novels in recent years in order to express her ideas semiotically.

Umberto Eco—the champion of "unlimited semiosis"—has also found it effective to write novels, parodies, and other fictional texts in order to demonstrate how semiotics works. Early on, Eco championed the "open work" as a way of avoiding delimiting and close-minded interpretations of literary and other works. He then turned to the role of the reader—what he has called the Model Reader—in order to demonstrate how semiosis works. In his famous *Theory of Semiotics*, he introduced the idea of sign and code production. While he worked primarily with a strict communication model in which a transmitter sends a message to a receiver, he also wanted to take account of the productive aspect of sign activity. The Model Reader is given the task of interpreting the work—but the Model Reader is not any particular person and, in this sense, sign production invokes such a Model Reader irrespective of any particular reading of the text or work. The Model Reader sets the "limits to interpretation" (a theme Eco has taken up in recent years).

Speaking of symbols, Eco writes:

> If we take it in the sense of logicians and mathematicians, then a symbol is either a signifier correlated to its meaning by a law, that is, by a precise convention, and as such interpretable by other signifiers, or a variable that can be bound in many ways but that, once it has acquired a given value, cannot represent other values within the same context. If we take it in the sense of Hjelmslev, we find as instances of symbol the Cross, the Hammer and Sickle, emblems, and heraldic images. In this sense symbols are allegories.[2]

The first sense of symbol—that of logicians and mathematicians—is singular and unique. It is designed to avoid alternative meaning, alternative interpretations. It follows a law, and it either means something determinate or can be interpreted by other signifiers. Similarly the notion of symbol can be variable, but once determined, its meaning or signification is set. A rose, for instance, might be a symbol for love, a woman, or divine Grace.

Once it is set, its meaning will be determinate literally or on different levels.

Eco derives the second sense from Goethe: "symbols are signifiers that convey imprecise clouds or nebulae of meaning that they leave continually unexploited or unexploitable" (*LI*, 8). This latter sense is perhaps closer to how Kristeva understands the semiotic and how Eco himself understands "unlimited semiosis," except in the end both want to understand—even tame—the unruly aspects of semiosis: Eco through semiotic analysis, Kristeva through psychoanalytic interpretation and understanding.

While I have attempted to trace this itinerary of the signifier through some of the major figures of the tradition in which it is inscribed, there are of course other names and theories that play an important role in this narrative. Merleau-Ponty—while not in any way a semiotician—was often tempted by the importance of signs, and it is no accident that his last collection of essays was entitled *Signs* (1960). Merleau-Ponty saw real connections between how he understood phenomenology and its relation to the semiology which had begun to appear in French thought as the 1960s approached.[3]

Beginning most substantially with *The Order of Things* (1966), Michel Foucault offers a critique of both hermeneutics and semiology by indicating that an archaeology of knowledge is not entrusted with interpreting signs but rather with developing the spaces of knowledge production as they occur within a historical context. While the epistemes of an epoch can be elicited from the multiplicity of discursive practices at a given time, the signifiers that proliferate within a discursive field make such an archaeology possible. Foucault would hardly give the name "cultural semiosis" to these discursive practices, but such a name might not be inappropriate.

Similarly Carlo Sini, whose own philosophical position arose out of the context of Enzo Paci's phenomenological marxism, has shown in recent years the virtues of linking phenomenology and semiology. The signifier is now to be understood as part of a semiological hermeneutics in which the enchantment of meaning is also linked to the adventures of the sign and to Eco's notion of "unlimited semiosis." Most recently, he has put this question in terms of an "ethics of writing" in which philosophy, as writing, questions its own status as writing and raises the problem of writing *per se*.

The last, but not least, figure to be mentioned here is Jean-François Lyotard. While we will devote an entire future volume of *Continental Philosophy* to his thought, it is worth noting how his sense of the signifier plays a role in the postmodern condition. The modern is full of signifiers, as were previous epochs. The marks of the postmodern operate in the interstices between signifiers which present their meanings but which also present the unpresentable. This latter presentation of the unpresentable in presentation itself is a postmodern event which occurs in the juxtaposition of signifiers: roses alongside churches and guns (as in "Guns and Roses"), alongside primrose paths and promises of rose gardens, alongside the "War of the Roses" and the Tournament of Roses. . . .

II. The Practice of Cultural Semiosis

This volume is divided into three parts: 1) Theorizing the Sign, 2) Cultural Signifiers, 3) Limits of Semiosis. The basic idea is to understand what is meant by the sign with its components: the signifier, the signified, and the signification that arises out of the relating of the two. Once it is clear what a sign is, it will then be possible to look at some examples of how the signifier operates as a cultural product and cultural effect—in art, in theater, in philosophy, in film. From there we will consider some implications of semiosis in alternative directions, such as those offered by Kristeva, Derrida, Levinas, and Foucault.

We begin with an account of Umberto Eco's *Theory of Semiotics*. Peter Carravetta reads Eco's tract in detail and traces the theory of the sign, keeping in mind the whole tradition I have outlined here. Carravetta looks at theory construction and how semiotic theory serves as a basis for a semiotic method as a device for interpretation. He indicates how theory and method are inextricably connected and interdependent in giving an account of signification and communication. And he demonstrates how a semiotic aesthetic can provide a basis for social and cultural criticism. For instance, Carravetta states that Eco's example of Gertrude Stein's line "A rose is a rose is a rose is a rose" (which we have examined in some detail) is a case of overcoding, since the excessive redundancy of the verse produces "an increase in informational possibilities." This happens, Carravetta claims, because a Reader or

Receiver is so "estranged" or "detoured" that he or she immediately begins connecting with different connotative subcodes, such as the allegorical and the iconological. Reading these codes and subcodes allows for a multiplicity of interpretations which elaborate the movements and dimensions of semiosis.

Alessandro Carrera follows with a further investigation of the question of "unlimited semiosis" as set forth by Eco and as placed in a phenomenological–hermeneutic context by the major Italian philosopher in that tradition today, Carlo Sini. Sini stresses the notion of gesture as an originary event and as what reveals itself in pointing out, in indicating, in fingering something, in signifying, in designating. By linking up the question of originary event and indication, Carrera shows how Sini brings together the ontological hermeneutics of Martin Heidegger and the semiotics of Charles Sanders Peirce. By beginning with Eco and Sini, we show the flexibility of cultural semiosis and the multiple directions that it can follow.

We then turn to the Saussurian tradition through the work of Lacan with a valuable essay by François Raffoul on the paradoxical role of the subject in Lacan's structural psychoanalysis and in the signifying chain. Raffoul claims that Lacan elaborates a theory of the subject, but that this amounts to a *calling into question* of the subject. He shows that the subject is a linguistic being and that it appears only in and by the signifier. This conception of the subject leads however to a circle: if the subject is no longer defined except in relation to the signifier, it is nevertheless also true that the signifier, in turn, is only defined in relation to the subject. Lacan's treatment of the subject seems then to oscillate between two poles: 1) the disappearance of the subject under the signifier which represents it and 2) its paradoxical preservation in Lacan's theory as a formation of the Symbolic.

Correspondingly, Kelly Oliver gives a detailed account of how Kristeva makes use of Lacan's notion of the signifier in the context of love and desire. She shows how Kristeva challenges Lacan's account of the logic or structure of identification in the mirror stage. Kristeva offers a material logic based on reduplication and metaphor, which prefigures Lacan's metonymy of desire. Oliver shows that Kristeva's semiotic operates somewhere between the Lacanian Imaginary and the Real. For Kristeva, love operates according to a logic of metaphor (and imaginary love) which is set up *before* the metonymy of desire. Kristeva's emphasis on imaginary love over desire (which is already implicated in the play of the signifier and therefore the Symbolic) affects psychoanalytic practice. Therefore Kristeva seeks to listen behind signifiers and their play of meanings to the music in language which "signifies" the operations of the Imaginary. An example of how Kristeva develops precisely this kind of attention to the Imaginary is given in her essay entitled "Psychoanalysis and the Imaginary" that opens the third part of our volume dealing with the Limits of Semiosis.

In the second part, we take up cultural signifiers, beginning with a Barthesian study of Botticelli's famous Renaissance platonic painting *Primavera* by Stephanie Sage. We feel that this essay provides an excellent sense of how Barthes' semiology works and how it can be applied to a specific visual example. Sage develops the concept she calls *écriture-vue* as a way of accessing the painting by contract to the study of writing (*écriture*) and verbal texts. She claims that Barthes' five codes—semic, symbolic, proairetic, hermeneutic, and cultural—arm the viewer to pursue the "magic of the signifier," to explore the richness of meaning in the text, and to reconstitute it through the language of lexical signs and codes. As we operate the text, we are forced to confront the culturally determined ways in which we see and interpret.

Continuing the theme of how to understand visual texts semiotically, Mark Roberts claims that two basic traditional ways to think about pictorial representation have tended to prevail: one considers the picture from the perspective of the psychology of visual perception, focusing on the process of image making; the other is based on language-oriented theories, which tend to analogize pictures to verbal narratives, emphasizing resemblance and symbolic formation. Roberts suggests that an alternative is provided by the aesthetics of Maurice Merleau-Ponty and Jean-François Lyotard. Roberts reports that various bodily, libidinal, figural, gestural, and perceptual experiences have primacy in their understanding of painting rather than static symbolic or theoretical constructs (created images or visual data that stand for something else). He points out that for Merleau-Ponty and Lyotard, pictorial representation is constituted by nonrational forces—desires, drives, affections, perceptions—which are not necessarily reducible to intelligible theoretical models. Merleau-Ponty and Lyotard seek ways of accessing these areas philosophically without offering accounts of image-making processes or accounts that are reducible to symbolic formations. As with Kristeva, the issue is one of getting at the processes of semiosis underlying symbolic forms, ways in which what Merleau-Ponty calls "visibility" operates without reduction to an algorithm, ways in which what Lyotard calls "figures"—image-figures, form-figures, matrix-figures—provide an articulation of desire, the libidinal, of gestures. Here semiosis is understood as getting at the difference between seeing and knowing, not reducing the pictorial to a symbolic system.

Another frame in which cultural signifiers operate is in the theater. Debra Bergoffen takes the example of Shakespeare's *Hamlet* as her point of departure. She notes three important features: 1) a woman is at the center of the play, 2) the issue of mourning is crucial to the drama, and 3) the theme of being at the hour/desire of the other pervades the play. She suggests that *Hamlet* may be read as the story of the usurpation of the place of the phallus by a widowed queen, a woman whose ambiguous place in the signifying chain allows her to play a game of *jouissance* while appearing to accept the law of patriarchy. Similar to the case of Antigone, patriarchy perpetuates the myth of the phallus as masculine by refusing to recognize that the legitimacy of the phallus depends on the mediation of the woman. Only when the woman refuses her invisible mediating role, only when she either is barred from mourning or refuses to mourn, does patriarchy discover the phallic powers of the woman. This invisible mediating role is once again a movement of semiosis which operates at the symbolic level only when mourning is refused—either by the woman herself or by her culture.

Alison Arnett makes this same point by looking at Kristeva's account of the *chora*. She focuses on spatial metaphors and particularly women's space understood in terms of the semiotic *chora*. It is noteworthy that just as Kelly Oliver looks for the nonsymbolic space between the Lacanian Imaginary and Real, so too Alison Arnett focuses on the spatial metaphors that characterize women's space. And one could say that Deborah Bergoffen reading Lacan directly emphasizes the invisible mediating role of women as other than the symbolic phallic centrality in which Hamlet's mother finds herself. In any case, each of these accounts of semiosis stresses the role of the signifier as engaged in a semiotic spatial process and not as a symbolic determination.

The final essay in the second part takes up cultural signifiers and unlimited semiosis in Umberto Eco's *The Name of the Rose*. The question of the rose has already been raised on a number of occasions here. The issue now is specifically the "rose" in the title of Eco's novel and the subsequent film. The rose could be described here and now as designating women's spatiality—a spatiality that is sometimes transformed into a religious, specifically Christian— understanding of semiosis. The internationality of the film's cast, its characters, and its scope places the question of semiosis also into a political context—a context in which semiosis spills over national boundaries, over the limitations of symbolic determination, over the specificities of a textual mystery, over the constitution of a name.

Kristeva's work plays an important role in the development of this volume of *Continental Philosophy*. In opening the final part of the volume, we include an essay by Kristeva herself as a way of both rounding out the first two parts and of signaling the question of the limits of a semiosis that turns into a scientific theory, that becomes symbolic, that closes itself off from cultural experience. Drawing upon some examples from her own therapeutic practice, Kristeva shows how certain emotional areas such as melancholy and artistic creativity are strangers to the kind of scientific, theoretical determinations that we rely upon in symbolic interaction. She shows how the imaginary opens up spaces—choral, semiotic, feminine, poetic—which require expression and understanding.

John Llewelyn develops semiosis in the direction of what he calls "semioethics," namely a semiotics informed by the work of Levinas and Derrida. Llewelyn points out that classical semiotics or semiology includes: *pragmatics* (the theory of the relation between signs and their users); *semantics* (the theory of the relation between signs and their meaning or truth); and *syntactics* (the theory of the relation of one sign to another). His essay outlines how a semioethics offers a pre-contractual approach as a "calling itself" or "calling as such," except that the "itself," the "as such," and the "as"—classically defined—are what semioethics disrupts by recognizing that "expression" necessarily results in exteriority (and this undermines all phenomenological and semiological claims to the interiority of expression). This exteriority of expression demonstrates in different ways in Derrida and Levinas the alterity of the subject, a point which is hinted at in Raffoul's account of the "eventual subject" in his reading of Lacan. With Llewelyn, through disruption of the various notions of the interior subject engaged in speaking (*parole*), semioethics brings classical semiotics to its limits.

Michael Naas links semiosis to the question of the status of a "natural sign." He attempts to rethink this paradoxical notion by looking at Jacques Derrida's "White Mythology." He shows how Derrida's understanding of metaphor and metaphoricity (what makes metaphors metaphoric) calls for a rethinking of the alternative between a natural and conventional theory of the sign. Although he might have chosen "a rose" (as in "a rose is a rose is a rose"), Naas takes the example of the scene in Homer's *Odyssey* where Odysseus establishes his identity before Penelope by means of the olive tree bed post that he himself had once fashioned. Naas shows how the bed post must be read as an essentially ambivalent "natural sign"—a sign that is rooted and grounded in the earth—absolutely certain and yet open to being read as a human cultural sign, as narrative, and, thus, open to the possibility of exchange, reproduction, and falsification. This means that all semiosis—even that built upon natural conditions—is always already cultural semiosis.

The final essay turns to Michel Foucault as offering another version of semiosis beginning as early as the 1960s. Adi Ophir points out that Foucault was seeking a coherent account of the way "power" and "subjectivity" were used. Spatial metaphors are often mixed with literal spatial descriptions. Different spatial frameworks or settings are distinguished as if space were a genus with its own species, and no explicit distinction is made between space and place. This spatial logic of power/knowledge and, more generally, the logic of social space, even though related to the economic, the political, and the institutional, cannot be reduced to any of these layers of analysis. To ignore the spatial factor is to ignore a crucial aspect in the history of discourse, and, more generally, of power relations. Ophir suggests that Foucault's famous formula "power/knowledge" should be amended and rewritten as "space/power/knowledge." This affirmation of the place of space in relation to knowledge and power is another access to the choral, semiotic space that Kristeva develops, the notion of spatial difference as in Derridean discourse, and the domain of unlimited semiosis that pervades Eco's and Sini's positions.

Through this itinerary—with various formulations of the signifier and signifying spaces—cultural semiosis begins to take shape. Key themes such as the role of semiotics, cultural theory, the deconstruction of the subject, and the choral space between the Imaginary and the Real establish the conditions for an unlimited semiosis. And this notion of unlimited semiosis becomes the basis for an account of cultural semiosis—reading paintings like Botticelli's *Primavera*, reading pictorial representation in terms of gesture and bodily spatiality, understanding women's role as one of invisible mediation as opposed to the symbolic and phallic domains into which she tends to be drawn, women's space as unspoken, and filmic space in which even a name can enter the field of semiosis. These notions of cultural semiosis are rethought in terms of the Imaginary, semioethics, metaphoricity, and the spatiality of knowledge and power. Cultural semiosis enters the spaces of everyday language, visuality, sexuality, and symbolization—reading them, interpreting them, seeking to understand them theoretically, and providing some tools for what has come to be called cultural studies.

Acknowledgments

Despite the hiatus since the appearance of the last volume of *Continental Philosophy* in 1993, we are pleased to reanimate the series at this time and with the hope that the subsequent volumes in preparation (CP-7: *Philosophy and Desire*; CP-8: *Lyotard: Aesthetics and Politics*; CP-9: *Foucault: Archaeology/Genealogy*; and CP-10: *Postmodern Ethics*) will resume the kind of rhythm established in the first half decade of the *Continental Philosophy* project.

Several occurrences have taken place in the interim. We are dedicating this volume to the memory of Lajla Lund, who served as Assistant Editor for a number of years after working first as Editorial Assistant. She devoted many hours to the completion of this volume while also attempting to write her dissertation in Philosophy at Stony Brook on Kierkegaard and Ricoeur. She died in January 1996. Lajla was enthusiastic about *Continental Philosophy*, and we are happy to remember her fondly here in print.

In 1993, Norman Bussiere joined us as Managing Editor. Without his dedication, persistence, and enthusiasm, we might not have been able to move ahead with these volumes. He has been a source of joy and delight. James Clarke's generous contribution over the years to the development of *Continental Philosophy* and to this volume is greatly appreciated. As always, I am also grateful to James Hatley for his help with the endnotes and his continued dedication to the *Continental Philosophy* project, which he helped to conceive back in 1985. Gary Aylesworth has provided some of his precious little free time to the volume in spite of his duties as Chair of the Philosophy Department at Eastern Illinois University. The newest Assistant Editors, Jim Keller and Michael Sanders, generously developed some late hours in the final stages of production. Finally, as for all of our volumes, thanks goes to Hélène Volat for providing the core of the bibliography. Contributors have also assisted us by providing their bibliographical recommendations, and I am of course very happy to acknowledge their generous support (and patience) over the years it took to produce this volume.

Each essay—as in all *Continental Philosophy* volumes—is extensively reviewed in order to maintain the highest quality and effectiveness of the contributions. Although invited and accepted in the light of the overall conception, each essay undergoes an extremely rigorous editorial and review process, often resulting in significant rewriting of essays for stylistic, syntactical, conceptual, and philosophical improvement. I am grateful to all the readers and referees of these essays—typically anonymous and therefore their names cannot be given here—who have helped to ensure the excellence of contributions to this volume. Because several of the essays were not originally written in English, we spent many exhausting hours bringing them to a readable English before asking the authors to consider our revisions. We hope that this effort will also be appreciated by our readers.

With this volume, Jim Watson of the Philosophy Department at Loyola University in New Orleans joins the staff as Associate Editor. His special contribution comes through the photos he has provided for each section and for his remastering of the Botticelli painting in connection with Stephanie Sage's demonstration of Barthes' semiological code theory. We are delighted to add this visual component, which he initiated in his own essay on "Uneasy

Images" for *Continental Philosophy V: Questioning Foundations: Truth/Subjectivity/Culture* (Routledge, 1993).

Maureen MacGrogan, one of the best editors in the business, has been rigorous yet supportive in seeing this volume along. Adrian Driscoll has continued to keep an encouraging and watchful eye on the project. Routledge is a new company now. We began *Continental Philosophy* under the aegis of the London office of Routledge and Kegan Paul in the mid-1980s. It subsequently underwent a number of changes under the Routledge imprint. Now one can expect another look in the new independent Routledge. We are especially grateful to Colin Jones for his support and decisiveness in continuing the commitment to *Continental Philosophy*.

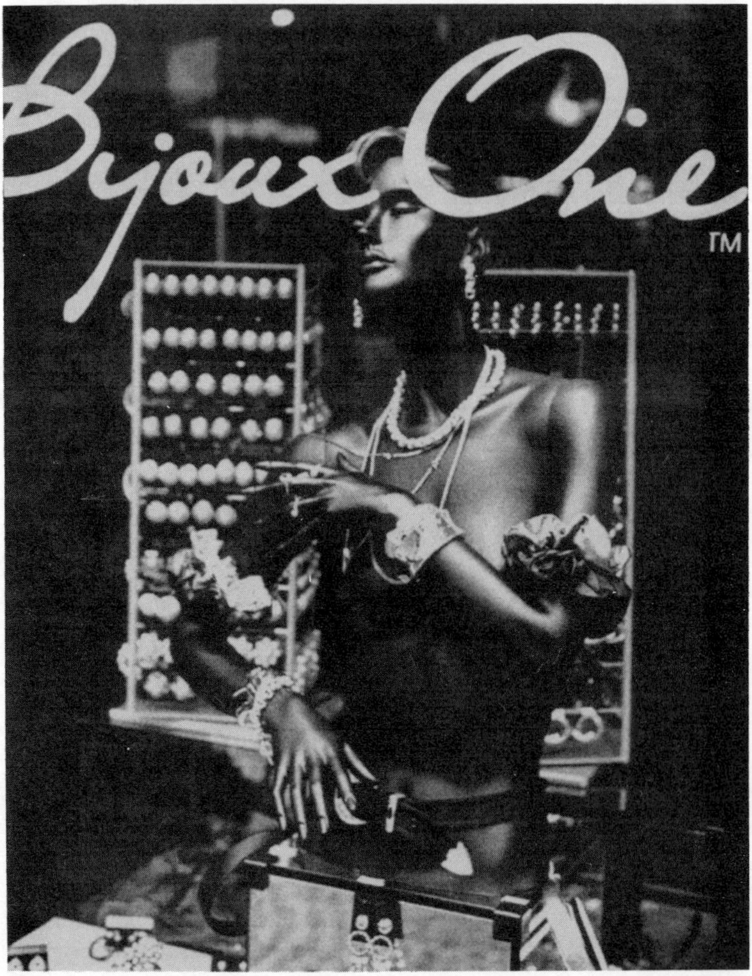
Bijoux One
TM

PART I
THEORIZING THE SIGN

Chapter 1

THE REASONS OF THE CODE: READING ECO'S *A THEORY OF SEMIOTICS*

Peter Carravetta

I Think I Am a Verb   —Ulysses S. Grant

Umberto Eco's *A Theory of Semiotics*[1] is widely regarded as one of the most comprehensive treatments of semiosis.[2] It is also a turning point in Eco's itinerary through various forms of interpretive thought.[3] Moreover, in the history and development of semiotics in Italy, Eco's opus is a milestone, a historiographical moment of consolidation as well as a compass needle that locates paths and sets agendas for subsequent study.[4] After a necessarily compressed synthesis of some fundamental tenets of *A Theory of Semiotics*, I propose to study three specific aspects:

First, how the theory *qua* Theory is actually constructed, taking into account its component elements, their definition, and their use.

Second, how a *semiotic method* is construed. Here I will consider its functioning and meaning with respect to the question of interpretation. The critical assumption (developed elsewhere)[5] is that Theory and Method are inextricably connected and interdependent. But theory is basically related to ontology and ideology, whereas Method is the formal–epistemological component necessary for grounding and legitimizing theory.

Third, how semiotics treats the arts and offers a semiotic aesthetic, or an aesthetic semiotic. This will bear on the relationship between semiotics and social and cultural criticism.

In general, then, I propose to reread one of the most important and successful texts in the discipline of semiotics in order to gauge its coherence against its claims to universal validity, to question its metaphysical underpinnings, and to point out some of the paradoxes of a semiotically informed cultural criticism.

I. Topos

According to Eco, a *"general semiotic theory* [should be able] to explain every case of sign-function in terms of underlying systems of elements mutually correlated by one or more codes" (*TS*, 3). Moreover, a general semiotics "should consider: a) a *theory of codes* and b) a *theory of sign production.*" According to Eco:

> In principle, a semiotics of signification entails a theory of codes, while a semiotics of communication entails a theory of sign production.
>
> The distinction between a theory of codes and a theory of sign-production does not correspond to the ones between *'langue'* and *'parole'*, competence and performance, syntactics (and semantics) and pragmatics. (*TS*, 4)

Stressing the shift *away from* structural linguistics,[6] Eco continues:

> It is not by chance that the discriminating categories are the ones of signification and communication. As will be [demonstrated], there is a signification system (and therefore a code) when there is the socially conventionalized possibility of generating sign-functions.... [T]here is on the contrary a communication process when the possibilities provided by a signification system are exploited in order to physically produce expressions for many practical purposes. (*TS*, 4)

If, as Eco indicates, semiotics comprehends and subsumes the other models of signification and communication, e.g., Chomskian, Saussurean, etc., he is also suggesting an even broader horizon, such that ideally it should replace philosophy itself.[7] The terrain disclosed to inquiry by this discipline is also a sweeping vision:

> semiotics studies all cultural processes as *processes of communication*. Therefore each of these processes would seem to be permitted by an underlying *system of signification*. (*TS*, 8)[8]

Eco goes on to explain that the two semiotics, that of communication and that of signification, are not "mutually exclusive approaches in opposition" (*TS*, 8).[9]

According to Eco, the communicative process requires that there be the *passage of a signal* from a *source* through a *transmitter* along a *channel* and *addressed* to a *receiver*. Following Jakobson's model, Eco naturally assumes that any message will entail different occurrences of the five corresponding functions: referential, emotive, imperative, phatic, and metalinguistic (*TS*, 262). It follows from these premises that *signification* is possible only if a code exists *already*, i.e., "if something stands for something else" that was or could be. We shall return to this key formulation again and again.

A first consequence of this axiom is that all the communicative stages acquire meaning, signification, or a reason to exist provided that the sign (or signal) represents or substitutes for something else. This raises some problems, as if whenever some sort of exchange is deemed to be meaningful, communication simultaneously hides or obscures something else. The *receiver* understands, or rather "decodes," what this sign (or cluster of signs) means[10] because it falls within a network of systems and rules which *the receiver* already knows and where the sign becomes the sole bearer of necessary information.[11]

II. The Field of Inference

Underlying Eco's book is what Ferdinand de Saussure *did not* say. Saussure never clarified what the signified was, "leaving it half way between a mental image, a concept and a[n undefined] psychological reality [*non altrimenti circoscritta*]," which is given within that global plenum called society (*TS*, 14–15). Therefore,

> according to Saussure signs 'express' ideas and provided that he did not share a Platonic interpretation of the term 'idea,' such ideas must be mental events that concern a human mind. Thus the sign is implicitly regarded as a communicative device [*artificio comunicativo*] taking place between two human beings intentionally aiming to communicate or to express something. (*TS*, 15)

Now we begin to perceive stress points in the unfolding of the Theory. We read that all semiological systems are "strictly conventionalized systems of artificial signs, such as military signals, rules of etiquette, and visual alphabets" (*TS*, 15). However, these systems make sense if the sign is taken as a communicative "device," that is, a man-made *art*ificial "thing" which entails intentionality and production and thus ultimately speaks to a consciousness! But if consciousness cannot be coded, it does not exist. Consciousness and intentionality are not thematized in Eco's *Theory of Semiotics*, and would at any rate follow upon the explication and adoption of the rationalist notion of *inference*: "there exist acts of inference which must be recognized as semiosic acts"[12] (*TS*, 17). Inference, however, needs the sign as a necessary support, as a floating *Grund* of sorts, and intentionality is subjected to the same kind of radical semiotic critique, as will be the intensional fallacy and the extensional fallacy, which Eco discusses later with reference to the *theory of codes* (*TS*, 58–59, 62–66).

Eco states that "semiotics is mainly concerned with signs as social forces" (*TS*, 65). Understanding these social forces is complex, owing to their multifaceted functions, their being originally polymorphous, capable of suggesting different conceptions of thinking and the universe. From ancient times down through Hobbes, "a sign was defined as the evident antecedent of a consequent or the consequent of an antecedent when similar consequences have been previously observed," but the sign was also reconceptualized as "an entity from which the present or the future or past existence of another being is inferred [and] as a proposition constituted by a valid and revealing connection to its consequent" (*TS*, 17).

Eco must therefore make some fundamental assumptions in order to proceed with any of these definitions of the sign and the connected problem of intentionality/inference–signification. He is well aware of the critical risks: "Probably this straightforward identification of inference and signification leaves many shades of difference unexplored: it only needs to be corrected by adding the expression 'when this association is culturally recognized and systematically coded'" (*TS*, 17). We must keep on referring to these "shades of difference" because they will help us in the two-fold task of seeing what semiotics includes, subsumes, explains, and what it ignores, expels, or cannot know.

For Eco, Saussure's ideas had this limitation: the problem of the *signified*, by remaining unresolved, continued to be an "open" question, a question he had addressed in his earlier work on the basis of non- or pre-semiotic philosophies and criticism.[13] Though the signified would later be the object of specific studies in the areas of semantics and pragmatics,[14] the signifier still took center stage in his research of the early seventies. And the signifier was traceable. After all Eco's historical–theoretical recollecting illustrates the ample and yet unharnessed possibilities of the notion of the sign, taking advantage of its concrete, empirical dimension. He can now transfer the notion of "communicative device" onto the plane of Peirce's logical conception of the sign.

III. Sign, Absence, Theory

Peirce's work is crucial to the theory of semiotics. Peirce's definitions appear time and again in Eco as in the following passage from the *Collected Papers* 5.488:

> By semiosis I mean an action, an influence, which is, involves, a cooperation of *three* subjects, such as [the] sign, its object and its interpretant, this tri-relative influence not being in anyway resolvable into actions between pairs. (*TS*, 15)

Hence the sign is, citing Peirce, "something which stands to somebody for something in some respects or capacity" (*Collected Papers* 2.228). Furthermore, "when—on the basis of an underlying rule—something actually presented to the perception of the addressee *stands for* something else, there is *signification*" (*TS*, 8). Eco adds that "the subjects of Peirce's 'semiosis' are not *human subjects* but rather three abstract semiotic entities, the dialectic of which is not affected by concrete communicative behavior" (*TS*, 15, my emphasis).

While Eco's account of Peirce seems to leave concrete behavior aside, his concurrent adoption of Morris suggests that something else must be going on here. First, Eco claims that "human subjects" are not involved. But how can this be if semiotics deals with cultural (or better yet: cultured, acculturated) communication (cf. Pareyson, *Apocalittici e Integrati*, 354–57)? The cultural is in principle a "human" product. Second, claiming that its dialectic is not affected by concrete communicative behavior suggests that it is removed, abstracted, or set apart from material or "real" communication. Such a position betrays formalistic and idealistic matrices.[15]

Given the exclusion of human subjects and concrete communicative behavior from the conception of semiotic entities, the question of the relationship between Theory and Method, of how ideas get translated into reality, forcefully reemerges. Is the Theory so metaphysical, so essentialist, so strongly inclusive (and therefore exclusive) and self-legitimating that, no matter what happens in actual human communicative intercourse, precepts will hold and validity will not be affected? Does not the "application" of the Theory need to be translated into a Method practiced through human agency? And doesn't this have an effect on the very Theory (Eco's *Theory*) from which it is derived?

Yet if we assume, as Eco seems to do, that method and theory are unrelated and can be studied as two autonomous areas of research, then does not semiotic theory aspire to timelessness, eternity, universalism, and totality?[16] This would make it a "strong" theory in the tradition of Aristotle,[17] Aquinas,[18] Locke,[19] and Kant, grounded in necessary but unprovable axioms and deducing everything from them. Even Peirce's triadic schema left the door open for a more existential and ontological conception of human agency. This trilateral epistemology which was potentially predisposed toward ontological hermeneutics[20] must therefore be reduced to a more manageable dualism, as in Charles Morris's semiotics.[21]

In *Theory of Semiotics*, Eco cites this key passage from Morris's 1938 essay on "The Foundations of a Theory of Signs":

> Semiotics, then, is not concerned with the study of a particular kind of object, but with ordinary objects insofar (and only insofar) as they participate in semiosis. (*TS*, 16)

This definition, resonant with the premises and the promise of one of the major efforts in twentieth-century culture to come up with a Unified Theory,[22] seems also to be the ontological–theoretical foundation of Eco's semiotics of the code. Such a semiotics is not preoccupied with the real, with any objects or things, unless they are first translated into signs and *exist as signs* . . . but not necessarily *for* something or for someone not readily present. The center of the universe, the *fundamentum inconcussum,* is an abstract concept/thing which necessarily harks back, or points forward, to something else, to an elsewhere. One gets the feeling that Hermes is showing only one side of himself, or telling half the truth.

Fortunately, this phantom is exposed and subject to discursive forces which can be contested or critiqued. If we read it metaphorically, as an imaginative *figura,* as the very definition of sign— *"something standing for something else"* (TS, 16)—it invokes its own ghost and acquires a double personality of which one is always present while the other gropes in the dark-infested background. In order to prevent the human interpreter from entering the space— time between Theory and Method, between signification and communication, he or she also must first be changed into sign-entities, into sign-functions. Thus Eco's final touch:

> The only modification that I would introduce into Morris' definition is that the interpretation by an interpreter, which would seem to characterize a sign, must be understood as the *possible* interpretation by a *possible* interpreter. (TS, 16)

In other words, this last gate open to a human subject is sealed off unless it is an instrument of the chain established by the sequence of signs during communication. Thus it can be analyzed within a verifiable statistical calculus, such as the model "Q," which appears in later sections of *Theory of Semiotics*[23] (TS, 121–124). The notion of "human" here is not very human at all because it exists and makes sense *only* as a sign—whether agent or reagent, shifter or variable, semantic marker or icon—*within* a preestablished code.

IV. Interpreter and Interpretant

The question of the status and function of the interpreter is discussed in detail in the chapter on a "Theory of Codes" (TS, 48–150, especially 68–72). Developing and adapting the Peirce–Morris axis—although not unresponsive to the most stimulating theories in linguistics, such as that of Hjelmslev (TS, 51–54)—Eco writes:

> *The interpretant is not the interpreter* (even if a confusion of this type occasionally arises in Peirce). The interpretant is that

> which guarantees the validity of the sign, even in the absence of the interpreter. (*TS*, 68)

Neither a "he" nor a "she," but perhaps more appropriately an "it," the interpretant is "another representation which is referred to the same 'object,' " in other words, another sign-function. Citing Peirce,[24] Eco writes that a sign is "anything which determines something else (its *interpretant*) to refer to an object to which itself refers (its *object*) in the same way, the interpretant becoming in turn a sign, and so on *ad infinitum*" (*TS*, 69). We may ponder here whether this understanding of the interpretant *as sign* doesn't make the interpretant somehow superfluous, contingent, and unnecessary to the basic ontology of semiotics. We have already seen how Peirce's triadic scheme was pushed toward a bipolar or dichotomous matrix. Eco attempts to make semiotics a philosophic and scientific discipline: "The idea of the interpretant makes a theory of signification a rigorous science of cultural phenomena, while detaching it from the metaphysics of the referent" (*TS*, 70).

Is this possible? Is reference so easily disposed of? Metaphysics means, if nothing else, reflection on something: thinking, deciding, referring, interpreting, understanding. If these aspects are removed, in what way can we still speak of a "semiotics of experience," or a "semiotic analysis of" anything, from meteorology to architecture to feminism? Current theories of reference explored by American linguists and analytic philosophers warn us of the danger of excluding the referent and of the complexities that arise from merely postulating the absence of reference in signification and communication, whether metaphysical, empirical, transcendental, positive, or rationalist.[25]

But let us continue with Eco's own synthesis of the possible ways in which an interpretant can be perceived, such as:

1. the equivalent sign-vehicle in another semiotic system. For example, I can make the drawing of a dog correspond to the word "dog."
2. the index which is directed to a single object, perhaps implying an element of universal quantification.
3. a scientific (or naive) definition in terms of the same semiotic system, e.g., "salt" signifies sodium chloride.

4. an emotive association which acquires the value of an established connotation: "dog" signifies fidelity (and vice versa).
5. the translation of the term into another language, or its substitution by a synonym.
6. the entire syllogism deduced from such premises as "All men are mortal" or "Socrates is a man." (*TS*, 70)

Without pretending to exhaust the implications of the above schemata of the interpretant, we can observe that:

1. *Correspondence* or *substitution* takes place even *before* we can speak of meaning or some sort of intrinsic qualities. Meaning is already and indeed always exchanged, transposed, and dislocated—in concrete historical cases—and tragically shortchanged the moment it enters the signifying chain. As the message, meaning can only be decoded within the enabling and justifying code. This code is marked fundamentally by ontological absence, by non-being. Signification can only occur on an *other* origin or site. In short, the correspondence theory of meaning goes through complex legitimizing procedures when it wants to connect with the real world of physical, emotional, and social existence.[26]

2. *Metonymic* sequential reasoning organizes the very structure of the thinking process.[27] Empiricalness, the presence of things, can only exist *as* a sign. Eco's *Theory of Semiotics* is, as its Italian title suggests, a *Trattato*, a treatise. The ordering of its real-world referents must follow the methodological rules typically employed in similar texts, such as those derived from set theory.[28] The development of the treatise from Aristotle to Wittgenstein's *Tractatus Logico-Philosophicus* achieves perfect abstraction, indifference, and silence.[29] Wittgenstein himself began to reject it by the early thirties. Eco also casts doubt on this persuasive model of exposition, magisterially deployed in the *Theory of Semiotics*, when, later in his career, he turns to writing novels.[30]

3. *Definition* is the standardization of a measure, the accepted currency for the social codification of what something *is*. This something can reasonably be exchanged without having to ponder what it *is*, *might be*, or *could be*. Though they may not be an anthropological necessity like food supply, incest taboos, and religion, we can argue that definitions are necessary in a social–cultural realm in order to get on with the business of living everyday life. Yet a definition is not meant to be questioned. The interpretant/

interpreter that might escape definition—as when it brings into the order of discourse foreign notions, logical impurities, semantic *écarts*, etc.—must be *re*defined (which is an intentional act) within the parameters of a code (even if this requires inventing one purposely). In short, the interpreter/interpretant as a socially and existentially given interlocutor or force is detached from the field of signification and exchange unless it plays by the rules and principles that apply to communication and signification *as such*. We don't have a choice—the formal system of sign relations matters foremost, *and reality is merely a hypothesis*. In this view, does not semiotics stretch a veil over reality, giving credence to Nietzsche's nihilistic assertion that the real world has become a fable?

4. *Association* manifests an obvious algebraic lineage, and an empirical–skeptical philosophical heritage, reiterated throughout this and later works. It comes perilously close to a behavioristic understanding of language use, insofar as *connotation* is sucked up centripetally to become, or to approximate, *denotation*, with all the "predictable" implications concerning identity, systematicity, typologies, forecasting, and manipulation. By the same token, it vindicates the relevance of the *pragmatic* aspect of communication and sign-production, which Eco takes up throughout the eighties.[31]

5. *Synonymity* is understood and defined solely with regard to preestablished, precoded correspondences along the signifying chain, e.g., A B C in code X (English) = A B C in code Y (Italian). Similarly, A B C in metalanguage P = A'B'C' in metalanguage S. When applied to a work of art, and aesthetics in general, this proposition will subject the entire semiotic edifice to strains and stresses, and possible fractures, as we will see below.

The Theory of semiotics thus far outlined is a *functional methodics* of formal definitions and relations grounded upon a *logical–rationalist epistemology*.[32] As such it is prone to all-inclusive and totalizing statements. Within this order of the universe, and insofar as the interpretant is a "category" that can accommodate both a theory of codes and a theory of sign production, "one should even consider as interpretants all possible semiotic judgments that a code permits one to assert about a given semantic unit, as well as many factual judgments" (*TS*, 71). And yet the interpretant also "defines many kinds of proposition and argument which, beyond the rules provided by the codes, explain, develop, and interpret a given sign" (*TS*, 71). The concept of interpretant is actually predisposed to the possibility that some interpretants may "escape" the semiotic universe, or even "enter" the system, though in the end, and coherent with Eco's logic, they must be incorporated into the fold of semiotic justification.[33]

Eco is not unaware of the "semantic" (if not altogether "hermeneutic") multiplicity of the concept of interpretant. The interpretant is such a broad category that it "may turn out to be of no use at all and, since it is able to define *any* semiotic act, may in the last analysis become purely tautological" (*TS*, 71). Nevertheless this vagueness may be its "force" and the condition of its "theoretical purity." This idea of a "pure" uncontaminated state is another rationalist and scientific chimera, though it is useful in guiding laboratory research as well as establishing metamathematical principles. The grounding presupposition of the two separate realms, that of ontology and that of the ontic are clarified once again and made to relate by means of correspondences and analogies of various types:

> The very richness of this category makes it fertile since it shows us how signification (as well as communication), by means of continual shiftings which refer a sign back to another sign or string of signs, circumscribes cultural units in an asymptotic fashion, without ever allowing one to touch them directly, though making them accessible through other units. Thus a semiotic unity never obliges one to replace it by means of something which is not a semiotic entity, and never asks to be explained by some Platonic, psychic or objectal entity. (*TS*, 71)

This may have appeared to be a liberating situation because, during the sixties and early seventies in Italy and elsewhere in Europe, as well as in America, the polemical interlocutors were still (neo)idealists, Platonists of all stripes, phenomenological rationalists, orthodox (pre-Lacanian) Freudians, Lukacsian theorists, and (dialectical) materialists. Whatever the case, the dualism, the dichotomous self-referring, including/excluding relationship, persists and the threat of tautology is turned inward to serve as mainspring and essence of its own validity: "*Semiosis explains itself by itself*" (*TS*, 71) or, in Italian, "*La semiosi si spiega da sola*" (*TSG*, 104).[34] Thus, "this continual circularity is the normal condition of signification and even allows communication to use signs in order to mention things" (*TS*, 71).[35] On Eco's premises, we do indeed get very close to the order of culture, and yet we cannot but observe how its explication, its *sense*, can only proceed on another plane.

The interpretant, when focused on cultural events, entities, and processes, is a function of the possibility of accumulation and of hierarchy. Its usefulness and persuasiveness grow as it exhausts or preempts all channels of communication within any given code. The signal does not have to elicit a simple stimulus, but ought to solicit an *interpretive* response or answer (*TS*, 8). But what is meant by interpretive behavior is the setting into a code (*codification*). The function of the interpretant consists in its switching or routing or placing a message within a receptive, specific code or sub-code. Therefore, the interpretant is charged with relating homologies, differences, deviances, and approximations to the necessarily pregiven conventions or codes. Such an interpretant is similar to an electric relay, a computer, or a psychological *dispositif*. The interpretant is not a person, a living interpreter: claims to theoretical purity are de-gendered, a-sexual, non-classist, anti-ideological, rationalist by election, and pluralist by default.[36]

V. Culture

There are three more broad areas of investigation which we must look at in order to have a more composite view of code semiotics. The first concerns the notion of culture, the second the dynamic of invention, and the third the question of the status of ideas.

From the semiotic point of view, an ambivalent relationship with culture is in question because communicating something with a meaning is actually irrelevant. What counts is that there *is* a communicative act or process. When Eco—with a pinch of irony—calls semiotics a "theory of the lie" (*TS*, 6–7, 58), he may be exacerbating Modern Rationalism, and he may be bringing out the paradoxical Socratic virtue of demonstrating how something must be *right* before it can be said to be *true*. If you can say the opposite of a statement, then it is a valid assertion, independently of whether it obtains in the order of the real. Hence the world is once again a hypothesis:

> *Every time there is possibility of lying, there is a sign-function*: which is to signify (and then to communicate) something to

which no real state of things corresponds. A theory of codes must study everything that can be used in order to lie. The possibility of lying is the *proprium* of semiosis just as (for the Schoolmen) the possibility of laughing was the *proprium* of Man as *animal rationale*. (*TS*, 58–59)

With neither intension nor extension, and deprived of reference, the cultural world "is neither actual nor possible in the ontological sense." Cultural critics seduced by semiotic analyses, take notice: your analyses are not about reality, but about signs! What is sought, what can function within a theory of codes is not the referent, but the *content*, which must in turn be "defined as a *cultural unit*" (*TS*, 63).

Cultural units are presumably capable of producing social effects. When they are transposed into signs, they exhibit semantic content; but semantics is not semiotics (*LI*, 54 ff.). Semiotics can only reveal *how* signification is obtained and comprehended:

Given two sentences such as "Napoleon died at Saint Helena on May 5, 1821" and "Ulysses reconquered the kingdom by killing all the Proci," it is irrelevant to a code theory to know that *historically speaking* the former is true and the latter is false. ... The fact that for us the second sentence connotes "legend" is semiotically analogous to the fact that it could yet be proven in some future civilization, on the basis of as yet unknown (or false) documents, that Napoleon died in a different place on a different day (or that he never existed). (*TS*, 65)

In this context, healthy Humean skepticism is enlisted to avoid totalizing sentences about anything at all. Thus culture is defined on the basis of the following four assumptions:

1. the production and employment of objects used for transforming the relationship between man and nature;
2. kinship relations as the primary nucleus of institutionalized social relations;
3. the economic exchange of goods (*TS*, 21);
4. the birth of articulated language.

The conceptual model, the historical paradigm, is furnished by Claude Lévi-Strauss, who is mentioned frequently by Eco. This had in part been done already in *La Struttura Assente* (1968). The author does little with the third entry on the exchange of goods and its semiotic aspect.[37] What draws our attention is the issue of the birth or origin of language, which brings Eco, when dealing with "radical invention," to meet up with and debunk idealist aesthetics.[38]

VI. Invention

Part Three of *The Theory of Semiotics* deals with "sign production." Here we are particularly interested in discussing "typologies of modes of production":

> We may define as invention a mode of production whereby the producer of the sign-function chooses a new material continuum not yet segmented for that purpose and proposes a new way of organizing (of giving form to) it in order *to map* within it the formal pertinent element of a content-type. (*TS*, 245)

Invention is "a case of *ratio difficilis*" brought forth "within a hetero-material expression." Since there exists no prior convention to correlate the various elements of the new expression with whatever the chosen content, "the sign producer must in some way *posit* this correlation so as to make it acceptable" (*TS*, 245), that is, intelligible or readable. Notice the word "posit." Invention is displayed against a spectrum of message production which includes *recognition, choice,* and *replica*, each requiring a particular mapping process (cf. Tables 40–44 in *TS*, 246–56). Invention occurs in the movement from physical givenness to stimulus to perception and thence to *in*forming, followed by abstraction in a semantic model and its *re*presentation or *trans*formation into sememes. Invention is conceived as that arrangement which places the greatest amount of stress on, and shifts the emphasis toward, the very institution of a comprehensive field of decodable sememes.

In the case of "invention as code-making" (*TS*, 250–56, ¶ 3.6.8), we find a further subdivision between a "moderate invention," predicated upon an interplay of coded semantic models (e.g., in figurative painting), and "radical invention," which is extraordinary insofar as "the sender more or less bypasses the perceptual model, and delves into the as yet unshaped perceptual continuum, mapping his perception as he organizes it" (*TS*, 254). Basically what takes place in this instance is that the sender produces and injects messages in the chain or field for which there is no existing code; in fact, the code is to be derived precisely from the expression itself. At times this creates confusion and, on the concrete historical plane, often rejection and destructive criticism:

> Take the case of the Impressionists, whose addressees absolutely refused to 'recognize' the subjects represented and said that they 'did not understand', that the painting 'did not mean anything', that real life was not like that, etc. This refusal was due to the addressees' lack not only of a semantic model to which the mapped items might be referred, but also of a percept to guess at, since they had never perceived in this way. (TS, 254)

The introduction of a radically new code of signification requires that the addressee (the viewer, the listener, or the reader) produce previously unthought notions of perception and semantization, and finally effect a decoding. This happens not only in the arts but also in the sciences, as in the not too dissimilar Kuhnian thesis of paradigm formation (see also TS, 188; ¶ 3.4.11). Meaning assumes some sort of correlation, such that the introduction of codes for the explanation of strange or radical inventions entails postulating artificial codes to determine what a message might mean. These codes are subsequently stabilized through convention by means of repeated analogous experiments and confirmations within a social group, or at the very least a specialized community where the code turns into a metalanguage.[39] The radical inventor gambles on the possibility of semiosis and often fails miserably.

The above assumption, however, may carry "speculation about languages back to the position adopted by Giambattista Vico, who proposed that languages arise as poetic inventions and are only accepted by convention afterward" (TS, 254). Eco is quick to point out that radical invention should not be understood according to an idealist model. Although Vico cannot be reduced to the idealist version of his thought, this observation makes sense primarily in the context of Italian culture.[40] Eco's problem appears to be the question of the origin of languages, an argument which semiotics does not typically address. In fact, consistent with its dualist rationality, code semiotics does *not* consider "invention" as a category or type of sign production—which would isolate and demonstrate *the* radical invention, the auroral moment that doubles as the prototype example of the birth of language. Rather, invention is "one among various modes of sign production, collaborating with others to correlate functives and to establish various sign-functions," thus avoiding the "idealist fallacy." On the historiographic plane, of course, this is accurate, insofar as "Croce's linguistics [overestimated] the creative power of the speaking subject" (*TS*, 256). Semiosis, in short, "never rises *ex novo* and *ex nihilo*," so that "in the semiotic universe there are neither single protagonists nor charismatic prophets. Even prophets have to be socially *accepted* in order to be right; if not, they are wrong" (*TS*, 256).

Certainly this position goes a long way toward demolishing myths about genius, supercreative talents, and the notion of truth as above human understanding. Indeed, if this position cannot be communicated, if it does not find a Receptor or Addressee, a truth (message) is not only meaningless, it does not even exist. Once extended to the interpretation of culture, it is a good antidote to notions of priority or superiority: "No new culture can ever come into being except against the background of an old one"[41] (*TS*, 256). Invention, we might even say creativity, is just one more way of arranging the relationships between Sender and Receiver, playing according to the particular case with replicas, stylizations, ostensions, and so on. The semiotic universe is ultimately a continuum of transformations wherein inventions are simply another (often exalted) way of changing something around.

VII. Basic Ideas

Looking at semiotics' treatment of ideas brings us one more step along the path to an understanding of how this Theory and its related Method betray a quintessentially modernist frame of mind. To even sketch the issues raised by the problem of ideas, their origins and their nature and structure becomes a major philosophical enterprise, which is not within the range of this exposition. Yet this may not be as daunting a task as might at first be expected: for, on the basis of the *Theory*, it is enough to consider whatever we think ideas are as signs.[42] We learn here that, since there exists a play of pointing and rebounding (deictics and reflection) from one image to the next, and since there is such a thing as a chain of concepts, the entire flow of thought can be looked at as a system of signs, and most cogently when—as is obviously the case with ideas—*something stands for something else*. In brief, *"even ideas are signs"* (*TS*, 166, ¶ 3.3.4). In retracing the history of this assertion, Eco writes that Peirce aligns himself along a very ancient and influential philosophical track, which comprises Ockham, Hobbes, and Locke:

> These ideas are not (as the Schoolmen believed) a mirroring image of the thing; they too are the result of an abstractive process (in which—let it be noted—only some pertinent elements have been retained) which gives us not the individual essence of the named thing but its *nominal essence*. This nominal essence is in itself a digest, a summary, an elaboration of the signified thing. (*TS*, 166)

It follows that:

> The procedure leading from a bunch of experiences to a name is the same as that which leads from the experience of things to that *sign* of things, the idea. *Ideas are already a semiotic product.* (*TS*, 166)

Therefore, though aware that in Locke's system "the notion of idea is still linked to a mentalistic view," we are authorized "to replace the term 'idea' (as something which takes place in the mind) by 'cultural unit' (as something which can be tested through other interpretants in a given cultural context)." In addition, Berkeley "also speaks of an idea as *general* when it represents or stands for all particular ideas of the same sort" (*TS*, 166–67).

When we turn to sign production, we are entreated to consider that "the notion of 'sign' *is a fiction* of everyday language,"[43] whose place should be taken by that of sign-function" (*TS*, 158, my emphasis). Here judgment also falls under the semiotic scythe. What happens when in a society a cultural unit is defined in terms of another for which no code is given? If it does modify the preexisting system, as it must,[44] how does it do so? Eco writes that:

> The analytic judgment is the one in which the predicate is contained implicitly in the concept of the subject, and the synthetic judgment is that in which the predicate is added to the subject as an entirely new attribute, due to a synthesis obtained from the data of experience.[45] (*TS*, 158)

He then goes on to ask:

> Why then, according to Kant, is "all bodies are extensive" analytic and "all bodies are heavy" synthetic? Simply because Kant referred to the 'patrimony of thought' which he presumed to be known to his contemporaries. It is worth noting that "body" for him was not a referent but above all a cultural unit. (*TS*, 158–59)

In other words, from Descartes through the Encyclopaedists, extension was attributed to this cultural unit as an "essential quality" which was part of its definition, whereas weight was thought to be an "accessory and contingent quality" not essential to the definition:

> *Judgments are either analytic or synthetic according to the existing codes and not according to the presumed natural properties of the objects.* Kant explicitly states in the first *Kritik* that "the activity of our reason consists largely . . . in the analysis of ideas which we already have with regard to objects." (*TS*, 159)

Drawing also on the work of Morton White,[46] who argued for the untenability of the analytic–synthetic dualism, Eco indicates that judgments are better understood in semiotic terms, where factual judgments must first be turned into metasemiotic or semiotic statements. This can be seen as another "logical" but somehow reductive appropriation, though we cannot explore its implications here.

The aesthetic text must also be studied as an "example of invention" (*TS*, 261–276, ¶ 3.7). Semiotically, the text is marked by the following processes:

1. Manipulation of Expression;
2. Reassessment of Content;
3. Code Changing;
4. Awareness of the World [*TSG*, 328 has: "visione del mondo"];
5. [Production and Representation of] a network of diverse Communicational Acts eliciting highly original responses.[47] (*TS*, 261)

Eco characterizes Jakobson's five functions of language[48] as merely *operative* or functionalist. In so doing, he must consider the poetic function as essentially "ambiguous" and "self-focusing" (*autoriflessiva* in *TSG*, 329). From within semiotics, ambiguity can be defined as a violation of the rules or a *deviation from the norm* in the message-bearing syntactic chain in such a way that the Addressee cannot make head or tail of it. Ambiguity seems crucial to aesthetic production and understanding, though it does raise some problems:

> Ambiguity is a very important device because it functions as a sort of introduction [*"vestibolo"*] to the aesthetic experience; when, instead of producing pure disorder, it focuses my attention and urges me to an interpretive effort [*"orgasmo interpretativo"*] (while at the same time suggesting how to set about decoding) it incites me toward the discovery of an unexpected flexibility in the language with which I am dealing. (*TS*, 263)

The definition of ambiguity is reductive because it cannot constitute a dimension of chaos or disorder, and yet chaos and the unknown may be precisely what is questioned by or linked up with the work of art. When Eco says ambiguity functions as an "introduction" to aesthetic experience, does he mean that there is a *first* moment in time, in consciousness, or in mind when a whole set of *other* and *different* processes go to work—curiosity, urge, labor, imaginings of sense, preliminary formulations or sketches—such that a coherent (semiotic) explanation and judgment may *later* be elaborated and cast into the network? But if this is so, why are not these same processes part of the semiotic process? Experience also may be rhetorically described, producing causes and explanations. Yet from the semiotic standpoint we can only learn *that this is the case*, that the signs for experience are related to the signs for the ordered universe of the (master) code. And from a methodological and pragmatic perspective, is not this "practice" very close to what philologists and hermeneuticians have always done?[49]

VIII. Aesthetics

Though he confutes Croce for basing his aesthetics on the time-worn categories of "expression" and "content," Eco nevertheless states:

> A first step toward an aesthetic definition of ambiguity might be represented by the postulate according to which in aesthetic texts an ambiguity on the *expression* [my emphasis] plane *must*

involve a corresponding ambiguity on the *content* [my emphasis] plane. (*TS*, 263)[50]

Eco's conception of aesthetic experience is greatly influenced by the Russian Formalists and Shklovskij in particular who "anticipates by some thirty years the analogous conclusions of so-called 'informational aesthetics'" (*TS*, 264). Aesthetic experience increases the "difficulty and the duration of perception" through devices of *estrangement* and *de-automatization* in language.[51] However, since perception itself becomes a sign (or is taken in its sign-function aspect), the main characteristic of the aesthetic experience is that it makes *pertinent* a particular artifact or cultural unit. This crosses somewhat over into the scientific domain, and would seem to confer on the aesthetic experience an epistemic capacity. In the section entitled "The segmentation of semantic fields" (*TS*, 76–81, ¶ 2.8.3), Eco explains and exemplifies the many possible ways in which a semantic field—in this case, concerning the properties of light— can be cut up, hierarchized, dissolved, and reformed: "science comes to know [the] reality [of wavelengths] after having divided it into pertinent units" (*TS*, 77). The Receiver (a reader, a scientist) decides to make the range of wavelengths from 430 mµ to 650 mµ *pertinent* to communication about light, because with those figures, those conferred attributes, we can speak more "scientifically"— from within a highly codified discipline, namely optics—of the colors everyone perceives every day. On a parallel plane, the aesthetic dimension lends itself to more structured and functionalist analyses. Its very ontology leans heavily on scientific models and practices. For example, aesthetic experience become sign takes up a position within a universe of signs in which what is important (what is made *pertinent*) is the very material that turns the work into matter or concrete substance. In linguistic terms, this means that art highlights the existence and force of the signifier over and above that of the signified. Through the fifties and sixties, in the wake of artistic avant-garde experimentation, critics from various branches in the humanities looked at all facets of culture under the revolutionary aegis of structuralism, a scientific approach which among other things brought out the theoretical and methodological importance of the signifier.[52] From a different historical and ontological grounding, an integrated structuralist–Marxist materialism also underscored the crucial role played by the very materials artists use and their function within an aesthetic theory.[53] For semiotics, things stand otherwise: "In the aesthetic text, the matter of the sign-vehicle becomes an aspect of the expression-form" (*TS*, 266). As any material employed is already charged with cultural signification, art manifests an aesthetic overcoding at both ends: the expression plane and the content plane. Eco's example of Gertrude Stein's well-known line "A rose is a rose is a rose is a rose" (*TS*, 270) clearly illustrates the case of overcoding, as the excessive redundancy of the verse actually produces "an increase in informational possibilities" (*TS*, 270). This happens because a Reader or receiver is so "estranged" or "detoured" that he or she immediately begins connecting with different connotative subcodes, "e.g. the allegorical, the iconological, the iconic. The work is thus 'open' to multiple interpretations" (*TS*, 270; here Eco recalls his own "pre-semiotic" 1962 work, *Opera aperta* [*OW*]).

IX. Interpretation

The many possible versions of an aesthetic experience (or object) brings semiotics to the limit, where the Theory attempts to master chaos itself. It is well known that Eco has done extensive work on labyrinths and abduction, and that later in *Semiotics and the Philosophy of Language* (1984) and *The Limits of Interpretation* (1990) he suggests the model of the encyclopedia as the plenum for unlimited semiosis, the interpretable social and cultural horizon of message exchange. In this "middle period," however, he is still staking out a *whole* that *must* be rendered in terms of codes and sign-production. To put some order into the infinite possibilities of interpretation raised by the work of art, it is useful, he argues, to have recourse to an *aesthetic idiolect*, which "must be postulated in order to comprehend the fact that the work works" (*deve essere postulato per comprendere il fatto che l'opera funzioni* [*TSG*, 340n]). Once again a willing or positing consciousness, some sort of subject, decides *a priori* (or at least *before* in time and context) that the work communicates something, something graspable solely in terms of its givenness *as* sign. To postulate anything is a *methodological necessity* which allows Theory to stand up. We should therefore be able to predict the methodological structure and the function of the aesthetic idiolect.

If we take an unreadable or impenetrable text, we must *suppose* a systematic ordering of its as-yet-unknown rules. There exists a *contextual solidarity* which requires that we perform semiotic commutation tests in order to arrive at a *systematic rule*. The explanation for this state of affairs rests once again on an analogy with the the basic tenets of structural linguistics:

> [the] work of art has the same structural characterists as does a *langue*. So that it cannot be a mere 'presence,' there must be an underlying system of mutual correlations, and thus a semiotic design which cunningly gives the impression of non-semiosis. (*TS*, 271)

Homology is the key critical concept here. It should not be too difficult to see how, with the growing demands of the pragmatic aspect of communication, and the greater focus on the Decoder/Receiver of the message(s), *langue* will have to be replaced by the *encylopedia* (in *SPL*). At every level and for every message, Eco writes,

> the solutions are articulated according to a homologous system of solutions, and every deviation springs from a *general deviational matrix*. Therefore, in a work of art *a super-system of homologous structural relationships* is established rather as if all levels were definable on the basis of a single *structural model* which determined all of them. (*TS*, 271)

Thus the aesthetic work, even when unreadable, also acquires a corresponding *super-sign function* which draws up a more complex cluster of correlations. We approach, define, even talk about some of these correlations by positing a new meta-concept attuned to the code:

> The rule governing all deviations at work at every level of a work of art, the unique diagram which makes all deviations mutually functional, is the *aesthetic idiolect*. (*TS*, 272)

In some cases, mapping out "all" these deviations can be very complicated indeed. Consider some of Eco's own deviational analyses in the *Theory of Semiotics* and in *The Role of the Reader*. Yet semiotics also borrows concepts from the more traditional and methodologically proven notions of genre, style, historical period, *Zeitgeist*, textual dominant, etc.:

> Insofar as it can be applied by the same author to many of his own works (although with slight variations), the idiolect becomes a general one governing the entire *corpus* of an author's work, i.e., his *personal style*. Insofar as it is accepted by an artistic community and produces imitations, mannerisms, stylistic habits, etc., it becomes a *movement-idiolect*, or a *period-idiolect*, studied by criticism or the history of ideas as the main artistic feature of a given historical group or period. (TS, 272)

Four idiolects—pertaining respectively to the *work*, the *corpus*, the *movement*, and the *period*—can be organized hierarchically and made manageable. But in order to be consistent with these premises, Eco must de-realize, de-ontologize the non-semiotic import of these categories, and define them in a manner analogous to the interpretant: "Insofar as it produces new norms accepted by an entire society, the artistic idiolect may act as a *meta-semiotic judgment changing common codes*" (TS, 272). A series of plausible meta-semiotic judgments on action and agency within the semiotic universe will allow us to grasp and define, to evaluate and explain how, for instance, the chosen idiolect—an author's preferred symbolism, the metaphors of a group—forms an underlying "hierarchy of competences" and executions. These can be identified at the molecular, or even the "molar," levels. They sketch a canvas *toward* a general interpretation, which is warranted by the (presupposed, or posited) methodological necessity of a *system of systems*.[54]

X. Critique

Eco's theory of interpretive acts, which is related to the work of art and its (re)generative power,[55] also demonstrates that a theory of interpretation cannot be disjoined from its methodological routes, from its epistemologically legitimizing steps:

> Inasmuch as the idiolect constitutes a sort of final (though never completely achieved) definition of the work, to read an artistic product means at once: i) to *induce*, that is to infer a general rule from individual cases; ii) to *abduce*, that is to test both old and new codes by way of a hypothesis; iii) to *deduce*, that is to check whether what has been grasped on one level can determine artistic events on another, and so on. Thus all

the modes of inference are at work. Like a large labyrinthine garden, a work of art permits one to take many different routes, whose number is increased by the criss-cross of its paths. (*TS*, 275)

This is an excellent characterization of a work of art: ample, suggestive, and acceptable by several different definitions of art. But one might want to underscore the reference to processes of cognition and the generation of common knowledge patterns, tropes that ensure the unencumbered linking up of lexico-formulaic statements about reality, culture, and the meanings that can be produced, processed, and reissued into an ever shifting communicative network.

Briefly summarized, Eco's *A Theory of Semiotics* introduces a number of key points:

1. A code is given on the basis of oppositional couples or dichotomies, distinguishing and contraposing "expression" and "content" (*TS*, 48–50).

2. In collapsing Frege's epistemological triangle (*Sinn, Bedeutung, Zeichen*) into a Sense/Symbol operative conceptual pair, a code divests the *Bedeutung* of any "real world" import, making it function as a 'type' (as opposed to a 'token') "very akin to . . . content" (*TS*, 60).[56]

3. The Referent is eliminated, insofar as the referential fallacy consists in supposing that the meaning of a sentence is in any way related to the corresponding object (*TS*, 58–9).

4. Intentionality is bracketed off as basically irrelevant to semiotic communication and understanding (*TS*, 15–19).

5. Code semiotics moreover does not deal with "extension," insofar as it falls within the precints of propositional calculus or of theories of truth (*TS*, 62–66).

6. Code semiotics recognizes as its ultimate epistemological limit the Indeterminacy Principle (*TS*, 28–9).

In Eco's later works, the definition of metaphor still remains structuralist: a complex, overcoded, and variously charged metonymic process of sense-production (or transfer) along a network of buzzwords, catachretic fields, and logically inferred associations within a recognizable and modellable code. Such a code can be called the cultural encyclopedia of a society. This has the advantage of shifting the emphasis to the addressee, at once rehabilitating interpretant *and* interpreter.[57] Nevertheless, Eco's interpretation of symbol in *Semiotics and the Philosophy of Language* (*SPL*, 130–163), as well as in *The Limits of Interpretation* (*LI*, 8–22), is still conceived in terms of a dualistic model for the decoding of *any* system of signification.[58] Furthermore, any grammatological or deconstructivist (let alone hermeneutic) sense of difference is lost. In its place difference assumes an empirical, commonsensical dimension: "the presence of one element is necessary for the absence of the other" (*SPL*, 23). Interpretation proceeds according to a system of formal presuppositions. The aesthetic artifact is ultimately a "closed work," an entity which can only exist in the interval between the theory of the code and the processes of signformation. Despite recent attempts to regain the extra-linguistic (or the non-semiotic) by extending the definition, range, and applicability of Eco's later theory, the great problem which underlies code semiotics is precisely the system of formal presuppositions. Axioms in a neutral (or logical) language do not allow for a thematization and *in concreto* response to stimulations coming from the subject, memory, ethos, and praxis.[59]

Chapter 2

CONSEQUENCES OF UNLIMITED SEMIOSIS: CARLO SINI'S METAPHYSICS OF THE SIGN AND SEMIOTICAL HERMENEUTICS

Alessandro Carrera

Any object is a finger, but the finger is not the finger. If the finger does not exist in the world, no object can be named object. I say that the finger is not the finger. If object does not exist in the world, is it possible to speak of finger?

I. Between Heidegger and Peirce

My task is to give a short account of the Italian philosopher Carlo Sini's theoretical work, which is still little known to American audiences. Sini's thinking, essentially devoted to a hermeneutics of the sign, engages in a constant dialogue with semiotics and phenomenology. The opening quotation here is from the Chinese philosopher Kong Souen Long-Tseu's treatise *On Finger and Object*, written between the fourth and third centuries B.C. Sini cites it in one of his most recent books[1] in the chapter entitled "Pointing Out" (*L'indicare*). The effect of the quotation of an Eastern philosopher in Sini's work is quite surprising, but it should not suggest that Sini is avoiding the Western tradition, looking elsewhere for the solution to problems that Western thought has left unresolved. On the contrary, Sini is deeply rooted in the main trend of European continental philosophy: Husserl, Peirce, Nietzsche, and Heidegger are his authors. Yet the quotation shows that Sini—a "conventional" philosopher using "conventional" methods—often achieves unconventional results.

The issue of the relationship between the act of pointing out and the result of opening a world, Sini comments, resounds in the pages of the Chinese philosopher. On the one hand there is gesture as originary event, on the other there is reciprocal constitution of world and body. It may be recalled that Heidegger, quoting Stefan George's poem "'The Word," had already said that there is no thing without a word that names it.[2] Even Saying (*die Sage*), the originary opening of language, is defined by Heidegger as pointing out (*NL*, 96). There is no thing without a finger pointing at it. Moreover, there is a thing only *for* a finger to point at. Any correlation between finger and thing results from such a pointing out. Gesture brings both finger and thing into being. Bringing things into being has a name in philosophy: event. Can we say that gesture is the originary event? Is it possible that an *originary event* exists? And why does it reveal itself in pointing out?

Linguistics and semiotics would perhaps change the too-prosaic finger into a sign or a signifying function. Some would speak of designation and designating. Following Peirce, another would call it "Index," since in Peirce's semiotics Index qualifies itself as a factual relationship, a physical connection between Representamen and Object. Even in Husserl's *Logical Investigations*, the sign is conceived as an Index. Heidegger adopts this very notion of the sign. Beginning with section 17 of *Being and Time*, which is dedicated to the notion of the sign, Heidegger discusses in many passages the meaning of pointing out (*Weisen*) and showing (*Zeigen*). Heidegger clarifies that pointing out is bringing something into manifestation, as he designates man *the pointer*.[3]

But in Peirce's semiotics, an Index is only one of the possible events of the sign. An Index does not exhaust a sign's essence. Every Index is a sign, but not all signs are Indices. Heidegger saw a fundamental experience in pointing out but, since he was satisfied with categorizing the sign only under Index, his philosophy lacked a real consideration of what a sign is. According to Sini, this is the weakest point in Heidegger's framework, making it necessary to supplement it with Peirce.

The correlation between Heidegger and Peirce is the basis of Sini's hermeneutical criticism of contemporary semiotics. The first problem of semiotics, according to Sini, is not the classification of various possible signs, but the appropriate understanding of a sign's essence.[4] In other words, semiotics suffers from the naturalistic *naiveté* common to all fields of knowledge not concerned with the issue of their foundations. Semiotics analyzes signs and groups them into categories. But, according to what criterion is "something" a sign and "something else" not? What makes a sign out of "something"? What is a sign? Why does semiotics use the sign without thinking of its essence?

Or is semiotics unable to answer to the issue of the sign altogether? Heidegger had warned that the sign is purely *a medium* and that its ontological foundation (*rimando*, according to Sini) could not be conceived as a sign.[5] That which allows a sign to be a sign is not a sign. But this statement does not solve the problem. Certainly, if the sign is an Index, its *rimando* is neither another Index nor a super-Index. But who establishes an Index as sign? How is it possible to establish a sign without "referring" (*rimandare*) to it, without "pointing at" it? How can *rimando* play in this game other than as a sign-relation (*relazione segnica*)? Is then *rimando* a sort of relation's link to the infinite?

As a matter of fact, according to Sini, not even Heidegger has been able to go beyond the traditional and metaphysical concept of a sign. In such a framework, the sign is just the instrument of an enunciation supposedly coming from "another" "non-sign" place. In Sini's opinion, Heidegger confuses the sign with the sign-relation, as he confuses the ontological *being-sign* with conventional signs that are based on language. But semiotics also ignores the necessity to see the difference among the three layers of the sign: *sign-relation, language, conventional signs* (*PS*, 25).

Such an evasion of the problem of the sign has brought philosophy and semiotics to three serious consequences:

1. Heidegger too found himself at a dead end and concluded his philosophy by theorizing the impossibility of a further philosophy, unless that philosophy is dedicated exclusively to the recalling of Being's event.

2. The ontological relevance of Peirce's philosophy has been discarded by the same semioticians who claim him as a founding father. Further, they fail to take the full implications of his thought seriously.

3. Heideggerian hermeneutics risks disappearing into mystical silence or a superficial relativism (interpretation is an infi-

nite process; any interpretation is legitimate; there is room for everybody).

In order to save philosophy from this collapse, Sini suggests as a first corrective an emphasis upon Peirce's *sign-relation* rather than upon the genus *sign*. Peirce's basic principles are perfectly suited to decide contemporary dilemmas concerning hermeneutics. Sini stresses the following points from Peirce's work:

1. Immediate intuition does not exist. There is no immediacy, no *adaequatio* between the supposed internal experience and the supposed external world. All knowledge is the result of inference. That which appears as intuition to common sense is just the result of previous inferences. Intuition is quick inference, based upon sedimentary layers of preexisting knowledge.

2. All inferences infer from signs and within sign-relations. In the sign-relation the subject does not stand before an object and acknowledge it "by means of" a sign. Rather, the Interpretant activates the relation between Representamen and its Object, i.e., between a sign and its meaning. The outcome of this process is not an object "in itself" staying "in the world," but the triadic relation of Interpretant, Representamen, and Object.

3. The truth of the sign-relation does not end in one meaning. The same meaning will become a sign for future Interpretants. In this regard, there is no difference between man and word. Both come from past interpretations and are destined to future interpretations. As Peirce was wont to say, "*Man is a sign.*"[6]

4. Interpretations are infinite. Semiosis is unlimited. It is impossible to establish the beginning or end of the interpretative process, for that would be just another interpretation.

5. There is no "true" interpretation in opposition to "false" ones. This does not mean that truth "does not exist" at all. The process of interpretation *is* truth in general. Truth is always in process and *public* in its essence. Nobody owns it but everybody is *in* it.

Peirce's unlimited semiosis and Nietzsche's perspective philosophy seem here in strong agreement. Nietzsche opened the path to hermeneutics in his Basel years, when investigating Greek rhetoric. One may also recall Aphorism 374 of *The Gay Science*, in which Nietzsche advances the hypothesis that the world is infinite to the extent that it includes infinite interpretations.

Correlating Peirce's unlimited semiosis and Heidegger's hermeneutical circle is likewise essential to Sini's purpose. Peirce's criticism of immediate intuition is matched by Heidegger's assertion that "understanding requires fore-understanding." In order to understand, one must have already understood. In order to infer, one must have already inferred. Both Peirce and Heidegger here reflect Nietzsche's notion of infinite interpretation. Although Heidegger did not develop a fully articulated semiotics, his emphasis on language after *Being and Time* goes in the direction of a hermeneutics of the sign. As for Peirce, man is a sign, for Heidegger (quoting Hölderlin), *"Ein Zeichen sind Wir"* ("A sign are we"). For Heidegger himself, "As he draws toward what withdraws, man is a sign"(*CT* , 351).

Nietzsche, Peirce, and Heidegger make up a triad on which Sini attempts to establish a rigorously hermeneutical habit of thinking. But this is not the conclusion of his philosophy; it is the beginning. In the development that follows, he encounters the aporias of hermeneutics, and comes to criticize the very concept of truth as public process.

II. From Semiotics to Cosmology

At the beginning of his philosophical enterprise, Sini opted for hermeneutics as an answer to the dead ends of Husserlian phenomenology, especially regarding the issue of the transcendental subject. Indeed, Sini's formative years as a student of Enzo Paci— the most important Italian phenomenologist after Antonio Banfi— were spent on phenomenology. Paci's Husserlism was an original confluence of phenomenology, dialectic, and epistemology. Appearing in the framework of Paci's thought, Sini's first work dealt with the scientific status of phenomenology, and with Whitehead's philosophy, since Paci was also interested in Whitehead's quasi-phenomenological approach to science.[7] After Whitehead, and after G. H. Mead, Sini approached American pragmatism in its historical development. Here he encountered Peirce, and the semiotic turn of his thought took place.[8]

Sini's first attempt to forge his own path appeared in *Semiotica e filosofia. Segno e linguaggio in Peirce, Nietzsche, Heidegger e Foucault*. First published in 1978, this book can now be considered the first part of a larger work, whose next stages were: *Passare il segno: Semiotica, cosmologia, tecnica* (1981), *Kinesis*: *Saggio di interpretazione* (1982), and *Images of Truth: From Sign to Symbol* (1985).[9]

In *Semiotics and Philosophy*, after investigating what Peirce, Nietzsche, and Heidegger have in common, Sini compared hermeneutics with Foucault's archaeology of knowledge, Lévi-Strauss's structural anthropology, and Ricoeur's semiotical challenge. In Sini's opinion, no one of these options provides interpretation of the much broader context required by semiosis. As Peirce said, if semiosis is unlimited, any statement leads eventually to a general explanation of the universe. Every interpretation implies, and moves toward, cosmology.

The term 'cosmology' is quite unusual in contemporary thought, appearing to belong only to the realm of astronomical sciences. This was not so, of course, at the beginnings of Western philosophy, when, as Aristotle indicated, speculation began in man's wonder at the starry sky. Sini's *Passare il segno* [Beyond the Sign], however, is not devoted to reconstructing this or that cosmology, but to the way the very cosmological sense of existence progressively vanished in the development of Western thought. For there was a time when cosmology seemed to be the natural conclusion of any philosophical inquiry. In his *Timaeus*, Plato still compares the cosmos to a Great Animal. What happened to that animal? What happened to the philosophy that could include the cosmos without being "anti-scientific"? From Plato to Bruno, from Vico to Hume, and from Kant to Feuerbach, Sini sketches out parallel movements in the history of Western philosophy: on the one hand, the feeling of the cosmos as man's house decayed; on the other hand, the growing and triumphant humanism which confined cosmological experience to an archaic chapter in man's history. At the same time, the very man who expelled the ancient cosmos from the realms of thought and science—the same *little man* who, to say it with Nietzsche, killed God—faced the meaninglessness of his own values. Just when it was blatantly affirmed that there was no other value than man and his history, the nihilistic background of that assumption revealed itself in all its crudeness. Man and history are relative values claiming to replace the eternal and supreme entities such as Plato's *Summum bonum*. But in metaphysical terms there can be no value unless it is absolute. If there are no eternal and immutable values, there are no values at all, nothing has worth, the world has no meaning.

Nietzsche and Heidegger showed how this nihilistic outcome has been achieved by way of a close interrelation between history and technology. Yet this ultimate accomplishment of Western philosophy turns out to be its very elimination. Now that cosmos and myth have been ruled out, our world's technological planning is ready to reduce philosophy to a role akin to that of the various human sciences which contend for supremacy in the hierarchy of knowledge. We are now living out the conclusion of what Sini called a psychological–historical strategy (*strategia psico-storica*), namely, a process that transferred pre-Socratic cosmological experience (a time when, according to Nietzsche, philosophy did not worry about being un-grounded) to the inner space of psyche. This innerness, where the untranslatable voice of metaphysics utters its hyperuranic truths, did not exist before Plato literally created soul in order to find a home for his anti-Sophistic idea of truth. Since then, the game of the world no longer takes place under the gods' heavens—it has to be reconstructed in psyche's laboratory. Plato's Socrates would ask Pan to help him to become *innerly* beautiful. Sini suggests that, since mankind today has experienced our exhaustion of that innerness and the triumph of the technological organization of the world and knowledge, our prayer should be: "O dear Pan, help us instead, and once again, to become *outerly* beautiful"(*PS*, 336).

Sini is aware that this criticism of nihilism, technology, and psychological–historical strategy must be based on a hermeneutics of the sign that can show how human sciences (which claim to have the last word on man and philosophy) remain entangled in the very metaphysics they believe to have overcome. This is the subject of the first part of *Kinesis*.

III. Sign, Symbol, and *Symbolon*

In his 1952 lecture entitled *Was heißt Denken?*, Heidegger formulates the fundamental questions: How do we keep holding on to thought? What is most thought-provoking (*das Bedenkliche*)? What is it that calls on us to think or, more simply, what is it that needs to be thought (*denk-würdig*)?[10]

We know the answers: we keep holding on to thought by not letting it out of memory, where memory is more properly thinking back or recalling (*Andenken*). What is most thought-provoking is that we are still not thinking—not even yet. What needs to be thought about is myth (*Sage*) as Saying, insofar as it speaks of the most-provoking. But what is shown in the fact that we are still not thinking? Perhaps some deficiency of man? No. We are still not thinking because the most thought-provoking constantly eludes (perhaps it has always eluded) man. What we see, what is shown, is not *das Bedenkliche* but only its *event*—the event of its eluding.

But, Sini asks, which was the most thought-provoking—the most compelling thought—for the pre-Socratics, for Pythagoras or Anaxagoras? The answer is truly cosmological: the highest task of thinking was the observation of the sky, of the movement of the planets and stars. They had to be *interpreted*. They were the most important *signa*. They needed to be deciphered, when cosmology still retained its philosophical meaning. But today? Today *signa* have descended upon Earth disguised as *signs*, and semiotics has replaced cosmology. Heidegger was right: the *event* of the most thought-provoking is the most thought-provoking, but (and this is Sini's departure from Heidegger) it is not Being's event, it is the *sign*'s event.

But the sign's event has always eluded thinking and language. Is it possible to think of it as just a new chapter in the philosophical enterprise? Has this enterprise remained unchanged since Anaxagoras raised his eyes and interpreted the sky? Sini's answer is no. There is no use in thinking of the sign's event in the same words and categories that Western rationality has shaped throughout its history. In order to come to a post-metaphysical philosophy, psychological–historical strategy must be removed from the game. That strategy alone killed *Timaeus'* Great Animal and secluded itself in the space of psyche and science, claiming that there was no other conceivable knowledge.

Sini is requesting here the most radical hermeneutics of *Logos* and its devices. First of all, the truth-value (*valore di verità*) of psychological–historical strategy must be questioned. Who owns its truth? Who administers it? Sini is forced to turn against Peirce, to the extent that Sini draws the most extreme conclusions from Peirce's own cosmology. As we know, according to Peirce no one *has* truth. Truth is the result of the general process of interpretation, retaining value only insofar as it is *public* and shared by the community of the Interpretants. Private man is just idiosyncrasy and error. Private truth is a contradiction in terms. But in this way Peirce shows how consistent was the original partition—the exclusion procedure that, with Heraclitus, has marked the beginning of philosophy. Heraclitus was the first to separate the truth of *Logos* that is common to everyone from the individual *phronesis* that is just idiosyncratic and mistaken wisdom.[11] Sini points out that Peirce's definition of truth as *public* is circular because only the already public *Logos* could establish that truth is public. Who *de-prived* the *private* man, not of his truth—because truth is only the result of the partition of public and private—but of his private rhetoric, of the ability to fashion his own persuasive and authoritative speech?[12] This question differs little from that of Nietzsche: Why did man never question his own will to truth? Are we sure that this will to truth is always *good*? What lies behind it? Foucault reshaped the question, asking what happened between the time of Hesiod and Plato. Why, Sini asks, did Plato so emphasize the distinction between "true speech" from "false speech"?

Even though it is probably impossible to know *why* the de-privation of truth occurred, it is likely that we know *how* it happened: precisely through Plato's invention of the soul. Only the institution of an inner space, removed from cosmic movement and from becoming, could find a place—a protection—for the public truth. The psychological–historical strategy is grounded in this *strategy* of soul. On these premises, in the second part of *Kinesis*, Sini prepares to think of the sign's event or, better said, the movement of difference between event and meaning.

The event of which Sini is speaking does not coincide with Heidegger's *Ereignis*. It is not the giving-of-itself of epochal Being. In terms of Peirce's semiotics, Sini sees the relationship of the first two elements of the sign, *Firstness* and *Secondness* (Quality and Fact), as the event of *Thirdness* (Law or Meaning). Here *Firstness* and *Secondness* seem to replace the concept of signifying. Although Sini's concept of "event" undoubtedly has something in common with the signifying event, his "event" is more, being in no way simply a sign or an Index of the signified. Essentially, Sini's event is the event *of nothing* or *of the nothing*. This *nothing* must not be understood as absolute negation but instead as *no-thing* (*niente, ni-ente, non-entity*): margin, edge, limit of the signified, its constitutive finiteness that *gives* meaning to the limited and finite relation. There is no signified without this occurrence (*accadere, ac-cadere*) of nothing.

The occurrence of nothing takes place in the sign-relation. But the sign-relation is not originary. It has to be grounded in the very source of *rimando* because sign is based on *rimando*, but *rimando* is not based on the sign. Sini places the event of the sign-relation in the primary structure of *rimando*. In *Images of Truth*, this structure is called *symbolic relation*. Sini's use of the term "symbol" does not refer to how symbols function in common language. His "symbol" is not a concept portrayed in an entity, as, for example, scales are a symbol of justice. He traces the symbol back to the etymological sense of Greek *symbolon*:

> The verb *symballein* means literally "putting together," "drawing near," "joining." Originally, *symbolon* was the broken part of an object. As an identification mark, it could join the missing part, recreating the unity. Then *symbolon* is the fragment of a wholeness that is not or is no longer. Because of these traits, symbol is a very peculiar sign: first of all it is a sign because, like any other sign, it "refers to"—*rimanda* (the fragment refers to the still unbroken object of which it is part, of which it is a sign). But, unlike any sign, symbol does not refer to "other," to something "different from itself." Instead, it still refers to itself, to "the same." *The other to which symbol refers is still itself.*[13]

Sini's thesis is that the real originary event is not the event of Being. Instead, the constant, silent occurrence of 'presence' is the symbolic relation: the crack, the fracture that connects and separates us from the totality that always eludes us since we exist (*ac-cadiamo*) only in its broken margin, in its "nothing." Sini calls *en-chantment* (*in-canto*) the emotional connotation of symbolic relation. What really happens is the enchantment of the world in both subjective and objective acceptation.

This enchantment precedes every statement about Being or thought. It is nothing less than sheer ecstasy (*ek-stasis*) in the margin of the sign and infinite interpretation. This explains how the original event emerges through the act of pointing out. To recall the quotation at the beginning of this paper, the correlation between finger and thing breaks the symbolic unity and allows the poles of relation to manifest themselves. But it is important to remember that this unity *does not exist before it is broken*. There is no "time" when it exists peacefully in its "togetherness." Only the fracture between *symbolon*'s two parts allows us to hark back to the unity that, in itself, never was. This lost unity is not; awareness of this lost unity's enchantment through the correlation between finger and thing is all that is. The event occurs in unison with the awareness of the event. What really happens is the awareness.[14]

The issue at stake is whether this conclusion can claim to go beyond metaphysics. According to Sini, Heraclitus' partition between public *Logos* and private idiosyncrasy (the latter being perhaps the last refuge of the awareness of symbolic relation) is based on Parmenides' decision to exclude nothing from thought. No philosopher, not even Heidegger, has deeply questioned Parmenides' postulate of absolute coincidence of Being and thought. It has always been assumed that thought had to be subsumed under Being and that only Being could be thought. The consequence of Parmenides' "decision" is that the constitutive "nothing" shaping the experience of world-enchantment has been confined within a truth-deprived privateness outside *Logos*' borders. On this basis, the "obvious" statement that equates Being and thought must be subjected to hermeneutical investigation as well. Which really came first, Being or *Logos*? Is *Logos* the product of Being's thought, or is Being the offspring of *Logos*? Sini wants to demonstrate that the will to truth actually preceded Being, and that Being sheltered *Logos*' public truth. Parmenides' Being was adaptable to the needs of Heraclitus' *Logos* at the same time that it satisfied Plato's requirements for right judgment. This Being did not exist before Parmenides conceived it and wrote about it in his poem. For Plato to write the *Sophist*, so that the truth, the science of truth, and philosophy could be, Being *had to be*.

IV. The Vertical Dimension of Event

In the preface of *Images of Truth*, Sini affirms that the journey begun with *Semiotics and Philosophy* has come to its "finite" conclusion. Peirce, Nietzsche, and Heidegger provided the foundation for Sini's criticism of metaphysics which brought him to the roots of Plato's strategy of soul. The next step is the genealogy of this strategy and the hermeneutics of some fundamental key-words of Western philosophy. *Silence and Word* and *Signs of Soul* (both published in 1989) begin to explore the new problematic.[15] With his definition of image, Plato created soul. But what is image? Why were philosophers never able to go beyond the psychological idea of image that Plato defined? Image and soul are intertwined in the same way as voice and gesture. These problems can be traced back to the primary partition out of which philosophy was born. Being, *Logos*, truth, image: philosophical discourse already *owns* these words. Hence, they cannot help us to find an external point of view. Therefore, the first question is: why did Parmenides shift from initiation into knowledge (*odos*) to the instituting of method (*methodos*)? Since Parmenides, the question of method *is* the philosophical question.[16]

The hermeneutics of method is thus the direction taken by Sini's philosophy in recent years. It seems also to be the way to begin again a dialogue with Husserl and Heidegger and, above all, *between* Husserl and Heidegger. After a long period spent consolidating his thinking about hermeneutics and semiotics, Sini came back to Husserl, because Husserl's phenomenology was, after all, the most consistent contemporary attempt to create a systematic philosophy. But what is Husserl's phenomenology? Path or method? *Odos* or *methodos*? How could Husserl claim that transcendental phenomenology was scientific philosophy? If scientific, why did it need (as Husserl said) a sort of religious conversion of thought? What is the reason for this ambivalence?

In his latest essay, *Mein Weg in die Phänomenologie,* Heidegger affirmed that phenomenology was not just a philosophical school. Much more, it defined the very question of thinking.[17] It seems time for phenomenology and hermeneutics to resume their dialogue. Beyond the personal break between Husserl and Heidegger, beyond differences and hostility between the two "schools," Sini affirms that, although they did not think alike (*das Gleiche*), they did think *the same* (*Dasselbe*).[18] And the crossroads of hermeneutics and phenomenology is reached only if it is acknowledged that phenomenon and event are the same and that "Thing and thing's event are absolutely the same"(*FF*, 204).

Actually, the fact that thing's event is a semiotic relation, subject to infinite interpretation, must serve as a warning: the greatest hermeneutical mistake is to believe that infinite interpretations *of the same thing* are possible. This is bad hermeneutics, repeating the metaphysical reduction of Being to an object of thinking. In Sini's opinion, contemporary hermeneutics, derived from H. G. Gadamer, is still affected by metaphysical historicism, since it claims that today's interpretation must achieve a "larger fusion of horizon" than previous ones. Such hermeneutics finds itself dangerously close to the most self-indulgent expression of relativism in which "anything goes," since everyone has his own little "public" truth. In reality, every interpretation defines a *different thing* not given outside that specific interpretation. The chain of Interpretants is not on a horizontal line whose extremes go to infinity. As odd as it may sound, every historical interpretation literally *creates* a different past:[19]

> In reality, the event of any interpretation occurs vertically, concentrating in itself the meaning of past and future. Past and future place themselves at the beginning of the event, they come out of the event, they *are* the very shape of the event. Any interpretative event becomes 'larger' when it puts at stake the interpretation from which it comes and because of this putting at stake.[20]

There is a strong faith in philosophy in all of Sini's work. The end of metaphysics, so he seems committed to repeat, is neither the end of philosophy nor of thought. He is deeply concerned about the danger of fostering a general distrust of philosophy based on a superficial acceptance of nihilistic assumptions such as, "There is no truth," "After Heidegger thinking is impossible." While agreeing that the central issue in today's thought is the ethics of writing, Sini dislikes any easy mixture of philosophy and literature. Following Husserl's admonition, he does not believe in the "literary philosopher." Sini reminds us that philosophy is essentially *methodos*, not *odos*, and his method is rigorously semiotical, hermeneutical, and increasingly phenomenological.

Yet the border between the reassuring field of the history of metaphysics (with all its "images," "truths," "Being(s)") and the Great Unknown of symbolic relation and private idiosyncrasy (always the preserve of poetry and literature) may become very unclear for a philosophy that claims to bypass Parmenides' equivalence of Being and thought. Where does this radical hermeneutics bring us? Beyond metaphysics? Below, above, beside? Or deeper in its heart? And how to reconcile (provided that reconciliation is needed) Sini's emphasis on method with Heidegger's assertion that "... in thinking there is neither method nor theme, but rather the region (*die Gegend*), so called because it gives its realm and free reign to what thinking is given to think" (*NL*, 74)?

Sini would answer that post-metaphysical philosophy has still a hard job ahead, leaving little time for nihilistic complaints or precious reveries. Metaphysics did not consign to oblivion only the ontological difference between Being and beings. Above all, metaphysics forgot a being's very transcendence, its event, its phenomenon. Not that metaphysics was unaware of that: from Hegel to Husserl, philosophy struggled constantly with the issue of the *this* and the *here and now*. It has been phenomenology's starting point, and there its search must conclude. Philosophy's goal (and Sini's too) is to understand what we "already" know—and especially what "already" means. Of course, what we already know is language. Ernst Bloch was wont to say that the nearest is always the farthest. Heidegger would say that *die Sage*, the originary Saying, "... has in fact already struck its target (*Sie hat schon getroffen*)—whom else but man"(*NL*, 90)? Zarathustra said, every speech is a circle, even speech that does not take for granted the Parmenidean identity of Being and thinking. In fact, the philosophical wall that no one ever overcame is not the Being–thinking equation.

In my opinion, Sini has seen something of tremendous importance in Heraclitus' separation of public *Logos* and private *phronesis* (Parmenides would have spoken of *episteme* and *doxa*). The issue awaits further development. It is no coincidence that the concept of *phronesis* is acquiring a new relevance in today's philosophical debate about ethics, in the face of the weakening of all "public" frameworks of morality. Although the classic source of *phronesis* is, of course, Aristotle's *Nicomachean Ethics*, it would be more appropriate to trace it back to Heraclitus. Much, perhaps all, is at stake in Heraclitus' division between *Logos* and *phronesis*, because the most insidious word of Western philosophy is not Being but *Logos*. Even Heidegger agrees that "Being" might be just a temporary word. According to him, the name of beings' Being is *Logos*, and he affirms that the answer to the question of how *Logos* came to signify "language" will decide many things.[21] Even though we go beyond the identity of Being and thinking, we are still stuck with the identity of Being and (public) language. The problem is that language is *only* public. *Private language* is a contradiction.

Poetry and literature speak *of* it but do not speak *it*. Psychology speaks *about* the language of folly, it does not speak the language of folly. Privateness and otherness seem to come very close, yet remain unattainable. Nonetheless, privateness *speaks*. Heraclitus admits that many men live only acccording to their *phronesis* instead of *Logos* (Frag. 2 B.). How do they live? What language do they speak? How does *phronesis* hide itself from *Logos'* panoramic eye? Sini's answer, as we have seen, is symbolic relation. But symbolic relation is just the analytics of privateness, not *phronesis* yet. Is it possible to come to an ethics of symbolic relation without forcibly inserting the existential richness of privateness into public philosophical speech? Is the relation between Being and (public) Saying the unsurpassable limit of thinking? Must radical hermeneutics give up at this point? That Sini's thought provokes these and other crucial questions, involving not only his own work but also the general destiny of today's philosophy, is just an indication that the path he has entered is a long one. Far from having been, it certainly deserves to be travelled.[22]

Chapter 3

LACAN AND THE EVENT OF THE SUBJECT

François Raffoul

A number of relatively recent readings have attempted to trace Lacan back to a certain subjectivist (and substantialist) tradition in philosophy, claiming that the Lacanian theory of the subject remains deeply indebted to, indeed determined by, a whole series of metaphysical presuppositions.[1] Such a case can no doubt be made (and I will try here to account for its necessity), but the question remains whether these interpretations do sufficient justice to what Lacan's work attempts to articulate in a way that is admittedly contradictory and uneven. My concern here is with the radicality and scope of the so-called Lacanian "subversion" or "destitution" of the subject with respect to its ability to disengage itself from such a tradition. Can one, for example, equate the Lacanian re-elaboration of the notion of subjectivity to a mere displacement (that is, from the ego to the unconscious) which would nonetheless maintain the value, function, and status of the classical subject? Can one interpret Lacan's expression "subject of the unconscious" as a substantification of the unconscious? Or, rather, should one see there the elaboration of an *original* figure of Selfhood, which is still called "subject," but which remains similar to the traditional subject in name only? Such questions, which might seem to be transposed from an order external to that of psychoanalysis (namely from philosophy), are in fact neither arbitrary nor forced. They emanate from the very definition Lacan gives psychoanalysis:

> Psycho-analysis is neither a *Weltanschauung,* nor a philosophy that claims to provide the key to the universe. It is governed by a particular aim, *which is historically defined by the elaboration of the notion of the subject.*[2]

Lacan elaborates a theory of the subject, but this elaboration amounts to a *calling into question* of the subject, insofar as it "poses this notion in a new way, by leading the subject back to its signifying dependence." (*FFCP,* 73/77). The Lacanian subversion of the subject, we know, resides in this very "leading back," in the sense that the subject finds itself thereby stripped of all the "privileges" that would constitute it as autonomous self-consciousness, master of itself, a subjectivity transparent to itself, and no longer able to "appear" except in and by the signifier. Indeed, Lacan has always maintained that the subject must be thought as a linguistic being, that is to say, *defined by and on the basis of* language. Among many examples, let us cite this one:

> Indeed, whether it is a question of being a self, being a father, being born, being loved or dead, how can one fail to see that the subject, if it is the speaking subject, sustains itself only on the basis of discourse?[3]

Consequently, and radically: "There is no pre-discursive reality whatsoever, for the very reason that what constitutes community, which I have referred to as men, women and children, are *nothing but signifiers.*"[4] This conception of the subject, symbolized by Lacan as $\cancel{S}$ in order to mark both its secondary character with respect to the signifier[5] and its division (to which we will return), leads however to a circle, which we find in the very definition of the terms *subject* and *signifier*:

> The subject is that which the signifier represents.
> The signifier is that which represents a subject.

If the subject is no longer defined except in relation to the signifier, it is nevertheless also true that the signifier, in turn, is only defined in relation to the subject. This circle could be thought of in various ways, either as the very hermeneutic position of the Lacanian theory,[6] or, more critically, as the sign of a certain presupposed subjectivism in the Lacanian theory.[7] If we develop the circle, we find the following situation: to the extent that the subject "is what the signifier represents," it finds itself subjected in this very subordination to a division which brings about its alienation, and to a "fading" which brings about its disappearance. The "subjective destitution" performed by Lacan's work lies in this two-fold effect of alienation and fading. But to the extent that the signifier is *only ever* the signifier *of a subject*, since a signifier is *what represents a subject* for another signifier,[8] the subject seems to maintain itself at the horizon of Lacan's theory, a horizon both presupposed and unsurpassable. Lacan's treatment of the subject seems then to oscillate between two poles: on the one hand, the subject "disappears as subject under the signifier it becomes" (E, 835). On the other hand, paradoxically the subject is preserved:

> If psycho-analysis is to be constituted as the science of the unconscious, one must set out from the notion that the unconscious is structured like a language.
>
> From this I have deduced a topology, the aim of which is to account for the constitution of the subject.[9]

Does this circle in which the subject and the signifier are reciprocally presupposed in effect either leave the subject unquestioned or does it make the subject precisely what is in question? The examination of this issue proceeds in three stages:

First, we must take into account the manner in which the Lacanian subversion of the subject is articulated, and how the alienation and fading of the subject in language are presented.

Second, we will consider the hypothesis of a maintaining or sublation of the motif of the subject by which the latter would not so much be "eliminated" as *displaced* from its traditional locus—self-consciousness—to the unconscious, where it now dwells under the enigmatic name of "the subject of the unconscious." In this case, the unconscious could be considered as the genuine subject, as the Lacanian expression, "the true subject of the unconscious," seems to imply.

Third, and finally, we will wonder whether it is possible to assimilate the unconscious, purely and simply, to a subject, in the sense of a *subjectum*, or whether, far from any idea of substance or ground, this "subject of the unconscious" should not rather be approached as an ek-static or disruptive "presence," in a sense that we will try to determine.

I.

The Freudian revolution, as Lacan always stressed, essentially consists in decentering the subject understood as self-consciousness by revealing the intrapsychic division which splits it. He explains, for example in "The Agency of the Letter in the Unconscious or Reason since Freud" (*E*, 524/171–2), that the "truth discovered by Freud" is the "self's radical ex-centricity to itself," the "radical heteronomy . . . gaping within man." Lacan's celebrated formula, "the unconscious is structured like a language," specifies this intrapsychic division, and draws our attention to the link between language, on the one hand, and the division of the subject, on the other, for the subject is primarily to be understood as a *speaking* subject, a *parlêtre*.[10] How is this formula to be understood? One might first consider that the unconscious, that "other scene" made thematic by Freud, is interpreted by Lacan as being ruled by the laws of language. This is, for example, what William Richardson seems to indicate when he writes that, by this sentence, "Lacan means that the unconscious follows the same laws that language does";[11] A. Vergote analyses this formula in the same vein: "First, it affirms that the contents of the unconscious consist in elements of language. . . . Second, according to this thesis, because of their linguistic nature the contents of the unconscious are organized and transformed *according to the laws of language*."[12] If such a reading is not incorrect, it nevertheless misses what is ultimately at issue here. Indeed, to contend that the unconscious is structured like a language does not simply amount to establishing a parallel between the order of the unconscious and that of language, nor to conform the former to the latter, but rather derives the very possibility of the unconscious from the effects of language on the subject. Indeed, for Lacan, the unconscious is not some deep level of the psyche, some animal or primitive force in human beings, but strictly "the dimension in which the subject is determined in the development of the effects of speech" (*FFCP*, 137/149). Therefore, the unconscious is structured like a language.[13] In *Psychanalyse et Médecine*, Lacan writes: "The unconscious does not exist because of the existence of some unconscious, obtuse, heavy, caliban, or even animal desire, some unconscious primitive desire brought up from the depths which would have to rise itself to the superior level of consciousness. On the contrary, desire exists because the unconscious exists, that is, because there is language which escapes the subject in its structure and effects, and because there is always something on the level of language which is beyond consciousness . . ."[14] In short, there can only be an unconscious for the speaking being. This is why Lacan goes as far as to say that "language is the condition of the unconscious.... The unconscious is the logical implication of language: indeed, there is no unconscious without language."[15] Lacan indicates through this formula that the division of the subject, or the recognition of an unconscious disrupting the unity of consciousness (a unity which for Lacan, as we know, is only imaginary), originates from language itself, from its effects on the subject. In other words, the formula is concerned with the *constitution of the subject*. This is why Lacan specifies:

> My saying that the unconscious is structured like a language does not pertain to the field of linguistics.... But if one considers all that which follows from the definition of language, *in regard to the foundation of the subject* ... then we will have to forge some other word. I will call that linguistery (*linguisterie*). (*Encore*, 20, my emphasis)

Accordingly, the subversion of the subject can only be understood on the basis of the effects introduced into the subject by language. If we take seriously the Lacanian definition of the subject as sustained by discourse alone, that is, possessing no consistency as a pre-discursive reality, but rather emerging from the structure of the signifier—where for Lacan "*everything* emerges from the structure of the signifier" (*FFCP*, 188/206, my emphasis)—we must then recognize that the subject is *literally* caused by the signifier.[16] No parallelism, then, but causation.

But with what sort of causality are we dealing here? Is it a traditional determinism, simply inverted, in the sense that the traditional relation between the subject and its meaning and language finds itself merely reversed?[17] Nothing could be less clear, for the very notion of causality seems to undergo a major transformation. For Lacan, causality does not constitute or close an order, but rather introduces or reveals a *gap*. He writes:

> There remains essentially in the function of cause a certain *gap*. ... Whenever we speak of cause ... there is always something anti-conceptual, something indefinite. The phases of the moon are the cause of tides.... Or, again, miasmas are the cause of fever—that does not mean anything either, there is a hole, and something that oscillates in the interval. In short, there is cause only in something that doesn't work (*qui cloche*).

Well! It is at this point that I am trying to make you see by approximation that the Freudian unconscious is situated at that point, where, between cause and that which it affects, there is always something wrong (*clocherie*). (FFCP, 24–25/ 21–22)

The subject, insofar as it is said to be "caused," will be affected by such a perversion of causality; the "hole," the "oscillation," and the "interval" will all become *constituting* features of the Lacanian subject. What "does not work" in causality, what does not work in the effects of language on the subject, is precisely that impossibility of reconstituting the unity of the subject, even in a reversed way, through the recollection of an order of reasons. It would thus be erroneous to think that Lacan limits himself to reversing the traditional hierarchy of cause and effect between the subject and language. In the recognition of a subordination of the subject to the signifier, there is no affirmation of a simple *inversion*, but more radically, of a *perversion* of the classical idea of a totalization of knowledge through causality, for the cause the signifier introduces into the subject determines it as *gap*, that is, the *gap* constituted by the non-coincidence of the subject to itself:

The effect of language is the cause introduced into the subject. Through this effect, the subject is not the cause of itself; it carries within itself the worm of the cause that splits it (*il porte en lui le ver de la cause qui le refend*). (E, 835)

Thus Lacan claims that the subject is constituted through the effects of language, which preexists it and in which that "subject-to-be" has to inscribe itself, that this constitution amounts to a division, and that only through this division introduced by the inner corruption of the signifier–cause must the emergence of the unconscious be situated.[18] The statement "the unconscious is structured like a language," states nothing less. . . . A reading of the Lacanian critique of the subject must then pay close attention to those "effects" of language by which the subject finds itself "divided," "destitute," and finally "eclipsed."

Lacan describes this effect of language on the subject through what he calls the mechanism of *alienation*. Alienation consists in that phenomenon by which the subject, first called into being by a signifier—which Lacan calls the "first" signifier, or "unary signifier" (*FFCP*, 199/218), also symbolized as S1—finds itself, as soon as it appears, congealed and petrified:

> The subject is born in so far as the signifier emerges in the field of the Other. But by this very fact this subject—which previously was nothing but a subject yet to come (*sujet à venir*)—solidifies into a signifier.... The subject is this emergence which, just before, as subject, was nothing, but which having scarcely appeared, solidifies into a signifier.[19]

The inaugural division of the subject hollows itself out in the gap which occurs between the "nothing" which the subject "was" before being taken into the signifier (but in which it is significantly said nevertheless to be "called")[20] and the unary signifier in which it solidifies. For if the subject is reduced, as soon as it appears, to "being no more than a signifier,"(*XI*, 188/207), it disappears in the same stroke as a "pure" subject, that is, in the authenticity of its being. The subject is alienated because, as soon as it appears, it is as *represented* by the signifier. "Of course, every representation requires a subject," Lacan explains, "but this subject is never a pure subject"(*FFCP*, 201/221). The impossible coincidence of the subject to itself as a speaking being is revealed in this "*vel*" of alienation, that is, in the gap between the emergence of the subject *called into being* and its (impure) represented being as signifier. The unconscious, as a pure effect of signifier, articulates itself in this rift of the speaking being. It is thus not surprising that the division of the subject is essentially formulated in Lacan's work as a separation between the level of the enunciation (*énonciation*) and the level of the statement (*énoncé*). He explains that "the presence of the unconscious ... is to be found in all discourse, in its enunciation"(*E*, 834). The subject, having no other reality than a discursive one, that is to say as a speaking subject, can only come to be and manifest itself in an enunciation. But to the extent that this coming forth solidifies or congeals in the signifier, that which *enunciates itself* as coming to be, is only henceforth *enunciated*. The impossible coincidence to itself of the speaking subject is thus to be understood as the impossible coincidence of the statement to its enunciation:

> Indeed, the *I* of the enunciation is not the same as the *I* of the statement, that is to say, the shifter which, in the statement, designates him. (*FFCP*, 127/139)[21]

The first effect of the constituting and alienating power of the signifier over the subject lies in the recognition that the subject is "petrified" in representation, and hence separated from its truth. This division is irreducible, for it is constitutive of the very being of the subject. I am never able, as a speaking subject, to be adequate in what I say to my saying, for, as soon as I speak, I am no longer the same:

> It is not a question of knowing whether I speak of myself in a way that conforms to what I am, but rather knowing whether I am the same as that of which I speak. (*E*, 517/165)

This description of the division of the subject through the fundamental mechanism of alienation is, however, still incomplete. The operation of alienation does not simply consist in this first fixation, but leads through the essentially *representative* structure of the signifier (the latter is essentially defined—or presupposed—by Lacan as representation), to the disappearing or *fading* of the subject *under* the signifier. If in a first moment the subject is petrified *in* the (unary) signifier, in a second, it falls from it and disappears *under* it. Hence the division of the subject: when the subject appears somewhere as meaning, it is manifested elsewhere as 'fading,' as disappearance. The subject is required to appear only in this division, that one could thus articulate as the play of the appearance–disappearance of the subject. The first signifier is only called a unary signifier to the extent that it refers to an *other* signifier,[22] or rather to the unity of all the signifiers (regrouped under the sign S2) a reference which constitutes a signifying battery S1, S2 (unary signifier, binary signifier) designated by Lacan as the "dyad of the signifying articulation." The subject which appears *in* the unary signifier duplicates itself and disappears *under* the binary signifier. Alienation then lies "in that first signifying coupling that enables us to conceive that the subject appears first in the Other, in so far as the first signifier, the unary signifier, emerges in the field of the Other and represents the subject for another signifier" (*FFCP*, 199/218). The latter provokes the fading of the subject. Lacan interprets this fading on the basis of a reappropriation of a phenomenon (the disappearance of sexual desire) designated by Ernest Jones as *aphanisis*:

> Now, *aphanisis* is to be situated in a more radical way at the level at which the subject manifests itself in this movement of

disappearance that I have described as lethal. In a quite different way I have called this movement the *fading* of the subject. (*FFCP*, 189/207–8, slightly modified)

This is why Lacan explains that it is "a matter of life and death between the unary signifier and the subject, *qua* binary signifier, cause of his disappearance" (*XI*, 199/218). The lethal character of the effects of the signifier on the subject is due no doubt to the way in which Lacan conceives of representation, as it intervenes in the definition: "A signifier is what *represents* a subject for another signifier." Indeed, Lacan conceives of representation in a quite classical way, as a holding-place of a reality in its absence, or as the murderous substitution of a symbol for a thing. As he writes, ". . . the symbol manifests itself first of all as the murder of the thing" (*E*, 319/104). This conception of representation commands the entire motif of the disappearance of the subject under the signifier: it is only because the subject is submitted to *representation* that it manifests itself as fading. Having thus posed (or presupposed) language as representation, defined in the sense we have just seen, the subject can only reveal itself as dead. A signified (represented) subject means: a dead subject. To lead the subject back to its signifying dependence is at the same time to present it as dead—a death which gives itself as the truth of the subject. On this point, Lacan places himself explicitly under the authority of Heidegger and the motif of being-towards-death.

> This limit [of the historical function of the subject] is death—not as an eventual coming-to-term of the life of the individual, nor as the empirical certainty of the subject, but as Heidegger's formula puts it, as that "ownmost, unconditional, unsupersedable, certain and as such indeterminable possibility of the subject." (*E*, 318/103, translation slightly modified)

The linguistic being, the *parlêtre*, is a dead being; the notion of a disappearance of the subject under the signifier then becomes clearer: As Lacan writes, ". . . it disappears as subject under the signifier it becomes" (*E*, 835). One could lay out the (de)constitution of the subject in the following sequence:

1. It appears, albeit solidified, in the first signifier: "For its cause is the signifier without which there would not be any subject in the real." (*E*, 835)

2. Its appearance amounts to a disappearance, due to the representative structure of the signifier.

On the one hand a petrification, on the other a disappearance: as we see, the speaking subject is indeed that *impossible* referred to by Lacan: "The path of the subject passes between the two walls of the impossible" (*FFCP*, 152/167).

II.

This very impossibility, in the guise of the petrification and fading of the subject, could be said to paradoxically *constitute* the new locus of the subject—a subject no doubt decentered or divided, but nevertheless maintained, if only in name. We are indeed constrained to observe, after the whole critique of the classical subject, the surprising reappearance of the term "subject," and in a place where we would least expect it (some would even say: "where it has no business being"),[23] that is to say, in the unconscious, as the formula "subject of the unconscious" indicates. This combination of terms seems at first quite paradoxical, in the sense that the term subject is usually associated with self-consciousness;[24] yet the matter becomes clearer if one considers that in the final analysis Lacan aims less at a destruction of the motif of the subject as such than at a denunciation of the identity or identification of the subject with consciousness, an identification that for him essentially represents a misrecognition (*méconnaissance*) of the subject's own division.

> You have spoken of the mirage engendered by the confusion of consciousness and the subject, a mirage that the psychoanalytic experience denounces. . . . How does the psychoanalytic experience take account of the misrecognition (*méconnaissance*) engendered in a subject by the fact that it identifies with its consciousness?[25]

The issue then becomes one of dissociating the subject from the ego. The so-called Lacanian subversion aims "only" at challenging the subject's identification with consciousness (which indicates that the very value of the term "subject" remains unquestioned— thus allowing Lacan to perpetuate its usage). The subject is then less "subverted" than "displaced." On the one hand, it is disassociated with and decentered from the ego, and on the other hand it is *re-posited*, to the exclusion of the ego, at the level of the unconscious. This is the sense of this passage from Lacan's seminar on "The Ego in Freud's Theory and Psychoanalytic Technique":

> If there is an image which could represent for us the Freudian notion of the unconscious, it is indeed that of the acephalic subject, of a subject who no longer has an *ego*, furthest from the *ego*, decentred in relation to the *ego*, and which is not ego-like (*qui n'est pas de l'ego*). And yet it is the speaking subject.[26]

But Lacan is not content simply to distinguish the subject from the ego. He inscribes them in a hierarchy in which the ego is devalued and severely criticized in its attempt to posit itself as the "true subjectivity"—we know Lacan's celebrated analysis with respect to the ego as an imaginary agency of misrecognition, an agency of alienation, and a deluding objectivation of the subject (*II*, 60/44). On the other hand, the subject, as subject *of the unconscious*, is set up as the genuine subject, the true subject of the unconscious (*E*, 417/128)[27] if not as an absolute subject (!), as Moustapha Safouan suggests:

> In contrast with this subject, the subject to which Lacan draws our attention, that of the unconscious, or else the one which is ex-centered in relation to the individual, could be called, rightly, an "absolute subject" in the sense that it does not posit itself in opposition to (*en face à face*). It has no need to posit itself, even less to oppose itself, to ek-sist. (*TD*, 146)

The subject "of the unconscious" would then be a subject excluded from the ego—which for Lacan is nothing other than an object,[28] or rather the subject having made itself an object—no longer referred to any objectivation or objectivity, which does not need to posit itself through an opposition. In short, an "acephalic subject" dwells in the unconscious. In a striking formula, Lacan writes that "the subject is *at home* in the field of the unconscious"(*FFCP*, 36/36, my emphasis). From that place, the subject poses its question to the philosopher:

> In the unconscious, which is less deep than inaccessible to a deepening consciousness, *it speaks* (*ça parle*): a subject in the subject, transcendent to the subject, poses its question to the philosopher since *The Interpretation of Dreams*. (*E*, 437)

What is this question? This question is as follows: " 'Who is speaking?', when it is the subject of the unconscious that is at issue" (*E*, 800/299, my emphasis). One might immediately object: How can this question even be posed when we know that the subject is *spoken*, that is to say articulated in and by the signifier? In this case, *id* speaks *the order of the signifier itself* . . . by which the subject constitutes itself as second and divided, takes the place of the subject, as subject of the unconscious. Lacoue-Labarthe and Nancy argue this very point in *The Title of the Letter*, where they seem to define the Lacanian subject as nothing but literal:

> To say that the letter is what implicates the subject means, even before "taking the letter to the letter" [see *E*, 495/147], taking the subject *in* the letter—which will soon appear, as one might expect, as a way of taking the subject to the letter. (*TL*, 27)

On this basis, the two authors advance the hypothesis of a *literalization* of the subject by which "the Lacanian subject is instituted . . . in and by the signifier," leading them to conclude that Lacan carries out a "destruction–reconstruction of the concept of the subject in the signifier"(*TL*, 70). However, the subject at issue here has nothing to do with the reflexivity of a self-consciousness; rather, its being exhausts itself in the structure of the letter which is only called a 'subject' through its function as *subjectum* or *substrate*. One would then be authorized to consider the subject of the unconscious as the literal order as such, which comes to replace consciousness in the establishment of a *subjectum*. We come across such a claim, for example, in the work of Serge Leclaire, who states that "it is the network of letters which will itself constitute the substrate."[29] If the unconscious is to be situated at the level of the literal order, the subject of the unconscious would then designate nothing other than the linguistic substrate of a divided subjectivity. The genitive "of" is implicitly recognized here as an agency in which the subject *insists* in the signifier, in the same way that the preposition "for," as it operates in the pivotal Lacanian definition of metaphor, is explicitly recognized as an agency of literalization of the subject. For example:

> Metaphor gathers in itself, then, the function of the subject and that of the word; it is the locus where the latter takes posses-

sion of the former and "literalizes" it in the form of an odd tropological or signifying literality. (*TL*, 75–76)

Metaphor, which is recognized by Lacan, at least in its operativity, as the originary mechanism ruling signifying substitution,[30] is to be considered the main mechanism of the operativity of the signifier insofar as the latter represents a subject *for* another signifier. This structure of the signifier is only possible on the basis of a constitutive metaphoricity. One must then recognize in the preposition "for," as it appears in the definition of the signifier, the same function that operates in the definition of metaphor, that of a literalization by which the subject is only ever an effect, and the signifying order, the "new" true subject of the unconscious, *as* unconscious. It nevertheless remains that the subject of the unconscious, as literal as it may be, that is, a thousand miles from any ego-subject, persists, or insists, but as substrate. What would remain unquestioned in Lacan's subversion of the subject is the essence of the subject as *subjectum*, its very "subjectness." Here the Lacanian subversion of the subject closes on itself and reaches its limit, in that it simply reposits the longstanding metaphysical figure of the *subjectum* elsewhere (that is, in the unconscious.) In this sense, it never questions its being.[31] Whether to rejoice,[32] or on the contrary to deplore a limit of the Lacanian theory, the result is the same: the subject remains, or as Lacan says: "It is there, it is always there. It is the subject" (*Ego*, 288/246).

How indeed can we fail to note a whole series of properly metaphysical presuppositions in Lacan's text, assumptions that need to be brought to light if we are to measure the scope and the radicality of his undertaking?[33] Let us single out a few of them:

1. The subversion of the subject that Lacan, after Freud, identifies as the "self's radical ex-centricity to itself"(*E*, 524/171) in fact results in a valorization of a "subject," under the name of "true subject of the unconscious," which is said to be more essential than any ego. The distinction that Lacan establishes between the ego and the subject makes possible, in the end (as *telos*), a reappropriation of the subject in its truth, as it finds its way through the sum of the alienating identifications from which it has to extricate itself. Lacoue-Labarthe and Nancy see both the place of a literalization of the subject and insistence of the latter as a *teleological* horizon of the signifying chain in the preposition "for," which

is found in the expression "one word *for* another," or in the expression "the signifier represents a subject *for* another signifier":

> One word *for* another, this means a word *in place* of another—a substitution of signifiers—but also one word *in view* of another—a sort of internal teleology of the signifying order. This metaphorical teleology is that through which the *subject* insists in the signifier, since it is, we know, "what a signifier represents *for* another signifier."(*TL*, 75)

This teleology would situate the Lacanian theory in the context of a hermeneutic,[34] through a dialectic of alienation and liberation between two subjective agencies. This motif of freedom (or realization of the subject in its truth) is present in Lacan's work as the promised recuperation of a subject *alienated* in the signifier:

> What the subject has *to free itself of* is the aphanisic effect of the binary signifier and, if we look at it more closely, we shall see that in fact it is a question of nothing else than the function of freedom. (*FFCP*, 200/219, my emphasis)

2. The notion of a *subject* of the unconscious, as paradoxical as it is, originates in the reintroduction by Lacan of the metaphysical schema of substance in the very heart of the gap opened in the speaking being, allowing henceforth a reappropriation of the category of the subject at the very level of language. This reintroduction is finally made possible only to the extent that Lacan presupposed the category of the subject, the one which remains as the very center and horizon of his theory. Before its being taken into the signifier, it was a subject to be. Once inscribed into the signifier, it is alienated in it and insists or persists there, as presupposed, that is, as posited underneath (for example, as underlying the meaning of symptoms). Moustapha Safouan recognizes this presupposition:

> For Lacan the subject is presupposed by the unary signifier which represents it for another signifier. As such it is the implication of this signifying relation, and it is presupposed in the sense of being posited underneath (*subjectum* or *hypokeimenon*). (*TD*, 226)

3. The division affecting the subject, and producing it as *fading*, far from constituting its vanishing point or disappearance, is re-

cuperated by Lacan as a gap whereby the subject maintains itself *as* a divided subject. Everything happens as if the Lacanian subject were sustaining itself as certainty from the gap which divides it but which nevertheless continues to allow its constitution. It is as if the very gap revealed by the effect of the signifier on the subject was reappropriated as a basis or a foundation (perhaps a more solid one than any ego could provide) instituting a "new" subject which is no longer an ego or a self-consciousness, and still less a person or an individual, but rather is designated as "subject of the unconscious." The impossibility of a subject to ever coincide with itself then becomes the very condition of *possibility* of its establishment, just as in Sartre's work the "for-itself," that negativity which is not what it is and is what it is not, becomes the very essence of subjectivity.[35] Such is, for example, the reading of Lacoue-Labarthe and Nancy: the gap of the subject becomes its very basis, in a quasi-Cartesian sense; "Even the gap of the *shifter* operates almost as a sort of confirmation of the subject adhering to its own certainty through the certainty of its noncoincidence to itself"(*TL*, 121).[36]

4. Finally, the very fading of the subject, constituting that subject as *lack-of-being*, amounts paradoxically to constituting the basis for a subject, or rather a subject lacking to itself, in the sense that this fading is reappropriated as a lack which the subject can and should under no circumstances... lack. This foundational character of the lack is taken up by Moustapha Safouan when he writes: "What man asks, what he can only ask if left to himself is, in the final analysis, to be deprived of something real"(*QS*, 263–4). And we know that man, left to himself, has to bear the ordeal of his lack of being, insofar as that ordeal represents the very ordeal of his truth, a truth which is nothing other than indispensable: "What is *Angst*-producing (*l'angoissant*) is not lack, but the lack of its support" (*QS*, 264). One would then be entitled to see in Lacan's theory no less than an ontology—"and this is indeed an ontology, as one might expect after having seen strategy borrow so many elements for its combination from the major history of metaphysical ontology" (*TL*, 126)—or more exactly a "negative ontology" articulated around lack, as truth and basis of the subject.

If it appears hardly disputable that the Lacanian subversion, through all these motifs, can lend itself to such a reading, we are perhaps justified in wondering nonetheless whether such is really the last word of Lacan, on Lacan? Do we not ignore here the profound transformations to which Lacan submits the metaphysical thinking of the subject, and through them, the elaboration of an original figure of subjectivity? And finally, *with regard to Lacan's texts,* are the hypotheses of a literalization of the subject (by which the subject *insists* in the signifier), and a substantification of the unconscious (by which the subject of the unconscious is understood as *subjectum,* or substrate), acceptable?

III.

The hypothesis of a literalization of the subject presupposes the (teleological) insistence of the subject in the signifying chain and reaffirms the persistence of the subject as an underlying support *(subjectum).* In this sense, we are led to the notion of a substantial unconscious. However, with respect to this so-called "insistence" of the subject in the signifying order, one should note that Lacan never failed to emphasize, on the contrary, that as soon as the subject is taken by the signifier, it can only be conceived as barred ($), that is, as *ecstatic* and *excluded.*[37] Each time the subject is represented by a signifier, and for another signifier, it is split once again in a kind of metonymical pulverization of its being:

> Through the effects of speech, the subject always realizes himself more in the Other, but he is already pursuing there no more than half of himself. He will simply find his desire ever more divided, pulverized, in the circumscribable metonymy of speech. (XI, 172/188, translation slightly modified)

One cannot, then, simply speak of the insistence or persistence of the subject, in the sense of a subject taken to the letter (*à la lettre*), since it appears on the contrary that the relation of the subject to the letter is not that of an insistence, but rather of an *ek-sistence.* Therefore, in contrast to what Lacoue-Labarthe and Nancy invite us to think, taking the subject *into* the letter does not amount to taking the subject *to* the letter, since this taking of the subject *into* the letter appears as a genuine expulsion *outside* of the letter. Following J. David Nasio, we are thus led to reconsider the genitive "of" (in the expression "subject *of* the unconscious"), as well as the preposition "for" (in the formulas of metaphor and signifier), as agencies of the exclusion of the subject:

In other words, the particle "of" has the same scope as the preposition "for" found in the definition which says "a signifier is what represents the subject *for* another signifier." Both the ex-centricity of the subject and the ek-sistence of the unconscious from the subject are based on this "for."[38]

This explains why Lacan asks in "The Agency of the Letter, or Reason since Freud,"

> Is the place that I occupy as subject of the signifier concentric or excentric, in relation to the place I occupy as subject of the signified? (*E*, 516–7/165, translation slightly modified)

His answer is unequivocal: the self's excentricity to itself is "radical." With such a "truth," he concludes emphatically, there is no "compromise" (*E*, 524/171-2). To deny it would amount to nothing less than bad faith, for the "radical heteronomy that Freud's discovery shows gaping within man can never again be covered over without whatever is used to hide it being profoundly dishonest" (*E*, 524/171-2).

The subject, as it appears, is excluded from the signifier. It falls out of the signifying articulation, refuses or resists articulation and literalization.[39] The being of the subject is here a *being in flight*, something like a remainder, as Lacan speaks of the *scraps* (*restes*) of the signifying articulation as that which falls outside of the signifier. Are these "scraps" to be thought as constituting some sort of substrate? Is the subject of the unconscious substantial, a subject within the subject? Nothing could be less certain. We already know that Lacan has never failed to reject this interpretation, professing on several occasions to avoid any formula which would overly substantify the unconscious. For example, in *The Four Fundamental Concepts of Psychoanalysis*, he explains:

> This makes it clear that, in the term *subject*—this is why I referred it back to its origin—I am not designating the living substratum needed by this phenomenon of the subject, *nor any sort of substance*. (*FFCP*, 116/126, my emphasis)

But in themselves, of course, these claims are not sufficient. More decisive in this regard is the question of knowing whether the so-called subject of the unconscious is of the order of a *stasis*, an underlying permanent support. Here Lacan's account of the unconscious does *not* seem to let itself be inscribed, purely and simply, in such a schema. On the contrary, Lacan constantly stresses the radically uneven, inconsistent, lacunary character of the subject of the unconscious:

> Impediment, failure, crack. In a spoken or written sentence something stumbles. Freud is attracted by these phenomena, and it is there that he seeks the unconscious. (*XI*, 27/25, translation slightly modified)

The unconscious is encountered at this level: there, where there is a disruption, where, as Lacan says, something "goes wrong," something "doesn't work." The subject of the unconscious is of the order of the discontinuous: "Discontinuity, then, is the essential form in which the unconscious first appears as a phenomenon."[40] This discontinuity, in turn, is so radical that it cannot be derived from or occur to some preexisting entitative subject, some preceding unity, in short, some "subject within the subject." The subject is split through and through: there lies the crack of the discontinuous. "Is the *one* anterior to discontinuity?" Lacan asks; the answer follows immediately: "I do not think so . . ." (*XI*, 28/25–26). The split is thus the split *of* the one ("You will grant me," Lacan declares, "that the *one* that is introduced by the experience of the unconscious is the *one* of the split, of the stroke, or rupture" [*XI*, 28/26]), not in the sense that it would divide or scatter an already extant unity, but as the very tracing of the one, a "folded" one, as it were.

> For any speaking being, the cause of its desire is strictly, in respect to its structure, equivalent, if I may say, to its *folding*. Namely to that which I have called its division as a subject. (*XX*, 114, my emphasis)

The subject, because of its relation to the signifier, is a "subject-with-holes (*sujet troué*)" (*XI*, 167/184). One should situate the unconscious at the level of what the holes imply in terms of loss, vanishing, or disappearance, therefore forbidding its repositing into a new essence. The hole that opens between the signifier–cause and the subject–effect is not able to consist as a stasis, or enduring support. The constancy of the self is here disrupted, interrupted. The Lacanian subject "ek-sists" in the vacillation where it appears (*by* the unary signifier) only to disappear (*under* the binary signifier), and only "consists" in such an oscillation. Lacan compares the mechanism of alienation to a "temporal pulsation," or a "beating," through which the subject of the unconscious—*as* unconscious—reveals itself in the flash of its own disappearance.[41] The subject of the unconscious, as "subject-with-holes," is coextensive to this movement of disappearance *by which* it gives itself, in the pure flash of its fading. The sole "status of being" Lacan recognizes with respect to the unconscious is that of the "evasive," the "inconsistent," or the "fragile." In that case, on what basis can one claim to fabricate a new consistency, or constancy? In a sense, the unconscious is nothing else than an *accident*, and cannot be distinguished from the way it gives itself, each time in an original, unique, and singular eruption of a gap, that is, in a "discovery" or "surprise." Such is the consequence of the Lacanian redefinition of the subject ("the subject is that which the signifier represents for another signifier"), that is, his referring of the subject back to its signifying dependence. Moustapha Safouan comments upon this definition as being an "indispensable definition putting an end to all substantialization of the subject, the latter being nothing but the movement of the disappearance by which it reveals itself" (*TD*, 209). The subject is not constant, but punctual. It is not consistent, but fading. It is not persistent, but appears only *as* it disappears. Lacan asserts: "the subject is only ever punctual and fading, for it is only a subject by the signifier, and for another signifier" (*Encore*, 130). The subject, in short, is "essentially" *elusive*; or, to use an expression from Lacoue-Labarthe, it is a subject in "desistance."

Perhaps then, when the subject of the unconscious is in question, there is no question less appropriate than: "Who speaks?" as if the position of such a question implicated immediately the position of the unconscious as a "subject in the subject" (as Lacan unhappily wrote) active in us and through us, and which would take the surreptitious form of a substantial entity. But it appears now that the subject in Lacan's work is to be thought less in terms of a metaphysical substance than as this "event" which, as it were, alternates presence and absence, appearance and disappearance, continuity and discontinuity. The unconscious is marked or delineated in the scansion of a discontinuous temporality, in the beat of an "each time." To the extent that the unconscious is not anterior to the folding of the subject and does not outlast it, one must think, with J. D. Nasio, of the unconscious in terms of the singularity of an event. "There is only an unconscious in the very event. It would then be erroneous to believe that before the slip of the tongue, for example, the unconscious waited to show itself, or on the contrary, that after the slip of the tongue, there remains a trace henceforth unconscious . . ." (*YL*, 41). The subject of the unconscious is not a "who" maintaining itself apart from its enunciation, but rather ek-sists in the very event of a saying which is ignited from its hemorrhaging disappearance. The subject of the unconscious is "equivalent" to this event. It is not a subject in the sense of a substrate, nor does it, in the end, appropriate that event. It is, rather, the ek-static place, trace or tracing, of such an event (and who better than Lacan should have taught us that):

> The saying comes to itself without its [the subject's] knowledge, and disappears, without finally being grasped. As if the speaking being was only at the moment of the event, the place of a passage, passage of a saying of which it is neither the author nor the recipient. (*YL*, 29)

Perhaps, then, the definition of the signifier from which we started, "a signifier is that which represents a subject for another signifier," should be taken as expressing this fact that the subject is present neither to its provenance nor to its destination; in short, it is purely immanent to its ek-static event.

Translated from the French by David E. Pettigrew

Chapter 4

TRACING THE SIGNIFIER BEHIND THE SCENES OF DESIRE: KRISTEVA'S CHALLENGE TO LACAN'S ANALYSIS

Kelly Oliver

Julia Kristeva's writings can be read as a mirror of the oscillation between the semiotic and symbolic, between negation and identification, between the two elements that constitute human subjectivity. For example, in *Revolution in Poetic Language* (1974) and *Powers of Horror* (1980) she emphasizes negation and the semiotic. In *Tales of Love* (1983), *In the Beginning Was Love, Psychoanalysis and Faith* (1987), and *Black Sun* (1987) she emphasizes identification and the symbolic. In *Strangers to Ourselves* (1989) and *Nations without Nationalism* (1990), she emphasizes the ways in which one is always implicated in the other.[1]

Kristeva claims that her work focuses on discourses that break identity. But she also focuses on discourses that constitute identity. She is concerned with the movement between negation of identity and constitution of identity, rejection and stasis. Her most famous distinction, the semiotic/symbolic distinction, points to this concern. Early in her writing Kristeva proposed that signification is composed of two heterogeneous elements, the semiotic and the symbolic.[2] The semiotic is the disruptive drive force that motives negation and difference while the symbolic is the stable position of judgment and grammar that fixes identity. These two forces move in a productive dialectic oscillation to produce signification.

Along with her revolutionary thesis that signification is heterogeneous, Kristeva maintains that both rejection and stasis, negation and identification—the two elements that are essential to subjectivity and human life—precede Lacan's mirror stage. Whereas Lacan sees the mirror stage as the onset of the subject through its entry into the world of the signifier, Kristeva hears the murmurs of subjectivity before the mirror stage in a subterranean world out of which the signifier develops.

Here I take up three arenas in which Kristeva's challenge to Lacan's analysis has a significant impact. 1) Kristeva challenges Lacan's account of the logic or structure of identification in the mirror stage. She suggests that there is a material logic, a bodily structure, operating to set up the identification in the mirror stage. This material logic is based on reduplication and metaphor, which prefigure Lacan's metonymy of desire. 2) Kristeva's challenge to Lacan's account of identification refigures the psychic play between the Symbolic, the Imaginary, and the Real. Kristeva suggests that her semiotic operates somewhere between the Imaginary and the Real. She also suggests that the three players are tied together by imaginary love. For Kristeva, love operates according to a logic of metaphor which is set up before the metonymy of desire. 3) Kristeva's emphasis on imaginary love over desire (which is already implicated in the play of the signifier and therefore the Symbolic) affects analytic practice. Kristeva listens behind signifiers and their play of meanings to the music in language which "signifies" the operations of the imaginary. She tries to work the imaginary in order to set up the love that is missing from the core of the narcissistic structure in borderline patients.

In order to bring the body, replete with drives, back into structuralism, Kristeva employs two very different strategies. First, she brings the speaking body back to signification by maintaining that bodily drives make their way into language. The notion of the semiotic element in language is developed in order to bring the body back into the very structure of language. Bodily drives make their way into language through the disruptive but necessary force of this semiotic element. Most commentators concentrate on Kristeva's theory of the semiotic in signification.

Kristeva, however, employs a second, perhaps more interesting, strategy for bringing the speaking body back into structuralism. Her tactic is to reinscribe language in the body, arguing that the dynamics which operate the symbolic are already working within the material of the body and the presymbolic imaginary. She concludes that these dynamics must therefore be material or biological as well as symbolic. In other words, her strategy is to trace the signifier through the body in order, at the same time, to reinscribe the body in language. Kristeva argues that the *logic* of signification is already present in the material body.

Kristeva moves behind Lacan's mirror and into the maternal function in an attempt to bring the speaking body back into structuralism. She suggests that Lacan's identification of the onset of the subject with the onset of desire, and its signifier the Phallus, sacrifices the body to desire. Kristeva suggests that Lacanian analysis, like structuralism and Husserlian phenomenology, engages in a kind of "necrophilia" by listening to "the narrative of a sleeping body—a body in repose, withdrawn from its sociohistorical imbrication, removed from direct experience. . . . Fascinated by the remains of a process which is partly discursive, they (structuralism and phenomenology) substitute this fetish for what actually produced it . . ." (*RP*, 13). Kristeva, on the other hand, attends to the process through which the subject is produced.

Kristeva criticizes structuralism in general which, she maintains, eliminates the drives from the semiotic and retains "only the image of the unconscious as a depository of laws and thus a discourse." While for Lacan the material of language points to an Unconscious which is structured like a language, for Kristeva it points to an Unconscious which is heterogeneous to language (*BS*, 204–5). It points to the semiotic body which both gives rise to language and destroys it. It points to the maternal music in and beyond language. For Kristeva, the Unconscious is structured like the maternal music in language. Was Kristeva's Unconscious beyond both Freud and Lacan because, as she says in *Tales of Love* (192), neither of them liked music?

Kristeva contests Lacan's thesis that the Unconscious is structured like a language and that it is the discourse of the Other. More precisely, she argues that if the Unconscious is structured like a language, it is not the language that Lacan imagines. Kristeva argues that language is not a system of pure signifiers, but is always made up of heterogeneous elements: semiotic drive force and symbols. The Other, then, is not a pure signifier. It too is made up of these heterogeneous elements. The Other, or the system of language into which we are born, is not the metonymical space that Lacan imagines, in which one signifier is associated with, or displaces, another. Rather, for Kristeva, the Other is the space of metaphorical shifting in which symbols are substituted for, or condensed with, drive force (*TL*, 38). Analytic interpretation, then, is not merely a matter of following a chain of signifiers or representations, but is rather a matter of listening to the unrepresentable within signifiers. Kristeva might say that meaning, like the Other, is "a condensation of semantic features as well as nonrepresentable drive heterogeneity that subtends them, goes beyond them, and slips away" (*TL*, 38).

Kristeva argues that Lacan's account of desire covers over its relationship to the heterogeneous semiotic out of which it comes. She complains that for Lacan the subject is constituted at the expense of "the real," the drives, from which this subject will be forever cut off (*RP*, 131). This leads to a "Kantian agnosticism" where the real cannot be known; it is impossible. Kristeva maintains that Lacan's Kantian agnosticism "castrates" the Freudian discovery. She seems concerned to protect the father of psychoanalysis from these castration threats from his most prodigal son (*PH*, 52).

For Kristeva, the Lacanian notion of desire combines Freud's topography with Hegelian negativity "but raises them out of their biological and material entrenchment into the domain of social praxis where 'social' means 'signifying'" (*RP*, 130). The result is that desire's basis in drives is "dismissed and forgotten" (*RP*, 131). Attention is focused on desire itself which is merely a reactivation on the symbolic level of a negativity that takes place in the body. In addition, the signifying process which is the movement and dialectic between the semiotic and symbolic "will be replaced by a nothingness—the 'lack' that brings about the unitary *being* of the subject" (*RP*, 131). The subject's being is seen as founded on this lack. And it is the lack alone which appears as fundamental to the human condition. The drives are lost:

> Desire will be seen as an always already accomplished subjugation of the subject to lack: it will serve to demonstrate only the development of the signifier, never the heterogeneous process that questions the psychosomatic orders. From these reflections a certain subject emerges: the subject, precisely, of desire who lives at the expense of his drives, ever in search of a lacking object. (*RP*, 131–2)

Desire is cut off from the living body; the living body is sacrificed to desire. The body itself becomes only a sign. As Kristeva passionately argues, when language is not mixed with drives, this subjugation to the Law of the Signifier turns the living person into a sign and signifying activity stops (*RP*, 132). Kristeva claims that the exemplary subject of Lacan's desire is the masochistic neurotic engaging in autocastration and bodily mutilation, or the completely catatonic body of the clinical schizophrenic (*RP*, 132).

Contrary to Lacan, Kristeva suggests that lack alone cannot motivate a move away from the maternal body and into language. She concludes that the logic of separation which is taken over in language is founded on pleasure as well as lack, or lack experienced as pleasure. If there were no pleasure in separation why would anyone leave the safe haven of the maternal body in order to enter the world of castration threats and paternal Law? Why wouldn't we all become psychotic?

In her essay "Place Names," Kristeva criticizes "a psychoanalytic practice that posits the subject as dating from the 'mirror stage' " because it minimizes the "function of the familial context in the precocious development of the child (before puberty, before Oedipus, but also before the 'mirror stage')."[3] Kristeva suggests that there are social relations prior to the mirror stage and language acquisition. These relations are not the specular relation of the mirror stage, but relations of transference, which she claims can be detected in the nonspeaking child before language acquisition and the onset of the oedipal complex (*PN*, 277). These pre-oedipal transferential relationships become the models for both negation and identification. The logic of signification includes both negation and identification. Within Lacanian analysis the logic of signification is put into place through the mirror stage, in which the infant both negates its image in the mirror and identifies with it. For Lacan, it is the mirror stage which first constitutes the child as a separate subject.[4] In the mirror stage, the child recognizes its image in the mirror. After some experimentation, the child realizes that the image reflected is its own image.

Prior to the mirror stage, the child does not conceive of itself as a unified whole. Rather, before the mirror stage, it "conceives" of "itself" as fragmented movements. The real body which stands on this side of the mirror experiences a fragmented body and fragmented desires. The image of the body in the mirror, on the other hand, is whole and perfect. When the child "realizes" that this other in the mirror is alien and beyond its control and yet constitutive of its own identity, a struggle begins. This results in a primary frustration that becomes the ultimate driving force behind human life and a model for subsequent relations and self-definition. What is paradoxical in the mirror stage is that the realization that the child is unified comes through its doubling in the mirror. In a sense, it must become two (itself plus its reflection) in order to become one (a unified self), hence Lacan's "split subject."

The mirror stage presents the subject with an image, which separate from himself, becomes the object, the Other. For Lacan, the construction of the Other is completed by the castration threat. The Other in the mirror stage is more or less "innocently" separate from the subject, while the Other which results from the castration threat is not merely separate, but the object of desire. That is why it is castration which forces signification: the subject is painfully separated from the object of his desire and must search for "stand-ins," alternative satisfactions. Founded on a lack and always inadequately, the child fills the gap between its previous imaginary gratification from the mother and its new separation from her, the other, with words. With the Other, the child can now name itself in relation to others. It becomes, through language, a subject proper. The ego is erected through the symbol. The subject imagines through the illusion of symbols that it has a unified ego, which is an actor, through which it can control its fragmented body.

Kristeva argues that the subject is not merely split by and through its entry into the symbolic, but also it is split between two heterogeneous modalities. The subject is split even before its entry into the symbolic. Upon its entry into the symbolic, the subject is split even more profoundly than Lacanian analysis indicates. In language the subject is split between drives and social practice.[5] The drives make their way into language through the semiotic, and the logic of signification is already operating in the body. It is this realm of bodily desires that Kristeva wants to bring back into Lacanian theory (*RP*, 30).

Kristeva takes us behind the mirror to the pre-oedipal manifestations of both negation and identification which make subjectivity possible. She analyzes the primary forms of these two elements which Lacan maintains are set up in the mirror stage. She develops a complex and detailed account of the negation and identification which make the mirror stage possible. Here I will limit myself to a discussion of Kristeva's account of identification in the mirror stage and what leads up to it.[6]

I. The Logic of Identification

Kristeva says that Lacan's "specular fascination is a belated phenomenon in the genesis of the Ego" (*TL*, 40). Whereas Lacan takes up the visible, Kristeva takes up the invisible. She takes us behind the specular image in Lacan's mirror. In an interview with Rosalind Coward, Kristeva claims that one of the ways that she goes beyond Lacanian theory is to "make more detailed the archaic stages preceding the mirror stage because I think that the grasping of the image by the child is a result of a whole process. This process can be called imaginary, but not in the specular sense of the word, because it passes through voice, taste, skin and so on, all the senses yet doesn't necessarily mobilize sight."[7]

What we find before the mirror stage are the maternal and the drive, both of which lie behind Lacan's signifier and desire (*TL*, 38). Lacan's identification of idealization solely within the field of the signifier and desire cuts off the drives. It underplays the importance of the maternal function. More than that, it makes it impossible to treat borderline patients for whom, for Lacan, the Law of signification is foreclosed. For Kristeva, on the other hand, idealization does not merely operate within the Law of signification. Signification is also the result of affect and drive which operate before the metonymy of desire.

The difference between identifying idealization—what takes place in the mirror stage—with desire or identifying it with affect and drive force is that desire "emphasizes lack, whereas *affect*, while acknowledging the latter, gives greater importance to the movement toward the other and to mutual attraction" (TL, 155). For Kristeva the difference lies between founding the social relation on a Hegelian notion of desire, which requires lack and struggle, or founding the social relation on a Freudian notion of eros or identification. Kristeva concludes that love is the only hope for the social relation (PH, 142). So she develops a notion of primary narcissism which is based on a metaphor of imaginary love, and which supports the child's movement away from the world of the maternal body and into the world of the Signifier.

Material Narcissism

In *Tales of Love* Kristeva looks for the primary psychic structure that sets up separation from the mother and the mirror stage. She looks for a structure that offsets the horror of the gap between the child's perfect unified image and its imperfect fragmented body in the mirror stage. This structure, which enables the child to negotiate between the maternal body and the symbolic, is the "narcissistic structure." As always, Kristeva constructs her narcissistic structure within a Freudian framework. As always, she reinterprets Freud and creates a new narcissism.

By rearranging and unfolding Freud's theories, Kristeva makes their tensions support a psychic space which guarantees all subsequent identifications. Following one Freud but not another, Kristeva rejects the notion that primary narcissism is a developmental stage (*TL*, 374).[8] Rather, she maintains that "neither screen nor state, primary narcissism is already a structure" (*TL*, 374). Insofar as it is a type of identification, and beyond an undifferentiated autoeroticism, it is intrasymbolic. The structure sets up the very possibility of symbolization. As such, Kristeva maintains that it is prior to the oedipal ego which begins to take shape with the mirror stage (*TL*, 22, 27, 44, 374). In other words, primary narcissism is a structure which preexists and sets up the identification in the mirror stage.

While an identification with the mirror image may be the *result* of the narcissistic structure, it is not the primary identification. The narcissistic identification in the mirror stage is merely the reduplication of earlier narcissistic identifications. These earliest narcissistic identifications are the result of mimesis in the mother–child dyad (*TL*, 22). This mimesis, however, is not an imitation. Because it is not an imitation, it does not presuppose an already constructed ego in relation with an already constructed object. It is not one being imitating another, the child imitating its object.

This primary narcissism cannot be the imitation of an object because for the child the object does not yet exist. Within Freudian psychoanalytic theory the mother becomes the first object. Kristeva challenges this thesis, suggesting that if we examine it closely we see that "no sooner [is such a thesis] sketched out, [then it] is exploded by its contradictions and flimsiness" (*PH*, 32). For behind this mother–object is the mother's semiotic body, filled with drives and pre-objects. Behind this mother–object is the anti-Oedipus, semiotic negativity, the logic of renewal, which takes us beyond Oedipus and the unitary subject. Behind the mother–object of Freudian psychoanalysis is an object, as well as a subject, always in process/on trial.

Behind the mother–object is one of the child's first identifications, the identification with the mother's breast. Kristeva explains, following Freud, that the archaic identification with the mother's breast is a pre-objectal identification. The infant becomes the breast through its incorporation. Kristeva maintains that this breast is not an object for the infant but a "model," a "pattern" (*TL*, 25). The infant's identification with this model or pattern of/through incorporation is not the *imitation* of an object or a pattern. Rather, Kristeva describes this identification as a *reduplication* of the pattern. This archaic identification, a strange identification indeed, is biological, or at any rate, semiotic. It is intrasymbolic only in a very primitive sense. It is as if here again Kristeva follows her logic of rejection backwards through the first semiotic negations now to discover the first semiotic identifications. This archaic semiotic identification with the mother's breast, which is merely a reduplication, becomes the first in a series of reduplications. It prefigures and sets in motion the logic of object identifications in all object relations, including both discourse and love (*TL*, 25).

The operator within this structure—the logic of reduplication, put in motion by the first identifications with the mother's body—sets up the logic of the psyche: repetition. The logic of reduplication itself becomes a pattern reduplicated by the psyche. Like Kristeva's earlier notion of the logic of material rejection (with which she explains how we separate ourselves from others), the logic of reduplication reproduces itself differently on different levels. Patterns are reduplicated on level after level until thresholds are crossed, the semiotic gives way to the symbolic, biology becomes culture, but like fractals in geometry, the patterns are recognizable.

With her theory of narcissism, Kristeva can explain not only how we break away in order to become individuals, but also how we come together in order to commune and love. In fact, she uses her notion of primary narcissism to reconceive the process of becoming a subject as a process which does not involve a break motivated by a threat that cuts off the possibility of love without fear. In Kristeva's story, Oedipus is really Narcissus turned lover. By retelling the tale of Narcissus, Kristeva creates a new psychic structure which will house the oedipal triad. Kristeva's narcissistic structure provides a new way to conceive of the oedipal situation as well as a new way to use it in the analytic situation.[9]

Narcissistic structuration, maintains Kristeva, is "the earliest juncture (chronologically and logically) whose spoors we might detect in the unconscious" (*TL*, 44). And, even before the first rejections, the structure of narcissism provides the first separation between pre-ego and pre-object in the form of identification. Narcissistic reduplication creates the space between the not-yet-subject and the not-yet-object so that they can become subjects and objects. This space is what gives rise to the symbolic. Narcissism protects and causes this space, this "emptiness" (*TL*, 24). The "elementary separation" intrinsic to reduplication guarantees borders. Borders are necessary for any distinctions between objects or symbols. Kristeva's Narcissus, or more precisely her reading of Freud's Narcissus, is an "infinitely distant boundary marker" (*TL*, 125). This boundary narcissism is the product of imagination. Kristeva's Narcissus imagines a love which is stable while receding always out of reach.

Kristeva maintains that it is imagination which comes to life in this space opened up by reduplication. This is why although "intrasymbolic," elementary reduplication is not a symbolic relation. Rather, it is an imaginary relation. This is also why Kristeva argues that the gap in Lacan's mirror stage is not a symbolic structure, but an imaginary structure which sets up the symbolic. She maintains that the "gaping hole" in Lacan's mirror stage, the space between the mirror and the infant, is guaranteed by the structure of narcissism through the separation in reduplication which comes before the mirror stage. The child's identifications are neither symbolic nor asymbolic, i.e., psychotic. Rather, they are narcissistic—before the mirror stage. Against Lacan, Kristeva argues that the narcissistic child does not merely need the symbolic in order to replace the missing real, but also it needs the imaginary, imaginary love:

> The child, with all due respect to Lacan, not only *needs* the real and the symbolic. It signifies itself as child, in other words as the subject that it is, and neither as a psychotic nor as an adult,

precisely in that zone where *emptiness and narcissism*, the one upholding the other, constitute the zero degree of imagination.[10] (*TL*, 24)

The child begins to distinguish the real from its symbolic substitutes through narcissistic imagination. Even though the narcissistic structure guarantees symbolization, it does so through a pre-oedipal, pre-objectal identification. Kristeva insists that human experience begins before what Lacan identifies as the Symbolic.[11] She complains that Lacan's all-encompassing Name of the Father removes the unnameable from childhood and places it in the impossible real (*PN*, 276–77). She claims that her research demonstrates that the unnameable drives are part of childhood. They show up in several aspects of pre-oedipal childhood experience (*SL*, 113). Kristeva doesn't argue that Lacan is wrong about the function of the mirror stage or castration. Rather, she emphasizes that Lacan's account does not analyze what is heterogeneous to the symbolic, which results from these functions on the "other scene" (*PN*, 276). Lacan's account of the mirror stage emphasizes the image of the body as other, the body as symbol reflected in the "mirror." It throws us into a hall of mirrors where we can no longer identify the real body—the real body is impossible.

Here once again Kristeva sets herself apart from Lacan. She maintains that the narcissist cathects a pre-oedipal pre-object rather than the paternal Phallus[12] (*TL*, 125). This cathexis precedes the oedipal identification with the paternal Phallus. Against Lacan, Kristeva argues that it is not the case that need gives way and is lost to desire. Rather, the semiotic "need" is a pattern which sets up the possibility of desire, not only chronologically, but also logically. In other words, there is an intrasymbolic structure which precedes the metonymy of desire. "The whole symbolic matrix sheltering emptiness is thus set in place in an elaboration that precedes the Oedipus complex" (*TL*, 27). For Kristeva, this narcissistic "elaboration" supports a semiotic reduplication which she describes as a type of transference.

Metaphoric Maternal Love

The fundamental transference, which sets up the ego ideal and thereby the metonymy of desire, is a transference to a metaphorical space. This transference, like all others, "transfers me to the place of the Other" (*TL*, 37). Through this type of transference the child's having the mother's breast becomes the child's being the mother's breast. Through the transference enabled by the structure of primary narcissism, the child is transferred to the place of the mother, to the place of the breast. The Other in this transaction is neither an object nor a "pure signifier." Rather, Kristeva breaks with Lacan when she claims that the Other is "the very space of metaphorical shifting," the space protected by the structure of narcissism (*TL*, 38). The structure of primary narcissism sets up the possibility of *metaphorical* shifting which in turn sets up the possibility of *metonymical* shifting (*TL*, 30). This metaphorical shifting is another form of transference.

In *Tales of Love*, Kristeva urges us to think of on the one hand ". . . modern theories of metaphor that decipher within it an indefinite jamming of semantic features one into the other, a meaning being acted out; and, on the other, the drifting of heterogeneity within a heterogeneous psychic apparatus, going from drives and sensations to signifier and conversely" (*TL*, 37). Later she suggests that "metaphor becomes antithetical, as if to blur all reference, and ends up as synesthesia, as if to open up the Word to the passion of the body itself, as it is" (*TL*, 277–78). Metaphor is where the drives burst into language. Kristeva calls metaphor "the economy that modifies language when subject and object of the utterance act muddle their borders" (*TL*, 268). It makes sense that if metaphor is language that does not refer to an object, then it expresses the objectless identification. The passion of the body itself has no object. This passion is pre-oedipal, pre-objectal, and pre-symbolic. It is prior to a distinction between subject and object. Kristeva argues that the metaphorical "object" is prior, both chronologically and logically, to the metonymic object.

In some sense, metaphor is the reduplication in language of the primary transference which takes place through the structure of primary narcissism. The pattern which is reduplicated is the pattern of displacement itself. Both the primary transference (as well as transference in general) and metaphor are patterns of displacement (*TL*, 27). The subject of utterance puts itself in the place of signs. The transference which once took place with an other now takes place with language itself. The result is the metaphor, particularly the synesthetic metaphor, where the subject's bodily passions are put into the place of language. Kristeva claims that the transferential displacement is at the heart of metaphor (*TL*, 275).

Kristeva maintains that in order to avoid tyranny in analysis we must postulate the formation of the unified subject within an "objectality in the process of being established rather than in the absolute of the reference to the Phallus" (*TL*, 30). She argues that Lacan locates the feature which unifies the subject "solely within the field of the signifier and of desire; he clearly if not drastically separated it from narcissism as well as from drive heterogeneity and its archaic hold on the maternal vessel" (*TL*, 38).

Separating the onset of the subject from the drives and narcissistic reduplication makes the process static rather than dynamic. The process is static insofar as it is anchored to the Phallus. This is why Kristeva argues that there are *various* ways in which the subject develops (although never completely). She suggests that there are advantages to untethering the onset of the subject from the Phallus. Above all, it allows the imagination of both analysand and analyst to intervene in the symbolic. It prevents the tyranny of the symbolic and tyranny in analysis:

> The object of love is a metaphor for the subject—its constitutive metaphor, its "unary feature," which by having it choose an adored part of the loved one, already locates it within the symbolic code of which this feature is a part. Nevertheless, situating this unifying guideline within an objectality in the process of being established rather than in the absolute of the reference to the Phallus as such has several advantages. It makes the transference relation dynamic, involves to the utmost the interpretative intervention of the analyst, and calls attention to countertransference as identification, this time of the analyst with the patient, along with the entire aura of imaginary formations germane to the analyst that all this entails. Without those conditions doesn't analysis run the risk of becoming set within the tyranny of idealization, precisely? Of the Phallus or of the superego? A word to wise Lacanians should be enough! (*TL*, 30; cf. 31, 125)

Paradoxically, the Lacanian analyst is a slave to the Word, the Signifier, or the Phallus; then a word should be enough to make the wise analyst realize that discourse is not absolutely dictated by the law of the Phallus or the Signifier. But which word will be enough? Or, perhaps any word will do insofar as it opens onto the imaginary. In any case, Kristeva suggests that wise Lacanians will heed her warning that the realm of the imaginary is more primary to psychoanalysis than the symbolic. Psychoanalysis should address the semiotic murmurs which support the signifier and not just the signifier itself. The imaginary allows the semiotic bodily drives to fuse with symbols in language. By attending to this imaginary—which is not reducible to the word—the analyst can touch the semiotic body, bring drives to language, and make it meaningful. The word to wise Lacanians, then, is that the word is not enough.

If the "unary feature" of the subject is a metaphor, then it is objectless, an objectality-in-process. In which case, the analyst is not dealing with a subject in relation to the Phallus, but with a pre-subject in a relation of reduplication to a pre-object, a subject-in-process in relation to an object-in-process. All of this takes place before the Law of the Father and not because of a lapse in the Law. In other words, it is not because the Law has broken down or been foreclosed that the subject has difficulty with the Law. Rather, because the sequence of reduplication, of metaphor, of imagination, has broken down before the Law is even set up, Kristeva claims that the breakdown which gives rise to psychosis is a breakdown of the narcissistic structure. What is needed is not the Law or the stern Father and his threatening Phallus. Rather, what is needed is the loving father, what Kristeva calls the "imaginary father." Perhaps Kristeva's word to wise Lacanians is "love."

II. Behind the Scenes of Desire

In a particularly fascinating seminar, Lacan describes the relationship between space and time and the two orders, the imaginary and symbolic. In the imaginary order, unity is based on spatial perceptions. But the name, the symbolic, provides unity over time. "The name is the time of the object" (*SII*, 169). Without the name, unity is fragmented and cannot be sustained. This is also why the symbolic order establishes the unity of the subject, "I." Although this "I" is always established as a split, and the symbolic is always founded on a lack, there is the appearance of unity. "Naming," says Lacan, "constitutes a pact, by which two subjects simultaneously come to an agreement to recognize the same object. . . . [I]f subjects do not come to an agreement over this recognition, no world, not even a perception, could be sustained for more than one instant." Lacan concludes that that agreement is the joint between the imaginary and the symbolic (*SII*, 169–70). The imaginary provides a momentary spatial unity which gives rise to a temporal unity within the symbolic which, in turn, supports it.

For Lacan, on the level of images the subject is in a precarious position in relation to the other. Lacan describes a tension between subject and other that is similar to the tension between Hegel's master and slave: before the subject enters language and a symbol can stand in for its desire, "desire is seen solely in the other" (*SI*, 170). This specular relation, where the subject can only see itself through the other, leads to an absolute rivalry with the other. The subject wants to annihilate the other so that it might exist (*SI*, 170–73). Ultimately, it is a dialectical struggle for recognition.

Kristeva replaces Lacan's Hegelian imaginary struggle for recognition, which plays dialectically between time and space, with a return to the imaginary space which supports the narcissistic structure, what she calls the "imaginary father." Kristeva distinguishes her imaginary from Lacan's by suggesting that while his imaginary is "blocked" by a representation in the mirror stage, her imaginary goes beyond the mere representatives of affect to its source in drives.[13] She emphasizes what is prior to the Name that provides the continuity of the subject. She returns us to a space that operates according to its own nameless time, a time before struggles, a space of imaginary love.

Certainly it is difficult to translate Kristeva's theory into the terms of Lacan's Imaginary, Real, and Symbolic; indeed, it is difficult to define these terms within either Kristeva's or Lacan's theories themselves. In an interview with *Critical Texts*, Kristeva claims that it is impossible to translate from one theory to another because it compromises the "specificity of each author." Kristeva wants to remain autonomous from Lacan. Yet she attempts a comparison between her notions of semiotic and symbolic and Lacan's notions of the Real, the Imaginary, and the Symbolic:

> But it does seems to me that the semiotic—if one really wants to find correspondences with Lacanian ideas—corresponds to phenomena that for Lacan are in both the real and the imaginary. For him the real is a hole, a void, but I think that in a number of experiences with which psychoanalysis is con-

cerned ... the appearance of the real is not necessarily void. It is accompanied by a number of psychical inscriptions that are of the order of the semiotic. Thus perhaps the notion of the semiotic allows us to speak of the real without simply saying that it's an emptiness or a blank; it allows us to try to further elaborate it. In any case, it is on the level of the imaginary that the semiotic functions best—that is, the fictional construction.[14] (*LL*, 7)

As Kristeva makes it out, her semiotic operates between Lacan's Real and his Imaginary. Kristeva's semiotic is, in some sense, the Real which makes its way into the Symbolic through the Imaginary.

In her essay devoted to Lacan's texts, "Within the Microcosm of the 'Talking Cure,' " Kristeva distinguishes Lacan's notion of *lalangue* ("the so-called mother-tongue," or the "real from which linguistics takes its object") from her notion of the semiotic by claiming that for Lacan even *lalangue* operates within a structure in which meaning is "*homogeneous* with the realm of signification."[15] In other words, Lacan's theory—even with its notion of *lalangue*—does not allow for nonmeaning, or what is heterogeneous to meaning, within the realm of signification. Kristeva criticizes Lacan for presupposing an "always already there of language" which prevents what is heterogeneous to meaning—the semiotic—from entering signification.[16] Her semiotic *chora*, on the other hand, "gives a different status to 'signifying' marks" (*TC*, 37).

Kristeva and Lacan have different conceptions of the Symbolic. For Kristeva, to enter signification is not the same as entering the Symbolic. To enter the Symbolic is to take up a position. Yet she argues that not all signification involves taking up a position; or, at least, there is more to signification than taking up a position. Kristeva has a narrower definition of the Symbolic than Lacan's. Her Symbolic is just one aspect of signification. And, she suggests that for Lacan signification is synonymous with the Symbolic. For Lacan everything interesting to analysis happens within the Symbolic. Lacanian analysis is concerned with the signifier and its movements through the metonymy of desire. For Kristeva, on the other hand, what is most interesting to analysis happens before the signifier is caught up in the metonymy of desire. What is most interesting happens on the level of the metaphor of love. The Symbolic, the Imaginary, and the Real are tied together by love (*TL*, 7).

III. Love at the Borders of Psychosis

For Kristeva, love is the foundation of the analytic situation. She develops Freud's suggestion that love is a "reciprocal identification and detachment . . . one open system connected to another" (*TL*, 14–15). She does, however, criticize Freud's notion that there is only one, male, libido because amorous discourse requires an interaction between heterogeneous elements (*TL*, 75–76, 80–82). Love requires two, the self and the other. Love enables the subject to cross the boundaries of the self and "be" an other (*TL*, 4, 6). The subject identifies with an other even while she remains detached from that other. In love, the other can retain its otherness, its alterity, and still provide the lover with an image of herself (*TL*, 33). The love that Kristeva describes provides an identification through difference without abolishing or assimilating that difference.

The play between identification and love eventually leads to the subject's self-identification and her identification of/with the object. Kristeva claims that the possibility of the amorous identification is the place of primary narcissism. Love makes primary identification possible. Pre-objectal reduplication, says Kristeva, sets up love (still without an object) (*TL*, 25). Love provides the *support* for the subject's separation, self-identification, and identification of the object. So, love sets up the possibility of the subject and the object. "The lover," says Kristeva, "is a narcissist with an *object*" (*TL*, 33). This is why, in her later works, Kristeva emphasizes the importance of love for the proper functioning of the psyche. She establishes the analytic relationship as the model of the love relationship.

For Kristeva, the love relationship is Freud's transference–countertransference relationship (*TL*, 8–14; *BL*, 3). Transference love requires three terms: the subject, the object (real or imagined), and the Other (the meaning of discourse) (*TL*, 13). Following Freud and Lacan, Kristeva suggests that in order for the child to move away from the maternal container, it must encounter the Third party, the Other. Kristeva's Other, the Third in the oedipal situation, however, is nothing other than the "Meaning of discourse" (*TL*, 13). The child must encounter the Meaning of discourse as the Other for/in "whom" it must speak, love, exist.[17] Kristeva claims that she departs from Lacan by describing the meaning of discourse as always constituted by nonmeaning. Meaning, like all of signification, is heterogeneous. It is constituted by both semiotic and symbolic elements.

Kristeva's Third party, then, is not just Lacan's stern Father of the Law who intervenes in order to set up the child's entrance into the Symbolic and the social. Rather, the Third is also a loving Third who intervenes on the level of the imaginary in order to support the child's move into the social. The analyst must concentrate on this imaginary loving support without which sociality and subjectivity break down for the analysand. The analyst must create the loving support with which the analysand feels brave enough to face the stern Father of the Law. Operating through language, the analyst reaches something that is heterogeneous to language. She reaches the affect and drive associated with the semiotic element of signification. Love is something spoken (*TL*, 277). It is through language that we can love each other. This does not mean that we have to speak the same mother-tongue in order to love each other. It does not necessarily mean that we have to speak to each other in order to love each other. Rather, it means that we are through language and that others are through language. Our relationship to others is constituted only through language. This, of course, is central to Lacanian psychoanalytic theory. Still, it is crucial in order to understand Kristeva's theory to remember that, for her, language is always heterogeneous; it is made up of semiotic and symbolic elements. It is through these heterogeneous elements that we can love each other. Love is neither merely semiotic nor merely symbolic. It is always and at the same time both. This is why Kristeva defines the effect of love as:

> a permanent stabilization–destabilization between the Symbolic (pertaining to referential signs and their syntactic articulation) and the semiotic (the elemental tendency of libidinal charges toward displacement and condensation, and of their inscription, which depends on the incorporation and introjection of incorporated items; an economy that privileges orality, vocalization, alliteration, rhythmicity, etc.).[18] (*TL*, 16)

Love—constituted through language—constitutes language in all its heterogeneous fullness (*TL*, 277). Kristeva claims that in the amatory discourse of transference love, the Symbolic, Imaginary, and Real (the realm of semiotic drive force) are tied together (*TL*, 7). Love links these three elements of signifying processes. Without love, the links break down, possibly to the point where the Symbolic is completely cut off from the Imagination and the Real in psychosis. Transference love allows the analysand to sort out the Symbolic, Imaginary, and Real, and to reestablish links between them (*TL*, 10). For Kristeva, love is the life of the psyche. Without love, inside analysis or out, Kristeva says that "we are living death" (*TL*, 15).

In order to satisfy and recharge love, Kristeva claims that the analyst must give in to countertransference and love her patients. The analyst must be able to put herself in the place of the analysand in order to feel her suffering and understand it. Love, transference love, requires a reciprocal identification and detachment. She sees psychoanalysis as "an infinite quest for rebirths through the experience of love" (*TL*, 1). Kristeva says that a word of love from the analyst may be more effective than electroshock therapy (*BL*, 48). With regard to love, psychoanalysis is privileged. Unlike other love relationships, it is not subject to the possibility of hurtful, even devastating, separation, breakup, or loss. Psychoanalytic love is beyond the "hazards of loves," and can, therefore, serve as a refuge against love's pain (*TL*, 382). Kristeva argues that analysis establishes the permanence of love which allows the analysand to turn the crises of failed and broken primary loves into fantasies with which she can live.

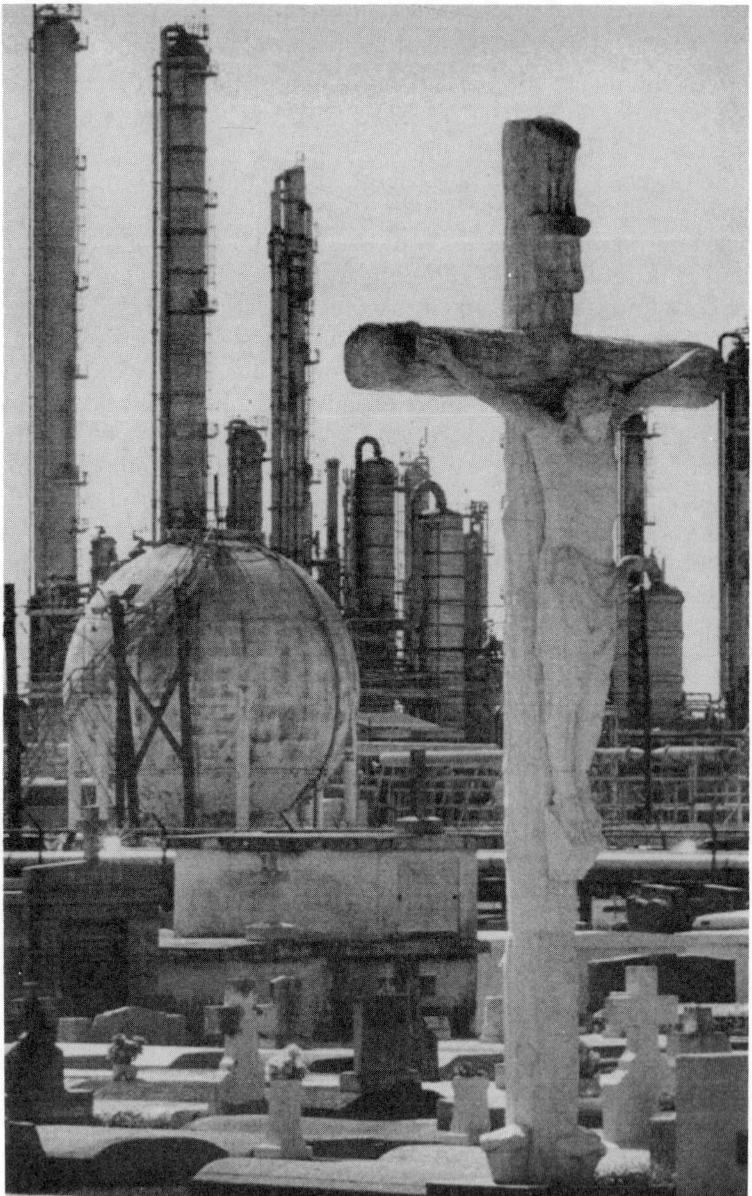

PART II
CULTURAL SIGNIFIERS

Chapter 5

ELIMINATING THE DISTANCE: FROM BARTHES' ÉCRITURE-LECTURE TO ÉCRITURE-VUE

Stephanie John Sage

> ... there is no question of "applying" linguistics to the picture, injecting a little semiology into art history; there is a question of eliminating the distance (the censorship) institutionally separating picture and text.
> —Roland Barthes (1969)[1]

I. Semiotics and Traditional Art History

Semiotics and traditional art history are reluctant bedfellows. One of the most recent (and comprehensive) discussions of this uneasy relationship has been provided by Mieke Bal and Norman Bryson.[2] Proposing a "semiotic turn for art history," the authors argue convincingly for the rich analytic possibilities arising when semiotic approaches are brought to bear on the study of visual art. Fundamental to this argument is the assumption that visual art is an "activity of the sign," an event in which semiosis occurs and is accessible to interpretation.[3] This concept traces its theoretical lineage to Peirce and Saussure and grants the art object—I speak specifically here of painting—an unprecedented autonomy. By conferring the status of sign to the painting, we acknowledge its vast communicative power. While both semiotics and traditional art history deal with paintings as expressive objects, the latter relegates them to a passive role in which their ability to actively engage the viewer as a discursive entity is curtailed.

If one were to review traditional art history's assumptions about meaning and interpretation in the work of art,[4] the painting would be regarded as ripe with meaning—intrinsic to the work and accessible through a process of dismantling or getting "inside" it. Moreover, it would be assumed that in order to apprehend the painting's meaning, the viewer must bridge the gulf between him or her and the work itself. In other words, the viewer stands before the painting, aware that it has meaning (it is communicating *something*), and must choose a way in which to get at that meaning. A space needs to be traversed—the viewer must "reach into" the painting to extract some kind of singular "truth." In the meantime, the painting remains passive—a mute object—awaiting the incision of the blade of art historical methodology. Two crucial elements are missing from this equation: 1) tradition does not acknowledge that the viewer cannot approach the painting innocently—in a purely objective mode—since the force of knowledge and the value systems operating in the person of the viewer must be accounted for; 2) the notion of singular truth is a fiction invented by positivists. Meaning is an ever-shifting phenomenon which cannot be pinned down by a univalent methodological approach. The viewer's gaze, shaped by his or her "cultural baggage,"[5] envelops the painting; in the all-consuming power of this socially determined gaze occurs the faceting and refraction of meaning.

Returning to the notion of "painting-as-sign" (or, more properly, "painting-as-text"), we can examine the kind of critical multivalence semiotics brings to art historical investigation and how it is equipped to reckon with the migration of meaning. By approaching the painting as a field of signifiers, the critical endeavor becomes an actual entry, as if into a physical space. What occurs in this space has been described by Bryson as a kind of collision, an interaction of discourses which shift and rearrange themselves as the viewer moves through the text. This movement comprises the "activity of the sign" mentioned earlier and is a force which grants discursive capacity to the painting in a way traditional conceptions of the work cannot. As Bryson asserts, the power of painting is "in the thousands of gazes caught by its surface, and the resultant turning, the shifting, the redirecting of the discursive flow . . ." (*Calligram*, xxviii). The painted text engages and is engaged by the viewer: we are invited to pursue the meanings spun *ad infinitum* through its web of signifiers.

Some would argue that because semiotics has its roots in linguistics, it is bound to negate the visual (formal) aspects of the work, hence doing it a critical disservice. The charge echoes through the halls of traditional art history's inner sanctum: dealing with painting as text violates its sanctity as an art object. I assert, however, that paintings can indeed be read and "rewritten"; that is, that looking can be transformed into a discursive activity through writing. The fact is that those of us who wish to make ourselves understood about works of art cannot escape language. We can have a wordless encounter with the work rich with realizations and revelations; in order to concretize that experience, however, we must resort to discourse. The silence will be broken, for art comes to life *only in words*. Ours is the realm of the visual, yet we are bound to language. As Louis Marin has pointed out, language "permits [painting's] articulation and constitutes it as a signifying whole."[6]

In order to arrive at this articulation, it is necessary to pull the painting apart. If we interact with painting as text and set out to trace its signifying activity, we will by necessity shatter its unity. (The semiotic embrace of polysemy demands this as it denies the notion of unified meaning.) To appreciate fully the plural of the text, we must first break it down into decipherable units and identify the various meanings resonating there. Having analyzed the text in this way, we then face the task of restoring it to a condition of integrity. I assert that this restorative act is missing from most semiotic analyses of visual art. It is a delicate operation, to be sure, and most crucial. How do we properly "operate" (to borrow Julia Kristeva's phrase) painting-as-text without irrevocably damaging painting-as-aesthetic-object? Does an analytic method exist which allows the work to function both textually and aesthetically?

The writings of Roland Barthes provide a key, for he is one of a handful of rare critics who can analytically dissect without destroying. His commentary on visual art manages to achieve the impossible. The work is treated simultaneously as "tutor text" (to be dismantled, analyzed, "worked over") and "work of art" (full of mystery and sensual beauty). Barthes conveys in his writing the sensation of vertigo we feel before the painting, in the moment when we are rendered speechless by the image before us. When critical methods have been put aside, what remains is the inexplicable capacity of the painting to move us, to rob us (if only for a moment) of the ability to explain its power. Traditionally, the critical endeavor happens when we have "recovered"; that is, after we have gathered our critical wits and armed ourselves with the proper analytical tools. Barthes manages to write *from the moment of speechlessness*. He allows his passion for the work (be it visual or literary) to shape his every word—his truly is a language of desire.

II. Barthes' Codes

And then our arrows of desire rewrite the speech. . . .[7]

Barthes has referred to writing as "the science of the various blisses of language . . ."[8] The seemingly paradoxical union of science and bliss distills a central quality of his critical approach, and is particularly evident in the strategy he employs in *S/Z* (1970). Published as the "trace of work" done in seminars at the École Pratique des Hautes Études between 1968–69, *S/Z* is a discursive penetration of the "galaxy of signifiers" of Honore de Balzac's 1830 novella *Sarrasine* through the application of five semantic codes. This application takes the form of what Barthes calls an *écriture-lecture*, or "writing-reading." Dissertational conventions are here abandoned in order to produce a discourse of reading. In effect, Barthes *rewrites* Balzac. His employment of the codes is not an attempt to locate and calcify structures of meaning in Balzac's text, nor merely to comment on the unfolding of the narrative. Rather, it "trace[s] zones of reading through the text in order to observe the migration of meanings, the outcropping of codes, the passage of quotation."[9]

The transitory quality of this language is telling, for it captures not only the essence of Barthes' criticality, but his conception of meaning as well. *S/Z*'s narratology is distinguished by a commitment to multiplicity and plenitude. The former characterizes the "non-positionality" of Barthes' position; in other words, he stresses that the field of the text can be entered from countless points of origin, without privileging one in particular. The commitment to plenitude is evident in Barthes' revelling in the "infinite productivity of language" (*Grain*, 73). He interacts with meaning as a limitless domain, endlessly full and ripe for discursive play. The *écriture-lecture* shapes this interaction, allowing Barthes to uncover the inner workings of the tutor text.

Bal and Bryson have acknowledged the contribution this method can make in the visual realm. They state that the codes "produce a . . . satisfying interpretation of the image in which every detail receives a place." They go on to describe this interpretation as a narrative produced by the reader which presents "the story through the processing of a strange image into a familiar mind set" (*SAH*, 203). I wish to expand upon Bal and Bryson's discussion and demonstrate the rich possibilities which can arise in the course of this "processing." Richard Howard has called the narratological approach of *S/Z* a "convinced, euphoric, even a militant critique of what it is we do when we read."[10] I am interested in bringing a Barthesian fusion of rigor and bliss to an inquiry of what it is we do when we *look*. We are faced, then, with the task of translating the *écriture-lecture* of *S/Z* into visual terms. It is instructive first to describe the codes as Barthes employs them in his reading of *Sarrasine*, then to discuss the repercussions of appropriating them for the purposes of what I will call *écriture-vue*.[11]

Barthes structures his literary investigation on a premise of division. He explains, "My gradual analysis follows the novella, dividing up the signifier which is the material text, and following along with it as the analysis unfolds" (*Grain*, 71). These divisions of text, or *lexias*, function as "reading units" through which pass a variety of meanings. The designation of the lexias is left to the discretion of the commentator; while it is not to be executed illogically, Barthes does allow a degree of flexibility in the textual division. "[It] can remain arbitrary," he explains, "purely empirical, and without theoretical implications . . ." (*Grain*, 71). For example, the 561 lexias of *S/Z* vary in size from only four or five words to lengthy paragraphs. The size of the lexia and length of the discussion concerning it vary according to its "density of connotations"(*S/Z*, 13). Once designated, these lexias function as loci of decoding. Barthes becomes both operator of the codes and witness to their effect. As he filters the tutor text (i.e., the material text as constituted by *Sarrasine*) through the codes, recording the rapid-fire interaction of signifiers and signifieds, Barthes simultaneously reinscribes it (in the literal act of writing Balzac's words in the form of sequential lexias). The act of reading—the event in which viewer, cultural baggage in tow, first confronts the myriad voices operating in the tutor text—is thus replicated, "performed," through the act of writing.

Here, then, are the five codes, discussed in no order of priority. The proairetic code (designated as ACT) deals with the narrative of the text and ensures, as Barthes tells us, "that we read the novella as a story"(*Grain*, 74). It is based on empiricism and consists of indicating the text's actions merely by listing them. This indication, according to Barthes, "will suffice to demonstrate the plural meanings entangled in them" (*S/Z*, 20). This code translates in a straightforward manner to the visual; where there is narrative in a painting, there are actions being performed which can be identified and recorded.

The semic code (designated as SEM) requires a bit more explanation, however. It functions within the text's orbit of connotations, pertaining specifically to character, to the person. In Barthes' words, the semic code "gathers together signifieds which are more or less psychological, atmospheric, pertaining to character . . ." (*Grain*, 74). As in the operation of the proairetic code, Barthes instructs us merely to indicate the significations revealed by the semic code; they are not to be organized or grouped thematically, merely listed and allowed a degree of instability. This code crosses over into a territory occupied by iconographic analysis in traditional art history. I am not suggesting a one-to-one substitution here but rather a strong parallel between iconographic readings and the application of the semic code. Traditionally, the iconographer dwells in the world of symbols, deciphering meaning as conveyed through the pictorial representation of literary, philosophical, and biblical themes. He or she may turn to the vast repository of images in the art historical continuum to assist in the identification of conventions used by the artist to communicate these themes. One such device is the use of attributes to signal the identity of a figure or theme from literature or history. For example, those familiar with Roman mythology will recognize Neptune by his trident; similarly, the informed viewer will know to identify a snuffed candle in seventeenth-century Dutch still life as a *memento mori*. We can conceive of attributes as "identity indicators" (of a character, place, or theme); this, as we have seen, is the province of the semic code. While iconography strives to uncover the deeper meanings intended by the artist in his or her use of attributes, the semic code merely identifies them as signifiers.[12] (The intention of the artist is not relevant here, but will be accounted for in a discussion of the cultural code.)

The function of the semic code can be thrown into relief by discussing it in connection with the symbolic code (designated as SYM). Unlike the proairetic and semic codes which clearly *indicate* within the text, the symbolic code *suggests*. Barthes stresses that "its logic differs radically from the logic of reasoning or of experience. It is defined, like the logic of dreams, by elements of intemporality, substitution, and reversibility" (*Grain*, 74). This code allows us to identify secondary sign systems in the text. For example, we can read the presence of Mary Magdalene in a painted text as signifying penance; how do we know, however, that the woman in the painting is to be identified as the Magdalene? Further, how are we to recognize her as penitent, as opposed to the pre-conversion Magdalene? Here we return to the semic code, uncovering clusters of signifiers indicating character. Through this code, we read the long tresses, brimming eyes, and nakedness of the woman—time-honored attributes of the penitent Magdalene—as positive indicators of her identity. We have thus established a primary signification. This sign system now functions as the signifier of a secondary meaning—that is, Mary Magdalene as penance itself. With the use of the symbolic code, we gain access to connotative systems such as this. Barthes states that this is "the place for multivalence," and that we should enter the realm of the symbolic from a variety of points (*S/Z*, 19). Perhaps the most intricate of the codes, its path to meaning is indirect and circuitous. All is unfixed, multiple, and connotative in the symbolic realm.

In contrast, the significations uncovered by the cultural code (designated as REF) can be tightly organized into sets; more specifically, "sets of references" which support the discourse of the text (*Grain*, 74). The cultural code identifies bodies of knowledge operating within the text (e.g., psychology, medicine, mythology, literature, history), all of which have a spatio-temporal resonance. As indicated earlier, this is the code which can accommodate the intentions of the artist; creative intention can, in fact, be subsumed in a set of references I call "art historical knowledge." A viewer positioned within the discipline of art history—or at least conversant with its terminology, practices, and documents—will be able to identify significations which might escape the notice of a viewer grounded in, say, cultural anthropology or theoretical physics. My intention is not to privilege the position of the art historian, for that would violate the multivalent spirit of Barthes' strategy. We must recall that implicit in this analytic strategy is the notion of polysemy: there is no singular meaning to uncover, hence, no assessments to be made about the "correctness" of the *écriture-vue*. The point is not what the text means, but *how* it means.

The final code is hermeneutic (designated as HER), which "covers the setting into place of an enigma and the discovery of the truth it conceals" (*Grain*, 74–75). With this code, Barthes provides a means of addressing mysteries of meaning in the text, as well as the barricades erected to complicate their unravelling. It is impossible to employ this code with regularity, as enigmas replicate themselves unexpectedly throughout the text and cannot be expected to appear in a fixed order. Barthes advises that "we list the various (formal) terms by which an enigma can be distinguished, suggested, formulated, held in suspense, and finally disclosed . . . they will not appear in any fixed order" (*S/Z*, 19).

Barthes does not claim universal applicability for these codes, for texts exist which resist the penetration of the codes. He identifies them as "modern," in contrast to the "classic" texts of which *Sarrasine* is an example.[13] The latter is characterized by a network of meanings which depends on a "revelation of truth and the coordination of the actions represented" for its discourse (*S/Z*, 30). Barthes refers to these two elements as "blocks" of truth and empiricism, and suggests that they create the closure of the classic text (*S/Z*, 30). In other words, what prevents a true plurality of disclosure (Barthes speaks in terms of the "limit of the plural") (*S/Z*, 30) is the necessary presence of the hermeneutic and proairetic codes. Unlike the other three, these codes only function in a logico-temporal fashion in order to sustain the narrative of the text. What is limiting about them is that they operate litigiously, in an irreversible sequence. Conversely, the symbolic, semic, and cultural codes have the capacity to function "outside the constraint of time" (*S/Z*, 30). Between the blocks of truth and empiricism, the modern text comes into being, distinguishing it from the classic. In the modern text, nothing constrains the order of reading and the irreversibility of the classic text is undone (*Grain*, 70).

How, then, are we to identify a painted text as modern or classic? The key is in the work's narrativity; its capacity to be read is an unfolding of visually recognizable actions and events. The painted text comprised of arrangements of figures and actions in this fashion will be receptive to the application of the codes. Although the classic painted text can be entered analytically at any point and allows random movement within, it is limited by the same closure as the classic written text. Its significatory power depends upon the "revelation of truth and the coordination of [its] actions." By contrast, a painting executed in a nonfigurative abstract style does not depend upon the unfolding of actions or the decoding of enigmatic gestures or identities for its meaning.

This is not to say that the non-figurative work cannot be enigmatic; quite the contrary. It is not possible, however, to operate the hermeneutic or proairetic codes in a non-representational work. We have only to imagine trying to identify sequences of actions in a color field painting by Barnett Newman, for example, or one of Wassily Kandinsky's "improvisations" of 1913–14. The moment that a painted text resists a narrative reading, it cannot be considered classic in Barthes' terms. The narrative of a painting must not be confused here with its *content*. There is no doubt that content can be found in nonfigurative abstraction; one obvious (and clichéd) example is the designation of "*Angst*" as the content of certain Abstract Expressionist paintings. Unless a figure/action construct can be recognized in the text, it cannot be read as a narrative and, accordingly, resists the application of the codes.

Fundamental differences between the internal structure of a novella and a painting demand further explication of the transformation of *écriture-lecture* to *écriture-vue*. The eye can move autonomously through a painting in a way it cannot in a novella; the successive nature of literary narrative limits this. Entering the written text, the eye moves *necessarily* from left to right across lines, from top to bottom through the page, from first page to last. The physical dictates of the act of reading a written text are compatible with logico-temporal codes. In the painted text, however, the path of interpretation is not governed by the unfolding of the narrative. The eye can move freely, even erratically, through the painted field in a way it cannot in the written text. Hence the aforementioned autonomy of the eye: the viewer has the freedom to choose his or her own point of entry into the field of signifiers, as well as the path followed once inside.

A question of misinterpreting Barthes arises here; after all, he speaks of following the unfolding of the literary narrative, not blazing his own trail. Is it inaccurate to assert, then, that the viewer of the painted text may choose the direction of reading at whim? Barthes' own words lay these concerns to rest: ". . . to take this entrance [into the text] is to aim, ultimately, not at a legal structure of norms and departures . . . but at a perspective (of fragments, of voices from other texts, other codes), whose vanishing point is nonetheless ceaselessly pushed back, mysteriously opened . . ." (S/Z, 12). The point is not how we get into the text, but what occurs once we are there.

Our destination within the text should be conceived as a "stereographic space," a three-dimensional locus in which writing occurs. A potential pitfall once we reach this destination is to apply mistakenly the codes to our own text as the analysis progresses, rather than to the painted text (e.g., commenting on the proairetic signification of our description of a gesture in the painting, rather than the gesture itself). This notwithstanding, the codes and lexia division transfer smoothly to the painted text, which I hope to demonstrate in the following exercise.

III. Primavera: une écriture-vue[14]

I choose Sandro Botticelli's *Primavera* (1492, *fig. 1*) as my tutor text. Beyond the fact that it meets the requirements of the classic painted text, I can offer no justification based on logic for selecting *Primavera* for this exercise. Perhaps my choice is motivated by my desire to "perform" the sheer gorgeousness of this painting, to reproduce its mysteries in the act of my writing. Or, perhaps—and more probably—*Primavera* simply chose me.

The path of decoding will begin with the title itself; this is a random choice (although a partial nod to Barthes, who begins his reading of *Sarrasine* in a like fashion.) The reading will continue through the painted text from right to left. This, too, is an arbitrary choice. The nine figures in the painting arrange themselves in groups of varying degrees of connectedness: the dancing Graces; the close-knit group of Zephyrus, Chloris, and Flora; finally, the loosely pyramidal trio of Venus, Cupid, and Mercury. I will interact with them as the following five lexias: (from right to left) Zephyrus–Chloris, Flora, Venus–Cupid, the Graces, and Mercury [*fig. 2*]

Figure 1. *Primavera*

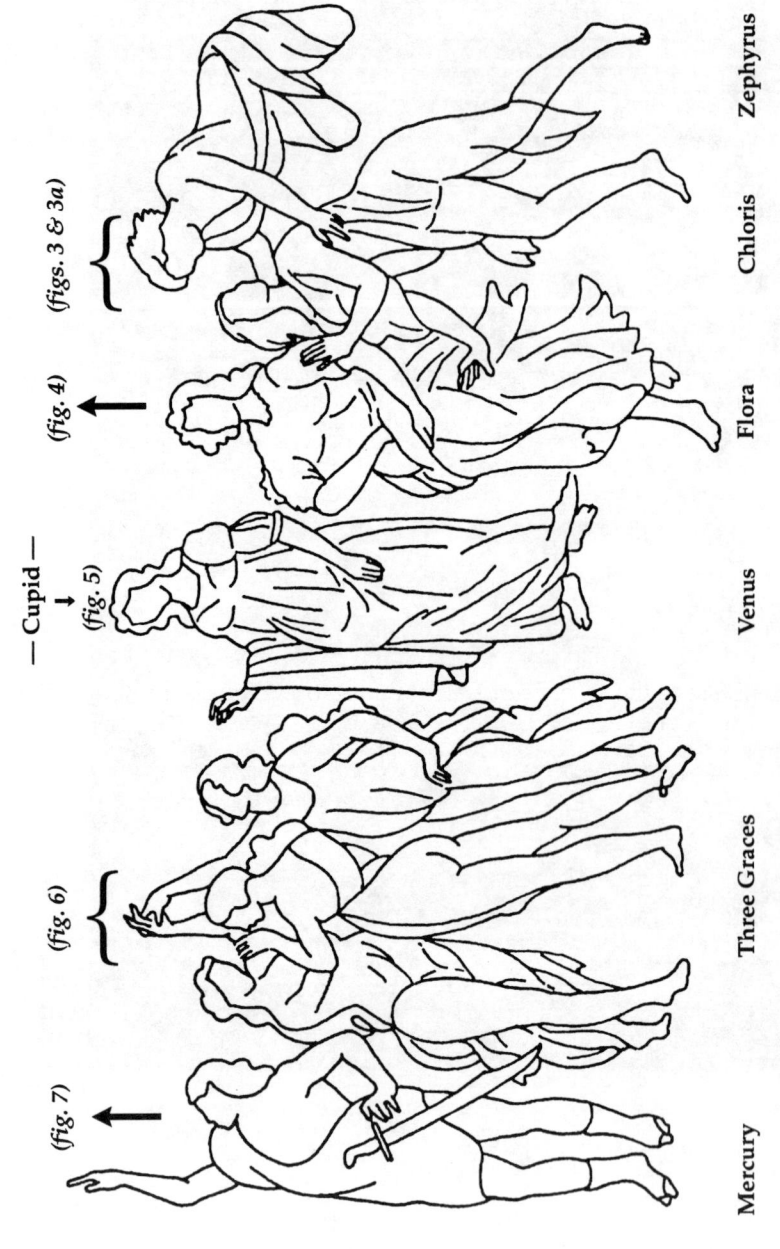

Figure 2. Schematic Drawing of *Primavera*

Mercury   Three Graces   Venus   Flora   Chloris   Zephyrus

As I operate the codes through each of these lexias, I will make subtle adjustments in the recording of the hermeneutic and semic codes; the other three will be inscribed as they would be in an *écriture-lecture*. The hermeneutic mysteries are proposed and resolved simultaneously in the painted text, in contrast to the more sequential unfolding of enigma in the written text. For example, a mystery in *Primavera* surrounds the stream of flowers flowing rather inexplicably from the mouth of the female figure in the right-most portion of the painting. We are instantly intrigued: Who is this female and what is the explanation for the flowers? Ironically, this very feature establishes her identity as Chloris, a figure from Greek mythology, and solves the mystery; hence, the simultaneity of enigmatic proposal/resolution in the painted text. Accordingly, hermeneutic significations will be indicated "all at once" in each lexia with their implicit simultaneity. As for the semic code, its activity will be recorded in a kind of "identity shorthand" (e.g., Chloris=nymph, or Venus=goddess of love). In other words, it will answer the question, "Who is this figure?" The function and connotative resonances of the figure's presence in the text will be left in the domain of the symbolic code. These are but minor modifications; the analysis of *Primavera* will endeavor to preserve the essence of Barthes' intention: "I pass, I intersect, I articulate, I release, I do not count" (S/Z, 21).

1. Primavera *[fig. 1 & 2]*

... an obscure and sublime song in every strophe...[15]

By way of entering the field of this text, I offer commentary on its title. A denotation in the language itself (it is an Italian word) allows connotations of all that nation represents (SYM. Nationality: "Italianness"). The flow of the sounds of the word is euphonious— the progression from syllable to syllable is a glissade of vowel sounds and the purr of an *m* and a *v*. This quality is mirrored in the graceful cadences of the painted text; hence, we see a reference to significations hidden elsewhere in the text (SYM. Beauty). The word "primavera" translates into English as "spring," which unleashes a flood of associations: renewal, fertility, romance, beauty (SYM. Seasons; REF. Art history: the renewal of the arts after the "darkness" of the Gothic era is conventionally identified as the Renaissance, itself a kind of "spring"—appropriately, the Renaissance is the chronological home of *Primavera*). Regarding the word "primavera" in its capacity as a title, I ask it to convey information about the text it names (REF. Art history: conventional function of artistic titles). I can read the various connotations indicated here as providing a prelude to the polyphony of the painted text; with the path into the field of signifiers thus prepared, what is left to do is follow its course.

2. Zephyrus and Chloris *[fig. 3]*

Was it affection or fear?

This pair is perhaps the most mysterious set of figures in the composition. The flight of the powerful male figure, the cerulean cast of his flesh, the distended cheeks, and furled brow—I marvel at his appearance and question his identity (HER. Ambiguous identity). He closes in on the ivory-skinned maiden (ACT. To pursue) and by the touch of his right hand on her bare shoulder, connects himself to her (ACT. To touch; SYM. Antithesis: male/female). Is the connection that also deepens the mystery of this pair's activity, the maiden's movement, the flight of a victim, or the gambol of a coy lover (HER. Ambiguous identity and motivation;

Figure 3. Zephyrus and Chloris

ACT. To run)? This particular proairetic configuration is sexually charged, and I attempt to anticipate the outcome of this pursuit (ACT. To rape, to consummate; SYM. Antithesis: virginity/non-virginity). The flowers cascading from the maiden's parted lips [*fig. 3a*] as she gazes at her pursuer raise more questions about her

Figure 3a. Chloris

identity (HER. Ambiguous attribute), which can be read as phallically suggestive (REF. Psychoanalytic theory; SYM. Sensuality). The flowers tell me who she is, and also lead me to identify her pursuer. She is Chloris, the nymph abducted by the amorous wind deity Zephyrus (SEM. Chloris=nymph, Zephyrus=deity of the west wind; REF. Mythology). The coupling of Chloris and Zephyrus strongly connotes spring (SYM. Seasons: the west wind heralds the balmy days of spring; the nymph Chloris is also the Greek goddess of flowers); their presence establishes a mood of loveliness, sensuality, and abandon (SYM. Beauty, sensuality). Finally, their evocation of sensual love signifies the lowest realm of the Platonic cycle (REF. Neo-Platonism).

3. Flora [fig. 4]

> ... her gauzy dress, her garlands of flowers, her softly curled hair ...

Zephyrus and Chloris tumble through the composition in the wake of a serenely smiling woman bearing flowers of all kinds (ACT. To bear, to smile; SYM. Seasons: the flowers that adorn the woman's gown and golden hair, as well as fill her arms, are identifiable as species blooming in April, May, and June; REF. Botany). Once again, my curiosity is piqued: Who is she and what is her relation to the other figures (HER. Ambiguous identity)? Her proximity to Chloris and Zephyrus, in addition to the blossoms that ornament her figure, tell me that she is Flora (REF. Mythology, quattrocento poetry; SEM. Flora=Chloris transformed, no longer virginal and now bride of Zephyrus and goddess of flowers; SYM. Matri-

Figure 4. Flora

mony, fertility, beauty, antithesis: virginity/non-virginity). Flora's presence is also key in the evocation of the Platonic cycle (REF. Neo-Platonism; SYM. Transformation: Flora, representing beauty, is the transformation of love, i.e., Chloris, forced to earth by passion, i.e., Zephyrus; REF. Gender stereotypes: note the encoding of culturaly determined, gender-based stereotypes, i.e., female Chloris, incarnation of chaste [passive] love is "victimized" by the male incarnation of profane [active] love).

4. Venus and Cupid *[fig. 5]*

> ... seductive eyes refuse, attract, speak or remain silent ...

Draped in the elegant robes of a Florentine matron (REF. Quattrocento costume; SYM. Matrimony: unlike single maidens whose hair flows free of headdress, the married woman wears a headcovering), a woman steps lightly into the center of the composition to the left of Flora (ACT. To walk). She extends her right hand delicately and inclines her head in the same direction (HER. Ambiguous gesture). Her visage tells me little—do I perceive her as aloof, crestfallen, dreamy (HER. Ambiguous expression)? Her central location and the framing effect of the tree branches around her present her as a focal point (REF. Art history: centering devices in artistic compositions, contextual significance of compositional focal point). The uncovering of centering as a recognizable convention triggers issues in related areas of knowledge (REF. Structuralism, post-structuralism: If this fig-

Figure 5. Venus and Cupid

ure is being "centered," are we to read her signifying activity as the "central" connotative system in this text? Or does she invite dislocation, de-centering, deconstruction?). There are several attributes identifying this figure as Venus (REF. Mythology, botany; SEM. Venus=goddess of love; SYM. Love: the myrtle trees behind her; the strawberries, violets, daisies, roses at her feet all signify aspects of love and courtship; SYM. Seasons: the aforementioned flowers bloom in spring months; SYM. Beauty). Her attire suggests that she is present in the text as Earthly Venus, traditionally depicted in sumptuous gowns and adorned with jewels (REF. Art history: iconography of Venus; SYM. Sensuality). My Venus, with her rich blue and red drapery, exquisite gold braiding, and pearl and ruby pendant, fits this description. Given her proximity to the Zephyrus/Chloris/Flora group, she can be implicated into the Platonic cycle and, concomitantly, assumes the identity of Celestial Venus (REF. Neo-platonism; SYM. Contemplation: in Ficino's conception, Venus represents the Love that transcends the physical world into the realm of the intellect). I am thus offered a dialectical view of the goddess (SYM. Antithesis: *Venus coelestis/Venus vulgaris*; REF. Mythology). Her graceful contrapposto stance and raised hand suggest that she is blessing the actions occurring around her (ACT. To sanctify; REF. Art history: the Gothic "S" curve stance of the goddess suggests medieval depictions of the "Beautiful Madonna" type, blonde and rosy-cheeked Madonnas who usually extend a hand in blessing). The signification of blessing signals another connotation: the painting may have been intended as a commemoration of the wedding of Lorenzo di Pierfrancesco de' Medici, who married Semiramide Appiani on July 19, 1482. If this is the case, Venus can be seen as Triumphant Love, sanctifying the couple's union (REF. Medici history; SYM. Love, matrimony, antithesis: virginity/non-virginity). Hovering above Venus is a blindfolded cherub, caught in the act of shooting a flaming arrow (ACT. To fly, to shoot). I recognize him as Cupid, whose presence reinforces the semic signification of Venus and the symbolic signification of love (SEM. Cupid=son of Venus, god of love; SYM. Love). His blindfold evokes connotations of random or impulsive desire—love is, quite literally, blind. Such a depiction of Cupid suggests the darkness associated with sin, which in turn connotes the baseness of carnal pleasures. At the same time, Cupid's arrow signifies the phrase *omnia vincit Amor* ("Love conquers all"); like his mother, Cupid here embodies the celestial and earthly aspects of love (SYM. Antithesis: sacred/profane love; REF. Art history: iconography of Cupid). I envision the course of Cupid's fiery arrow (HER. Ambiguous action; REF. Psychoanalytic theory: like the flowers streaming from Chloris' mouth, Cupid's arrow can be read as a phallic symbol, especially as it is aimed at one of the female figures in the text [SYM. Sensuality] and at one of the dancing maidens below him [HER. Ambiguous identity]). The arrow, quivering tautly in the bow, not only leads me to the next lexia of the text but co-opts Cupid into the Platonic cycle as well (REF. Neo-Platonism; SYM. Transformation: Ficino holds that desire—Cupid's bow—will be transmuted to a higher plane through the movement of the Three Graces; SYM. Love, contemplation).

5. The Three Graces *[fig. 6]*

> Light, rustling movements, voluptuous steps ... the gauzes float around their delicate forms.

The target of Cupid's arrow seems to be the central figure in a group of achingly beautiful maidens. Fingers intertwined and diaphanous gowns fluttering, they dance with the intimacy of sisters (ACT. To touch, to dance). This activity, along with their configuration (two in profile, one with her back to the viewer) and their placement near Venus inform me that they are the

Figure 6. The Three Graces

Three Graces (SEM. Maidens=Graces, handmaidens to Venus; SYM. Beauty, love, chastity; REF. Art history: iconography of the Graces). In addition to their symbolic connotations of beauty and love, the Graces are sometimes conceived of as the first three months of spring (SYM. Seasons). Further, they can be read as emblems of the Medici family (REF. Medici history: the favorite country home of the family was often referred to as *Charitum ager*, the field of the Graces). Two more symbolic significations link the Graces to the Medici: Renaissance literature reveals not only that the dance of this trio often accompanied wedding celebrations, but that they traditionally offered orange trees as nuptial gifts (SYM. Matrimony; ACT. To give, to celebrate; REF. Quattrocento poetry). These significations signal references to the marriage of Lorenzo and Semiramide (REF. Medici history elsewhere in the text. The presence of orange trees functions not only to signify a Medici wedding; like the Graces, the trees serve as emblems of the family itself (REF. Botany, Medici history: oranges were associated with the balls on the Medici crest and the name itself; i.e., *citrus medica*=Medici). Yet another evocation is the blooming time of orange trees: May (REF. Botany; SYM. Seasons). Finally, the trees interact with the branches of the myrtle tree to created a backdrop and frame the figure of Venus (REF. Art history: compositional device). Returning to the Graces themselves, an identification of them as Beauty, Chastity, and Pleasure interacts with Cupid and his flaming arrow to signify a Platonic elevation of desire to a more celestial realm (SYM. Beauty, sensuality; antithesis: virginity/non-virginity; SYM. Transformation). Their physical beauty has a referential resonance, particularly when connected to the other female figures in the painting. The Graces, Venus, Flora, and Chloris all embody the same kind of beauty—golden tressed, small breasted, long of limb, and fair of face; the sextet signifies the bodily ideal of quattrocento Florence (SYM. Beauty; REF. Florentine cultural history; REF. Art history: the proliferation of this physical type extends beyond this text and signals an idealization trend in art at this time period). As I describe the activity of the cultural code in relation to the presence of a physical "ideal" in this text, I must pause and interrogate my own interpretation (REF. Gender stereotypes: How is my designation of the female figures in this text as "beautiful" culturally determined? What social constructs allow the privileging of the blonde-haired, blue-eyed, slender women as a physical ideal)? Five of the six female figures share a striking physical feature, a gently swelling abdomen. This can be read as a sign of pregnancy (SYM. Fertility; antithesis: virginity/non-virginity), reinforced by the fact that the central Grace (signifying chastity) does not appear to display this feature.

6. Mercury *[fig. 7]*

> ... when an olive complexion, strongly defined eyebrows, and the fire of velvet eyes give promise of future male passion, of brave thoughts ...

The gaze of the central Grace directs us to the next lexia, where I encounter the third of the painting's trio of male figures (ACT. To gaze; SYM. Antithesis: male/female). The swarthy beauty of this youth and the plasticity of his supple musculature belie a sense of aloof, Polykleitean introspection (ACT. To contemplate; REF. Art history: the figure's far-away gaze and graceful contrapposto recall the cool perfection of Polykleitean statues such as the *Doryphorus*; SYM. Beauty; REF. Gender stereotypes: note my automatic assumption that this male figure embodies physical beauty—based on what standards?) I gather from his winged boots, helmet, and caduceus that he is Mercury (SEM. Mercury=messenger of the gods; REF. Mythology, quattrocento poetry). His presence near the dancing Graces is instrumental in two different referential significations. He can be viewed as a representation of the bridegroom Lorenzo, basking in the adoring gaze of Semiramide (in the guise of the central Grace), hence signalling the Medici

Figure 7. Mercury

marriage (REF. Medici history; ACT. To gaze; SYM. Love, matrimony, antithesis: male/female). There is mystery in this signification: Is this indeed a portrait of the newlyweds? How true to life is the representation (HER. Ambiguous identity)? In addition, Mercury signifies the final phase of the Platonic cycle (REF. Neo-Platonism; SYM. Transformation: desire, transformed through the mediation of Venus and the dance of the Graces, is guided by Mercury back to its ideal sphere). In this respect, the god functions in his role as psychopompos (leader of souls—less specifically, a guide), as well as an emblem of reasoning and eloquence (REF. Mythology; SYM. Contemplation; REF. Gender stereotypes: note the inscription here as contemplation—a "higher" faculty is represented in a male persona, while love is the provinces of females). The signification of contemplation sheds light on the reason behind Mercury's upward jab with his caduceus (HER. Ambiguous gesture; ACT. To reach). The clouds toward which he reaches can be read as symbols of confusion or unenlightenment which he is attempting to dispel (SYM. Antithesis: confusion/understanding; ACT. To dispel). Referentially, the clouds signify the stormy threat of the Pazzi conspiracy of 1478 (REF. Medici history). Mercury, garbed in a military cloak of brilliant crimson (REF. Art history: iconography of Mercury) and carrying a magnificent sword (REF. Medici history: the black scabbard is an emblem of Lorenzo and his father Pierfrancesco; REF. Psychoanalytic theory: To what extent is the sword and the upwardly stabbing caduceus phallically encoded?), reaches in this case to repulse the Pazzi threat with his caduceus (REF. Quattrocento poetry: the caduceus is often described as an instrument of peace; SYM. Antithesis: good/evil). Mercury also operates as a signifier of spring: he is the son of the nymph Maia (May), a patron goddess of fertility, and is adorned with flowering cress, a symbol of fecundity (REF. Mythology, botany; SYM. Seasons, fertility). As is true with each of the figures in the painting, Mercury also signifies an aspect of love. The combination of the flame motif on his robe and the flax which grows at his feet evokes the eternal fire of celestial love (REF. Neo-Platonism, botany; SYM. Love).

7. *Post-view*

Having operated the lexia comprised by the figure I call Mercury, I end this essay as arbitrarily as I began it. Having indulged my probings and intrusions, the text folds back in upon itself as I withdraw. I have stalked its mysteries like a poacher, but ultimately the enigma of the signifiers eludes me. As Barthes states, "the classic text is pensive . . . replete with meaning. . . . [I]t still seems to be keeping in reserve some ultimate meaning. . . ." After the multiplicity and multivalence have been explored, the plenitude and plurality engaged, what remains is the closure of the classic text. Just as the pensive Marquise metaphorically provides the final "meaning" of *Sarrasine*, so does my Venus. Her gaze attracts and engages, her visage is expressive; ultimately, she discloses nothing.

IV. Postscript

The *écriture-vue* is, of course, only one of countless ways this infinity of meaning can be penetrated. The *écriture-vue* is simultaneously complete and also incomplete—my writing has come to an end, but there is no end to the significations within the text. The question arises: What sense do I make of the discourse I have just produced? Of what use is my "operation" of this text, and how can it contribute to existing discourse about looking, Botticelli, Barthes, or criticality itself?

Following is a list of the results of my reading; that is, what was generated by the operation of the five codes:

- SYM: Nationality (Italianness), Seasons, Male/Female, Virginity/Non-virginity, Mythology, Sensuality, Beauty, Matrimony, Fertility, Transformation, Love, Contemplation, Good/Evil, Sacred/Profane
- SEM: Zephyrus, Chloris, Flora, Venus, Cupid, the Three Graces, Mercury
- REF: Art history (compositional devices, iconography), mythology, Neo-Platonism, botany, Quattrocento poetry, history (of Florentine culture, of the Medici family), gender stereotypes, psychoanalytic theory
- HER: Ambiguity of expression, of gesture, of identity, of intention
- ACT: To touch, to run, to rape, to consummate, to bear, to smile, to walk, to sanctify, to fly, to shoot, to dance, to give, to celebrate, to gaze, to contemplate, to reach, to dispel.

Here, then, is what I produced. There is nothing final or definitive about this information. In fact, presented this way in list form, the results of my *écriture-vue* throw into relief the eternal elusiveness of meaning. While the list above can give us a kind of visual shorthand of *how* the text offers meanings, it can never pose as an explanation of *what* it means. The results of my reading are obviously incomplete, for how can I properly distill the multivalence and reversibility of the painting's signifying activity? If we accept incompleteness as intrinsic to the *écriture-vue*, we can appreciate its true critical power. Barthes' codes arm us to pursue the "magic of the signifier," to explore the richness of meaning in the text and reconstitute it through language. More importantly, the codes are a relentless reminder of the charade of "true" critical objectivity. As we operate the text, we are forced to confront the culturally determined ways in which we see and interpret. The *écriture-vue* is thus simultaneously an odyssey into the enigmas of the text, and the equally mysterious realm of our own subjectivity.

Chapter 6

THE END(S) OF PICTORIAL REPRESENTATION: MERLEAU-PONTY AND LYOTARD

Mark Roberts

Although there are numerous traditional theories of pictorial representation, contemporary thinking on the subject is dominated by only two. One, based on the psychology of art, examines the constitution of the picture from the perspective of the psychology of visual perception, taking into account what is involved in the process of image making.[1] Of course, what is actually involved in the process of image making is always open to controversy, and theories based on the psychology of art range across a great number of hypothetical models of visual perception. The other approach to pictorial representation is based on language-oriented theories, which are likewise varied, but have certain common features.[2] Most notable among these is a tendency to analogize pictures to verbal narratives, and to attach importance to resemblance and symbolic models and their various components. Obviously, both theories take pictorial representation as the result of certain symbolic or cognitive operations that are intelligible and analyzable. It might, however, prove interesting to follow a line of thought that provides an alternative to these predominant theories of pictorial representation—one which is perhaps best expressed in the writings on aesthetics of Maurice Merleau-Ponty and Jean-François Lyotard. Generally speaking, their approaches to this subject, though differing in certain important ways, take as a starting point not the picture as a symbolic construct—as a collection of created images or visual data that stand in place of something else—but rather various bodily, libidinal, figural, gestural, and perceptual experiences, which, taken along with a picture's formal elements, constitute the pictorial surface. Thus, in their general view, pictorial representation cannot be seen wholly in terms of some static theoretical construct (e.g., a psychological hypothesis or an analogous linguistic model), since, on the contrary, it is constituted by nonrational forces—desire, drives, affectations, perceptions, etc.—which are not necessarily reducible to intelligible models, to theorization. In fact, we could say that both of these thinkers stress the very elements which tend to undermine the traditional idea of the unity and intelligibility of the pictorial surface, and thus the very distinction between knowing and seeing.

I. Merleau-Ponty

Three key conceptions appear at virtually every stage of Merleau-Ponty's work: perception, the visible, and the body. Their importance was evident as early as the *Phenomenology of Perception*, where Merleau-Ponty tried to provide a philosophically functional and psychologically accurate account of consciousness. This required an analysis of founded acts of cognition, so as to reveal the primordial perceptual encounter that must occur before we can even have a subject–object distinction. The encounter is always of a specific kind, revealing a relation between ground, figure, and the world. The latter presents itself in any one perception as a figured totality in which each instance or moment has a meaning as it functions in this totality. Each partial view of the world, then, provides a part of a larger dynamic whole and vice versa. For example, the brilliant orange ball which characterizes a sunset does not in and of itself constitute the perception "sunset," but rather functions as an intensely perceived element, carrying with it the sense of a sunset. What is directly confronted, or "lived," by our entire psycho-physical system, is "brilliant orange ball" in a sunset landscape. The setting sun is only a moment in the sunset landscape, yet, combined with other moments—purple sky, elongated shadows, silhouetted trees, etc.—it constitutes a sense of the whole, of sunset landscape.[3] Thus any one element within a perceptual field serves as a micro-totality, in that it conveys the full sense of the whole of which it is a part. And what guarantees this sense of fullness is our perceptual and therefore bodily presence to this experience, or as Merleau-Ponty puts it, "our presence at the moment when things, truths, values are constituted" (*EM*, 161).

We also find ample evidence of the above three conceptions in Merleau-Ponty's aesthetic theory, especially that expressed in two later essays, "Cézanne's Doubt" and "Eye and Mind." In the former, it is precisely the question of the artist's position regarding sensation and judgment, or more specifically, his position with regard to the faithful representation of his own experience of nature, that fascinates Merleau-Ponty. He begins by asking why Cézanne required one hundred sessions for a still life and five hundred sittings for a portrait. Not, Merleau-Ponty stresses, for the reasons most conjectured; not because Cézanne was unsure of himself, obsessed by a need to reaffirm his vocation, or for some deep psychological reasons—not, in short, for anything having to do with his life. Rather, Merleau-Ponty speculates, Cézanne was trying desperately to work through the "ready-made" distinctions that were handed to artists: the distinction between nature and composition, between sensation and judgment. In his deepest desires, he endeavored to depict "matter as it takes on form, the birth of order through spontaneous organization."[4] For him, then, painting was not merely a reproduction of reality or the convergence point of sensation and understanding, of seeing and knowing, but rather a direct presentation of nature itself, which had a peculiar way of producing its own order, of ordering sensation.

Cézanne found another route to understanding this "productive" character of nature through his intense, almost fanatical, study of perspective, which, in the end, led to some seemingly curious conclusions. In brief, he proposed that systematic distortions on the actual surface of the picture do not effectively distort the picture itself. On the contrary, seen in a "global framework," they tend to contribute to an emerging order, of an object in the act of appearing, rather than one set in a predetermined framework. Cézanne thus took perspective to be an active rather than a static force, revealing the processes of nature within a temporal horizon. This could, moreover, be extended to other formal devices used to transfer the experience of nature to canvas or paper. Volumes, colors, lines of force, etc. are not rediscovered or constructed by the sensory apparatus, but, as "lived objects," they present themselves to us as the center from which sensations radiate. The sensations are thus discovered in the world, since our bodily perceptions are equally in the world and in us (*CD*, 15).

An even more detailed account of the relation between perception and representation appears in "Eye and Mind." Here Merleau-Ponty not only takes into account the painter's position regarding the world, but also seeks to establish an ontology of seeing and the visible. The text, consistent with his earlier works on perception, is modeled on the distinction between reconstructed and originary experience. What is striking about this particular work, however, is its strident denunciation of operationalist or scientific method as inadequate for describing what Merleau-Ponty calls "brute meaning." The main question posed by the text, then, is: What *is* adequate for describing this sort of meaning? Merleau-Ponty proposes that art, and especially painting, gives access to it. Painting, unlike science or even writing, is nondiscursive and thereby need not take a stand with regard to what it expresses. A painting is neither a statement nor a scientific claim; its objects are self-explanatory and it can hold them in suspension without being obliged to appraise them in a universally intelligible language. In fact, Merleau-Ponty suggests that, "for the painter . . . the watchwords of knowledge and action lose their meaning and force" (*EM*, 166).

Merleau-Ponty's notion of the act of perception is already a primitive act of creation, and the painter, through the involvement of both vision and the body, is able to present this act in its most immediate, primordial form, foregoing the terms of "knowledge and action." The painter's vision thus approximates a primordial state, which contains each nuanced response to color, volume, tone, light, darkness, space, etc. This sort of painterly vision consists of far more than just imitating reality, or consciously organizing the contents of visual experience. Such an authentic way of "being in the world" is not dependent on prefigured mental activity. Painting does not begin with some preset rules or techniques that preexist the actual seeing and making visible of the event. The painter never calculates what will be presented, nor does he organize his subject-matter—apples, mountains, geometric planes, etc.—according to knowledge derived from some other field (*EM*, 161–62). The geometry of Mt. St. Victoire is not borrowed from Euclid's theorems, but is rather the result of Cézanne's intimate encounter with the very process of nature's appearing, through the medium of perception and its locus, the body. For Merleau-

Ponty, then, the process of pictorial representation necessarily involves an active, dynamic relation between the artist and the world. In this regard, the artist does not stand at a distance from the scene and formulate a way of reproducing it on a two-dimensional surface. Rather, the artist *is* the scene, the focal point of convergent experiences and events. A painting is never described as a thing separate and distinct from the artist, as an aggregate of forms, volumes, etc. that signify something. Indeed, at times it seems that, for him, the painting virtually emerges out of perception and its presence to the world through the body. For example, in describing the genesis of Cézanne's later landscapes, he writes:

> Then he began to paint all parts of the painting at the same time, using patches of color to surround his original charcoal sketch of the geological skeleton. The picture took on fullness and density; it grew in structure and balance; it came to maturity all at once. "The landscape thinks itself in me," he said, "and I am its consciousness." Nothing could be farther from naturalism than this "intuitive science." Art is not imitation, nor is it something manufactured according to the wishes of instinct or good taste . . . a picture is not a *trompe-l'oeil*. Cézanne, in his own words, "wrote in painting what had never yet been painted, and turned it into painting once and for all." Forgetting the viscous, equivocal appearances, we go through them straight to the things they present. The painter recaptures and converts into visible objects what would, without him, remain walled up in the separate life of each consciousness: the vibration of appearances which is the cradle of things. (*CD*, 17–18)

"The landscape thinks itself in me"; "The painter recaptures and converts into visible objects." These phrases, among others, point toward a notion of *representation* (or more properly, *de-representation*) based on viewing the pictorial surface as an active inscription of the painter's experiences—a "tracing" which has neither an outside nor an inside, but which stands somewhere at the juncture between the two. The painting is not entirely exterior to the processes that formed it, nor are those processes absent from the picture. The pictorial surface consists of gestures, disorganized perceptions, rhythmic patterns, etc., which are presented as the raw, brute, originary products of seeing and "making visible" rather than in a symbolic way. These "products" are, moreover, concretized in the formal expressions of the painting. The lopsided orthogonals of Cézanne's still lifes, the impossible contortions of his "ill-proportioned" bathers, are all pictorial indications of the above-mentioned processes. They are not attempts to imitate reality, to create resemblances, but are traces of a process which takes place somewhere between the world, the eye, the hand, and the body of the painter, and the surface of the canvas.

Ultimately, this conception of pictorial representation can be traced to Merleau-Ponty's existentialism. This is evident in his continual stress on the active, originary, brute experiences associated with perception, especially aesthetic perception. Aesthetic perception does not present a ready-made representation of reality, that is, the world outside the artist, but rather actively works upon the reality experienced by the artist, his "total field," which, for Merleau-Ponty, involves both inner and outer experience. The surface of the picture, as far as Merleau-Ponty is concerned, is a site where this active engagement is inscribed. The painting is thus not a calculated, isolated solution to the problem that is perceived, experienced, examined, and then more or or less resolved by the artist—i.e., the problem of expressing a feeling, vision, or an idea in two-dimensional terms. Rather, it is an active inscription of the very problem of the artist's existence, the problem of reconciling thought, feeling, expression, and material in the process of making visible.

For Merleau-Ponty, a painting which successfully "represents" something would not be a result of the artist's ability to find equivalent forms and unique significations for a series of spatial, linear, and chromatic formations. Rather, it would result from those aleatory, barely detectable experiences—those brute meanings that present themselves to aesthetic perception, those brute meanings that the artist had experienced at the "moment of creation," at the moment when eye, mind, and body were in perfect accord with nature, with the external world. Each of the recorded images—Cézanne's apples, Giacommetti's figures, etc.—are traces of these moments of accord, of silent understanding, and of what Klee calls the "*Urbildliche*," the very birth of seeing in contact with its newly formed image. Or, to cite Klee further: "painting does not represent the visible, it makes visible." Thus, for Merleau-Ponty, painting is a kind of record of the process of becoming visible, rather than a *depiction* of the visible. And representation (if we can even use this term) is not a means of symbolizing certain artistic experiences, but an inscription of those experiences in the very process of formation.

II. Lyotard

Lyotard's early work in aesthetics, especially *Discours, figure*, is indebted to Merleau-Ponty's,[5] especially his later writings. His approach to pictorial representation is, however, more complex, augmenting Merleau-Ponty's approach in certain respects (especially in the social and political implications of representation). Whereas Merleau-Ponty's concept of pictorial representation takes into account the fundamental relationship between subject and object, between painter, world, act, and artwork in the formation of the painted surface, Lyotard tends to propose a rather more anonymous and non-dialectical formation. He takes the pictorial surface to be "a space" in which libidinal desire and its figures play, tear discursivity apart, transform, and metamorphosize, forming certain unforseen and unspecified images. Consequently, Lyotard's early writings focused largely, though by no means exclusively, on articulating and exploring the idea of figure in both art and literature, and in its relation to discourse. *Discours, figure*, for example, treats this problem in terms of the difference between "seeing and reading." For Lyotard, to see something, to form an image or figure of some perceptual object, is nothing at all like understanding that object intellectually: seeing yields something inexpressible in the discursive, linguistic register. This claim obviously owes something to the phenomenological assertion, that perception involves a discursively unmediated given which is irreducible to operationalist discourse—a "brute meaning" originally manifest in some primordial experience founding all secondary acts. Lyotard extends this phenomenological insight to art and especially painting. For him, art, like seeing, indicates a function of the figure that is entirely nonlinguistic. The "symbol's transcendence" in art is the figure of a spatial manifestation which cannot be inscribed in a linguistic space.[6] Or, to use Lyotard's example: "when Cézanne contemplates Mt. St. Victoire, it is not the given but the donation, the event which immobilizes him before the mountain." The term "figure," then, covers the formal play of art within and beyond figuration (*Discours*, 21).

Perhaps the best illustration, in art, of what Lyotard means by "figure" appears in both the work and the theoretical writings of Paul Klee,[7] whose thought occupies an important place in *Discours, figure*. Klee's theories were by and large based on the expressive values inherent in the various formal elements (compositional, linear, chromatic, etc.) that constitute artworks. In his mature works—consisting mainly of small paintings and collages—Klee handled these elements in an intentionally childlike manner, letting his tools lead him until an image began to emerge. He would then tighten up this emerging image in a conscious way, and, more often than not, allow it to once again become diffuse. This process imparted a kind of "life" to the pictorial forms, and it depended more on the transformation of visual and imaged material than on the transposition of some concept onto the pictorial surface. In effect, Klee's figures exceeded the spatial situation in which they were set, constituted "a movement of the organic in the geometric," as well as a movement away from the specificity of objective representations. Klee's figures might take on any form that the eye and the internal transformations of formal constituents (line, color, modulation, etc.) lent them. The figure in Klee's work is not merely symbolic or metaphoric. Rather, he "freezes" the process of creation on the surface, dynamically playing out its drama before the viewer's eyes: the figural, for Klee, consists in those forms created by the free transformation, repetition, and dissolution of certain energies "in" pictorial elements, perhaps best exemplified by the famous "line taking a walk" phenomenon.

Although, as Klee's art illustrates, figure is essentially unordered and aleatory in art, Lyotard allows that it can, in principle, be organized. He thus divides figure into three categories, all of which may be distinguished according to their thematic and imagistic content. The "image-figure" is what appears in dreams and hallucinations, what is set aside or at a distance, within some figural format, like a film or painting. Lyotard, following André L'hôte, calls this the "revealing trace" because it sets the theme for the artwork but lacks the components necessary to complete it. One of the missing components is what Lyotard calls the "form-figure," which is present in the perceptible material. It may even be invisible but is usually concealed within the Gestalt or hidden architecture of the work. The third category is the "matrix-figure," which is perhaps the most complex (and problematic) of the three. In principle, the matrix-figure is invisible (perhaps in Merleau-Ponty's sense). It is subject to primal repression and immediately intermingled with discourse. Yet, for Lyotard, the matrix-figure is not a structure (as in Lévi-Strauss), in the sense of a form-figure which is always available to mental apprehension. Rather, the matrix-figure is the devilish component of figure that tends to rip discursivity apart. It does this primarily because it consists in a violation of discursive order, in an upheaval of the transformation authorized by this order. And, according to Lyotard, to imagine this other of discourse in a textual sense would be to entertain a double fantasy: "first that of an origin, and then that of an utterable origin."[8]

If, as Lyotard proposes, these three categories of figure constitute the basic visual "theme" of the picture, a painting would take its specific "representational" form from the relative dominance of any one of these categories, i.e., image-figure, form-figure, or matrix-figure. Thus, for example, if the image-figure—which infringes the set of rules regulating the constitution of the perceived object—is dominant, we would have the following type of "representation":

> This [the dominance of the image-figure] is conclusively illustrated in the Picasso sketch where the object of deconstruction is the edge, the line which shows that there is a single and reifying point of view; the coexistence of several contours infers the simultaneity of several points of view. The scene where this woman is sleeping does not belong to "real" space; it allows several positions of the same body in the same place and at the same time. Erotic indifference to time, to reality, to exclusive poses. (*Driftworks*, 58)

Or, in the case of the form-figure:

> Pollock's "action painting" . . . could give us an idea of what "bad form" might be like. A plastic surface entirely covered with chromatic flows, no stroke, not even a "trace," no effects of echo or rhythm coming from the repetition or reentry of form, values or colors on the surface of the painting, thus no recognizable figure: all of this suggests that we have passed

> over to the side of Bacchic delirium, descended into the substratum where the plastic "invariables," the linear invariable at least, become a whirlwind, where energy circulates at top speed from one point of the pictorial space to another, prohibiting the eye from resting anywhere, from investing here or there, be it only for a second, its phantasmagoric charge. (*Driftworks*, 64)

Hence, for Lyotard, the artist's task of representation is really one of *de-representation* in that he must strive not to depict or recreate reality but rather "produce figures within reality." In this case, the artist does not take the artwork as a representation of *anything* that *stands in place of* something else. To take a painting as representing something is not to take it seriously in its own right; it is to remain within the order of representation, within a theological and teleological perspective, which has very little to do with art itself. But the production of figures within reality escapes this order of representation; it is, as Lyotard suggests, the play of forms above or beyond representation, the auto-figuration of a unique, aleatory world, which also serves as a critique of representation itself:

> I believe that the true art–fantasy relation is not direct: the artist does not externalize systems of internal figures, he is someone who undertakes to free from fantasy, from the matrix of figures whose heir and whose locus he is, what really belongs to the primary process, and is not a repetition, a "graphy." (*Driftworks*, 64)

By involving "repetition" and "graphy," representation falls on the side of discourse or secondary process. It lends power, meaning, and substance to ideology by its very capacity to create the illusion of a parallel, well-regulated order behind what is expressed. But, for Lyotard, a painting is not an expression of rational order but of desire, a product produced largely out of primary, unconscious material. In this regard paintings are expressions of a "libidinal economy," an economy based on the investment of certain energies in the form of figures. Thus, a picture consists in a vast array of desires—expressed in figures—that indicate the concerns of artists, both in terms of the expression of fantasy and social consciousness. But these expressions are not those of any one particular artist. Rather, they are expressions of an anonymous libidinal economy of painting—to the extent that the expression of figures on a surface is, as in dreams, a collective force, which is not specific to any one individual consciousness. Piero della Franscesca, for example, handles perspective as a direct expression of the need for mathematical precision and heralds the coming age of scientific discovery. By contrast, Jackson Pollack stresses the dissolution of form, the dissolution of painting. Both are instances of libidinal economy—the figures are different, the expressions and fantasms are different. Thus for Lyotard, as for Merleau-Ponty, pictorial representation takes the form of an inscription, an active record of a vast number of registers. However, for Lyotard it does not carry the indelible mark of the subject, only the traces of a subjectivity.

The significant difference between these alternative conceptions of pictorial "representation" and the previously mentioned dominant theories should now be clear. Instead of reference and cognition, Merleau-Ponty and Lyotard regard representation as subject to ontology and ideology, respectively. For Merleau-Ponty, representation is tied up with the being of the painter, the creator. This being cannot be reduced to an ulterior and partial unit, like a linguistic statement, a symbolic re-presentation of something which is absent. Similarly, for Lyotard, representation is not a way of organizing referents or a precise isomorphic equivalent of the artist's perception of the world in Rudolph Arnheim's sense. For Lyotard, painting is a way of not "making visible," of jamming signification and meaning, of deconstructing the very order in which ideology and theory thrive. Hence Merleau-Ponty and Lyotard both propose an alternative to the end(s) of pictorial representation.

Chapter 7

MOURNING, WOMAN, AND THE PHALLUS: LACAN'S *HAMLET*

Debra B. Bergoffen

> ... the theater raises the familial relation to the condition of a universal metaphoric structural relation, whence the imaginary place and interplay of persons derives.
> —Gilles Deleuze and Félix Guattari, *Anti-Oedipus*

I. A Beginning

This is a story reading chain. Lacan reads *Hamlet*. I read Lacan reading *Hamlet* and use this reading, its psychoanalytic structure and its focus on a woman, to read the drama as an account of the woman as mourner within partriarchy. Accepting Lacan's notions of the phallus, *jouissance*, the symbolic, the imaginary, and the signifying chain, I suggest that Shakespeare's tale may be read as a story of the usurpation of the place of the phallus by a widowed queen, a woman whose ambiguous place in the signifying chain allows her to play a game of *jouissance* while appearing to accept the law of patriarchy.

Staying within Lacan's framework, I accept, for this reading, the idea that the phallus as the symbolic law is gender neutral, but pursue the idea that the phallus depicted in *Hamlet* is not the symbolic law of the third (Lacan refers to the third as the father, but this belies its gender neutrality and moves the symbolic into the symbolics of the patriarchal-imaginary) but the imaginary law of the father, the one whom patriarchy recognizes as the only possible third. This law equates the phallus with the penis, the man, and refuses to recognize the woman's claims to signifying power. Under this rule of the imaginary, a woman must play the role of the silent other, the mourner. She must accept the myth of the masculine by appearing to be inessential in the ritual of the transference of power. By refusing to mourn, *Hamlet*'s Gertrude challenges the imaginary phallic structures of patriarchy. She shows us the way woman's complicity is essential to the patriarchal order as she provides a glimpse of a woman who steps outside its parameters.

This distinction between the imaginary and the symbolic calls for another differentiation, the difference between mourning and grieving. In insisting that within patriarchy men cannot mourn, I do not intend to say that men neither feel nor express grief. Grieving is a personal psychological expression of loss enacted by both men and women. Mourning, however, is a social act. Within patriarchy, mourning is the role through which women mediate men's recognition of each other as they obliterate all signs of their own power. In claiming that *Hamlet* shows us that men cannot mourn I do not intend to say that the men of *Hamlet* feel no grief but rather to say that they cannot, within the structures of patriarchy, perform the public rituals of personal loss required by the signifying chain.

From distinctions to definitions. As used here, the term phallus designates that signifier which controls and situates all signifiers and significations within the patriarchal order. Further, within the context of this piece, the term *jouissance* designates that desire, that excess, which breaks into and disrupts the code of patriarchy. These distinctions and designations are simple sketches. The texts—mine, Lacan's, and Shakespeare's—provide the context within which they slide. They tell the stories of the ways in which a woman and her desire interrupt patriarchal significations and the ways in which the power of the imaginary phallus reasserts itself as it covers over the marks of *jouissance*.

II. The Reading

In "Desire and the Interpretation of Desire in *Hamlet*," Lacan directs us to follow Shakespeare's tragedy along the axes of mourning, desire, and the phallus. Challenging traditional wisdom, he asks us to see Ophelia as the pivotal character. Challenging traditional psychoanalysis, he displaces the oedipal motif. According to Lacan, it is not the desire for the mother, the guilt of this desire, or the envy of the uncle that delays Hamlet, but rather the fact that he is always at the hour of the other. Instead of tying *Hamlet* to the psychoanalytic structures of familial sexuality, Lacan links it to the dynamics of mourning and melancholia.

By focusing on mourning rather than mating, Lacan opens the way for a political reading of *Hamlet*; for mourning, unlike the oedipal fantasy, is a public and ritualized act. Further, by situating a woman at the center of the play, he invites a feminist interpretation. Pursuing this invitation, and stalking this opening, I suggest that *Hamlet* be read as the drama of woman as mourner. Following the Lacanian reading I place a woman at the center of the play. Departing from that reading I argue that Lacan has given the wrong woman center stage. It is Gertrude, not Ophelia, who is pivotal to understanding *Hamlet*, and her action—not Ophelia's, or Claudius', or Hamlet's—knots and untangles the plot.

Pursuing Lacan's decoupling of Hamlet and Oedipus, I would like to propose that psychoanalytic readings of *Hamlet* which link the intrigues of the play to the drama of the Oedipus complex can only present the woman as the passive object of man's desire. A reading focused on mourning, however, sets us in other directions. If we begin from the mourning motif, we discover inadequate/inappropriate mourning everywhere. Instead of mourning Gertrude marries. Hamlet, who persists in wearing mourning clothes, is reprimanded by the queen for being inappropriately melancholy and reproached by the ghost for mourning instead of acting, that is, taking revenge. Polonius is hastily buried and cannot be properly mourned. Ophelia is denied proper burial rites. Hamlet and Laertes make a mockery of mourning in their gravesite antics. Looking at these incidents we discover that they are not scattered episodes, but part of a thematic movement whereby women are re-situated from their passive position within the oedipal triangle to an active role within the drama of the transference of phallic power.

We discover the ways in which mourning directs us to a feminist reading of *Hamlet* by seeing that the questions of proper burial, funeral rites, and appropriate mourning lead not to Oedipus but to Antigone, and that in *Antigone* as in *Hamlet* we are confronted with the question of transference of power and forced to recognize that the power of the patriarchal phallus, though lodged in the male, must pass through the female. No longer the passive object of man's desire, women here are an integral part of the game. Men may try to pass the phallus amongst themselves, but, as *Antigone* and *Hamlet* reveal, without the complicity of women, legitimacy is impossible.

Between Antigone and Gertrude we are presented with two women who are required to sacrifice themselves so that the power of the phallus may be "rightfully" established. Or perhaps these women are required to sacrifice themselves so that the power of the "rightful" phallus may assert itself. These women display divergent responses to an "illicit" transference of phallic power. Antigone insists that her brother be properly buried. Her quarrel, at least at the onset, is not with the fact that the power of the phallus now resides with her uncle, but that in acquiring this power her uncle refuses to recognize its source in her brother. Her overt demand is that her uncle recognize her brother. The drama of the play, however, reveals that there is another demand at work, the demand that her role in the transference be recognized. For in refusing her demand, Antigone's uncle is transformed from the legitimate heir to the illicit phallus. Without Antigone's recognition he cannot reign.[1]

In Gertrude we find a woman whose pursuit of *jouissance* undermines the requirements of mourning. Unlike Antigone who demands that the rites/rights of mourning be fulfilled/recognized, Gertrude is an accomplice to the illicit transmission of power. Her rejection of the law of the father foils the imaginary phallic structure. After open defiance of the law kills her, her death restores legitimacy to the patriarchal phallus. But, as we shall see, though things are no longer rotten in Denmark the phallus remains displaced. The woman's threat to it has been put down, but the wrong man rules.

In *Antigone* and *Hamlet* we are presented with variations on a single theme: though men go to battle to conquer and/or avenge each other, the victories of male violence are secured by the female. Though the structures of patriarchy require that phallic power be transferred from man to man, the transference is not direct. It is always and necessarily mediated by the silent power of the woman. In her role as mourner this power is played out, and in the disruptions of this role, this power is made manifest.

Hamlet and *Antigone* argue against the possibility of direct mutual male recognition. Within the structures of patriarchy as depicted in these dramas, the mutuality of male recognition is female-mediated. The female mediator, however, is the sacrificial other. Her role is silenced, not celebrated. If she mourns/mediates as she is supposed to, phallic power passes from father to son, brother to uncle, male to male. Her role is not recognized (because its recognition would threaten the myth of the male phallus?) and she is reduced to the invisible medium through whom the phallus passes. If she does not perform her function as prescribed, if she does not properly mourn, the power of the phallus cannot assert itself. Now her role is made evident. Though she is always at the center of the drama of phallic power, her centrality only becomes visible at the breaks/discontinuities of transference. As her role becomes manifest, so does her sacrifice. For now the sacrifice must be literal. Only the death of the woman who will not mourn (Gertrude) or cannot mourn (Antigone) resets the phallus to its "legitimate" path.

If we follow this line of thought we see that though Lacan bemoans the fact that Hamlet is always at the hour of the other, he misses the fact that as mourner, as silent mediator, the woman is always at the hour of the other, and that the tragedy of Hamlet may be understood as the tragedy of a misplaced man whose only route to legitimacy lies in occupying the place left vacant by his mother. Put differently, the tragedy is not simply that Hamlet cannot act, but that the ghost asks too much of him; for Hamlet is not simply asked to avenge his father's murder, he is asked to legitimize the phallus of the father. Hamlet seems to understand that the issue lies with his mother for his thoughts move, much to his father's dismay, from Claudius to Gertrude. It is as if Hamlet understands what his father does not, that is, that the plan is too simple, that it is fraught with danger, that it cannot succeed without his mother's compliance, and that it threatens his masculinity.

The idea that men are emasculated by mourning—although suggested—is not central to the drama. The idea that women are obliged to mourn pervades *Hamlet*. There are constant references to the queen's hasty marriage, i.e., refusal to properly mourn; there is the suggestion that Ophelia's madness is triggered by her father's death and sudden burial, i.e., inability to properly fulfill her role as mourner; and there is the portrait of the perfect queen in the mousetrap play, an idealized woman who promises never to remarry, i.e., to be the constant mourner. Women as mourners are expected to be at the hour of the other. They are threatened with madness or worse if this position is closed to them and scandalized if they attempt to escape their fate.

But what of men who try to mourn? Here the play is less constant but nevertheless suggestive. The queen simply tells Hamlet to give up grieving. She finds his behavior inappropriate, too sentimental. Everyone dies. The king is more specific. He accuses Hamlet of "impious stubbornness" and "unmanly grief." The graveyard scene is also telling. The church has refused Ophelia full burial rites. The only woman on the scene is Gertrude, a reluctant mourner at best. Laertes tries to fill the gap. Hamlet, acting as if challenged to a duel, tries to do Laertes one better. A burial turned into a brawl. No, mourning is not for men. They cannot be at the hour of the other. But what if they have no choice? What if father and mother conspire to corner the son? What if the man is Hamlet, under obligation by the ghost to remember the father but thwarted by the mother who will not hold the place of remembrance open?

The ghost's parting words, "Adieu, adieu, adieu. Remember me," speak to the complexity of the case. Since Hamlet as mourner has been remembering the father the words must mean something other than what they say. Within the context of the discussion between Hamlet and the ghost, "remember" seems to mean avenge. The ghost is telling Hamlet to remember him by taking revenge. Within the context of the play, however, the words are a rebuke. In mourning, Hamlet has not been properly remembering, or has not been remembering like a man. Laertes shows us how men remember their fathers. The question of remembrance, however, is triangular. How can Hamlet remember like a man when his mother obliterates the memory with her cheerfulness (Act III, Scene ii)? To whom is the "Remember me" really addressed?

On this reading, it is not the murder that calls forth the ghost but the lack of mourning, the hasty marriage which allows the meat from the funeral to serve as refreshment for the wedding. "Thrift Horatio. The funeral baked meats did coldly furnish forth the marriage tables" (Act I, Scene ii). Could we ask for a clearer indication that the issue is the issue of phallic transference? Gertrude is the source of upheaval, not Claudius. Her refusal to mourn properly raises the question of the place of the phallus. The murder may have been accomplished without her, but its goal—

phallic power—cannot. The ghost has no understanding of this. For him Gertrude's affront is personal, not political. Had Hamlet acted and taken his (the ghost's) throne he could lie in peace. No return would be necessary. The ghost must return because Gertrude acted where Hamlet should have. Or, more accurately, the ghost must return because Gertrude's action, substituting marriage nuptials for mourning rituals, immobilizes Hamlet. The ghost sees the immobility but does not understand its source. He does not understand that Gertrude's refusal to mourn brings back the ghost and fuels its impossible request: that the son do what the mother will not, legitimize the father.

We find Hamlet, at the opening of the play, committed to mourning his father and obsessed with the remarriage of his mother. Though he does not yet suspect foul play in his father's death, he is sure that his mother is befouled. The marriage is an affront on two counts. It violates the father who has not been properly remembered, and it violates the son who is denied his legacy. What is curious, however, is that only Hamlet is truly scandalized. The court seems to buy Claudius' story. Affairs of state, he says, require the stability conferred by the marriage.

Gertrude's role here is unclear. Whether she is the victim of a seduction or an adulterous accomplice is left to speculation and innuendo. Critics have come down on one or the other side of the question depending on whether they see her as passive or wanton and oversexed. The ambiguity of Gertrude's character, at times passive (e.g., exiting at the king's command, asking Hamlet what to do) at times appearing spirited (e.g., her defence of Claudius to Laertes, her open defiance of Claudius in drinking the wine) may be reconciled if we see her as a woman who understands the limits of the woman's role and who pushes against those limits without overtly challenging the patriarchal structure.

Whatever the relationship between Gertrude, King Hamlet, and Claudius may have been, however, Claudius is correct. Only the marriage can legitimize his claim to Denmark. Only the queen can make him king. But why would the queen prefer the brother-in-law to the son? Prince Hamlet is certainly old enough to rule. Why deny him? Though there is much in the play to indicate Gertrude may be passive, there is nothing to indicate that she is stupid. We cannot say that she does not know that a son who is old enough to go abroad and old enough to marry is not also old enough to be a head of state. (That he is old enough is emphasized in Act IV, Scene v, when the people proclaim Laertes, Hamlet's contemporary, king after Polonius' murder.) We cannot suggest that she does not know that the marriage is hasty. The text is clear here. She knows the causes of Hamlet's grief and she knows they have as much to do with her as with the death of his father. Without clear text we cannot be certain of Gertrude's motives. Neither can we definitely ascertain what this marriage means to her. We can, however, use the text to speculate. If we put together what we know she knows with what she does, we can suggest that Gertrude's decision to marry may be understood as a rebellion against the dictates of phallic power and/or as an expression of a non-patriarchal sense of the phallus. That is, we can suggest that Gertrude refuses to mourn the death of King Hamlet in order to effect the death of the patriarchal phallus. We can suggest in other words that the woman who showed her rebelliousness in drinking the wine at the end of the play was a woman who understood and was capable of acting against patriarchal power at the beginning of the play. Further, that she never gets embroiled in affairs of state indicates that the marriage, for her, serves no patriarchal function. Her desire lies elsewhere.

Women must mourn. Women may marry. Gertrude may escape the requirements of mourning without appearing to invalidate them by invoking the privilege of marriage. She may invoke the marriage right to challenge the mourning rite. Never appearing to step outside the law, she undermines it from within by refusing to comply with the patriarchal dictates of phallic transference. She, not the law, will determine legitimacy. But she will not show her hand. Claudius will speak of the marriage, not Gertrude. *Jouissance* will cloak itself in the law. Affairs of state, the law, require that the incest taboo, the law, be broken. The law itself requires its own violation. No outside forces at work here.

If we can accept that Gertrude uses her female identity to challenge her woman's role in the patriarchal structure, we can also suggest that this marriage is more an act of affirmation than rebellion. While we may use the drinking episode to support the possibility that Gertrude's decision to marry is her way of escaping the demands of the imaginary phallus, we may look at the various descriptions/discussions of her sexuality to suggest another meaning of the marriage.

From Hamlet's perspective she is wanton. But Hamlet is the voice of the patriarchal law. Having resolved his oedipal complex, he accepts the sensual dimensions of the relationship between his parents. When his mother's pleasure transgresses the law of the literal father and threatens the place of the masculine phallus, he is thrown off track. He is scandalized by the face of *jouissance*.

Rather than seeing the incest motif as indicative of the oedipal structure of *Hamlet*, we may see this motif as expressive of the complexity of the power relationships initiated by the rhythms of sensuality. Claudius presents the court with the story of a marriage of convenience, but his story is not supported by the play. Passion, not politics, links him to Gertrude. In his words: "She is so conjunctive to my life and soul that, as the star moves not but in his sphere I could not but by her"(Act IV, scene iv). The incest motif suggests the power of the passion and the new laws it provokes. This is no ordinary marriage. As husband and king Claudius dominates, but Gertrude is not only his wife and queen. She is also his "sometime sister" and as such his double and equal rather than his subordinate. More than a subordinate, more than a double and equal, however, Gertrude is also a threat. As Hamlet's mother she may challenge Claudius' legitimacy any time. Indeed as the end of the drama makes clear, the legitimacy of the phallus lies with her. In this marriage the complexity of the otherness of woman replaces the woman as the object–other of the patriarchal demand.

Talk about a shifting signifier! The hasty marriage in violation of the laws of mourning justified in the name of the state enacted at the insistence of desire. The phallus as law passed from king to brother through the wife, denied the son by his mother. The phallus as law tempted by the phallus as *jouissance*. The woman, mediator of the law, playing with the phallus. No wonder the ghost is scandalized. The woman will not mourn; the son cannot take revenge.

We would of course like Gertrude to tell us what she is up to. She does not. *Jouissance* cannot speak in this phallic register. It can only show itself obliquely and this it does in two critical scenes, the mousetrap play and the closet encounter. As director of the mousetrap play, Hamlet intends to unmask the guilt of mother and uncle. He succeeds with the man but not the woman. The play's reenactment of the murder does not touch her. She responds instead to the idealization of mourning. Her reaction, "The lady doth protest too much methinks" (Act III, Scene ii) indicates, I think, that she does not accept the legitimacy of the law that demands that women mourn. Further, the straightforward way, the innocent way, in which she expresses herself indicates that in not accepting the role patriarchy reserves for woman she does not feel guilty and does not experience herself as transgressing a limit. Rather, she accepts a dimension of herself that she believes the mousetrap play queen also experiences but represses.

Gertrude accepts her *jouissance* as a legitimate mode of otherness, as a way of being open to her, until the closet scene, a critical moment in this reading of the drama; for here Hamlet finally succeeds in re-inserting his mother into the patriarchal phallic order. Reproaches regarding her hasty marriage and lack of mourning having failed to move her; Hamlet takes another tack. He accuses his mother of being too old to love (Act III, Scene iv). Her mode of otherness de-legitimated, her undoing is begun. In the next scene, she speaks to Ophelia, a young woman, a woman still young enough to love, of feeling guilty. The patriarchal noose has been lowered and begins to tighten.

Reenter the law. The ghost who believes that ignorance is the source of the problem enters to tell Hamlet the truth about his death. The ghost who believes in the power of knowledge assumes that Hamlet has taken on the role of mourner rather than avenger because he did not know his father was murdered. But the ghost, absent at his son's birth, does not know his issue. He does not understand the power of the woman (having known her only as his wife) and does not recognize the play of *jouissance*.

Knowledge does not produce action. So much for Socrates. It suspends Hamlet between the masculine and feminine demands of patriarchy. Before the ghost's appearance we find Hamlet playing the woman's role. He must mourn his father for his mother will not. The ghost demands that Hamlet act like a man—like a warrior. Hamlet, we discover, cannot meet his father's demand. Why not? Oedipal conflict says Jones. He is always at the hour of the other says Lacan. He needs to be sure of the veracity of the ghost's accusations (more knowledge) say the Socratic-like critics. Or perhaps, and more simply: his mother won't let him. So long as Gertrude confers legitimacy on Claudius, Hamlet's action is barred.

Hamlet, in playing the role of the mourner, is engaged in more than an act of remembrance. He is reminding the queen of her role and holding it open for her. Unless and until she moves to occupy this place revenge is impossible.

Hamlet's inaction here is not indicative of an inability to act, but of his awareness that his revenge cannot accomplish its end without the complicity of his mother. The old ghost believes that destroying Claudius will reestablish his legitimacy. Hamlet understands that this may be mere fantasy on his father's part, that King Hamlet has not confronted the possibility that the queen may still thwart his phallic claims. In the ideal play, the script intended by the ghost, Hamlet kills Claudius, the queen renounces her illicit liaison, that is, withdraws her recognition from Claudius, and mourns her "rightful" king. In this play King Hamlet, though wrongfully murdered, remains the rightful possessor of the phallus and transfers its power to his son (through the invisible mediation of the queen). But Hamlet has learned what his father has not; the queen may not follow her script. While the ghost understands that the queen must not be harmed because she is needed to mourn and provide the medium for the recognition and transference of power, Hamlet understands that so long as she remains on the scene the transference cannot be guaranteed. What if, instead of renouncing Claudius, she does for him what she would not do for the king? What if she mourns Claudius? Gertrude is pivotal. So long as she remains alive she is both promise and threat to King Hamlet's legitimacy. She may recognize the father of her son or not. Her decision determines the place of the phallus. Then why not eliminate the risk by destroying her? Because the risk of her absence is even greater than the risk of her choice? Because without her the line of transference is destroyed? Because without her the power of the phallus is permanently displaced?

By reading Hamlet as a drama of mourning and seeing Gertrude as the inverted double of Antigone, we find woman at the heart of patriarchal phallic power. We find her critical to the transference of the phallus and the stability of the law of the father. We discover a structure in patriarchy where woman is not the passive object of man's desire, but where she is a necessary partner in the rule of the law. Far from discovering the equality or recognition of woman, however, we discover a complex masking process as work. Instead of acknowledging woman's mediating role, patriarchy conceals it.

Again the play's the thing. Gertrude, the key to the drama, is a woman of few words and long silences. Appearing in half of the scenes of the play, she has less dialogue than any of the other major characters;[2] less dialogue even than Ophelia, who appears in half as many scenes. She is never the central figure on stage.[3] In her one big scene, the closet scene with Hamlet, Gertrude is completely overshadowed by her son (*HM*, 241). The overwhelming impression we are left with is that of a passive woman of extensive silence (*HM*, 244). In the words of Baldwin Maxwell, ". . . however important the part of the Queen in *the story* of Hamlet, her role in the play is definitely subordinate"(*HM*, 236). The discrepancy catches our attention. We seem to be given a portrait of absent presence. For some reason Gertrude must be on stage. For some other reason her presence must be silence. For some reason Gertrude is necessary for the efficacy of phallic power; for some other reason her necessity must be hidden.

Hamlet provides phenomenological descriptions of the woman's mediating role. It shows how woman's refusal of the mourner's role disrupts everything around her. It shows how things go wrong when she refuses her role, for it shows men to be incapable of mourning and unable to maintain the law without the mediating presence of the woman. It does not go beyond the phenomenological, however. It neither explains the necessity of women's mediation nor the requirement that the mediation be masked. But the showing suggests an intentionality at work. It suggests that the role of the woman as mediator must remain hidden in order to give credence to the myth of the male phallus—the myth that the power of the phallus is the power of the literal father.

It does this in two ways: one, by presenting the woman as simultaneously central and peripheral, the other by portraying direct male transferences of power as either impossible or misplaced. The ghost cannot confer the kingdom (which he identifies as his) on his son. Hamlet cannot legitimize his father without his mother's consent. When the phallus passes from Hamlet to Fortinbras in the absence of women, Denmark comes under the rule of its enemy.

Throughout the drama the ghost is incapable of motivating Hamlet. What should also be clear is that Hamlet acts only after his mother gives him permission. Only after she has been poisoned and strips Claudius of his legitimacy, does Hamlet kill the pretender to the throne. What frees Hamlet is not the knowledge that Claudius murdered his father but the guarantee that Gertrude will not mourn Claudius. With Gertrude's death one barrier is pulled down as another arises. Now there are no women to mourn or mediate the transference. The final scene might make it appear that a world without women is possible. Indeed we might see this scene as the epitome of the male fantasy of phallic power—the fantasy of a world where even the silenced presence of woman is unnecessary. Now that there are no women left all the roles are open to men. Horatio is entrusted with the story. Fortinbras arranges the funeral rites. It will be a military mourning. No hysteria over grave sites. Order will be restored. And yet on second look we discover that this portrayal of phallic power passed from man to man is a portrayal of the undoing of the law. The phallus passes to Fortinbras, the son of the ghost's enemy. The resolution accomplishes nothing. King Hamlet is avenged but not legitimatized.[4]

From this perspective we might read *Hamlet* as attempting to pose an answer to the question: What do men want? The answer would seem to run something like this. Men want to control the phallus. They want to be the law, possess the law, and determine the place of the law. They do not want to deal with the complexities of the relationship between themselves, women, and the law. But the answer has another part. Men cannot get what they want. If they succeed in realizing their fantasy of the phallus without woman, the place of the phallus eludes them. Hence the dilemma of patriarchy: how to recognize the role of the woman without compromising the myth of the male phallus. In *Hamlet* the workings of the resolution of the dilemma are played out as the breakdown of its structure is unveiled. Women will be recognized as the silent, controllable other. They will be portrayed as marginalized though not as marginal. Though their movement from side to center stage will be veiled, their refusal to remain peripheral determines the tragedy.

Between Ophelia and Gertrude we are given the story of patriarchal woman from beginning to end. The young woman passed from father to husband under the guarantee of virginity bears the son to whom the phallus will be passed. The legitimacy of the transference depends on the legitimacy of the issue, hence the daughter must be chaste. Polonius' concern is to assure his daughter her rights within this patriarchal chain. He fails and with his failure Ophelia escapes the structure completely, first through madness and then by death. Why she goes mad is the subject of extended debate. Because she could not bear the loss of the father? Because she could not mourn him? Because she has been betrayed by father, brother, and lover? Because having been loosened from the structures of patriarchy she is lost? Or because madness and death are the only acts of rebellion open to her?

Were Ophelia the only woman in the drama the ideology of male domination and female passivity might be secure. Women could be reduced to "womb men . . . walking repositories for the male seed."[5] But Ophelia is not the only woman, she is only one of the women, the woman at the beginning of the patriarchal chain. The other woman, Gertrude, situated within the chain as the legitimate mother, stands at the other end of the line. Her child may be the property of the father, but the king cannot stake his claim without her. Virginity and monogamy legitimatize the marriage and the birth, mourning legitimizes the heir. From marriage to mourning the active passivity of the woman is essential. Her mediating powers must be masked.

In Shakespeare's *Hamlet*, however, one woman tries to play another game. Rejecting the role of passive mediator Gertrude plays the game of *jouissance*. The play destroys her. Patriarchy is not easily undone. We would be wrong to conclude, however, that the only lesson of Hamlet is that tragedy follows the woman who refuses her place. For though neither Ophelia nor Gertrude succeed in extending the limits of the woman's role, they do succeed in exposing the myth of the male phallus. And there is a time in the play, however brief, when Gertrude provides us with a glimpse of a signifier placed outside the patriarchal structure of silenced mourning women, i.e., with a view of *jouissance* playing outside the law of the King.

Chapter 8

A METAPHOR OF THE UNSPOKEN: KRISTEVA'S SEMIOTIC *CHORA*

M. Alison Arnett

Successively, and in regulated fashion, the center receives different forms or names. The history of Metaphysics, like the history of the West, is the history of these metaphors and metonymies. . . . The event I called a rupture . . . would presumably have come about when the structurality of structure had to begin to be thought.
—Jacques Derrida, "Structure, Sign and Play"[1]

People have often reproached me for *spatial obsessions*, which have indeed been obsessions for me. But I think through them I did come to what I had basically been looking for: the relations that are possible between power and knowledge.
—Michel Foucault, "Questions on Geography"[2]

The *mirror stage* is a drama whose internal thrust is precipitated from insufficiency to anticipation—and which manufactures for the subject, caught up in the lure of *spatial identification*, the succession of phantasies that extends from a fragmented body-image . . . to the assumption of the armour of an alienating identity.
—Jacques Lacan, "The Mirror Stage"[3]

We can think of the "wild zone" of women's culture *spatially* . . . stand[ing] for an area which is literally no-man's-land, a place forbidden to men . . . [which] must be the address of a genuinely woman-centered criticism, theory, and art.
—Elaine Showalter, "Feminist Criticism in the Wilderness,"[4]

> I could go on giving examples. But they all converge on *the problematic of space*, which innumerable religions of matriarchal (re)appearance attribute to 'woman,' and which Plato ... designated by the aporia of the *chor*, matrix space, nourishing, unnameable, anterior to the One, to God and, consequently, defying metaphysics.
> —Julia Kristeva, "Women's Time"[5]

I. Space and Woman as Metaphors

Many contemporary thinkers have adopted spatial metaphors to represent particular hypotheses or relationships between various theoretical concepts. As Jacques Derrida suggests above, this choice is perhaps not a new one—the whole history of metaphysics coinciding with the history of these very metaphors. Michel Foucault concurs, adding that "[a] whole history [could be and] remains to be written of *spaces*."[6] Yet the preponderance of these metaphors at this particular time should not be passed over as merely another moment in this history, as if the importance of space as a theoretical model has remained constant. Foucault, through his historical analyses of the human sciences, recognizes a period, from which we are now emerging, in which space was less useful to philosophy:

> Among all the reasons which led to spaces suffering for so long a certain neglect, I will mention just one.... At the moment when a considered politics of spaces was starting to develop, at the end of the eighteenth century, the new achievements in theoretical and experimental physics dislodged philosophy from its ancient right to speak of the world, the cosmos, finite or infinite space. This ... reduced philosophy to the field of the problematic of time. Since Kant, what is to be thought by the philosopher is time. (*EP*, 149)[7]

If indeed space has been reappropriated, it remains to be determined why this neglected characterization of the world has now become, to philosophy, at least acceptable and perhaps even necessary. What can the construct of space offer the post-structuralist philosopher? Alice Jardine provides a preliminary response in describing the current inclination of philosophy toward self-reflection:

> In general, this [recent crisis in legitimation] has brought about, within the master narratives . . . a questioning and turning back upon their own discourse, in an attempt to create a new *space* or *spacing within themselves* for survivals. . . . [The] other-than-themselves [which the, most often male, narratives work to incorporate] is almost always a "space" of some kind (over which the narrative has lost control), and this space has been coded as *feminine*, as *woman*.[8]

Julia Kristeva, the last philosopher in the "history" presented above, returns to what is essentially the advent of metaphysics, of philosophizing—to Plato. She does this to incorporate his spatial conception of a primary cause of the cosmos, the *chora*, into her own philosophy, which desires, like that of Derrida and Foucault, to "defy" or deconstruct metaphysics, and, as suggested by Jardine, to disrupt master (male) narratives. Examining Kristeva's notion of the semiotic *chora*, and therefore inquiring as to what exactly women's space is, how it works, and what kind of discourse it engenders, I hope to answer, although perhaps only in a limited way, the question posed above regarding the current necessity of spatial metaphors. Finally, it must be asked what other philosophers have to say about Kristeva's particular appropriation of space and woman; what, in fact, are the limits or boundaries of her own theory?

II. Women's Space

> It often happens that neurotic men declare that there is something uncanny about the female genital organs. This *unheimlich* place, however, is the entrance to the former *Heim* [home] of all human beings, to the place where each one of us lived once upon a time and in the beginning.
> —Sigmund Freud, "The Uncanny"[9]

"Woman" is rightly, according to Kristeva, referred to as a place, that is, a place familiar yet forgotten, or long departed from, and positioned in opposition to the here neurotic "man" and his realm, time.[10] With regard to discursive practices, which will be Kristeva's main concern,

> The symbolic order—the order of verbal communication, [is] the paternal order . . . a temporal order. For the speaking animal, it is the clock of objective time: it provides the reference point, and, consequently, all possibilities of measurement, by distinguishing between a before, a now, and an after.[11]

Women's time, referred to by Freud as "the beginning" above, is, according to Kristeva, unlike the symbolic order, and therefore not temporal at all. By nature of their reproductive functioning, women participate in a monumental time which crosses individual boundaries, becoming the time of a whole species. This time fails to follow a linear progression, exhibiting rather a cyclical activity throughout eternity. Woman is further:

> a *pregnancy*: an escape from the temporality of day-to-day social obligations, an interruption of the regular monthly cycles, where the surfaces . . . are abandoned in favor of a descent into the depths of the body. (*ACW*, 154)

The signifying process arising from this ultimate return to the maternal body produces what Kristeva calls a genotext, operating prior to and then within the signifying structures of the paternal, symbolic order. Here signification is determined not in relation to a fixed reference point in the temporal sequence of speech but to the primary processes we experience in relation to the maternal body, which:

> The very word 'temporality' hardly fits: all encompassing and infinite like imaginary space, this temporality reminds one of Kronos in Hesiod's mythology, the incestuous son whose massive presence covered all of Gaia in order to separate her from Ouranos, the father. (*WT*, 191)

As implied by the myth, then, woman is a space, defined or delineated after the birth and separation of the child.[12] The child's separation is an identification with the paternal law, the symbolic order, but is accompanied by a desire to return to the mother. Thus, women's time, Kronos, which is massive and all-encompassing, is really a kind of place, situated outside of the domain of the father.

Jacques Derrida concludes his essay "Structure, Sign and Play" with some curious remarks about birth, perhaps the very birth of this sort of uncanny space that is woman and mother:

> Here there is a sort of question, call it historical, of which we are only glimpsing today the *conception*, the *formation*, the *gestation*, the *labor*. I employ these words, I admit, with a glance toward the business of child-bearing—but also with a glance toward those who, in a company from which I do not exclude myself, turn their eyes away in the face of the as yet unnameable which is proclaiming itself and which can do so, as is necessary whenever a birth is in the offing, only under the species of the nonspecies, in the formless, mute, infant, and terrifying form of monstrosity. (*SSP*, 242–43)

For Derrida, the conception and birth of *differance* is a difficult one to watch, as it disrupts the established order. For Kristeva, this is the symbolic order of language, thus this space is "the as yet unnameable." It offers itself as a not-a-self—for Kristeva, not a "phallic," speaking subject[13] but "the formless, mute infant"—and implies the "monstrosity" of the incest taboo which Derrida describes in his essay as destructive of the nature/culture distinction. For Kristeva, this is that which forces the child, like Kronos, to desire to return from the paternal law to the space of the repressed mother.

In her essay "Stabat Mater," Kristeva provides her readers with an example of the maternal space, which "re-establish[es] what is non-verbal and show[s] up as the receptacle of a signifying disposition that is closer to so-called primary processes."[14] This essay reveals her meaning in not only its language but its visual and formal qualities as well:

FLASH—Instant of time or of dream without time; inordinately swollen atoms of a bond, a vision, a shiver, a yet formless, unnameable embryo ... WORD FLESH. From one to the other, eternally, broken up visions, metaphors of the invisible.

Christianity is doubtless the most refined symbolic construct in which femininity, to the extent that it transpires through it—and it does so incessantly—is focused on *Maternality*. Let us call 'maternal' the ambivalent principle that is bound to the species, on the one hand, and on the other stems from an identity catastrophe.... Augustine, Bernard of Clairvaux, Meister Eckhart to mention but a few, played the part of the Father's virgin spouses, or even, like Bernard, received drops of virginal milk directly on their lips. Freedom with respect to maternal territory then becomes the pedestal upon which love of God is erected. (*SM*, 161-2) [15]

As each of the two texts struggles for recognition within the essay, it is space that is at stake. Kristeva's academic text on the importance of the cult of the Virgin within Christianity represents the language of the symbolic order—clear, logical, and subject to rules of grammar. The second text represents the more spontaneous, irregular, non-theoretical "language" of the maternal body, the semiotic realm, which is prior to the symbolic but can appear only as flashes or bursts within it. The essay, and indeed, meaning itself (*signifiance*), is nothing more than this dialectic between the symbolic and the semiotic,[16] this "heterogeneity that cannot be subsumed in the signifier [and that] explodes violently with pregnancy" (*SM*, 182). The maternal is the "FLASH" of meaning exploding into the greater text. But it is also the "ambivalent principle" that arises from an "identity catastrophe," seen firstly in the very body of the pregnant (m)other, secondly in our own inability, as readers, to maintain any consistent identification with the symbolic text due to the compelling interruptions of the semiotic, and finally in the move all speaking subjects make into the symbolic order, the acceptance of the "name of the father," and the simultaneous positioning of the semiotic, the maternal, in opposition to (t)his law.

Kristeva redefines this maternal element, calling it the semiotic *chora*, from the Greek word for space:

> not yet a position that represents something for someone (i.e., it is not a sign); nor is it a *position* that represents someone for another position (i.e., it is not yet a signifier either); it is, however, generated in order to attain to this signifying position. Neither model nor copy, the *chora* precedes and underlies figuration and thus specularization, and is analogous only to vocal or kinetic rhythm. (*RPL*, 94)

She borrows this term *chora* from Plato, who in the *Timaeus* details a tripartite origin of the cosmos. In addition to a "maker and father of this universe," that is, an intelligible and unchanging model who shapes the universe into a copy of himself, there exists "a third form . . . the receptacle and, as it were the nurse of all becoming."[17] The *chora*, this "invisible and formless, all-embracing" receptacle, produces meaning, its own signification, as seen in "Stabat Mater," but not through the reasoned and ordered structures of the paternal law. Rather, it "precedes" this kind of "specularization" and remains akin only to "vocal" or bodily "rhythms." Plato is open to this gendered interpretation, even suggesting:

> We may indeed use the metaphor of birth and compare the receptacle to the mother, the model to the father, and what they produce between them to their offspring. (*T*, 69)

Plato's *chora*, the indeterminate cause of the universe, has become for Kristeva the "nonsymbolic, nonpaternal causality" that is motherhood which is "no more than the place where the subject is both generated and negated, the place where his [sic] unity succumbs before the process of charges and stases that produce him" (*RPL*, 95).

III. Spatial and Maternal Identification

As intimated earlier, in the myth of Kronos, the child is only able to achieve identification through a separation from the mother, from the semiotic, which, due to its heterogeneity, is no-thing and offers no real space against which to assert oneself. The *chora* establishes "the period of indistinction between '*same*' and '*other*,' infant and mother, as well as between 'subject' and 'object'. . . . [N]o space has been delineated (this will happen with and after the mirror stage—birth of the sign)."[18] The mirror stage, as described by Lacan, is invoked here as the beginning of separation and thus identification. Through accepting the image in the mirror as one's own, one "permits the constitution of objects detached from the semiotic *chora*." This break is finally completed in the oedipal stage in which "the subject, finding his [sic] identity in the symbolic, *separates* from his fusion with the mother, *confines* his *jouissance* to the genital and transfers semiotic motility on to the symbolic order" (*RPL*, 100–01). What is significant for our purposes here is to recognize the very spatial nature of these primary identifications which make of the semiotic *chora* the space that allows for all positioning, or the space that is no space until the child regards itself as positioned somehow in relation to it, and thus necessarily outside of it.

The child, repressing the semiotic and becoming a speaking subject, and having thus been successfully brought into the symbolic order, leaves the mother behind.[19] What can be said of the identity of the mother? Kristeva suggests that we should listen more attentively to what mothers are saying for an answer. Listening then to her own words, as a mother, in "Stabat Mater," we hear the experienced "weakness of language" and the desire for "Someone of either sex, *before* the id speaks, before language, who might make me be by means of borders, separations, vertigos" (*SM*, 176). Thus, the mother, the semiotic, depends upon this spatial separation of the child for her/its own identity. This identity must not, however, become fully subject to the symbolic order; it is a *sujet en procès*, a subject in process/on trial (*RPL*, 91) that is desired, a "fluid and free subjectivity" (*WT*, 209) "a demented *jouissance* . . . [filled] with overflowing laughter where one senses the collapse of some, ringing, subtle, fluid identity or other, softly buoyed by the waves" (*SM*, 179–80).

It must be recalled here that Kristeva is a psychoanalyst and her concern for signifying practices is related to her desire to aid individuals in crisis to a better understanding of themselves through language, through "the talking cure." This subject in process, a "fluid subjectivity," becomes the a goal of psychoanalytic therapy. As Richard Kearney describes in his *Poetics of Imagining*:

> The purpose of analysis, therefore, is not to terminate imagination [Lacan's imaginary realm, Kristeva's semiotic realm] but to restore its free play. So that if it is necessary to demystify certain *imagos* of the self—as self-sufficient and sovereign cogito—it is equally necessary to recall imagination to its Heraclitean vocation of "acting like a child, of playing." This is the most healing lucidity, after all the idols of dogmatic "truth" have been toppled. . . . We become confident of our own desires as we enact the transfer between narcissism towards the other [recognize this as the very act of the mother who cares for the other within herself]. For to acknowledge our imaginary discourse, the discourse of loving play, is to acknowledge the discourse of the other in us.[20]

IV. A Space for Revolutionary (Re)Production

The semiotic, marked off through this primary repression, refuses to remain silent: "Although originally a precondition of the symbolic, the semiotic functions within signifying practices as the result of a transgression of the symbolic (*RPL*, 118). Thus, the semiotic, the mother, remains as surplus/sur-place, capable of transgression of the "law of the father." As indicated in the title of her thesis, this revolution will come in the form of poetic language: *poetic*, "to demystify the identity of the symbolic bond itself, to demystify, therefore, the *community* of language as a universal and unifying tool, one which totalizes and equalizes" (*WT*, 210), and *language*, as "The very existence of the subject is due only and entirely to language, thus it is only through language that the subject can be redefined."[21] The goal of this poetic language is to reveal the sacrificial nature of the symbolic contract, to show that, "While the Symbolic is predicated upon the rejection of the mother, the semiotic ... re-presents or recovers the maternal body in poetic speech.[22] Here we again see the desire to return to the maternal body (recall the Kronos myth) and can infer the risk which the subject takes in using this kind of language:

> Because the subject of poetic language only exists as such by constantly risking the reactivation of the "repressed instinctual, maternal element (the chora)," there is a constant threat of slipping completely under the influence of the chora. This absence of (after there once was) the symbolic disposition is the equivalent of becoming psychotic, where all that remains is semiotic, rhythmic non-sense.[23]

Kristeva refers to the successful transgression as a secondary repression done in the face of death (loss of identity), thus effecting a second birth. In order to remain transgressive, the semiotic must always be that which is defined negatively in relation to the symbolic[24] and conceived of as a space which, unlike a moment in time, can be returned to in some way.

V. Kristeva's Problematic of Space

We can step back at this point to consider the profusion of spatial metaphors Kristeva has employed. Characterizing the maternal, the semiotic *chora*, as a place, albeit an uncanny place, or a place that is originally no place, in fact, prior to placing, has allowed Kristeva to speak of constructed borders surrounding a repressed territory of signification and its revolutionary transgressions. Is space, however, the only way to illustrate these ideas? Why has she chosen to frame her discourse with this language and this concept? And again, what does the metaphor of space offer the poststructuralist philosopher?

As a French psychoanalyst, Kristeva is indebted to the thought of Sigmund Freud, who posits metaphorical spatial divisions within the mind (the Conscious/the Unconscious, the Ego/the Id/the Superego) as well as Jacques Lacan, who, as we saw earlier, establishes spatial identification as the basis for ego formation. We must also investigate her knowledge of and responses to Hegel to more fully understand why space is a fitting construct for her to utilize. While Kristeva does outline the signifying process, with Freud and Lacan, as something that occurs in the child's development temporally and, if successful, sequentially, she insists that the child's prior states, although repressed or surpassed, have not been wholly eliminated (thus the possibility for revolutionary language born out of the negated semiotic *chora*):

> This explosion of the semiotic in the symbolic is far from a negation of negation, an *Aufhebung* that would suppress the contradiction generated by the thetic and establish in its place an ideal positivity, the restorer of presymbolic immediacy. It is, instead, a *transgression* of position, a reversed reactivation of the contradiction that instituted this very position. (*RPL*, 119)

The two opposing discourses, like the two stages of the women's movement she identifies in "Women's Time," are not subsumed under some final movement, one grand synthesis which resolves the contradiction in time, but together produce a third

> 'generation' [think of the reproductive connotations of this word], impl[ying] less a chronology than a *signifying space*, a both corporeal and desiring mental space . . . which does not exclude—quite to the contrary—the *parallel* existence of all three [movements, moments] in the same historical time, or even that they be interwoven one with the other. (*WT*, 209)

This third movement destabilizes the notion of the singular subject, for whom the first space provided unity with the Other, be it the mother or the opposite sex, and the second pronounced the sexual difference required for self-identity. Recall here the identity catastrophe, seen in "Stabat Mater," of the maternal body, which admits the heterogeneity of subjectivity and, through a fundamental act of transgression, reveals the primary space from which all signification arises, the semiotic *chora*. Thus, for Kristeva, the predominant philosophical construct, time, as part of the master (male) narratives of Subjectivity and Identity, fails to satisfy:

> the Father is: sign and time. It is understandable, then, that what the father doesn't say about the unconscious, what sign and time repress in the drives, appears as their *truth* (if there is no 'absolute,' what is truth, if not the unspoken of the spoken?) and that this truth can be imagined only as a *woman*. (*ACW*, 153)

VI. Placing Woman

The question remains to be asked whether, in the name of transgression, Kristeva is not merely using woman, as she uses space, to evoke that other, the truth, behind our false *imagos* of identity, behind the structured and thus repressional symbolic order. If the spatiality of the semiotic *chora* is to be only the negative defined in relation to the temporality of the symbolic order, then must woman, to be effectual as a transgressive metaphor, remain only the negative defined in relation to man? Need she be, as Simone deBeauvoir describes, "the Other [who] is not to regain the status of being the One, [who] is submissive enough to accept this alien point of view"?[25] Does not even Kristeva's conception of a *herethics* of "loving towards the other" rest upon essentialist notions of woman as being, in Nietzsche's words, a riddle with only one solution: that is pregnancy."[26]

Among other problems with Kristeva's theories[27] Judith Butler voices this concern. She insists, in Derridian fashion, that for Kristeva merely to move to the less privileged side of a binary opposition is for her to fail to examine the construction of this opposition and thus to pronounce liberation where there is none:

> In asking whether a prediscursive libidinal multiplicity is possible, we [must] consider whether what Kristeva claims to discover in the prediscursive maternal body is itself a production

of a given historical discourse, an *effect* of culture rather than its secret and primary cause. (*BPJK*, 80-81)

Here, amidst the nature/culture distinction, one cannot assert the existence of the maternal body as primary to cultural construction, for to seek the liberation of this body could very well be to free "yet another incarnation of that law, posing as subversive but operating in the service of that law's self-amplification and proliferation" (*BPJK*, 93). Butler insists that none of her criticisms seek to "invalidate [Kristeva's] general position that culture or the Symbolic is predicated upon a repudiation of women's bodies" (*BPJK*, 93), yet Kristeva's work is, as Nancy Fraser suggests, in no way "useful for feminist politics."[28] It is trapped in various dualisms and bound to assert essentialist notions of women and exclusionary models of motherhood as revolutionary.

I believe that Kristeva avoids some of these criticisms as she is calling for a liberation of the speaking subject, man or woman, from the dogmatic structuralist discourses of unity, which make men of all subjects. Her philosophy is never a "feminism" per se; one should not conflate the fact that she is a woman and that she uses woman as a metaphorical construct to mean that she is seeking a particularly political feminist end. This is not to say that she ignores the position of individual women in society. She writes on the feminist movement from a distance, yes, but with a respect for its accomplishments and a concern for its future:

[If] in this fantasy, where a woman, intended to represent Truth, takes the place of the phallus . . . she ceases to act as an atemporal, unconscious force, splitting, defying and breaking the symbolic and temporal order . . . [a] crude but enormously effective trap for 'feminism': to acknowledge us, to turn us into the Truth of the temporal order, so as to keep us from functioning as its unconscious 'truth.' (*ACW*, 155)

As deBeauvoir posits woman as the epitome of the existential subject (i.e., one who cannot escape the ambiguity of being a subject sure of her ability to create herself, yet at all times being objectified and defined as the other), I would suggest that Kristeva posits woman, the maternal body specifically, as the quintessential example of the *sujet en procès* (i.e., she who recognizes herself as a split subject; in the symbolic order as a speaking subject yet harboring the other, that without language, that from which new language will come, within her). With this notion of a fluid subjectivity as the goal, Kristeva stands closer to Butler and Derrida than it would seem, as she insists upon no victory over the binary opposition, but a ceaseless play between the symbolic and semiotic. Kristeva's project, perhaps more properly called transgressive than revolutionary, is just this:

> let us . . . refuse all roles to summon this 'truth' situated outside time, a truth that is neither true nor false, that cannot be fitted in to the order of speech and social symbolism, that is an echo of our *jouissance*, of our mad words, of our pregnancies. But how can we do this? By listening; by recognizing the unspoken in all discourse, however Revolutionary, by emphasizing at each point whatever remains unsatisfied, repressed, new, eccentric, incomprehensible, that which disturbs the mutual understanding of the established powers. (*ACW*, 156)

Chapter 9

THE SIGN OF THE ROSE: FILMING ECO

Hugh J. Silverman

> It is not true that a code organizes signs, it is more correct to say that codes provide the rules which *generate* signs as concrete occurrences in communication intercourse. Therefore the classical notion of "sign" dissolves itself into a highly complex network of changing relationships.
> —Umberto Eco, *A Theory of Semiotics*[1]

One cold January day in Vienna, I saw *The Name of the Rose* (*Il nome della rosa*)—the film—for the first time in the German version. At the box office not only could one purchase a ticket but also an elegant booklet in the *Neuer Filmkurier* series (published in Vienna) with a color photo of Sean Connery on the cover along with the words *Der Name der Rose*. On the back of the booklet is a stunning black and white frame of the unnamed abbey in the background with Bernardo Gui (E. Murray Abraham) and William of Baskerville (Sean Connery) in the foreground. In the manner that one comes to both appreciate and expect in major professional theatre and opera, the booklet contains detailed descriptions of the principal actors, a biographical sketch of their acting careers, and a list of the *international* production staff—including the French Director, the West German Producer, the Italian Production Designer and Photographer, et alia. The personal histories of the actors are remarkable for their diversity: Sean Connery from Scotland (surely the best of the 007s); E. Murray Abraham from Pittsburgh (whom one came to dislike, yet pity, as Salieri in *Amadeus*); Michael Lonsdale, from a French mother and British father (making it possible for him to comfortably perform in both English and French language films, including Orson Wells' *The Trial*, Truffaut's *Baisers*

Volees (Stolen Kisses), Luis Buñuel's *Fantôme de la liberté*, Joseph Losey's *Galileo* and *Monsieur Klein*); Christian Slater—the sixteen-year-old New Yorker (who plays Adso of Melk and was later admired for films such as *Pump Up the Volume* and *Broken Arrow*, opposite John Travolta); the peasant girl and would-be rose of the *civitas terrena*, Valentina Vargas from Chile; and the celebrated (now late) Viennese, Helmut Qualtinger—known for his role in films made from Kafka and Durenmatt fiction and for the almost mythical Herr Karl—as the secretly heretical and ultimately burned-at-the stake Remigio di Varagine. The supplement to this universal—"catholic" one might as well say—cast and production staff is the author of the book from which the film was made, namely the Italo-international semiotician Umberto Eco.

This international *dramatis personae* amply matches the multiple coding that Eco himself anticipated in the novel. The traditions, connections, and achievements of the film's staff and cast correspond well to the fame of the Benedictine, Franciscan, Papal, heretical Dolcinite, and simple peasant crowds that people the novel and film. The characters—the Grand Inquisitor Bernardo Gui, the wise Franciscan (and obviously British) William of Baskerville, the youthful Adso from the magnificent now Benedictine monastery of Melk along the Danube in the Lower Austrian Wachau, the Papal emmisary Cardinal Bertrand Poggetto (played by Lucien Bodard), the heretical hunchback and deformed polyglot, Salvatore (Ron Perlman), not to mention the local Abbot (Michael Lonsdale), the blind Spanish librarian Jorge de Burgos (clearly coded to correlate with the Argentinian Jorge Luis Borges, played by Feodor Chaliapin Jr.)—come from "everywhere," or at least what would have been everywhere in 1327! Eco's contemporaries are mapped onto the medieval 1327 polylinguistic, multicultural, multiple origination of the novel–film. The novel–film itself is a performative (i.e., illocutionary) denial of Eco's own (ironic) claim that he "commends the tale to his readers because it is 'gloriously lacking in any relevance for our day.' "[2] Indeed, this double coding is only the framework for a whole network of semiotic patterns that constitute the film.

I. Naming/Anonymity

The second time I saw *The Name of the Rose* was in the United States, on video—this time in English, a language which many of the characters were actually speaking. Sean Connery, E. Murray Abraham, Christian Slater, et al. could now speak with their own voices. One could hear the determinate, slightly Scottish accent of the James Bond 007 character whom Eco so greatly admires.[3] The dubious and unequivocally hateful Salieri speaks through the voice of E. Murray Abraham. By contrast, the youthful, uncertain, apprenticed words of Adso are first heard as those of a boy, then in the mature voice of the narrator remembering the events of his adolescence in the fateful Abbey. In English, they are now less eerie, less artificial, in short, undubbed. For obvious reasons, the voice of Salvatore does not change. Will he be the salvation that his name names? If so, it cannot be because he is *not* burned at the stake. As if he were constructed by the James Joyce of *Finnegans Wake* or some sort of Esperanto, Salvatore has the same chaotic, dispersed, and distracted sound in English as he did in German. Like the fool in Shakespeare, he offers himself in ignorance, marginality, and self-indulgence as he catches, plays with, and eats rats—as he is kept in line by the Qualtinger-Remigio character in something like a master keeping his semi-tamed beast in check. Whether Salvatore is speaking English, Latin, French, German, or full Italian phrases—well-known idioms that seem to fit—they are all uttered in a discontinuous interrupted chain of signifiers. And what of Salvatore's salvation? Can he be saved? Can he be saved from his heresy, his deformity, or his linguistic dislocations? Is he burned as a Giordano Bruno at the stake, or as a Christ on the cross?

And what of the peasant girl who does not speak—even though the program notes tell us that the Chilean Valentina Vargas herself speaks English, Spanish, French, and Italian equally fluently? In the film, she only grunts and makes sounds of pleasure as she makes love to Adso. She is saved from the burning by the peasants who have been kept at bay until the corresponding fire inside the Abbey distracts Bernardo Gui and the soldiers from their task of maintaining the fires of execution outside. Is she saved from the fire because God has answered Adso's prayer to the voluptuous statue of the Virgin on her behalf? Is she saved because the other fire is more compelling? Is she saved because there will have already been the theologically conventional *seven* deaths at the monastery? Is she saved because she has no voice? Is she saved? For in the end, Adso cannot stay with her—he has a higher calling, a mission that he must fulfill, if not as monk, then certainly as narrator of the story. Perhaps she is ultimately saved like Goethe's Gretchen—as the "eternal feminine"—not so much by an act of God, but by an act of memory, narration, and fabulation. Throughout her role in the film, she remains silent—never speaking, never complaining, never asking for any more than is given. In her, there is a quiet peacefulness and warm understanding despite the nasty, brutish, and presumably short existence she lives. She is a repetition of the statue of the Virgin and she is the instantiation of the feminist's "woman without a voice" in a world designed by men. The male patristic view is expressed in Brother William's remark that when God created "so foul a creature" he had to endow her with some redeeming features.

In the novel, the girl is not saved. She burns at the stake. Like a Jeanne d'Arc, her martyrdom brings a kind of victory. The difference between the film and the novel is crucial here. The girl's salvation from the stake is her condemnation to a life of poverty and desperation. But the difference is a genre difference. A Hollywood-like experience prescribes the exchange of Bernardo Gui's death for the girl's salvation. The novel can support her death. Furthermore, a palimsest involves a covering over—for Eco, a rewriting of the novel; the rewriting of the girl's fate is itself a cover-up and a disclosure of the multilayered codes inscribed in the event. It provides for an alternative reading—like the various "expectorations" in Kierkegaard's *Fear and Trembling*. With each rereading, the girl's identity in the "network of changing relationships" is itself transformed.

As is characteristic of monastery life, the monks and friars themselves come from many corners of the earth, all gathered together in support of the monastic and/or devout life. Their very names signal their multiple provenances. So by contrast, one is lead to ask about the name of the peasant girl. And her name is not given, never uttered. She does not need a name. What's in a name anyway? She is a kind of allegory or *figura* of carnal love, of what Brother William calls at first "lust" but later, when he recognizes Adso's care and concern, admits must be "love." He feels that she needs his attentions—and so he prays for her. But in the end, Adso cannot *give himself* to her—she even remains nameless to him—she is the *vox populi*—again without a voice, with only her physical presence.

She is not alone in namelessness in the novel–film. The abbey itself—presumably situated in northern Italy, though the set was made outside Rome on a hill (not, apparently, on one of the *septem*)—was designed to look like many medieval monasteries, but also with a tinge of a medieval castle worthy of *The Lion in Winter*. Yet the abbey is also quite precise in its uniqueness, especially with its Norman-like turrets and imposing high tower. Indeed, the monastery set was itself patterned after the 1240 Castel del Monte, thereby again mixing the codes between the secular and the sacred; murders are not supposed to happen in cathedrals or abbeys, but on the other hand, castles are *loci classici* for murders—the murder of the Duc de Guise in Blois and Thomas à Becket in Paris are only two such examples.

Also nameless is the "name" of the murderer who is in question from the opening of the film. Yet Brother William's purpose in travelling to the fateful abbey is not to solve a murder. Like the Angela Landsbery character in *Murder She Wrote*, Brother William just happens to be there for another reason: in this case, on the occasion of a debate between Franciscans and Benedictines (officiated and judged by the Papal legate on the question as to "whether Christ *owned* the clothes he wore" and the related matter as to "whether the Church should be poor"—an issue not irrelevant to the doctrine of the Dolcinites presumed to have taken St. Francis' view to the extreme, namely that all should be poor and those members of the Church who have become rich should be killed). Upon arrival with his novice Adso of Melk, Brother William finds that he must sleuth out the matter of a murder that has putatively occurred in the abbey. Brother William (of course British, like his Sherlock Holmsian prototype) is so observant that he is even able to tell Adso where the men's room is located. This leads Adso to ask whether his mentor had been to the abbey before. The reply in the negative comes with an explanation indicating that upon arrival he noticed a monk disappear hurriedly behind a door then return with an air of contentment. This evidence—a sign of William's powers of perceptiveness—is an important clue to his skills. He notices details. Hence it will be no surprise when he detects the black mark on the dead monk's forefinger. Or that he observes the absence of books in the manuscript working room. Or that he understands very quickly that lemon paper was used for taking notes so that the information would not be available to the naked eye. At one point, William retorts when Adso asks how his master knows what he knows, "Elementary, . . ." We can hear the "my dear Watson" in what is *not* said. And then a picture of Eco himself (in a

German study of the film by Hans Baumann and Arman Sahihi in the *Psychologie Heute* Filmbuch series) shows the author of the novel standing with the Director Jean-Jacques Annaud and several members of the cast, himself duplicating the Holmsian code with a rumpled version of the classic sleuth's cap. Eco's book, entitled *The Sign of Three*—published along with Thomas Sebeok—includes Sherlock Holmes among the three as it again repeats the code. And were one to look more deeply into the author of Holmes, the historical medieval novel *The White Company* which Arthur Conan Doyle also authored would certainly also appear. Yet the sleuth code does not, as Eco states in his *Theory of Semiotics*, organize the signs of Sherlock Holmes, his synecdochal hat or his metonymical "Elementary, ... ," rather the sleuth code provides the rules which *generate* signs of the mystery to be solved—murder, intrigue, clues, etc.—throughout the novel–film. Yet despite the good work of Brother William, the name of *the* murderer is never given. This is not to say that there are no murders for whom the killer is disclosed. Indeed, it becomes evident that the second death—not the first after all—*was* a murder. The black monk Venatius (played by Urs Althaus) was killed for what he saw, and the fourth death was also a homicide. Severinus (the "coroner" monk who performs an autopsy on the black monk) has also seen something for which he must die. Severinus tries to inform Brother William, but before he is able to do so, he is killed by the Head Librarian Malachias von Hildesheim (played by Volker Prechtel) for having seen too much. One cannot however really say that either is the name of the murderer.

While one cannot call either killer *the* murderer, one can however say the names of those who died. For instance, the name of the first death is known. Although he is already dead before the scene opens, Brother William rather easily discovers that the monk had thrown himself from the tower out of guilt for having engaged in a homosexual relationship with Berenger, the "moon-faced" gay monk. The second death we already know to have been a murder—killed by Berenger and dumped head-first in a large jar of pigs' blood. As to the third death—that of the moon-faced Berenger—it becomes evident that it was not a murder but rather the result of drowning in his own bath (poisoned by his guilt and anguish as well as by the onset of the hitherto undisclosed chemical). By then Adso—Sherlock's Watson—begins to suspect that something supernatural is happening—events foretold according to Revelation and the seven days of the Apocalypse. Yet the Apocalypse is only one of several possible sets of rules which *generate* or in some way "correspond to" the sequence of deaths. Another set of rules would be the sequence of the deadly sins: jealousy, lust, greed, etc. that result in death. Another set would have to do with the conditions of quest—as in Kafka's *Castle*—for some unattainable object of desire, some holy grail, some fulfillment of *nostos*, some search for a hidden treasure. Each bears a different set of rules constituting the code in question. On the other hand, the account of the deaths could be related to the desire to protect, to cover up, to keep from view. Truth—as in the Heideggerian *Unverborgenheit*—both discloses and remains undisclosed, hidden from view, unnamed, anonymous. . . .

II. Roses/Books

The third time I saw *The Name of the Rose*, it was again on video, but this time in England. The setting of the film—although based in Italy—repeated many features I already knew from the castles and abbeys of Yorkshire. One need only think of Bolton Castle, Scarborough Castle, or Fountains Abbey. But also this time, it was the mystery of the rose and the *topos* of books that took primacy in the reading of the film.

The novel–film is entitled *The Name of the Rose*. Yet in the *Postscript* which Eco published in 1983, he remarks: "My novel had another, working, title, which was *The Abbey of the Crime*. I rejected it because it concentrates the reader's attention entirely on the mystery story and might wrongly lure and mislead purchasers looking for an action-packed yarn. My dream was to call the book *Adso of Melk*—a totally neutral title, because Adso, after all, was the narrating voice. But in my country, publishers dislike proper names, and even *Fermo and Lucia* [the first title of Manzoni's *I promessi sposi*] was, in its day, recycled in a different form. . . ."[4] Eco then goes on to give an account of why he decided to call his book *The Name of the Rose*:

> The idea of calling my book *The Name of the Rose* came to me virtually by chance, and I like to think because the rose is a

symbolic figure so rich in meanings that by now it hardly has any meaning left: Dante's mystic rose, and go lovely rose, the Wars of Roses, rose thou art sick, too many rings around Rosie, a rose by any other name, a rose is a rose is a rose is a rose, the Rosicrucians. The title rightly disoriented the reader, who was unable to choose just one interpretation; and even if he were to catch the possible nominalist readings of the concluding verse, he would come to them only at the end, having previously made God only knows what other choices. A title must muddle the reader's ideas, not regiment them. (*Postscript*, 3)

The Name of the Rose is a connundrum. One is lead to ask: What is the name of the rose? (as did my daughter after she saw the film in Britain). As Eco would himself admit, even his own account of all those roses does not close down the options. Indeed, Dante's Rose in the heart of the Empyrean of *Paradiso* correlates with the stained-glass rose windows of Gothic cathedrals, and Guillaume de Lorris/Jean de Meun have their Lover seek after the Rose (the object of love). The rose, understood according to Hugh of St. Victor's fourfold method of interpretation, which Dante himself reports in his letter to Can Grande della Scala, could be read literally (as a flower), allegorically (as the object of love), topologically or morally (if one seeks after one's love and one has faith, one will surely attain it), and anagogically (having faith in God can bring His free gift of Grace in return). But if one follows this line, how does one answer my daughter's question: What is the name of the rose? Could the rose be the flower which is absent from the unfortunate Abbey surrounded by snow (as well as sin, guilt, and despair)? Is the rose the unnamed peasant girl (added to the film for Hollywood effect) whom Adso has come to love? Is the rose the path that one must follow to lead one out of the sin, the guilt, and the despair of the Abbey beset by crime, an overzealous Inquisitor, and a corruption that is eating the insides out of the Abbey? Or is the rose the hope and the faith that William must have, and the love that will surely save the inhabitants of the Abbey (by lifting them up to the *civitas Dei*) or raze them (like the Abbey itself) to the ground? But this is only one set of codes, established by a certain theory of interpretation. What if one were to think of the rose as the mystery itself: the question that is posed, the answer that is never really given, the interpretation that has no univocal sense?

Or what if—as the *American Film* article suggests—the rose is a ruse? Substituting a "u" for the "o" in the Rose produces a "ruse." Throughout the novel–film, there is always something at the end of the tunnel, an end to the labyrinth, a way out of the maze, the Piranesi/Escher-like staircases that lead somewhere—just as Adso's ingenious Hansel and Gretel scheme in which he unravels his undercloth returns him (temporarily) to where he began? Or what if the rose is Brother William's answer to Adso's question concerning love? William says that his love is a love of Aristotle, Ovid, and Thomas Aquinas. Or what if, by contrast, it is his other answer: "How peaceful life would be without love; life without woman would be safe and tranquil; and how dull!" Could one say that the rose is the answer to the connundrum which Plato had posed in the *Symposium*? But then, as Brother William also says, "If I had all the answers, I'd be teaching theology in Paris." So once again to possess the rose would be to hold the position of central office theologian—and the rose window at Notre Dame Cathedral may as well be its symbolic expression. The point is that none of these roses is the very rose whose name one could surely possess. The rose is elusive and possibly even unnamable. Perhaps its place is in silence or in the Wittgensteinian fire.

One might say—according to the secular reading—that Adso threw his rose into the fire even though he saved her from the fire. Hence "fire" operates as a hinge term between roses and that which (when thrown into the fire) signifies a destruction of culture, an offence against humanity, namely the burning of books. It could even be hinted that the name of the rose is the very book which everyone has been fighting over—not the *Romance of the Rose*, but the "truth" of the rose, the rose that is the lost second book of Aristotle's *Poetics* (on the topic of "Comedy"). The book then is a kind of binary pair that matches the rose, that is kept hidden, that is fought over, that is killed for, that brings terror, destruction, and ultimate despair. Those who see it, die. Only Jorge de Burgos—the blind Borges figure (the Keeper of Special Books)—is able to protect the book from the investigative eye of both the Benedictine monks *and* the medieval private eye Brother William. And when William does see it, he reads, and he reads with a glove—so that he will not be poisoned by the device of reading (licking the thumb that turned the poisoned corner of the page). And when Jorge "sees" (does he see?) that William will not be poisoned, he begins to eat the pages (thereby, like the first and third deaths, killing himself—and resembling the "lover" in Greenaway's *The Cook, The Thief, his Wife, her Lover* who also dies eating books—revolutionary books). But Jorge's demise is only the fifth death. The other two—since there must be seven—are the two heretics burned outside the Abbey at the stake. And they were guilty of excessive Robin Hoodism: stealing from the Church to give to the poor. That they were willing to kill members of the Church to satisfy their end was where they went too far.

The burning of heretics and the burning of one's love, the historical fear of nazism, the rebirth of fascism, and the terror of some cultural revolution that incites the burning of books looms heavy over the human spirit. And Brother William's recogition of loss is devastating—the burning of the abbey tower is the destruction of the greatest collection of books known to the West at that time. To save only a few books is evidence of his profound despair. He may have solved the medieval riddle of the Sphinx: that the book in question was the second book of Aristotle's *Poetics*, the presumed lost book on Comedy, a book which only the monastic translators of Greek—*cognoscendi* of classical culture—could read. And in seeing it burn, he sees the very culture that he loves burn. For if, as he says, Aristotle is one of his loves, then this rose cast into the fire is the burning of his love. In a way, *The Name of the Rose* is a medieval version of the Bradbury–Truffaut *Fahrenheit 451*, in which books are burned in favor of the propaganda that Bernardo Gui the Inquisitor—if he had access to the same technology—would surely have employed. But we uncomfortably delight in Bernardo Gui's harsh end: impaled on spokes of a farming machine, a technological device to help free the peasants from the tedium of their toil. Four hundred fifty degrees fahrenheit is the temperature at which books would burn—the firemen come to burn all the books that they find—only people can save the books by memorizing them, by becoming the books themselves. Brother William does not become the books that he saves. The mystery of the rose is, among others, the unattainable library that vanishes before William's very eyes. The trial of faith is a trial by fire: but it is also a loss. According to the "trial by fire," if the accused does not die, then he/she is not guilty. According to this medieval catch-22, if the accused actually dies, then guilt can be presumed! The book—which is the answer to the murders—dies in its discovery. Hardly a laughing matter. A sorrowful end to the book of Aristotle that follows the one on tragedy. Where Dante was convinced that his poem—the *Commedia*—should be a Comedy because it ends well, Eco's rose (the Book on Comedy) brings despair and destruction. As Jorge de Burgos comments with wry cynicism: "the book will make it possible to laugh at everything." Like the Borges cartographer who discovers that a total map of the whole world will destroy all representation, Jorge de Burgos fears that laughter will eliminate all difference in the world. We shall not be granted such a luxury. If we could laugh at everything, we would be able to keep our distance, to take whatever happens with a grain of salt, in short to not worry about anything. So when Nietzsche says that philosophy ends in laughter, he implies as well that a herd morality could not live with comedy, and only the *Übermensch* could go beyond such a collective morality. This book of Aristotle's—which, it might have been surmised, could have been burned in the fire of the Library in Alexandria—is now definitively burned.

As William guessed, it was a book which kills and for which one kills. The Book of Revelation would hardly fit such a description—as William informs Adso early in the narrative. Even the book mentioned as "the masterpiece," the *Beatis of Lebena* by one Umberto of Bologna, would doubtless have been destroyed as well. Is Umberto Eco as author the name of the rose? In this fictional masterpiece, Eco himself is marked in the film. But even Hitchcock, when he made his cameo appearances in his own films, did not kill himself off in the course of the events. Fortunately, the other book—the one corresponding to the "palimpsest of Umberto Eco's *The Name of the Rose*"—is saved. If the book by Umberto of Bologna does not survive the fire, will it survive in another form? As Victor Hugo suggests in *Notre Dame de Paris*, "*ceci tuera cela*: this will kill that," the book will kill off the reading of stained glass windows, and perhaps the film will "kill off" (or perhaps just burn), or at least mark the end of, the book. For the book is a rose, a signifier whose traces weave throughout the film, inscribing itself not only as the irretrievable Holy Grail but also as the textuality of the book behind the film.

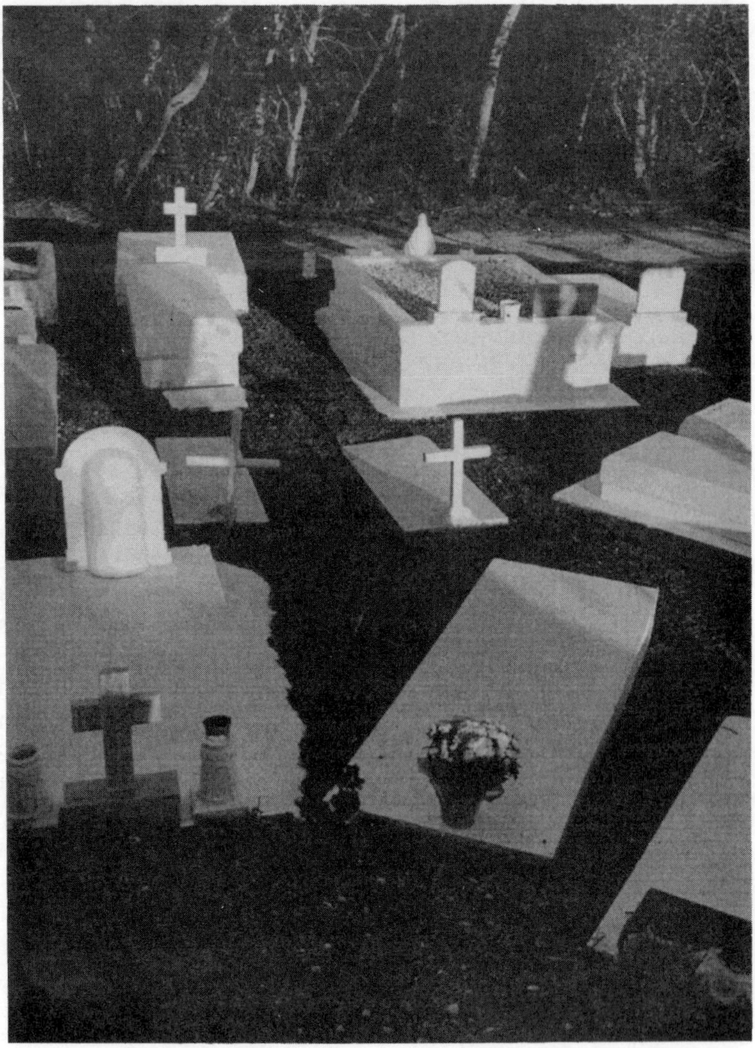

PART III
THE LIMITS OF SEMIOSIS

Chapter 10

PSYCHOANALYSIS AND THE IMAGINARY

Julia Kristeva

When speaking about the imaginary in psychoanalysis, I am committed to a discourse that I would like to be as close to the imagination as possible: a discourse I wish to address to your own imagination, to provoke images in you, and hence, the eventual acceptance of my conclusions—only beyond and because of your imaginary participation in my arguments.

This means that I will try to be as concrete as possible and tell you some stories that nourish analytic theory but which are kept from the public by the necessity of secrecy, as well as by the tough metalinguistic ambition of theoreticians.

The imaginary is generated by transference, by identification between patient and analyst (the strongest moment), just as it can be generated by identification between teacher and student, artist and muse, etc.

What happens in transference? I will refer only to one aspect of this huge problem, which will bring me to the imaginary: What is transference time? Three moments can be differentiated to it.

I. Transferences

1. What Is Transference Time?

a. One immediately thinks of the linear time of the patient's narrative—a time belonging to memory, which attempts to reconstruct the links, reestablish a continuity.

b. And then, and this is my second point, suspended time springs to mind, the zero time of silence—empty, blank from trauma or pleasure or dizziness. This break is beyond the line of discourse. Lacan was brave—or exhibitionistic—enough to claim the right to this dizziness, this idiocy of pleasure which marks the patient's discourse at the same time as the analyst's listening.

c. Finally, and necessarily, we come to the third point—the interpretation: to give a meaning to memory, but also to suspend of memory. To be within the line of discourse *and* in the blank of dizziness–pleasure, and then to come up again for an instant in an identity with a provisional meaning. This third interpretation time is a time belonging to resurrection.

There is a rejuvenation particular to transference and countertransference which sometimes takes place quite perceptibly within the patient. But first, a few words about the analyst: Through identification, we assume or assimilate the memory, as well as the pleasure–suspension of the patient's discourse: We assume the line and the pause. As a result, our temporality is multiplied, and we live several lives within our life. And yet the regenerative effect of transference seems to me to stem less from the plurality of time sequences than from what I have called suspension and resurrection: from pleasure beyond time and from the resurgence of a provisional meaning to that pleasure. When I speak of rejuvenation, you will no doubt think of that perpetually youthful look the analysts have, inhabited as they are by regression, adolescence, and even silliness—all, more or less, acted—which never fails to strike in a gathering of analysts once the theoretical super-ego has been torn away. This rejuvenescence, which I attribute to the various temporalities intersecting in the transferential dynamic, appears most clearly and quite logically in what I would call the explosive discourse: in the joke as quintessence of analytical speech, steeped in instinctual pleasure beyond time and "logical conclusion." Freud's own style evidently had this quality of explosiveness, of *Witz*. I simply wish to make clear which temporality it rests upon—a temporality which, while being a personal characteristic of the orator, is nevertheless intrinsic to the very logic of the cure.

2. *Other Signs of Other Times*

If one accepts this varied temporality of the transferential dynamic, one is led to ask the following question: Since speech, with its linguistic signs and their linking together, assures linear time and the memory in transference, then in what signs (other than silence) do the zero time of temporal suspension (the time of pleasure) and the resurrectional time of interpretation find their support?

Infra-linguistic signs occur to me at once, as they seem to me to mark this zero time of pleasure: modulation or vocal intensity, phonatory gesture, or facial expression. Particularly when dealing with sufferers of depression or melancholy, it is essential that each of these signs be considered and interpreted.

However, I would like to emphasize, above all, the appearance in certain cures of nonlinguistic signs (for example, images, photos, or paintings) which (as secret objects) aggressively reveal this zero time of pleasure, but keep it split apart from verbal expression. Discourse remains in the power of repression or splitting, and, if one limits oneself to verbal communication only, one risks keeping the cure within the domain of discourse and the superego, of that which cannot be analyzed. Taking into account these pictorial works, however, can bring the split pleasure—for it is more a question of "splitting" than of "repression"—onto the manifest scene of transference, thus altering the transference itself. For as long as the implicit or implied elements of the transference remain unnamed, there can be no analytical transference strictly speaking.

I have a patient who is a painter in his spare time, a draughtsman by profession, married, but with no sexual relationship, either marital or extramarital, masturbation being his only access to sexuality. He has a few intermittent somatic symptoms, like eczema and migraine. He came to me after his mother died, and for two years he left the deceased's apartment closed, without touching it, neither visiting it nor even thinking of selling it, despite his financial difficulties. Now, his discourse on the couch was voluble, even well-informed about psychoanalysis. He did all the talking, he knew everything, he didn't expect anything from me. Masturbatory speech of complete infantile power, without silence—and yet it was continuous silence, without emotion or affect, even when he was speaking about erotic or phobic dreams or memories. I soon had the feeling that the secret lay in the space of the mother, of course, but at the same time in this means of trans-linguistic expression his paintings represented, which he used to show to his mother while she was alive. (He'd never exhibited or sold them, he always gave them to his mother.) During the transference, and because I took on the place of the mother, the patient (Didier) expressed the desire to show me his works. I accepted, and several sessions took place in which Didier displayed his photos and paintings: lying on the couch he showed them to me, showed them to himself, explained them to me, explained them to himself. The pictures represented bodies cut up, arms and legs floating, collages made from posters of well-known actors and actresses within the painting, the posters themselves cut up and rearranged by the patient. He spoke to me of the shapes and of the technical aim of his pieces, about his aesthetic sources and his style. His discourse was always neutral, but this time the neutrality was in the content, since for once the tone of his voice grew lively, as did his gestures and the color of his skin. I had the feeling I was watching the transferential time of the autoerotic pleasure in the presence of the mother—a time beyond time, removed from speech—now flowing into the actual transference cure.

It was my task to give meaning to it. I constructed, in place of the aesthetic and formal disclosure of the patient, the fantasy that was missing in the speech, but which seemed to be present in the dizziness of the pictorial display and in the excited voice. I talked about his masturbatory pleasure, about the fear of seeing his own member cut off, about how this fear was counterbalanced by cutting to pieces the two parents—the "actors" of the posters. Contrary to the silent complicity of his voyeuristic mother, I introduced an interpretative discourse that was the discourse of perversion: I grafted it on a perverse fantasy absent from the operative speech of the patient.

"Result": the mother's apartment was opened and her heritage distributed. Didier found himself seduced ("amorously, not sexually, I don't dare" he said) by a young girl, an "almost teenager" from his office. His eczema was cured . . . by a trip to sunny Morocco.

To come back to the fantasy-craft I performed, and which many of our interpretations in the transference/countertransference perform: it is a resurrectional moment when pleasure and meaning are brought together for the analyst, and, consequently, for the patient.

I was in the deadened time of his memory, a time frozen in a linear discourse, void of affect and steeped in the super-ego. I plunged into the beyond-time of his pictorial pleasure—wordless, full of a violence of fecal matter, full of references to color, fragments he uses in his works, secret and aggressive, and of the cutting up of his own body as well as the maternal body—into a time inscribed in images, but not in speech. Affect had remained signifiable in images—in return, speech could not signify affect. Finally, the interpretive discourse I held was that of perversion, a discourse which created the link between language void of affect, and affect simply rendered in images.

I constructed fantasies: now instincts made image through speech. I did this by reconstructing a meaning to the formless and wordless images of Didier's works. Was the meaning I suggested also mine? Or was it his? Didier accepted it.

The transferential dynamic demands of the analyst are a veritable fantasy-construction: a passage through perversion to assure the flow between affect and language, sometimes passing through nonlinguistic signs. This dynamic of analytical perversion (a perversion since it is already named and analytical) is the outer side of the explosiveness, or *Witz*, shown to us by Freud. In other words, the *Witz* is the logical aspect, the a-perversion—the thematic appearance—of the transferential dynamic, as long as it is capable of crossing through the various temporalities I mentioned at the beginning. The moral is to let ourselves be puzzled, and to look for meaning where there is no more language. How? By trusting our perversion and by making it apparent in a discourse which reflects the secret side of our wit (witticism, being witty).

This is the imaginary aspect—necessary and unavoidable—of the analytic interpretation. There is, however, another countenance assumed by the imaginary in its role of guiding the rebirth of the subject during the analytic cure.

II. The Role of the Imaginary in the Acquisition and Utilization of Logical and Grammatical Norms

1. The Child with Unutterable Sense

Certain cases of slowness in language acquisition, or of difficulties in learning logical and grammatical categories, seem to have physiological causes, which are difficult to identify, and even more difficult to treat on a somatic level. However, in the radial structure of the brain, these lesions, if minor, do not hinder access to the symbolic, provided we allow the child a wide and intense use of the imaginary.

The term "symbolic" indicates the practice of discourse according to the logical and grammatical rules of interlocution. "Imaginary" refers to the representation of strategies of identification, introjection, and projection, which mobilize the image of the body, the ego, and the other, and which make use of primary processes (displacement and condensation).

The imaginary is, of course, dependent on the mirror stage. It constitutes the self-image of the subject in the process of formation, and, in order to do this, the imaginary mobilizes, through the play of the representations proposed to the child, the whole range of identifications: narcissistic identification accompanied by a hold over the maternal image or a reduplication of it; primary identification with the ideal benevolent father of the "personal prehistory" (Freud); secondary identification during the Oedipus complex and notably its variant, the hysterical identification with a phallic role, etc. (Subject to the fluctuating rules of assimilation and rejection, of condensation and displacement—a kaleidoscope of images of the ego—the subject of utterance comes into being.) This should not however allow us to forget that the imaginary extends its effects as far as the psychical representatives of the affects. We can hypothesize that this imaginary level of semiotic meaning, as opposed to linguistic signification, is closer to the instinctual drive representatives specific to the lower layers of the brain. The imaginary level could then serve as a relay between these layers and the cortex governing linguistic performance, thus constituting supplementary cerebral circuits in a position to remedy possible bio-physiological deficiencies. This is why, in a child who has no active use of symbolic communication—and in whom the exact passive comprehension retained is uncertain—the imaginary is a means of access, if not immediately to linguistic signification, then at least, and to start with, to the meaning of more archaic affective representations and to their dramaturgy, which continues to dwell in him, to torment him, or to afford him pleasure.

I am thus making a distinction between, on the one hand, the instinctual and affective meaning organized according to primary processes and indicated by sensory vectors often different from language (sound, melody, rhythm, color, odor, etc.), which I am calling semiotic, and, on the other hand, linguistic signification which finds realization in linguistic signs and their syntactic and logical organization, and which requires certain biological and psychical conditions in order to occur. The imaginary, as understood in imaginative or fictional works, stems from linguistic signification and cannot be dissociated from grammar and logic. However, this level is not specific to the imaginary strategy in curing children. On the contrary, looking beyond linguistic performance, the prerequisite psychical conditions are what interest me in the conception of the imaginary: conditions which do not seem to be innate in certain children, or which have been damaged during intra-uterine life or at birth, and which the therapist could attempt to bring into being precisely through the use of the imaginary.

I will go one step further. The difficulties to which I am referring, difficulties in gaining access to the symbolic, which mean that some children have no natural and spontaneous access to signification—although they still may have access to meaning—give rise to a depression which may be more or less recognized and more or less serious in these children. Now, where language is concerned, a depression is characterized by the denial of the symbolic. "Language doesn't count, your signification doesn't matter to me, I'm not one of you, I'm withdrawing, I'm not even fighting you like a child suffering from a character neurosis would; no, imprisoning you in my unutterable meaning is killing me." This is what the child with "linguistic problems," who is often not recognized as a depressed child, seems to be saying. Because he doesn't use the symbolic, the young "infans," who prolongs the period of babyhood well beyond the canonical age, buries himself in the crypt of his unsignified affects, exasperating those around him, exasperating himself, or taking pleasure in his hiding place, without however allowing the adult to recognize the secret signals of his infra-language of distress and regression. Neither autistic nor suffering from character neurosis, these children are more likely to give the impression of being seized by a phobic inhibition which hampers access to discourse. It appears as if language frightened them, whereas what frightens them is perhaps their depression at being unable to use it, at being incompetent in the world of other speakers, at being a "bad speaker." The task of the therapist is thus double: on the one hand, becoming an analyst in order to bring about the desire (and of course the desire to speak) which lies beyond the inhibition and depression; on the other hand, becoming a speech therapist in order to facilitate paths specific to the child in question (for whom he has understood that "universals" don't occur universally) and to help him acquire linguistic categories which will enable him to give symbolic realization to his being as a subject.

Precipitating cognitive requirements (in our terminology: symbolic requirements) onto such an economy is not only useless, it censors the situation in which this "infans," with meaning but without signification, finds himself, a situation where he has no alternative but to elaborate in the imaginary the semiotic conditions necessary for access to discourse.

After all, the economy of the imaginary brings the subject of utterance into existence, and so this economy of the imaginary is the psychical prerequisite for language acquisition.

I had been acquainted with Paul's neurological difficulties from the time of his birth, and at the age of three he was still unable to utter a single word, only some vocalic echolalia in which a few unidentifiable pseudo-consonants could just be discerned. He couldn't stand dialogue between his parents, and of course refused to accept the exchange of words between the therapist and his mother, these situations sending him into dramatic states of screaming, tears, and distress rather than rage. I was able to interpret these reactions as an oedipal refusal of the sexual relation between his parents, and, by extension, of any verbal exchange thought to be erotic between two adults from which Paul felt excluded. Not only did this interpretation have no effect on him, but very quickly seemed to me to be premature. I began to think that Paul was refusing a signifying chain he was incapable of managing, and the perception—or should I say the precocious consciousness?—of this incapacity was de-valorizing him, depressing him, inhibiting him through fear. I decided to communicate with him, but also with his mother, by using the means available to him: singing. The operas we improvised, which must have appeared ridiculous to any possible spectators, certainly carried the signification that I wanted or that we wanted to exchange, but they also carried the meaning of the representatives of affects and instincts coded in the melodies, rhythms, and accentuation which were more (if not exclusively) accessible to Paul, which were his element, more than the linguistic charm itself ("come and see" (do-re-mi); "how are you" (do-ti-la), etc.). Gradually, through this vocal game, which was actually multidimensional (semiotic and symbolic), the child overcame his inhibition, and started to vary his vocalizations more and more. At the same time, he began to listen to a large number of records, and to reproduce the melodies and gradually the words. I felt as though I was tuning a musical instrument, getting to know him, and making more and more unexpected and complex possibilities surge forth from his resonant body. Thus, through the opera, we developed the precise articulation of phonemes while singing, without there being any technical work on pronunciation strictly speaking, but rather by counting on the possibility of articulating and hearing oneself in the melody. Once sure of knowing how to pronounce while singing—therefore with the breath, the sphincters, his motor functions, his body—Paul agreed to use his phonemes, already established in the opera, in everyday speech, and this with a precision in his articulation that few children possess. The singer had become a speaker.

I shall not be talking to you about the actual analytical work we did, but I do insist upon the fact that it cannot be dissociated from the arrival of language which it favored.

Some problems arose during the following stages, which once again the imaginary enabled us to solve. One example among others: the distinction between first and second person personal pronouns, I/you, me/you. The confusion in this case revealed Paul's dependence in relation to his mother, and the participation of the young woman—who was thereby able to detach herself from her child, from a narcissistic prosthesis invested in the depression she had suffered due to her son's deficiencies—was the key to his cure. However, the crucial point of the distinction I/you was Paul's identification with Pinocchio (the character from the famous children's tale), particularly in the episode where the little boy saves his father Gepetto from the jaws of the whale Mostro. "Help, Pinocchio," begged the old man. "*I'm* coming, *Father* wait for *me*, don't be afraid, *I'm* with you," replied Paul.

This story allowed the child not only to dominate the voracious whale, but to cease to be the victim. Paul took his revenge on the father. He could now say "I," provided that he no longer felt threatened with engulfment or castration. The "you," that is, the sign by which Paul—the poor child, the victim—was designated, was another in this tale. This unfortunate soul, the dreaded other ("you"), which fused with the bad part of Paul himself, could now be somebody else and receive love; for in the tale it was Gepetto, the benevolent and gifted father, who was the victim. Through this displacement of the suffering over another onto a signifier ("Gepetto"), the other ("you") could be separated from the self ("I") and given a different name from oneself. At the same time, Paul took on the role of the hero, and only in this way was he able to refer to himself with an "I" rather than a "you" coming from his mother's lips. In addition, the "you" also had its place, which was no longer confused with the bad "I": it was the place of the other (Gepetto), not the other as impotent child, but with and through the acknowledged misfortunes associated with this victim position, the "you" indicated the role of a dignity certainly in danger but sovereign and kind ("you" was another hero, the other of the hero) with whom Pinocchio could converse as one equal to another, that is, as one different person to another.

I have given you here a few brief elements of my conversations with Paul, but a number of conclusions can be drawn from this information. Discourse is a complex psychical affair which cannot be reduced to the dimension of grammatical categories and their combination, a dimension which I have called symbolic. It also comprises the semiotic modality, which is extraneous to language, but in which the psychical representatives of the affects unfold, and with them, the dramaturgy of the desires, fears, and depressions which make sense to the child, but which do not manage to enter the coded signification of everyday language.

In order to hear this infra-linguistic semiotic sense, the analyst *cum* speech therapist needs to have an optimal maternal ear. I put my faith in Paul's mother, or rather she convinced me of the existence of meaning in her child because she said that she understood him, and she used to answer him without his having spoken to her. I adopted her way of listening and of deciphering this meaning. In this day and age, when science is able to make almost any woman a child-bearer, let us try to revalorize the maternal role, which manages to ensure a path towards signification for the child. This despite the fact that mothers often use the child as a narcissistic prosthesis, a counter-phobic object, or a provisional antidepressant. In generating the language known as maternal, the mother is often alone. She relies on therapist-teachers especially when neurological difficulties arise to complicate what is already a problematic passage from meaning to signification in all speaking beings. In the best of cases, the mother arrives with the meaning. It is up to us to find the signification. The therapist's role is more-than-maternal: through identification with the mother–child relation, we recognize and often anticipate the meaning of what is not said. However, through our ability to hear the logic of buried affects and blocked identifications, we allow suffering to come out of its tomb. Only in this way can the signifier we use—the signifier of everyday language—cease to be a devitalized envelope that the child cannot assimilate, and become invested with meaning for a subject whose second birth, after all, we have accompanied.

Rare are the mothers who manage single-handedly to give signification to the unutterable meaning of their handicapped children, because their own unutterable suffering, present or past, clings to it. When this naming occurs, we must seek the help of the third party which encouraged it (this could be ourselves, or the father, or some other person who led the mother herself to recognize, name, and lift her unspeakable depression) before supporting her child as he travels a similar path. For even if the essential causes of the depression in one (the child) are biological and in the other (the mother) psychical, the result, where language is concerned, is similar: we find the same inability to translate psychical representatives of the affects into verbal signs.

In reality, the imaginary plays the role of theatrical director of the psychical conditions which underlie grammatical categories. The imaginary prevents language, which is sometimes acquired through imitation or forced by parroting, to act as an artifice for the use of a false-self. Despite his backwardness, Paul never presented the symptoms of the "as if" personality, and all his performances—modest in the beginning, and "beneath his age"—were striking in their authenticity and in the child's ability to use them creatively.

2. Story: The Time of the Imaginary

The time of the imaginary is not that of speech. It is the time of the story, of "mythos" in the Aristotelian sense—the time where a conflict arises and is resolved into an outcome, that is to say, a way out, a path for the subject of speech to follow. It is a tortuous time, which encompasses the non-time of the unconscious, the tiresome repetition of the eternal recurrence, the sudden irruption of suffering, which can assume the face of anger, and lastly, the bright spell of comprehension, against which the earlier conflict can be seen differently from the way in which it appeared initially, in the confusion of the unutterable. The conflict now appears as a latent project, as an implicit advancement towards a goal. But in the internal labyrinth of this imaginary time, how many dark nights of expectation and exasperation! Until the time of speech (of the symbolic) arrives, the linear time of syntax (subject/predicate), where he who speaks positions himself, brings about [so as to advance] the representation of an act which is the act of judgment. However, since in hearing the utterance by the child of this luminous time of judgment, we are comforted, let us not forget—when it becomes blurred, when the child suddenly hides from us, once again, this syntactic signification of judgment we believed to be already established once and for all—let us not forget how to find once more the labyrinth of imaginary time. For, by marking time inside him once again, by implanting a new imaginary graft, the imaginary will be able to help us clear the logical impasse where the child has been blocked.

Paul used the tenses of verbs (present, past, and future) correctly in conjugations and grammatical exercises. But when he himself told a story, he always used the present, the adverb alone indicating that he actually saw himself in a before, a now, or an after. His personal expression of the verbal system had not yet assumed this distinction. "Before, I am a baby," he said; "now, I am grown up; afterwards, I am a rocket pilot." The categories of tense remained established in the abstract, for he could recite them in conjugations, but they didn't occur creatively in Paul's speech. It was with tales of metamorphosis that we were able to integrate the use of temporal shifters into Paul's discourse.

To take but one example, there was Sleeping Beauty. The princess was sixteen years of age when the Wicked Fairy put her to sleep; a hundred years went by; and she was awakened from her slumber by the love of the prince, to find herself at the same age, still with all the youthful freshness of her sixteen years, but not in the same era. This theme of resurrection, where a character finds herself unchanged but living and transposing her past across the caesura of sleep into a new context, unknown and surprising, enables us to measure the passing of time. The child identifies with the past childhood of Sleeping Beauty ("she was"); later, he identifies with the massive zero time of her sleep, which perhaps also represents the stagnation of the present moment where, in his difficulties, he is marking time, not understanding, "sleeping" ("she is sleeping"); finally, he identifies with the time of her revival, which amounts to a project, to a future life, a life which is however already realized ("she is coming back to life through love, she will live") without any threat of separation, but on the contrary with the reassurance of the future as reunion, as resurrection. Even more precisely, it seemed to me that it was the distinction the fairy tale makes between a present hiatus or a confusional present (sleep) and a present launching, act, and realization (waking up). The first receded into the past, the second opened the future life, the real trigger, positioning the past and the future, and allowed Paul to travel on the path of temporal categories.

You will notice that these stories, which structure the subject and thus create the conditions necessary for linguistic categories, are love stories. Let us consider this for a moment and remember it whenever a child—or somebody else—with unutterable meaning comes to see us. The imaginary here is the language of the love relation—solid and nevertheless distant—that the analyst establishes with his patient.

After having given you these imaginary examples and understanding the importance of love in enabling us to produce them, let me conclude with a more abstract statement.

III. "Beyond" Signification: Metaphysics and the Imaginary

To posit the existence of a primal object, and even of a Thing or of a pre-linguistic meaning anterior to signification, which is to be conveyed through transference into a new capability—isn't that a fantasy of a melancholic theoretician enamored of a lost paradise?

Certainly the primal object, the Thing-in-itself—the meaning always remaining to be conveyed beyond signification—this ultimate cause of conveyability, only exists for and through discourse and the already constituted subject. Because what is conveyed is already there, the conveyable can be imagined and posited as in excess and incommensurable. Positing the existence of that other language, and even of an other of language, indeed an outside-of-language, is not necessarily setting up a preserve for metaphysics or theology. The postulate corresponds to a psychical requirement that Western metaphysics and theory have had, perhaps, the good luck and audacity to represent. That psychical requirement is certainly not universal. Chinese civilization, for instance, is not a civilization of the conveyability of the Thing-in-itself, neither of the pre-language, it is rather one of sign repetition and variation, that is to say, of transcription.

The obsession with the primal object, the object to be conveyed, assumes a certain appropriateness (imperfect, to be sure) between the sign and the nonverbal experience of the referent (not the referent itself) in the interaction with the other. Through this, I am able to name truly. The Being that extends beyond me—including the being of affect—may decide that its expression is suitable or nearly suitable. The wager of conveyability is also a wager that the primal object can be mastered. It is an attempt to fight depression (due to an intrusive pre-object that I cannot give up) by means of a torrent of signs, which precisely aims at capturing the object of joy, fear, or pain. Metaphysics, and its obsession with conveyability, is a discourse of a pain that is stated and relieved on account of that very statement. It is possible to be unaware of, to deny, the primal Thing; it is possible to be unaware of pain, to the benefit of signs that are written out or playful, without innerness, and without truth. The advantage of those civilizations that operate on the basis of such a model is that they are able to mark the immersion of the subject within the cosmos, its mystical immanence with the world. But, as a Chinese friend recognized, such a culture is without means for facing the onset of pain. Is that lack an advantage or a weakness?

Westerners, on the contrary, are convinced they can convey the mother and the archaic in language—they believe in her, to be sure, but in order to convey her, that is, to betray her, transpose her, be free of her. Such melancholy persons triumph over the sadness at being separated from the loved object through an unbelievable effort to master signs in order to have them correspond to primal, unnameable, traumatic experiences.

Even more so, and finally, the belief in conveyability ("mother is nameable, God is nameable") leads to a strongly individualized discourse, avoiding stereotypes and clichés, as well as to the profusion of personal styles. But in that very practice we end up with the perfect betrayal of the unique Thing-in-itself (the *Res Divina*). Why is the nomination a betrayal? Because if all the fashions of naming it are allowable, the verbal reality, the Thing postulated in itself, becomes dissolved in the thousand and one ways of naming it. The posited conveyability ends up in a multiplicity of possible conveyances. The Western subject, as potential melancholy being, having become a relentless conveyer, ends up a confirmed gambler or potential atheist. The initial belief in conveyance becomes changed into a belief in stylistic performance for which the near side of the text, its other, primal as it might be, is less important than the success of the text itself.

Thus, if the belief in a pre-linguistic reality is metaphysical, it ends up with a profusion of the imaginary, of infinite possibilities to play.

Question: Does Western religion integrate this lucidity, is it a Divine comedy? Or is the imaginary lucidity alien to religion, its opposite, its enemy?

Allow me to leave you with this choice: How are we to answer those questions?

Chapter 11

APPROACHES TO SEMIOETHICS

John Llewelyn

> So that we are left wondering whence it came, from within or without; and when it is gone, we say, "It was here. Yet no; it was beyond." —Plotinus, *Enneads*, 5, 11, 8

I.

The now classical theory of systems of signs called semiotic, semiotics, or semiology includes: *pragmatics*, the theory of the relation between signs and their users; *semantics*, the theory of the relation between signs and their meaning or truth; and *syntactics*, the theory of the relation of one sign to another. This essay outlines how according to Levinas and Derrida classical semiotics and its signifier are traced by what I shall call *semioethics* and how the study of interpersonal movement and touch, that some of the contributors to the collection entitled *Approaches to Semiotics*[1] would call proxemics, calls for a proto-proxemics or a semioethics of what might be called "calling itself" or "calling as such," were it not that the "itself," the "as such," and the "as," as classically defined, are what semioethics disrupts. Approaching semioethics one encounters a difficulty concerning culture. This *approche* is at once a *rapprochement* and an *Auseinandersetzung* in which some of the strands of Derrida's and Levinas's ichnographies are brought together in a plait or *plethyn* or *tresse*. As with Derrida, one might well say that in the moment of moving together—and a moment is a movement—the strands also move apart.

II.

The word signifier is ambiguous. Sometimes it is used synonymously with "sign," sometimes for one aspect of a sign, for what is called the *signifiant* or the acoustic image in the semiotics of Saussure. In this second sense the signifier is contrasted with the concept, the signified, the *signifié*. But since it is natural to say that what a sign is used for on a particular occasion of its use is what is signified on that occasion, it is not unnatural to refer to the complex sign as a signifier. Saussure warns his reader of the risk of confusion when he makes it explicit that on his definition of the linguistic sign: "The linguistic sign unites not a thing and a name, but a concept and an acoustic image."[2] This is another way of saying that the subject matter of his *Course* is not acts of speech, *parole*, but *langue*, the system of signs to which recourse is made in performing acts of *parole*. This explains why he prefers not to call the sound-image a phoneme. To do so would imply that an act of speech is performed and that, as he puts it, the interior image is necessarily realized in discourse.

Saussure sometimes says that this interior image is material, but he asks his readers to take care not to be misled. The adjective "material" is employed only in contrast to the "generally more abstract" concept with which it is paired. This phrase implies that the so-called material is generally less abstract. But it is abstract. The sensory (sonal) image must be in principle applicable to more than one case of the concept with which it constitutes a sign.

Saussure observes further that although which signifier is associated with which signified is originally arbitrary, in the sign there is necessarily both a signifier and a signified. Derrida takes this to be the traditional understanding of the nature of the sign despite Saussure's arguments for replacing the substantivist *signum-signatum* account of signification given in Stoic semiotics for a diacritical account according to which signification is a function of the lateral interrelations among signifiers and the lateral interrelations among signifieds. Because of the traditional understanding, in Derrida's discussion of the theory of *Bedeutung* in the first of Husserl's *Logical Investigations*, he does not refer to this as a theory of signification. For "significant sign" is pleonastic whereas *bedeutsame Zeichen* is not, and to say that a sign has no signification is a contradiction in terms, whereas Husserl argues that some signs, indicative ones (*Anzeichen*), are without *Bedeutungen*.[3] Indicative signs belonging to a historical culture are necessary, Husserl maintains, only for communication (compare Saussure's acts of *parole*), but are in principle effaceable in his envisaged science of purely expressive meanings (compare Saussure's science of *langue*).

In a note in Levinas's *Otherwise than Being* there is a sentence that may be partially translated as follows:

> A word has a *"Meinung"* which is not simply a *visée*. M. Derrida has felicitously and boldly translated this word by *vouloir dire*, uniting in its reference to (the) *vouloir* (which every intention remains) and to the exteriority of language (*langue*), the allegedly interior aspect of meaning (*sens*). See Derrida, *La voix et le phénomène*.[4]

The phrase "exteriority of language" would present a difficulty if the exteriority intended were that of a factual historical language. Derrida's endeavor to avoid begging the question against Husserl in the manner just described would have been undermined immediately by his recourse to *"dire."* The saying must be the phenomenologically reduced expression which would allow phenomenological semiotics to be a phonemology and which we shall find Husserl distinguishing from the empirically audible speech of communication. The exteriority Levinas refers to must therefore be understood as the non-real (*irreal* but *reell*) exteriority of a systematic field of meanings relative to the *vouloir* of the subject intending meanings in that field. Only when understood in this way can saying be an exteriority within what Levinas refers to as the alleged interior aspect of meaning. This reference to the interior aspect of meaning is reminiscent again of a phrase we have encountered in Saussure. It confirms both that there is a basis for Derrida's assimilation of Saussure's project to Husserl's and the fidelity of the following description of a doctrine they share (and share with Hegel, but the present essay will no more than touch on the latter kinship in passing):

> When I speak, not only am I conscious of being present to what I think, but I am conscious also of keeping as close as possible to my thought, or to the "concept," a signifier that does not fall into the world, a signifier that I hear as soon as I emit it, that seems to depend upon my pure spontaneity, re-

quiring the use of no instrument, no accessory, no force taken from the world. Not only do the signifier and signified seem to unite, but also, in this confusion, the signifier seems to erase itself or to become transparent, in order to allow the concept to present itself as what it is, referring to nothing other than its presence. The exteriority of the signifier seems reduced.[5]

Here Levinas's reference to the exteriority of language is matched by Derrida's reference to the exteriority of the signifier. Both defend the claim of a certain noncontingent exteriority that is underprivileged if not outrightly denied in Husserl's theory of the signifier and at least threatened in Saussure's. A certain kind of exteriority, the kind of exteriority that Saussure disclaims for the signifier when he enters his caveat regarding his own talk of the signifier's materiality, and that Husserl disclaims when he explains why he says that the expression "expression" is a remarkable form. If by "expression" is meant the verbal sound (*Wortlaut*) or the sign understood as signifier, we must not forget that it owes its expressiveness to the fact that the meaning it expresses (the *Wortbedeutung*) is already an expression, an expression of a *Sinn*. Hence "one may *not* say that an expressing act *expresses* a doxic act, if by expressing act one understands, as we do here at every point, the act of meaning (*Bedeuten*) itself." The expressing act *is* the doxic act. "If, however, the phrase "expressing act" relates to the verbal sound, one could very well speak after the manner in question, but the sense (*Sinn*) would then be altered."[6] The ex- of expression (the *aus-* of *ausdrücken*), thus understood, grants the expressing that is the meaning an interiority safer from external intrusion than either Derrida or Levinas is ready to allow. According to Derrida, expression thus understood as an ideal interior act of meaning has a radical—and at the same time superficial—sense; so perhaps rhizomatic exteriority is necessarily, and not just contingently, inscribed into it, a necessary contingency and an exposure to risk. According to Levinas, expression is absolute exposure, not the safety of phenomenological interiority but the danger of an ethical outside.

This complaint about Husserl's and Saussure's failure to do justice to exteriority—and we shall see that Levinas presents this as a failure to do justice to judgement and ultimately to justice itself—is one with their reservations over the exaggerated voluntarism of

Husserl's phenomenology of the intentionality of meaning and sense. This brings us back to the footnote cited earlier from *Otherwise than Being or Beyond Essence* (footnote 4), but via the one that comes next:

> The Medieval term intentionality, taken up by Brentano and Husserl, does indeed have in scholasticism and in phenomenology a neutralized meaning with respect to the will (*volonté*). It is the teleological movement animating thematization that justifies the recourse, however neutralized it may be, to voluntaristic language. (*AE*, 47; *OB*, 189)

Not wishing for the reason given earlier to say *signification* where Husserl has *bedeuten*, Derrida can write: "Without forcing Husserl's intention we could perhaps define, if not translate, *bedeuten* by '*vouloir-dire*'" (*VP*. 18; *SP*. 18). But how in view of this does one explain why Levinas writes that Derrida proposes *vouloir dire* as a translation of *Meinung*? This question merits more detailed consideration than there is space for here. Although one could say simply that Levinas is mistaken on a matter of fact, something may be learned about what motivates Levinas's own doctrine of the signifier if it is asked whether someone who proposes "vouloir dire" as a translation or—and the distinction is not unimportant here—definition or analysis of Husserl's *bedeuten* could be expected to offer it as such for *Meinung* or *meinen* as well. That Levinas would give an affirmative answer to this question is suggested by what he writes in the essay "Language and Proximity" published eight years after the first edition of *Otherwise than Being or Beyond Essence* and four years after the second edition which retains the footnote we are trying to explain.

"Language" in the title of this essay translates "langage," not "langue." Whoever approaches Husserl's doctrine(s) of meaning quickly discovers that it overflows Saussure's definition of "langue" and requires account to be taken, if not necessarily of acts of *parole* as audible utterance, at least of the doxic acts of meaning mentioned above. Now in "Language and Proximity" the intentionality, hence voluntarism, of Husserl's interpretation of *bedeuten* is shown to be subject to the authority of his "principle of all principles" (*Ideen*, § 24). The authority vested in intuition by this principle is not the authority that psychologistic empiricism invests in sensory content. The authority of intuition is that of the hermeneutic *as*. It rests, in the words of Levinas's exegesis, on the fact that objects are meant and *understood as (entendus en tant que)*, thought *as (comme)* this or *as* that and *as* present, so that their presence is not their occupation of a field of consciousness which is passively struck by them.[7] To say that consciousness is consciousness of something is to say that something is not merely seen or sighted, not *visé*, as Levinas puts it in his puzzling note, but, as he puts it in "Language and Proximity," *prétendu*, where the *tendu* picks up the tension and tending of intentionality and where the *pré*, as well as echoing the anticipatory character of the protensionality that Husserl holds is associated with all presence, marks the apriority that is, citing Levinas again, "a *kerygma* which is neither a form of the imagination nor a form of perception," but "primary *Meinen* which proclaims meaning while sovereignly postponing it," *l'ajournant souverainement*—deferring it, one is tempted to say in deference to Derrida, except that *différance* is never sovereign. What is proclaimed is selfsameness which, prior to resemblance, maintains domination over the images and percepts one has of an individual thing, although they "promise always to be *other* and other."

This proclamation exceeding the given appearances is announced in the Saying—*Dire*, writes Levinas provocatively—that makes use of the systems of signs of the culturally and historically contingent languages whose real existence Husserl's phenomenological semiotics purports to reduce. Semiosis, signification as such, remains the unreduced formal structure without which there could be no appearing, no *phainesthai*, of the phenomenal as such. Within this structure *meinen* or *Meinung* is the movement through alterity toward the ideal *telos* of identity. Because without *Meinung* there can be no *bedeuten* or *Bedeutung*—since the former is the essence of the latter in the sense that it is constitutive of the being of every being that is meant—it is perhaps not surprising that Levinas should suppose that it is as a translation of *Meinung* that Derrida proposes *vouloir dire*. But more important for our purposes than this explanation is the vocabulary encountered in reaching it. Of especial significance are the capitalized Saying, or "To-say," and the italicized "*other*" just cited. Levinas will argue that this alterity admitted in Husserl's semiotics is going to have to be supplemented by an alterity in semioethics. This semioethical alterity will exceed that of the accounts Husserl and Heidegger give of *Seinsinn*, the meaning of being and the being of meaning. Levinas will also argue that there is more to be said about Saying than is said in connection with Husserl, though in very Heideggerian words, when he writes that "Conferring a meaning on being . . . is from the first a function of a Saying which, far from falsifying being, lets it shine in the truth." This non-dialectical superlation, production, or emphasis of "Saying" by Levinas is accompanied by his earlier mentioned emphasis of Husserl's word "expression."

III.

Levinas will emphasize another key word of which no mention has yet been made. The key words in our list so far have occurred in paragraphs stressing the projective aspect of signification, the reference ahead to a sameness in what is to come. Another key word is met in paragraphs of *Otherwise than Being* where what is stressed is reference to the past. These paragraphs include the one to which is appended the footnote that has been the point of departure of the present essay. In them the topic is the same as in the paragraphs of "Language and Proximity" at which we have been looking, but they give an extra turn to what is said in the latter about the relation between identifying expressions and culturally instituted signs. They turn one hundred and eighty degrees the orientation of the word on which what is said there pivots, the word *entendre*.

Levinas writes that, contrary to the view Husserl seems to have held in the first of the *Logical Investigations*, an identifying expression is not a sign of a *Sinn* but a predication in the etymological sense of *praedicatum*, from *praedicare*, to announce, publish, or proclaim, though predication does proclaim the identification of a this with a that or a this as that in the *praedictum*, the already said. "Identification is *understood* on the basis of a mysterious schematism, of the already said, an antecedent *doxa* which every relationship between the individual and the universal presupposes" (*AE*, 45; *OB*, 35). Here "is understood" translates "s'entend," which Levinas wants to be read also as "is heard." Identification is *ouï-dire*, hearsay, and *oui-dire*, yea-say, affirmation of a sedimented, understood, *sous-entendu déjà dit*, subscription to a historical linguistic culture. Someone's meaning to say ("*j'entends dire ceci ou cela*") is an obedience at the heart of wanting, *obéissance au sein du vouloir*, and so an obedience at the heart of *vouloir-dire*. This obedience, *obaudire*, is the listening and heeding to cultural norms assumed even where a norm is being challenged, judged, and disobeyed. However—and with this we arrive at his judgment of semiotics—Levinas proclaims that before this disobedience, and the obedience disobedience assumes, an older obedience is called for, namely an obedience to an in principle unrecollectable past that is older than any, in principle, recollectable protodoxic past of history and culture, an obedience, as Derrida and Kafka say, *before the law*. The *e-normity* of this obedience is more anarchic than the breaking of, or departure from, a law. For it is the breakup of legality *as such*, the departure from the *as such* of essence, the undermining of the hermeneutic *as*.

With the undermining of the *as* and the *as such* of essence, we would be undermining the making mine of *meinen*. As with Hegel, we might say, what we might call a *deinen* (a making thine) and a *dienen* (a serving) per-form the formality of Husserl's *Formal and Transcendental Logic*. This "for-the-other" before the "for-oneself" would ex-press, exteriorize, utter, force out of itself the expression of meaning as described in the *Logical Investigations* and *Ideas*, whether "meaning" here be translated by *Bedeutung*, *Meinung*, or *vouloir-dire*. Paradoxically, older than the most *proto protodoxa*, this pro-position of the "Sayer" before proposition of the "said" undermines the meanings of cultural semiosis by being, before and beyond being, its quasi-transcendental condition. That is to say, it makes possible the signification of the said by supplementing it with a *signifiance* of a semioethical Saying or To-say without-and-with which the signification of the hear-said and the semiotic identificatory *Dire* cannot be complete. That is to say, the semioethical Saying beyond being and the thinking and meaning of being is beyond the possible. It breaks up *pouvoir* and *vouloir*. It interrupts *Seinkönnen* and "I can." It prefaces, pre-faces, traces the bad infinite of "the other and other" (*autre*), the never fully fulfilled desiring to say (*vouloir dire*), with a To-say of Desire for the Other (*Autrui*) which is the Infinite of the Good.

IV.

For both Derrida and for Levinas, but not obviously following the same route, the tracing of the so-called signifier is its resensibilization, its re-exteriorization, the quasitranscendental reduction of Husserl's eidetic and transcendental reductions—a resensibilization, however, that is not only not opposed to, but is the condition of, the ideality of sense as meaning. Derrida's strategy is to work through Husserl's texts to bring out that—despite their expressed intention—they themselves are a living proof that the allegedly pure *eidos* of expressive meaning is exposed to the historicality and materiality of the signifier, though here historicality is not opposed to logic and materiality is not opposed to spirit, mind, or life. The intrication of an allegedly pure signified with a historically material signifier is necessary, as Saussure already shows, even if for him the materiality is that of a sound-image. Saussure's sound-image, less abstract than the concept but abstract all the same, is an essence, a universal. However, if, as Derrida argues, the "essence" of essence and universality is iteration, the apparently enclosed interiority of semantic possibility is exposed to the intrusion of eventuality in new contexts. Does not even the father of transcendental phenomenology, in declining to answer or even put the question "What is the essence of a sign?", betray his suspicion that there is no such essence, no such "thing" as a sign (*VP*, 26; *SP*, 25)? Is he not rather—as the midwife (*Hebamme, Sage-femme*) of the phenomenology of spirit—pursuing the teleological ideal where writing is subsumed within the temporality of the voice, yet, in passing and in parentheses (those very parentheses that are the metaphor of transcendental phenomenological reduction, the metaphor of the metaphor of empirical fact), concede the irreducibility of punctuation, shape, and other marks of spatiality when (s)he writes in the course of a commentary on Leibniz "(and hieroglyphics are used even where there is alphabetic writing, as in our signs for numbers, the planets, chemical elements, etc.)"?[8]

Purely expressive meaning according to Husserl is meaning from which allusion to the empirical and hence to indexical and otherwise indicative signification has been suppressed. Husserlian phenomenologically expressive meaning is suppressive meaning. Why does Derrida question this suppression? He notes that the author of the *Logical Investigations* and *Ideas* himself goes on to acknowledge in *The Crisis of European Sciences and Transcendental Phenomenology* that the experience of original evidence attains and sustains a tradition of objectivity only because, as we can put it, inquirers have obeyed the request the author of the *Phe-*

nomenology of Spirit makes to the defender of sensible certainty: "Write this down." The critical dilemma is that writing is a "salutary threat" (*VP*, 92; *SP*, 82); it is exposed to a "bad" infinity of readings in which the putative original evidence is missing, forgotten, or betrayed. Literary culture is both a rescue and a risk, a risk to transcendental phenomenology itself which, even when it becomes a phenomenology of culture, is, as Husserl sometimes admits,[9] a part of culture itself. Derrida's intervention in this dilemma traces something like writing, arche-writing, in the alleged pure transcendentally signified evidence. No signified can escape the eventuality of becoming in its turn a signifier. That is to say, his intervention reinstates sensibility, though in a way that no longer regards it as the simple opposite of intelligibility. For sensibility is now the essence of the intelligibility of signification. Signification can now be reinscribed in the discourse of meaning and sense with the recognition that sense as meaning is inseparable from sense as sensibility. This reinstatement of sensibility, however, is not a restatement of sensible certainty. Nor is it that for Levinas. But both he and Derrida take the beginning of the phenomenology of spirit as a challenge. They move away from sensible certainty in different ways from Hegel, different ways that are the same as each other insofar as they both insist on the irreducibility of the sensibility of the signifier.

Derrida saves the sensibility of the signifier by losing the simplicity of the opposition of its sensibility, e.g., audibility, and the meaning of the sense signified, that is to say, by losing the classical notion of the sign. The hierarchical notion of the sign as a signifier–signified dyad betrays itself as a theatrical, fictive effect of a hyletic flux, a serial (an)arche-trace which is archic in that, unlike a trace in the traditional sense, it is not derived from a primal presence, but is anarchic because what it gives primacy to is the secondary, the derivative. This trace or tracing is not a neutral synthesis of signifier and signified or of sensibility and intelligible sense. For the signified form, idea or *Sinn*, precisely because of its intelligibility, is itself indicative signifier, remarkable mark re-marked. Precisely because it is a meaning represented by the signifier it is itself representing signifier. It is itself not a self-identical self opposed to difference. For its self-sameness is, as Saussure says, its differing from other meanings that are likewise constituted by this and a multiplicity of other differences. An infinite nonterminating multiplicity which, as Levinas was seen to show, Husserl himself recognizes in fact; but only as fact, rather than *de jure*. Husserl does not quite come to recognize that, as Derrida shows, the *de facto* and *de jure*, history and logic, cannot be simply opposed once the expression of ideal meanings cannot be opposed to in principle unprincipled, infinitely indicative reference.

Nevertheless, Derrida's introduction of the pseudo-concept or conceit of arche-trace seems at first sight not to lead beyond a revision of our ideas of ideas, concepts, predicates, terms, and what is said through the syntactico-semantic system of signs of which Saussure's semiotics was to be the science. In giving the "materiality of the idea" and the spacing of marks their due it is most apparently and initially semantics and syntactics that are desystematized. On the other hand, the pragmatic aspect of semiotics is more obviously and initially affected when, in the semioethics of Levinas, the arche-trace saves sensibility by revealing it as that which makes sense rather than as that which is opposed to it. For the sensibility emphasized by him is not so much that of the lexical or graphic signifiers as that of the utterers of these. And what these Signifiers signify is not abstract noematic Objectives which get fulfilled by what Husserl and Merleau-Ponty describe metaphorically as the "flesh and bone" of *Gegenstände*. The Signifiers of the semiotics of Levinas are and stand for other Signifiers which are made of non-metaphorical flesh, bone, and vulnerably sensitive skin. His semiotics is a somatics, and a somatics less directly of the body of signs used, a semiosomatics, than of the human beings who use them. And that is why it is a semioethics. More exactly, if ethics is conceived on analogy with a systematic legal code, it is a proto-ethical semiotics which precedes and transcends the proto-doxa of Husserl's transcendental phenomenology and the sensible certainty that remains over from and is left behind by the phenomenology of spirit. For the essence or *Wesen* of this an-archic proto-ethics is a past and a passed or *Gewesen* that was never a present and cannot ever be "retained" as Husserlian proto-doxa are when they are re-presented in a livingly present act or passion of consciousness. Nor can it be *aufgehoben* in a dialectic of determinate negation which cancels and kills it only to transmit and transfigure it into a new phase in the life of consciousness. Somatico-semio-proto-ethics is prior to consciousness. The phenomenology of spirit, in which the voluntarism of German Idealism culminates, remains teleological. Even the Austrian phenomenology that succeeds it retains in its memory the Idea in a Kantian sense and bolsters its teleologism with the doctrine that all consciousness is an active intending of something and all expressive meaning a wanting-to-say.

Yet in the many pages Husserl writes about passive synthesis and sensory hyletic data, Levinas discovers pointers toward a phenomenology of sensibility that exceeds the epistemological and ontological polarities of certainty and uncertainty, subject and object, being and nothingness, passivity and activity, and exceeds phenomenology itself when it reaches a semiotics where meaning as erotic *conatus dicendi*, *désirer-dire*, finds itself harking back to a signifiance which is Desire to say and to answer for the other human being who addresses me, to stand and substitute for him or her with a patience whose passivity is greater than that of the passivity opposed to activity in the dynamics of the struggle for existence, the war of each against each, including the war of words. Before the war of words and the word of war, already before any initiation of hostilities and before any initiative at all, resounds the word of peace.

"Shalom," "Salaam," "Hullo," "Bonjour," or, at exits and entrances, "After you." This last expression expresses most simply what Levinas means when he says that I am always in a certain sense anachronistic. Not anachronistic in the sense that, for example, in the history of a given culture for a man to give way to a woman may be out of date. Indeed, the noncultural absolute anachronism that Levinas has in mind is such that it is always, figuratively, a woman who says "After you." The *signifiance* of this expression of patient deference is feminine. The mater-iality of maternity is bearing par excellence, the bearing of responsibility, antenatal sensibility, and suffering before nature, before *phusis*, and before being-in-the-world. We must forego an examination of this contentious issue here, referring the reader to the most immediately relevant texts,[10] and, because in commenting on the chance or mischance that *Sa* is an abbreviation for the *signifiant* etc., Derrida also illustrates the syntactics of the remarking and tracing of the signifier, to his reminder that:

> I have composed an entire book with *ça* (the sign of the Saussurian signifier, of Hegel's Absolute Knowing, in French *savoir*

absolu, of Freud's Id [the *Ça*], the feminine possessive). I did not, however, think of the s.a. of speech acts, nor of the problems (formalizable?) of their relation to the signifier, absolute knowing, the Unconscious or even to the feminine possessive.[11]

However conventional and convenient expressions of politeness may seem, perhaps they indexically signify an ex-position of oneself in which a dominant philosophy of one's self as dominant is exposed. This exposition is attempted by Levinas and Derrida, both of them departing from Heidegger's attempt, and each of them departing from the other. How they depart from and are traceable in each other is not at all easy to say, not easy, by his own admission, for Derrida himself.[12] He declares in an interview published in 1986 that he is ready to subscribe to everything Levinas says on the subject of alterity and the alterity of the subject. The only difference between them, he suspects, is one of "signature," for example the difference between Levinas's readiness to use the word "ethics" and his own unreadiness because of the charge the word carries from its philosophical past. Even this recourse to that word would worry him less so long as we articulate how that word is being, as Levinas would say, emphasized or pro-duced—where the word "production" is also being pro-duced.[13] Levinas remotivates philosophical paleonyms, for after all it is metaphysics that his "metaphysical ethics" would "produce"; but he is not averse to introducing into this allegedly Western lexicon biblical words associated with the East. Nor is he entirely averse to introducing neographisms like "illeity," from French *il* or Latin *ille*, and "trace," if the latter can be called a neographism in view of the fact that it has a remote ancestor in Greek. Derrida is more inclined to prompt philosophical paleonyms to betray the play of forces that produce their apparently oppositional pairings and to allude to that play whereby neographisms are introduced.

This word "play" may make us want to ask how Derrida can subscribe to what Levinas says about responsibility. Bearing in mind that primary signifiance in the semioethics of Levinas is self-substitutive responsibility for the other, we could begin answering this question by returning to the sentences cited from *Limited Inc*, after which Derrida goes on to refer to the limited responsibility alluded to in the acronym Sarl, standing for the limited liability company (*Société à responsibilité limitée*) incorporating John Searle,

John Austin, and, among others, himself. How can the semiotics of Derrida, we might ask, allow room for even limited responsibility, let alone the infinite responsibility of which Levinas speaks?

In a preliminary note in *Otherwise than Being or Beyond Essence* Levinas confesses that he was tempted to write the last word of that title with an "a." This spelling would have marked the etymological connection the suffix has with *antia* and *entia* from which abstract nouns of action are derived, and so with the mixed verbal substantivity of *Sein*, the German word for "being," which Levinas's "essence" is meant to translate. That suffix with an "a" is retained in the word "signifiance" that both he and Derrida use, thereby signifying their recognition of the difficulty of giving meaning to the words "beyond being." When used in the interview with the authoress of *Semiotike*, Julia Kristeva, entitled "Semiology and Grammatology" and included in *Positions*, the "ance" of "signifiance," as too of "mouvance," restance, *revenance, differance*, etc., indicates the supplementary plus or minus of impower brought to the power of the subject through the subjection of the subject's sign-giving to the expository explication of the text and the interminable extension of its tissue in the way the structural semiotics of Saussure is stretched when it is educated out of its "congenital expressivism" by Peirce's redefinition of a sign as that of which the interpretant becomes in turn a sign and so on *ad inifinitum* (*P*, 46; *P-trans*, 34).[14] Grammatology would be semiology minus expressology and phonology. It would not only disestablish the personal transcendental subject and the transcendental thing by transliterating them as effects of textual play, but would also transcribe the impersonality of *die Sprache spricht* into *die Urschrift schreibt*. This leaves us with an impersonality which might well seem, and has indeed seemed to some of Derrida's readers and non-readers, incompatible with personal responsibility.

This impersonality could seem to be incompatible, for example, with a person's *standing by* his or her word and with a *person's* standing by his or her own word, being *present* at it, as described by Levinas and in those parts of Plato's *Phaedrus* (276) to which both he and Derrida so frequently refer. For Levinas, *signifiance* is primarily a sign of the Other assigning to me the responsibility for what I say. This sounds like a personalism, indeed a Personalism of the highest majuscule degree. Although I am less of—and more than—an "I" (such as is posited in transcendental egology), I am accused as a "me" (made by the Other's call to stand out in relief, unrelievably, beyond possibility of being *aufgehoben*, beyond possibility of being, *seinkönnen*, beyond being, beyond possibility, and without anything to identify me) to say who or what I am, other than my saying without wanting to say, the *dire* without *vouloir-dire*. I am accused not exactly as an accusative *case* but as a unique elected singular *one* that cannot be confused with the impersonal one of *das Man* and with another person who, by the laws of traditional and dialectical logic, could substitute for me. Although in semioethical signification I cannot not substitute for the other, no other can substitute for me. Here my singularity is not that of a subject persisting in its will to have its say, but of a self subjected to a categorical imperative that categorizes me in the quasi-legal sense of the Greek word, selecting and summoning me above all to go to the assistance of the other in whose place in the sun I find myself and who has always already called for my help. Me above all. And below all, because the other is the Other in the majesty Descartes attributes to the Infinite—though (it must be added at once) this majesty is attributed by Levinas to the Other's being the hungry stranger, the orphan, and the widow. The service to which I am called is not slavery, for the asystemic semioethical "relation" before the systemic relations of structural semiotics and the asymmetrical "communication" before the symmetrical intercommunication (*Mitteilung*), which Husserl would exclude from phenomenological expression is not a being-with, not a *Mitsein* or communication between powers. *Ipse* rather than *idem*—no longer am I the single-minded ego anxious to mark its property by leaving its scent on the gateposts of its world. I am both host and hostage, ex-tradited to the other by a trad-ition that is betrayed by the tradition of culture—betrayed in the sense of represented, not only betrayed in the sense of misrepresented, if cultural gifts are no less *donanda* than bread. I am in exile in my own home, hospitable to the point at which possessions make sense only in being given gratuitously to the ungrateful, outside the economy of recompense by thanks, as the gift of bread from my mouth, on the point of becoming part of myself, I am the sign of my self and my word already having been given. The *Sinngebung* of semantic signification, a signifier standing for a signified, is given its sense by the senselessness inspired by love, the madness of the fourth kind distinguished in the *Phaedrus* which expresses itself as the *signifiance* of a human Signifier standing for the other human being, both of them both transcendent of being and possessed of the flesh and the bone without which no one can labor or have hands (with which) to give.

However, is not this humanism of the other human being phonological? So when the Signifier Emmanuel Levinas signifies to the Other, Jacques Derrida, *Me voici, Hineni*, "Here, hear, see, send me," will Derrida not have reason to suppose, as he says of Husserl and Hegel and Saussure in the words of *Positions* reproduced above, that the Signifier supposes himself to be hearing the signifier as soon as it is pronounced? Not if we hear and understand *obaudire* as an obedience prior to hearing and to the doxic obedience Levinas, following Husserl and Hegel, ascribes to the understanding of intentional meaning, *meinen* or *vouloir-dire*. Not if, in the words of *Otherwise than Being or Beyond Essence*, "Obedience precedes any hearing of the command" (*AE*, 189; *OB*, 148). Not if we can accept "the possibility of finding, anachronously, the order in the obedience itself, and of receiving the order out of oneself. . . ." Not if the semioethical is prior to the semio*tic*. So, appearances notwithstanding, this is no return to a phenomenology of self-consciousness or of speech and phenomenon, for "the appeal is understood in the response" (*AE*, 190; *OB*, 149) and the response is not vocal words. However, going to the other in Kant's universalistic ethics of free will is called autonomy or non-pathological, practical love, and Levinas's pre-principial semioethics of singular signification prior to the freedom of will is called hetero-affection, sensibility, susceptibility, responsibility, or being called.

But is proto-semiotic heterography of the Derridian trace prior to the trace of Levinasian semioethics? Or does the latter come first? We have already cited a remark of Derrida's about Levinas which suggests that these questions are mal-posed. The notion of a pre- or proto-ethical semioethics of being called, of *Geheiss* before *Meinung* and *vouloir-dire*, is a topic in Derrida's writings at least from the late 1970s. In the late 1960s, he has already written of his concept of trace and with reference to "The Trace of the Other" of 1963: "I relate the concept of *trace* to what is at the center of the latest work of Emmanuel Levinas and his critique of ontology: relationship to illeity as to the alterity of a past that never was and can never be lived in the originary or modified form of presence" (*G*, 102–103; *OG*, 70). But how does Derrida relate his concept of trace to relationship, to alterity? This is a question we can here do little more than pose, telegraphing merely in the directions from which one might gather a response.

Levinas's arche-trace looks or sounds less like arche-writing than like arche-speech, the "vocative absolute" that the Derridian arche-trace suspends (*G*, 164; *OG*, 112). For Levinas the arche-trace is that which supplements with obliqueness the directness of the face-to-face with *Autrui*. Derrida's topic is less often *Autrui*, the other human being, than alterity in general, *l'autre*. Of course, like Levinas and many other readers of Husserl, he is provoked by what is said in the fifth meditation of the *Cartesian Meditations* about the other human being. But what Derrida is provoked to write about can be said without the need Levinas stresses to get further than thinking of the other human being as another *ego*. Thus the approach to the trace made in *Speech and Phenomena* hinges on the manner in which the subject's self-affection demands a predicative or pre-predicative alterity with respect to itself. The ideality of the living self-presence that is demanded by Husserl's account of expressive meaning is found to demand the possibility of the subject's morality. The appearance to me of ideality, the infinite possibility of repetition, demands my finitude, the possibility of my disappearance. In Levinas's response to Husserl's Fifth Meditation, priority is given to the death of the other. For Levinas the primary relation is for-the-Other, *pour Autrui*. Derrida, moving to the *Cartesian Meditations* in order to treat questions about the alleged independence of expressive meaning from indicative signification put in Husserl's *Logical Investigations* and his *Ideas*, is understandably preoccupied with the more general question of something standing for something else, *für etwas*. So expressive meaning is shown to be dictated by indicative signification when it is shown that if "I am alive" is written down, its expressive meaning implies the fact of my being dead; it is not dependent on my being alive for its meaningfulness. That is to say, and Derrida says it, the written *I* is anonymous, even when endorsed by the signature I append to my will. For my signature too is something of which, of necessity, I can be dispossessed; it is liable to become a common noun or name, as Derrida demonstrates in *Signéponge* and elsewhere. And when I am dispossessed of my life, the signatory of the death certificate is not I. This seems a long way still from the uniqueness of the *me* accused by and elected to responsibility for the Other and expressed to him when I say "Here I am" or perhaps already in saying only "I" or "me" or "only me." Yet Derrida claims to be interested in a certain uniqueness. He writes: "To think the unique *within* the system, to inscribe it there, such is the gesture of arche-writing: arche-violence, the loss of the proper, of absolute proximity . . ." (*G*, 164; *OG*, 112). How is this uniqueness related to the illeity to which Derrida relates the concept of trace? We begin to answer this question when we begin to understand that the Derridian trace and Levinasian illeity are both ways by which something like the primacy of singularity (defeated by mediating universality in Hegel's treatment of sensible certainty) may be rediscovered *within* the system of semiotics: Hegel's, Husserl's, or Saussure's; and they both attempt this by exposing a paradoxical unprincipial principle of uncertainty which allows or conditions non-causally and non-logically the metaphysical oppositions of sensibility and intelligibility, passivity and activity, particularity and universality, rendering these oppositions undecidable except as surfacial effects.

V.

Alongside or, rather, in chiasmus with Levinas's statement in *Otherwise than Being or Beyond Essence* that "Yes" is the first word of "spirit" that makes "negativity," "consciousness," and all the other words possible (*AE*, 156; *OB*, 121–2), can be put the reference in Derrida's essay "*Nombre de oui*"[15] to a Yes before the Yes one opposes to No, a first Yes, a tremendous unheard Yes, a *oui inouï*, by which this second Yes is pre-echoed, foreshadowed, ghostridden, ghostwritten.[16] In several other fairly recent publications, for example, his dis-phenomenology and dis-ontology of spirit, *Of Spirit*, Derrida reworks Heidegger's reflections on the promissory affirmation (*Zusage*) that, like an excluded middle of responsibility, *Ent-scheidung* before *Entscheidung*, calls into question the primacy of the question, the question to which the answer is either a Yes or a No. There is no decision without dis-scission, the undecidability of the incalculable risk which proliferates in the moment—and the moment is always already past—that my response to the face of the first other implicates an unforeseen unnamed third for whom nevertheless I am called to respond. This perhaps is how the third person pro-nominality of illeity figures on the scene as non-seen, non-figure, non-face, not even archi-face, if it is prefigured by the arche-back of God whose face, according to Exodus 33:23, Moses will never see.

Derrida's first published book, the *Introduction to Husserl's The Origin of Geometry*, because it is concerned with Husserl, is inevitably concerned with responsibility, as is another book on Husserl written earlier, but published only in 1990.[17] The last words of this book (which, incidentally, contains a note referring to and not subscribing to something Levinas writes in his book on Husserl) report the conversation Husserl had with his sister during his last illness when he said "I did not know it was so hard to die.... [A]t the very moment when I feel totally penetrated by the feeling of responsibility for a task ... I have to interrupt that task and leave it unfinished. At the very moment when I reach the end and everything for me is finished, I know I have to take everything up again from the beginning" (*PG*, 283).

Emmanuel Levinas and Jacques Derrida are among the writers who take everything up again from the beginning (or still earlier) on Edmund Husserl's behalf. Both of them readers of Franz Rosenzweig's *The Star of Redemption*, they both refer back to a passage in that book which suggests that maybe the first semioethical word, the foreword, is the one that usually comes at the end: "Amen." Perhaps it can be said of "Amen" rather than of "to be" that it "is the first or the last word to withstand the deconstruction of a language of words" (*VP*, 83; *SP*, 74). This would not mean that it would succeed in withstanding deconstruction, at least if success is opposed to failure. The last word is only the latest, always too late and too early. Even "deconstruction" is exposed to the trace of penultimacy, antepenultimacy, and so on. And so is "trace." The pseudonyms for the shaking of foundations themselves shiver and shake. Where the identity of "trace" is sealed in promissory marks, what is to prevent Derridian trace, as we have been calling it, finding affiliated to itself the trace of Levinas, not being and being it in a non-Parmenidean way, the way Levinas tells us the father and son are related (*TI*, 255–56; *TI-trans.*, 278–79)? What is to prevent these traces from getting grafted onto Rosenzweig?

"Amen," Rosenzweig suggests, is the silent accompaniment to every word in a proposition, a "sic"—or, Derrida might suggest, a "sec," a proxy secretarial signature *p.p.*, primary process in a non-psychoanalytic sense or in the sense of a new psychoanalysis, the analysis of *psychisme* as conscience before consciousness, super-superego—like the process of initializing the disk of a computer before it will process words. Ad- or pre-pending a sign of affirmation to Frege's sign of assertion, witnessing thereby with a *firma* to a truth older than the truth of propositional representation and even older than the truth of a-lethic presencing, the four-letter foreword "Amen" may be what makes the judgment of cultures possible. There is a twofold difficulty with the statement to this effect that Levinas makes in an essay in which he reverses the priority of meaning over signification claimed by Husserl, the priority with which our own essay began. Levinas's statement appears to imply the possibility of a context-free universalism, that cultures can be judged from a neutral point of view (independent of cultures), and that all cultures are not equivalent, but require that they be judged. This sounds like ethnocentrism. The context-free universalism to which it appeals seems to be an outdated ideal of Platonism that is difficult to sustain even in its updated Husserlian version, as has been shown by, among others, Derrida and Levinas himself.

The dedication of *Otherwise than Being or Beyond Essence* is more than enough to show that Levinas is no less aware than others of the violence of ideological colonization conducted in the name of emancipation and supraculturally objective truth backed up perhaps by a conviction that one has heard that truth pronounced over the telephone by God.[18] How can this awareness be reconciled with his assertion that whereas the perceived and scientific world do not permit us to rejoin the norms of the absolute, "the norms of morality are not embarked in history and culture? They are not even islands that emerge from it—for they make all, even cultural, signification possible, and allow Cultures to be judged" (*CPP*, 101–102)?

Can Levinas be meaning moral principles when he refers here to "the" norms of "ethics"? And can he be denying that the norms of morality depend for their content on culture? If he is denying this, he is exposing himself to the objections of modern cultural historians and ethnologists. If he replies that he means moral principles of a purely contentless kind like the Kantian moral law, he is exposing himself not only to the objection that such a principle is useless because vacuous—an objection that he could meet by saying, like Kant could, that it gets its content from the maxims to which it applies—he is exposing himself also to the objection that this very principle of universalizability is a product of the discredited universalism of Plato, a Western ideal, even if, through its being assumed and applied to the abstract idea of the human being as such, it prescribes respect for personality in whatever historical and ethnic context it manifests itself.

Levinas does not want to be committed to morality founded upon universalistic Kantism or Platonism, but he does see himself to be rejoining Platonism in a way different from the way of Kant and Husserl. When he writes that the norms of morality are not "embarked in" history and culture he means that they are not founded in meaning either as what one wants to have said, the *dit* of a *vouloir-dire*, or as doxic or non-doxic intending, *Meinung*. Before culture, before purporting to say, before the expounding of opinion, before meaning intentions, even before the alleged immediacy of pointing that Hegel and Wittgenstein and Levinas question, is the signifying of myself for the other in the immediacy of the separation in proximity of the dyadic face to face: the *vis-à-vis* before *avis* and *visée*. Not, however, before *visitation*: a strange visitation, because the face-to-face is endorsed by the illeity of the trace of absence in the eminence of the ab-solute, separated past before culture (*EDE*, 199, 202; *CPP*, 104, 106).

Before culture, but before in a new way. For the priority of saying over the said is a priority that is "in" that which is posterior to it, "in" in a new way. The very historiality of history, the very acculturation of culture, its *Bildung*, even the nativity and nature of a nation is alter-nation. Culture is anarchy. As is so-called human nature. Levinas is no personalist if personalism presumes personal identity which allows alteration only as change. The ego maintaining itself ec-statically, ahead-of-itself up to its death, has its monadic existence expanded by human and other beings it is *with*. But the oneness—and, Levinas would say, wonderfulness—of the self is the uniqueness of my election to responsibility for the other who calls me in the voice of absolute conscience absolved from absolute knowing, heard in me yet as though coming from without, from above, and from a never present past. Not expansion, but unevadable invasion of the identical ego, turning it inside out into a self that is not a self-possessed psyche, but the psychism of owing my self to the other, heteropossession, psychosis.

If the dyadic face-to-face, which is the society of the self, is what makes multiple society possible, then the latter and the cultural and historical meanings that go with it and which Husserl treats in the fifth Cartesian meditation and in the *Crisis*, are never out of crisis, ever under de-cisive judgement, *Ur-teil*, as is the judge himself. Thanks to semioethical signifying, the vanishing trace (the always passed) of the nonappearing face that the mask of the *persona* betrays—and, Levinas would add, thanks to God, provided "God" is not heard as a theological or ontological name, but as the infinite illeity that is perhaps said by the word God "pronounced without 'divinity' being said" (*AE*, 206; *OB*, 162),[19] without uniqueness being sacrificed in gaining universality and justice as it is sacrificed in gaining universality and justice by what Hegel calls "the divine nature of language"—there can be criticism and judgment of history understood as the narratable deposit of events. Such a judgment of culture and civilizations can be understood as the systematic semiotic structures of institutions, as criticisms of those Values and Worldviews so dear to the Neo-Kantian philosophy (of which Heidegger's fundamental ontology was meant to be a criticism). For such criticism to be possible for philosophy, Levinas is saying, philosophy must somehow be beyond being, *epekeina tes ousias*. If this is so, and if philosophy is itself within history and culture, then although history and culture are self-contained like the chapters of a book, they also face out from themselves as when in a book's preface the author addresses the reader. There is an oscillation between dis-sedimentation and its interruption, between said and saying or unsaying; a chiasmus of *Einbildung* and *Abbildung*, forming and deforming, imaginative construction and deconstruction, at the difficult, hard place or non-place under the skin of *to on* where *to agathon* is neither idea nor value, not even the value of universality or respect for persons as such. Permitting real newness and creation, not just a make-believe and makeshift novelty such as is produced when, to use Levinas's and Blanchot's metaphor of the "there is" (*il y a*), furniture is shifted from place to place, Levinas's return to Platonism "in a new way" is not vacuously formal. For it is not formal. It is performative, and de-formative of Platonic Forms. Without a basis in universal reason, Levinas's Neo-Neoplatonism of newness and creation by the Good is an ultimately baseless and, by the norms of formal and dialectical logic, incoherent, unfundamental deontology of the uniquely signifying signature retracing the trace (*ichnos*) of the Plotinian One, as the trace that is said to be the form of the formless in the *Enneads* is retraced by the anarche-writing of Derrida (*Enneads*, 5, 5, 5; 6, 7, 33).[20]

To the extent that we *do* judge and criticize history and culture, a favorable judgement upon philosophy itself would not be amiss if Levinas's philosophy of "facism" can show, albeit not without enigma, that this practice escapes vicious circularity thanks to the re-facing of signification. By testifying to what is admittedly a certain pre-predicative madness and incoherence, philosophy would be demonstrating that my judgment of cultures or culture as such is not without coherence, provided I acknowledge that it is me above all who calls to be judged—and is responsible for the judgments made by others!

It remains to ask ourselves whether we *should* judge and criticize history and cultures, for instance, our own or the Cultures of Fascism, which Levinas no doubt had indelibly in mind when (in the French text of "*Signification et sens*") he spells the word with a capital "C." And how should we justly judge this "should" unless semiotics is, to speak the language of Husserl and Hegel, animated or inspirited, *beseelt* or *begeistert*, haunted, as Derrida and Levinas enigmatically indicate, by the semioethical afterword Amen? As has already been said, Amen is also a foreword, in particular here a foreword to a response to the question this essay has hardly more than posed, the question that returns to the Yes opposed to No but without being able to silence the other Yes or the Yes of the Other. Is the trace of the signifier as pursued in the writings of Derrida complemented by, that is, does it just let there be space (*chora*?) for the trace of the Signifier as pursued in the writings of Levinas, or does either or each supplement, that is, call for the other?

Chapter 12

STUMPING THE SUN: TOWARD A POST-METAPHORICS

Michael Naas

Signs are not proof, since anyone can produce false or ambiguous signs. Hence one falls back, paradoxically, on the omnipotence of language: since nothing assures language, I will regard it as the sole and final assurance: *I shall no longer believe in interpretation*. I shall receive every word from my other as a sign of truth; and when I speak, I shall not doubt that he, too, receives what I say as the truth. Whence the importance of *declarations*; I want to keep wresting from the other the formula of his feeling, and I keep telling him, on my side, that I love him: nothing is left to suggestion, to divination: for a thing to be known, it must be spoken; but also, once it is spoken, even very provisionally, it is true.
—Roland Barthes, *A Lover's Discourse*[1]

I. Instead of Nature

In Book II of the *Physics*, Aristotle helps illustrate the position of those who "hold that the nature and substantive existence of natural products resides in their material" with the example of Antiphon, who

> took as an indication [σημεῖον] of this that if a man buried a bedstead [κλίνην] and the sap in it took force and threw out a shoot it would be tree and not bedstead that came up ... and this is why they say that the natural factor in a bedstead is not its shape but the wood—to wit, because wood and not bedstead would come up if it germinated. (193a, 193b)[2]

Antiphon's logic seems quite sound, even natural—indeed what could be more natural than a tree sprouting from the earth to illustrate what nature really is? But curiously, it is not a simple, naturally sprouting tree that provides Antiphon with this "indication [σημεῖον]" of nature, but a work of culture, of artifice, which, *by being stripped* of its accidental properties, reveals the natural substance residing beneath or within it.

Yet even if the bedstead comes first in the order of demonstration, it would seem that the demonstration still indicates that the tree is ontologically prior to the bedstead, that through demonstration and indication one can gain access to what is beyond or before demonstration or indication, the silence of the sprouting tree that precedes all artifice and language. Stripped bare of all artifice, able to strip itself of all that is not proper to it, would not indication, in the end, still indicate or demonstrate what is truly natural within or before it? In other words, might not a certain indication, like a certain bedstead, be able to overcome itself as indication in order to reveal the prelinguistic substance at the root of it?

Such questions suggest not that Antiphon's demonstration or indication is unsound or unnatural but that the nature of indication is complicitous with the indication of nature. In other words, the question of nature and artifice is inseparable from the question of the sign. For what if the sign of Antiphon, or even of Aristotle, were itself structured like a bedstead, with a husk of artificial language concealing a sap of natural meaning that would *in fact* never see the light of day but would always *in principle* be there before and without it? What if the very indication of what is natural versus artificial already itself reproduced or doubled the opposition that it was supposed to indicate?

From these questions comes the *inclination* to ask about the bedstead and the sign *together*, to take Antiphon's example at face value and to read on it and not yet behind it all the differences between nature and culture, inside and outside, essential and accidental, that seem to structure both its content and its form—as well as the difference between content and form. And one way to follow such an inclination would be to turn things around, or upside down, by means of an hypothesis:

For what if a bedstead *were* to spring out of the earth when planted, what if not only more bedsteads, but an entire bed, indeed an entire bedroom, an entire home, an entire cosmos, grew out of it? What if the most natural thing in the world were a bedstead? And what if this bedstead grew to the point of detaching itself from the earth, from itself, in order to become a sort of signpost that would always suggest, or point back to, yet another bedstead detaching itself from itself, always another instead of itself, in the stead of a unique nature that it would always figure but to which it could never refer? What if Antiphon's distinction between nature and artifice, material and form, was itself the result of a bedstead that will have already been buried, and from the beginning, providing not the prelinguistic force or sap of a natural language but the very possibility of a stead of nature, of a bed in the stead of a tree trunk, a signifier in the stead of a signified, a name in the stead of an identity, a scar in the stead of flesh, a narrative in the stead of a home, a metaphor in the stead of a definition? Would we rest more comfortably, would we rest assured, knowing that language does not grow on trees but is from the beginning crafted and polished, cut with an ax, turned with an augur, spun round a bedstead that is always being uprooted, that can be a sure sign only insofar as it is instead of itself?

In what follows, I will try to show that the bedstead is the *focus* of the sign, the axis of its revolutions, the stump at the center of the sun that makes for the seasons, for the seasoning of wood, humans, and stories. The bedstead itself, the crafted stump itself, such is, such must be, the focus of a paper on the relationship between signifier and signified, the husk of meaning and its kernel, a paper on the possibility of a return to an already constituted identity or to a natural language that would precede all cultural institutions.

Planted in the ground to mark the difference between the horizontal and the vertical, the present and the past, such a bedstead can be dated, I will argue, indeed must be dated, and located, indeed must be located, though it itself accounts for all dates and locations. Armed with the best tools of the archeological dig, I will try to locate it on the island of Ithaca in the Mediterranean, some three thousand years ago. Unless, of course, everything the reputedly blind poet says is there to stump us—a narrative to be plunged into our eye at the moment when we see too well that of which he speaks.

The aim of this paper, then, is to give a certain figuration of *seasoning* through a rereading of certain signs, sure signs of the seasons, signs anchored in the ground, like a tree trunk, but already crafted, like a bedstead, their legibility assured by their unfathomable truth: sure signs that can be disrupted or uprooted only by the seasoning that they will have assured; sure signs that uproot themselves from the very beginning, already at their root; sure signs that revolve not around the sun but around the bedstead that eclipses and stumps the sun. This bedstead does not grow beneath and toward the sun but out of it; it is that from which the sun itself rises each morning and into which it sets each evening; it is that about which even the sun, this greatest of eyes, cannot keep posted, that which marks youth from old age, present sap from lost bloom, departure from return, the spring of life from its autumn. It is that which precedes, then, the journey away from home, away from Ithaca, away from a natural or private language, into metaphor and narrative; it is that about which we must tell stories since we can never really know what a bedstead means.

II. Stumping the Reader

To show that stumping the sun is no mere metaphor but the origin of all metaphor, the axis of metaphoricity itself, I will begin by sketching out the opposition between the sun and the earth as it develops in Derrida's "White Mythology." At the very end of that essay, Derrida speaks of two heliotropes, the plant that turns to the sun, the *tournesol* or sunflower, the emblem of the metaphysics of presence, and the reddish purple stone that we in English call the bloodstone. In the final paragraph, these two heliotropes are opposed in the forms of anthology, the book or logic of the flower collection, and lithography, the writing in or of stone. Yet situated between these two heliotropes, between a rock and a hot place, is, we will see, a certain stump, a sort of petrified tree or growing stone, more solid than a rolling stone and yet somewhat organic, personal or private, a kind of jewel or pet rock, the bedrock of narrative itself.

Derrida opens "White Mythology" with the image of a flower "turning away, as if from itself, come round again, such a flower engraves [*grave*: or such a serious flower—*grave* can be either a verb or an adjective]—learning to cultivate, by means of a lapidary's reckoning, patience...."[3] The virtue of this patience—as opposed to the impatiens, the touch-me-not or jewelweed, which bursts open and scatters its seed when ripe—is not that we will ever, by practicing it, get beyond metaphor, or even slow down the process, but that we might use it to engrave, without jumping to conclusions or over our own shadow, the stumped eye at the center of the sun, to carve out a space for what is always a stumped narrative.

Derrida begins by showing that the text of philosophy, of metaphysics, is full of metaphors, that philosophy never escapes figurative language. Metaphor can thus never be understood completely from within philosophy since metaphors will always have been used to explain metaphor. Philosophy can never dominate the metaphorology it uses and thus can "perceive its metaphorics only around a blind spot or central [*foyer*: hearth] deafness" (*MP*, 228). But since metaphor itself is an old philosopheme, no metaphor from outside philosophy can come to dominate an understanding of metaphor in philosophy.

Neither inside nor outside, then, but this is not all, for Derrida tries to mark, inscribe, draw attention to a metaphoricity that would precede any particular metaphor, the condition of possibility, so to speak, of all metaphor. "To mark," "inscribe," "draw attention to," these too are, of course, metaphors, but metaphors of what? At the same time as we are led toward a *mise en abîme* of metaphor, the text figures or gestures the metaphoricity of metaphor, that which produces metaphor, the trunk from which the flowers of rhetoric and philosophy grow. We are always too late for metaphoricity, for seasoning, and already in metaphor, in some season. But to explicitly deny a metaphoricity that would precede metaphor would be to treat it as something whose presence, actual or possible, can be denied. Since metaphoricity does not precede metaphor as a literal meaning might, it cannot be denied in an unambivalent way. Metaphoricity leaves its trace in the metaphor, a trace that can only be described or figured by more metaphors, themselves the result of metaphoricity. To say either that all metaphorical language is based on some literal meaning that precedes it, or, to reverse the proposition, to say that all meaning is based on some primitive, figurative language that, through usage, has been effaced, is itself to efface the metaphoricity that gives metaphor. It is already to know what "likeness" is, what links the vehicle to the tenor of the metaphor, what it is to "share" a quality or to have a characteristic "in common."

In the first scenario, which Derrida labels in shorthand Hegelian, the "turning" of metaphor is risked only with a view toward reappropriation in the overcoming of metaphor in literal language. In the second scenario, the empirical version of heliocentrism, an original, figurative language gives access to a realm of immediate, sensuous experience that is more real, more evident, more powerful, and, of course, more natural. According to this latter, abstract, metaphysical language effaces not only the material figures of language but the very fact of this effacement—thereby taking its own literal language as transparent, prompting Anatole France to say that metaphysicians live a white mythology.

But Derrida shows that the apparent opposition between what is characterized as the Hegelian overcoming of metaphor and the empiricist retrieval of it rests upon the same unquestioned ground. Both want to recover an experience or realm of thought that is identical to itself, a realm wherein things are identifiable because they resemble themselves to the point of being taken for themselves. But what about the metaphor of resemblance? Derrida writes, "Metaphor has always been defined as the trope of resemblance; not simply as the resemblance between a signifier and a signified but as the resemblance between two signs, one of which resembles the other" (*MP*, 215). The metaphor of resemblance thus eludes the system that is supposed to contain it. As Derrida demonstrates, the foundational metaphor that would claim to be the origin of figurative as well as literal language "cannot dominate itself, cannot be dominated by what it itself has engendered, has made to grow on its own soil, supported on its own base [*socle*] (*MP*, 219)." (In architecture *socle* refers to the base of a column, in geology, to a layer of rock, a bedrock, beneath the surface. It could also be used, I add in passing, to describe the base of a bed.)

According to Derrida, then, base or fundamental metaphors can never account for themselves since there is always one more metaphor in this "interminable *dehiscence* of the supplement" (*MP*, 219). This dehiscence multiplies metaphors, breaking them open to a metaphoricity that will have preceded them. Like splitting a piece of wood with an ax—but an ax ground from within—this dehiscence gives rise to a stump that will have preceded the tree from which it came.

The stump of both language and being, of both words and things. Derrida writes:

> Already the opposition of meaning (the atemporal or nonspatial signified as meaning, as content) to its metaphorical signifier ... is sedimented—another metaphor—by the entire history of philosophy. Without taking into account that the separation between sense (the signified) and the senses (sensory signifier) is enunciated by means of the same root [*racine*] (*sensus, Sinn*). One might admire, as does Hegel, the generousness of this stock [*souche*: stump]. (*MP*, 228)

This stock, this stump, is the "tropic and prephilosophical resource" (*MP*, 229) that cannot be a proper origin since it precedes propriety itself. (This resource, this resourcefulness, might already be read in relation to that man of many resources who returned to Ithaca after nineteen years of absence to discover, to invent through his *metis* or ruse, not a signified that he once left behind but the signs that he will have inscribed, the sure signs of a stump. Odysseus will discover not the thought, the *dianoia*, behind the language or *lexis* of Penelope who is trying to stump him with the question of the bed; he will not unveil some thought buried deep in the mind, waiting, as Derrida writes, to be "brought to the light of language" (*MP*, 233). No, he will discover, he will invent, the resource or source of both thought and language, a source that breaks out of the earth and yet, if it is to be sure, must remain within it. And what will link the past stump to the present will not be an assumed, theoretical apprehension of resemblance, of *homoiosis*, but the stump itself, the center or prephilosophical *foyer* (called the "sure sign").

Metaphysics, therefore, according to Derrida, has conceived of metaphor in terms of *either* the sun, presence and light, *or* the ground, in terms of *either* "dialectical idealism ... the *relève* (*Aufhebung*) ... the memory (*Erinnerung*) that produces signs, interiorizes them in elevating, suppressing, and conserving the sensory exterior" *or* foundationalism, "the desire for a firm and ultimate ground, a terrain to build on, the earth as the support of an artificial structure" (*MP*, 224). An artificial structure, as we will see, like a bed "anchored" in the earth or a scar "carved" on the body or inscribed in narrative. *Either* the sun *or* the earth: this is the logic of the sun, the logic of presence as origin, *arche*, foundation, or ground. But to think earth and sun together, earth as that which hides and harbors the sun and sun as that which has the earth in its eye, in its face, another logic is required, a logic that can never dominate or master itself but must always rely on risking a story, on erring in language. For if "language is the house of being," if the earth is the gatherer and house of the sun, then the foundation of the house of the sun is the stump at the center of the sun, the moment of eclipse that gives rise to narrative.

In the section of "White Mythology" entitled "The Ellipsis of the Sun," Derrida concludes that, for Aristotle, metaphor, as an effect of *mimesis* and *homoiosis*, is a means of knowledge. It must work in the service of truth, even though, or precisely because, it is inferior to philosophical discourse. And yet Derrida cites an example from Aristotle's *Rhetoric* that would seem to call this claim into question: "When the poet calls old age a 'withered stalk' he conveys a new idea, a new fact, to us by means of the general notion of 'lost bloom' which is common to both things" (*MP*, 238–39).[4] The poet in question here is, of course, Homer, and the man who is compared, who compares himself, to this stalk [καλάμην] is Odysseus, who says to the swineherd Eumaeus in Book 14 of the *Odyssey*, "Now all [my] strength is gone; yet even so, in seeing the stubble, methinks thou mayest judge what the grain was [ἀλλ' ἔμπης καλάμην γε σ'ὅιομαι εἰσορόωντα γιγνώσκειν]."[5] Homer's Odysseus seems to say that the old stalk, the stubble, is a sign, or signifier, of what was once contained within it—the grain or sap of youth. Like Antiphon's bedpost, the example chosen by Aristotle to illustrate metaphor doubles the structure of the illustration (it is not merely an example of metaphor but the metaphor of metaphor), the exterior stalk or stubble of the metaphor referring to an interior meaning that allows for the substitution of grain for the sap or strength of youth. Thus while the line in Greek is literally, "I think that seeing the stubble ye may judge," the liberty taken by the English translation in putting grain there where it is not seems justified since the metaphor establishes a relationship between the grain and the sap of youth.

And yet it would seem that Aristotle's interpretation of this line implicitly calls all this into question. For unlike the example of the bedpost that would refer to a present sap within or before all artifice, the stubble of old age refers not to some youth still present, not even potentially, nor to some youth once present but now lost, but to the general notion of "lost bloom." But can one ever grasp such a notion—itself expressed here as a metaphor—detached from any particular signifiers? Does not the very notion of "lost bloom" depend on a difference between past and present, what is absent and what is present? Is the notion "lost bloom" ever present as such—uncontaminated by either the categories of youth or flowers? It seems that what makes metaphor possible here, what makes the above translation possible along with the movement from the particular to the genus, is an impossible notion that two things share—a literal "lost bloom." This impossibility compels us to ask whether the Homeric line might not suggest that it is on the basis of the stalk *itself* that one may judge the strength now gone, that the stubble *itself* inscribes the general notion of lost bloom— right on its surface, on its husk—and that one can think the oppositions particular/general, presence/absence, signifier/signified, only on the basis of this husk or stalk.

Derrida concludes that metaphor in Aristotle "does not just illustrate the general possibilities" of *lexis* but

> risks disrupting the semantic plenitude to which it should belong.... Marking the moment of the turn or of the detour during which meaning might seem to venture forth alone, unloosed from the very thing it aims at however, from the truth which attunes it to its referent, metaphor also opens the wandering of the semantic. (*MP*, 241)

Return, Derrida claims, is always disrupted by the turning or trope of the sun, the sun that provides the light of resemblance for all metaphors and, even before metaphor, for all identities—including, and first of all, the proper name. "The proper name ... is the nonmetaphorical prime mover of metaphor, the father of all figures. Everything turns around it, everything turns toward it" (*MP*, 243). All metaphorical wandering is done with the retrieval of the proper name in view. "Like *mimesis*, metaphor *comes back* to *physis*, to its truth and its presence. There, nature always refinds its own, proper analogy, its own resemblance to itself, and takes increase only from itself. Nature gives itself in metaphor" (*MP*, 244). But the discourse of presence and propriety is sustained by what Derrida calls "a secret narrative" (*MP*, 243). For Derrida in "White Mythology," this secret narrative is a blind spot around which the sun turns; for me here, it is a stump at the center of the sun, the stumping of the return of the sun to its origin, to the identity of a proper name. To be a master of metaphors, a polytroper so to speak, is to be able to perceive resemblances in order to substitute one term for another—the *telos* always being the retrieval of univocity through the risking of metaphor and polysemy. This desire for univocity depends, as Derrida shows in Aristotle, on the presence of the sun, on presence itself, on that which illuminates the resemblances or similarities between things. But the sun is not always present. Just when one might think that it, like metaphor, would return to itself, return from its wandering circuit across the sky to join up with itself in a perfect circle of light and presence, it sets, or even worse, hides beneath the earth. We can thus never know that which makes all things proper—that is, the proper of the sun—because the sun turns and hides. The metaphor of the sun is thus not the proper of metaphor but the metaphor of metaphor, since all metaphor is opened to setting, to hiding, to an endless wandering away from proper language. Derrida concludes: "metaphor means [*veut dire*] heliotrope, both a movement turned toward the sun and the turning movement of the sun"(*MP*, 251).

At precisely this point in "White Mythology" (*MP*, 251), Derrida turns around, for what I believe to be the first and only time in the essay, to address what one might assume to be us, the reader: "But let us not hasten to make of this a truth of metaphor. Are you sure that you know what the heliotrope is?" Having just said that metaphor *means* heliotrope, Derrida turns, advises caution, and then asks us a question intended, I think, to stump us, the reader—a certain kind of host. For heliotrope is not, we will come to see, a proper name with a univocal meaning; it means *both* the turning of the sun *and* the earth, *both* turning toward the sun *and* the bloodstone, *both* anthology *and* lithography. Hence we can never be sure what heliotrope *means* for it "is" both anthology and lithography, both sun and stone. Both at once, since reducing the ambivalence of the heliotrope to a masterable polysemy determined by context would be to turn away from the earth, away from the stump, to the sun alone. In other words, it would be simply to repeat the heliocentric gesture of philosophy that aims to reduce the "both . . . and" to an "either . . . or" in the name of univocity, which is to say, in the name not of the name but of meaning.

Thus Derrida turns toward us as if he himself were a heliotropic plant and we were the sun, as if this reserve of turning could itself turn our heliocentric desire to find the truth of metaphor back to earth, back to the lithographic text. With this question, this apostrophe, Derrida turns us away from meaning back toward writing, toward an unmasterable graphic ambivalence. In this apostrophe, Derrida is in our face—to blind us with the stake of writing, to drill writing into us, to write across our Cyclopean eye with the drill or *mochlos* of ruse, to turn us toward the blindness at the root of our vision, our wanting to know. For as Derrida writes, the sun, as the unique referent, is always already metaphorical, always already non-proper, always already in relation to the earth in which it hides. The sun "eclipses itself, always has been other, itself: father, seed, fire, eye, egg . . ." (*MP*, 253). But also, perhaps, the mother, the womb, the fire-hardened stick that pokes out the eye, the night that blinds the sun—the arrow that pierces the skull at the dark of moon.

"All that these tropes maintain and sediment in the entangling of their roots is apparent"(*MP*, 253): roots, plural, for neither the stump nor the root is ever singular. And it is this multiplicity, this opening onto narrative, that, paradoxically, makes for sure signs.

> If there were only one possible metaphor, the dream at the heart of philosophy, if one could reduce [the] play to the circle of a family or a group of metaphors, that is, to one 'central,' 'fundamental,' 'principal' metaphor, there would be no more true metaphor, but only, through the one true metaphor, the assured legibility of the proper. Now, it is because the metaphoric is plural from the outset that it does not escape syntax, that it gives rise, in philosophy too, to a *text* which is not exhausted in the history of its meaning. (*MP*, 268)

A text, then, that is always at a loss, always stumped.

III. Signstump

Like metaphor, Odysseus is always trying to return home, always trying to come back to himself, to reappropriate himself. To cite Derrida's description of du Marsais' understanding of metaphor, Odysseus is "a being-outside-one's-own-residence, but still in a dwelling, outside its own residence but still in a residence in which one comes back to oneself, recognizes oneself, reassembles oneself or resembles oneself, outside oneself in oneself"(*MP*, 253). Still in a residence, still with a name, a story, an identity, though always in disguise, never truly home, in his own place, Odysseus would always long for the overcoming of his longing, for an eclipse of nostalgia.

And yet like metaphor, Odysseus would always risk *not* returning home. Although he would always have reappropriation in mind—the return to his dear native land, to proximity itself, to the undisguised home, the hearth or inner chamber, the natural stump at the center of the *kosmos*—he would always risk not only delay but non-return, perpetual wandering or erring in language. And perhaps this is not simply a question of getting lost along the way. For it just may be that when Odysseus—like metaphor—finally returns to his proper abode, to Ithaca, what he finds or reappropriates is not himself, but himself as other, himself as the opening onto narrative.

Let us turn then to this man of many turns, to this sort of "wandering signifier," at the very moment in the *Odyssey* when, after having returned to Ithaca and killed the suitors, he is ready to reveal himself to Penelope. In this scene of Book 23, it would seem that the master of ruses and disguises faces his final uncovering and discovery, the moment when he can peel off the last layer of artifice, the last thread of false identity, in order to be home, truly home, with his wife. As Jean Starobinski notes, Odysseus' "mastery derives from his ability to appraise, while moving through an almost ubiquitously hostile world, the exact portion of himself that can be externalized."[6] Now that he is home, he can, it seems, portion out all of himself without remainder, externalize everything, hold nothing back.

And yet this is not what happens. Bathed and well clothed after the slaughter, Odysseus sits opposite Penelope in the palace, holding himself back from embracing her, from pouring himself out completely in front of her. And Penelope too, as if she were a mirror in front of Odysseus, remains implacable, not yet satisfied with the signs the stranger has given her to assure his identity as Odysseus. Hence the final encounter, the final mediation, the moment when Odysseus is recognized as himself, as being truly home, does not occur spontaneously (as it perhaps did with Argos) but requires a sign—and not just any sign, but the sign that gives meaning to all other signs. What Penelope thus wants, in the end, is a sure sign, a sign that cannot be repeated, imitated, or reproduced, a sign that only Odysseus could give. What she wants, then, is the revelation of a private sign: "we have signs," she says, "which we two alone know, signs hidden from others" (I, 23. 109–110). What she wants is a final sign, a final proof, beyond all signs and proofs. Penelope thus orders the nurse to remove her and Odysseus' bed from out of the bridal chamber and prepare it in the hallway for the stranger to sleep on. Taken in by this ruse, Odysseus, this most suspicious and ruseful of men, recounts in indignation the story of the bedpost that he had once built, the bedpost that had been at the center of his universe, the magnetic pole that had oriented his nineteen years of wandering:

> Woman, truly this is a bitter word that thou hast spoken. Who has set my bed elsewhere? Hard would it be for one, though never so skilled, unless a god himself should come and easily by his will set it in another place. But of men there is no mortal that lives . . . who could easily pry it from its place, for a great token [μέγα σῆμα] is wrought in the fashioned bed, and it was I that built it and none other. A bush of long-leafed olive was growing within the court, strong and vigorous, and in girth it was like a pillar. Round about this I built my chamber. . . . I cut away the leafy branches of the long-leafed olive, and, trimming the trunk from the root, I smoothed it around with the adze well and cunningly, and made it straight to the line, thus fashioning the bed-post; and I bored it all with the augur. Beginning with this I hewed out my bed. . . . Thus do I declare to thee this token; but I know not, woman, whether my bedstead is still fast [ἔμπεδόν] in its place, or whether by now some man has cut from beneath the olive stump, and set the bedstead elsewhere.
>
> So he spoke, and her knees were loosed where she sat, and her heart melted, as she knew the sure tokens [σήματ' . . . ἔμπεδα]. Then with a burst of tears she ran straight toward him, and flung her arms about the neck of Odysseus. . . .
> . . . since thou hast told the clear tokens [σήματ' ἀριφραδέα] of our bed . . . thou dost convince [πείθεις] my heart, unbending [ἀπηνέα] as it is. (O, 23.183–208, 225–26, 230)

Penelope accepts the man before her as Odysseus only when she hears the sure signs. Only Odysseus could have known about the bedpost and thus have told the story about it. But there seems to be some confusion here about what is the sign of what. Odysseus says at line 188 that a "great token [σημα] is wrought in the fashioned bed," while Penelope is said to have melted when she knew, or had revealed to her, the sure signs (plural), those that Odysseus, it seems, had just recounted. Is the tree the sign, then, or is the story about the tree the sign, or signs? If the latter, what would ever make these signs sure if they were simply the signs of narrative—signs that could be mimed, imitated, stolen, inspired by the gods, made into instruments of deception? In other words, what would anchor the sure sign, what would give it its sureness? What would ensure that the sign could not be uprooted and placed outside its proper context, outside its private chamber? Just as the sign seems to apply to both the tree and the story of the tree, so the notion of sureness or steadiness seems to apply to both the sign and the bedstead itself. Odysseus asks whether his bedstead is still fast [ἔμπεδον], still bound or anchored where it was, or whether some man has cut it at the root, stolen or usurped it: his bed, his wife, his rule. But the signs are also said to be ἔμπεδος, steady. Odysseus thus makes manifest the sureness of signs, the private language that he shares with Penelope alone, the idiomatic language of their bedroom, which has not been uprooted by some other man and put into the general economy of language and the state. Yet to assure his identity, Odysseus must make this private language manifest, make it public, make the idiomatic story a story for an outside ear—or voyeuristic third party, a narrator, perhaps, who might now spy *on himself*, being both hero and narrator, able at once to seal and unseal his own private language, to overcome the sureness of time while opening narrative. As Starobinski writes,

> it is through the outside, through the mediation of exteriority, that the hidden part, the dissimulated identity, can become manifest. . . . [T]he narration of external activity stands *in place of* (in the fullest sense of that term: it develops in space, it establishes itself in space) the expression of internal identity. (*I/O*, 348, 350)

In the final book of the *Odyssey*, the recounting of sure signs once again persuades—the recounting of sure signs rooted once again in narrative and trees. Old Laertes says to his son, "If it is indeed as Odysseus, my son, that thou art come hither, tell me now some clear sign [σῆμά . . . ἀριφραδές], that I may be sure [πεποίθω]" (O, 24.328–329). And so when Odysseus has shown his father the scar, told him the story of it, and named the various trees that his father had once given him, Laertes' "knees were loosed where he stood, and his heart melted, as he knew the sure tokens [σήματ΄ . . . ἔμπεδα]" (O, 24.345–46).

IV. Turning-Posts, Flesh Wounds, Planted Oars

What is the effect, then, of the conjunction of sign and sureness, σῆμα and ἔμπεδος, in these final scenes of the *Odyssey*, and what does this conjunction tell us about seasoning, about this spring or resource of metaphor that makes language go round?

In Homer, a σῆμα is a sign, spot, or mark of some sort, either in the sky or on the earth. Odysseus puts a σῆμα along a path during the night raid of the *Iliad* so that he will not miss the place upon his return (10.466-68). The Greeks decide who will face Hector in man-to-man combat by casting lots, each man putting his own σῆμα on a stone—a mark known only to him (I, 7.189). A σῆμα is thus a distinguishing mark;[7] it marks the distance of a throw during a discus contest, for example (I, 23.843; O, 8.192, 195). It is a token that provides a guest-friend with his credentials (I, 6.176)—even though it may turn out to be an "evil token σῆμα κακον]" (I, 6.178), the "baneful tokens [σήματα λυγρά]" of writing (I, 6.168). Zeus' thunder is a σῆμα for men, as is the appearance of certain snakes (I, 2.308) or birds.[8] In Book 4 of the *Iliad*, "Zeus turned the [Myceneans'] minds by showing them tokens of ill" (I, 4.381). A σῆμα is also a tomb, a mark on the earth that indicates, or so it would seem, the presence of buried bones and ashes.[9]

Finally, a σῆμα be a signal for action (O, 21.231), or else something offered as proof—like a scar [σῆμα ἀριφραές] (O, 21.217; cf. 23.73). Thus when in Book 19 the disguised Odysseus describes in detail the clothes and manners of Odysseus whom he feigns to have met in a foreign land, Penelope weeps "as she recognized the sure tokens [σήματ΄ . . . ἔμπεδα]"(O, 19.250)—the words of the beggar but also, it seems, the clothes, the fabrics and brooch that she herself had taken from the store-room and given to her husband before his departure. Hence narrative seems to provide sure signs as long as they are anchored in experience, or else woven into it. Indeed the weaving of Penelope, the metaphor or emblem for narrative throughout the *Odyssey*, is perhaps the female counterpart of the crafting of the bedpost. One female, one male: it is as if the tree stump knits its way through the fabric of narrative, weaving and unweaving the narrative web, like the moon that waxes and wanes.

In the next to last book of the *Iliad*—once again the next to last book—a σῆμα functions as both an indication in speech and an external mark, both a mark on the earth and a tomb. Instead of being the mark of the linear flight of a discus, however, it is the turning-point of a chariot race. Nestor says to his son Antilochus:

> Now will I tell thee a manifest sign [σῆμα ... ἀριφραδές] that will not escape thee. There standeth, as it were a fathom's height above the ground, a dry stump whether of oak or of pine, which rotteth not in the rain.... Haply it is a monument [σῆμα] of some man long ago dead, or haply was made the turning-post [νύσσα] of a race in days of men of old; and now hath ... Achilles appointed it his turning-post [τέρματ']. (*I*, 23.326–33)

Once again, the sign is manifest, can't be missed, though it still needs to be pointed out. The μ thus seems to refer here both to the indications of Nestor and to the tomb or monument that will serve as the turning-point for the race, both to the manifest sign of a speaker and to the seemingly exterior sign of an object, that is, both to the signifying process and to the signified.

In the *Odyssey*, the sure sign and the manifest sign merge in the bedpost and the scar. But there is yet one more manifest sign that points us outside or beyond the narrative itself. This sign is recounted in Hades by Tiresias, the half-male, half-female, blind seer. Tiresias tells Odysseus that to appease the wrath of Poseidon, the god of the sea, angry because Odysseus had blinded his son the Cyclops with a well-turned stick, he must leave Ithaca once he has returned, travel back to the mainland, and journey inland bearing an oar on his shoulder.

> And I will tell thee a sign right manifest [σῆμα ἀριφραδές], which will not escape thee. When another wayfarer, on meeting thee, shall say that thou hast a winnowing-fan on thy stout

shoulder, then do thou fix [πήξας] in the earth thy shapely oar and make goodly offering to lord Poseidon. (*O*, 11.126–30; 23.273).

(The verb πήγνυμι, interestingly, is used in Homer to describe a spear, for instance, when it sticks into the earth, a spear that is fixed but not actually rooted—not unlike Antiphon's bedpost.) And so Odysseus must once again leave Ithaca, and when he has been given a manifest sign—someone mistaking his instrument of seafaring as one of agriculture—he must plant or anchor his oar and make offerings to Poseidon. At that point, with that point, that sign, Odysseus' journey will end, says Tiresias, and he will return to Ithaca to die a comfortable death in old age.

But Odysseus' bed—this bed on which Odysseus will probably die if he fixes his oar in the ground for Poseidon—is not only a manifest sign but a sure sign. Sure, ἔμπεδος, has a variety of meanings in Homer. As an adjective, it denotes firmness, steadiness, safeness, or protection against decay; it is used to describe things or men who are vigorous, unimpaired, well balanced, secure, assured, unfailing. Thus chains, men in battle, and even the human heart can all be steady, firm, secure, ἔμπεδος. As an adverb, ἔμπεδς means unceasingly, steadily, without hesitation or break. Hence snow can fall continually, or sticks and stones can rain down steadily from a city wall during a battle. Ἔμπεδος thus indicates both steadiness at a particular moment in time, steadfastness of or in space, and continuity across time: like a seasoned stump that reaches down to another time, like a spacing or inscription of time in flesh, like a scar provoking narrative, a scar as the emblem of narrative, that is, not just another sign but the place from which the sign—and the likeness of the sign—is given.

Indeed what could be a surer sign of someone's identity than a cicatrix, a scar, a trace? Remember that it is precisely at the moment when the scar is discovered by the aged nurse during the washing scene of Book 19 that the poet breaks into the narrative, interrupting Odysseus' reaction to the discovery, cutting in like a scar across the narrative, to tell the story of Odysseus' birth and name. Hence Odysseus' name, "child of wrath," itself cuts into the narrative like the boar's tusks once cut into his flesh. To stump the host is, it seems, to cut his flesh and give him a name. This is the cut of the name and of language, the unique cut that provides certainty and yet must be manifest, that is hidden in the flesh and yet must be decoded on its surface. This is the point where the body is opened to and inscribed in narrative: my name, my body, my bed, my wife, my house, my kingdom . . . but then, my story, my narrative, the story of my name, of my body, of my bed . . . of my kingdom. To be given a name, even if unique, is already to be inscribed in the flesh of narrative.

And so the tree stump, the sure sign, seems to refer back to itself in the past, back to the experience of making the bed. This duration, this relation between past and present, is what would give the sign its sureness and stability. But this past is not given in a non-linguistic moment that would precede all signs; it is open to experience only in the experience of narrative, while narrative is itself opened up only by means of the sure sign that gives to all signs their light and legibility, their stability and identity with themselves. Thus, what assures the stability of the bed is not the presence of an experience, not the making of the bed under the light of day, but the fact that the bed is half buried, its roots reaching down into the stable earth. This is an impossible sign, a sign that can become manifest, that can become in fact a sign only by uprooting itself, by detaching itself from itself. On the one hand, then, signs in the present link up with signs or things of the past to produce sure signs. On the other, a sign in the present supplements, but does not reveal, the sure sign, for it produces that which precedes it, and thus gets its sureness not from a past once present but from its own auto-affective movement, the sure sign being not the tree once and still present but the narrative about the tree. The narrative thus substitutes itself, must substitute itself, with its own signs under the light of the day, signs that can be learned, mimed, imitated, and repeated, for sure signs offer no proof and possibility of reference, for roots plunge down into the earth. To make these roots present, to make them manifest, would be to destroy the hidden, private signs that they ensure; and yet how else to offer proof? The sure sign must become manifest. It must become itself by becoming other than itself—so that its sureness is never sure, never absolute, never inimitable, always repeatable. The sure sign is not, then, simply the limit of experience; it is not some idea or intuition that would precede experience and narrative; it is, rather, that which gives the difference between experience and narrative, experience of the present and tales of the past; it is that which first gives the sign, and thus is both the first sign and the impossible sign.

The sure sign refers, then, only to itself; it is the unfathomable trace of itself: both narrative and root, both artificial and natural, both the object of human artifice and the nature that precedes artifice. The stump of the bed is the first sign and the first metaphor, which is to say that it is already multiple, the divided center of a private language. This language recognizes itself, indeed becomes itself, only in being brought back to itself after a circuit (of some nineteen years) around the stump at the center of the sun, around a certain *seasoning* of time and space. Levinas writes in *Meaning and Sense*, "in a trace has passed a past absolutely bygone. . . . A trace is the insertion of space in time, the point at which the world inclines toward a past and a time."[10]

V. Post-Metaphorics

The stump is indeed an *axis mundi*, not just the center of the world but a worldly axis, the very difference or ax cut between nature and culture. It grows beneath the sun toward itself, toward the stump at the center of the sun. The sun thus turns on itself around the stump that precedes it. As the sun goes down beneath the earth, the stump grows at the center of the sun, a line at the center of the circle. The stump of the sun is thus no mere metaphor but the inclination of metaphoricity itself. While the circle of the heliotrope is the dominant metaphor of metaphysics, the ambivalent heliotrope, the stumping or posting of the heliotrope, would be the metaphor of the metaphor of post-metaphysics, of post-metaphorics. Thus the metaphoricity that is overcome in metaphysics, that is made into a mere metaphor, is but reinscribed in a *post*-metaphysics.

At the end of "White Mythology," just before introducing the other heliotrope that is a rock, Derrida summarizes the two auto-destructions of metaphor, the first, that of the Hegelian *Aufhebung*, and the second, it seems, that of deconstruction. Of this latter he writes: "The *other* self-destruction of metaphor thus *resembles* the philosophical one to the point of being taken for it" (*MP*, 270). "Other" and "resemble" are in italics, indeed must be in italics, for the similarity between these two self-destructions can no longer be a simple resemblance. The other self-destruction of metaphor is taken for philosophy because it resembles it—resembles it both without and with italics—that is, both resembles it and resembles this resembling. What Penelope welcomes home at the end of the *Odyssey*, what she tries to stump even after the beggar has doffed his disguise and donned the appearance, voice, and memory of Odysseus, is an Odysseus both with and without italics, an immovable center that nonetheless inclines, slants away from itself, and in this inclination first becomes itself.

As the poet Richard Wilbur puts it, "Odd that a thing is most itself when likened." Odd that Odysseus is most himself when likened to himself, when he is both disguised and revealed, both hero and poet, both with and without quotation marks, both the object and subject of discourse. Odd that Odysseus is most himself when he has returned to himself, to his proper name, when he must at last recall and cite himself, tell his own story, put himself in italics, resemble himself to the point of being taken for himself, to the point of stumping not only us but himself, since he must now put even himself on, and, like Penelope, weave an identity by day that is unwoven at night, the sun no longer there to assure the transparency and property of his name, the bed now uprooted and put into narrative.

Chapter 13

THE CARTOGRAPHY OF KNOWLEDGE AND POWER: FOUCAULT RECONSIDERED

Adi Ophir

Commenting on his "obsession with space," in several interviews Michel Foucault clarified his ideas concerning the spatialization of knowledge and power, adding new insights, but in such a way that further explication is called for.[1] But nowhere in Foucault's texts or para-texts can one find a systematic account of the way spatial analysis is employed and spatial relations are to be understood. This lack of an explicit, unequivocal meaning characterizes Foucault's use of other concepts, most notably the concept of power. Although Foucault, in some later interviews, tried to spell out a coherent account of the way *power* and *subjectivity* were used,[2] space has nevertheless remained an orphan notion. In Foucault's text, spatial metaphors are mixed with literal spatial descriptions;[3] different spatial frameworks or settings are distinguished as if space were a genus with its own species,[4] and no explicit distinction is made between space and place.

This apparent muddle is worth an explication since more than the consistency or clarity of Foucault's writings is at stake. Indeed, the conceptual ambiguity is superficial, and when adequately elaborated it not only provides new insights into Foucault's own philosophical project, but it also leads into a new domain of questions and problematizations: the spatial logic of power/knowledge and, more generally, the logic of social space. Foucault's contribution to theory in this domain may be closely linked to the pioneering work of a historian of science like Shapin, a social theorist like Giddens, or a theorist of architecture and urban planing like Hillier. These links will only be hinted at in what follows, for my reading will be limited to the Foucaultian corpus; however, my argument will be general and somewhat speculative. I will argue that spatial conditions in the production of knowledge and the exercise of power are constraining–enabling, and it is as crucial to articulate and understand the embodiment of discourse in social space as it is to spell out its historicity. The spatial aspect of Foucault's archaeology and genealogy of discourse should not be the exception in intellectual history but the rule. Studies in intellectual history, even when thoroughly contextualized, tend to subsume spatial analyses under the reconstruction of political or economic formations, structures of institutions of discourse, and the like. I will try to show that the spatial factor, even though related to the economic, the political, and the institutional, cannot be reduced to any of these layers of analysis. To ignore the spatial factor is to ignore a crucial aspect in the history of discourse, and, more generally, of power-relations. I would like to suggest that the famous formula, "power/knowledge" should be amended and rewritten as "space/power/knowledge."

A sweeping generalization of this kind is all too often trivial if not false. However, I do not think it is easily falsifiable, nor trivial. I will examine three aspects of my claim, three ways in which it must be tested: 1) with regard to our understanding of particular events in the history of discourse; 2) with regard to other components of the theory to which it is related; 3) with regard to its status as a truth claim.

These three aspects will be examined in three separate, yet related moves:

A *historical* move, inspired by Foucault's notion of *heterotopia*, in which I propose a contribution to a (speculative) description of the emergence of modern science, may be told as a story of the transformation of "places of knowledge" in the West, of their inner spatial organization and their relation to social space.

A *theoretical* move, in which, inspired by some clues from the archaeology of the clinic, I propose a topology of social space that situates the above historical transformation of places of knowledge in a broader theoretical context. Within this framework, it will be possible to reinterpret Foucault's dissemination of the modern subject as a series of spatializations. I will claim that the deconstructive genealogies of the subject can be read as reconstructions of the changing patterns and the different, interrelated dimensions of the spatialization of subjectivity.

A *meta-theoretical* move, in which I propose to understand the claims about spatialization of knowledge, power, and the subject as transcendental hypotheses, that is, as falsifiable claims about the limits of experience. I will start, however, with Foucault's own spatial analyses.

I. The Clinic's Three Spaces

Foucault was first explicitly concerned with the relationship between space, knowledge, and power in *The Birth of the Clinic*, "a book about space, about language, and about death; ... about the act of seeing, the gaze" (*BC*, ix). He distinguished there three spatial layers.[5] The first is the *phenomenal* field in which diseases are "localized" (hence "a space of localization"), the domain in which they appear to an observer (*BC*, 3–10). Foucault claims that it was not always the case that this space was the space of the concrete human body; this occurred only after the emergence of the medical clinic in the late eighteenth and early nineteenth century. In a second, spatial setting the very *objects* of medical discourse are located; this is the space in which diseases, and later organic pathological processes, assume their specific form, are "configured," "a space of configuration." Before the emergence of the clinic, Foucault tells us, this space was constituted by nosological tables (*BC*, 3–16). The third space is the social space in which diseases are socially governed and controlled, epidemics are tackled, and public health is taken care of (*BC*, 16–20). Social space pertains both to the territory under the control of a political regime and to specific demarcations inscribed within it, e.g., between public and private spheres, the ecclesiastical and the secular, etc.[6]

Using this spatial language, it is possible to reformulate Foucault's most general argument in his "archaeology of medical perception." Foucault actually gives a spatial twist to the description of the schism between theory and practice that characterized classical medicine. Before the birth of the modern clinic, "the patient [was] a geometrically impossible spatial synthesis, but for this very reason unique, central, and irreplaceable" (*BC*, 15). The individual was so unique that he could be an object of care, but not of knowledge. The transformation of relations between medical theory and practice meant overcoming the gap between academic charts and tables of diseases studied from ancient, authoritative texts and the practitioners' acquisition of direct knowledge of the human body through daily exposure to the sick and the dying. This required the reorganization of a large terrain within social space. This new privileged place of medicine, the clinic, was demarcated within social space and designated as a site in which the treatment of diseases and their scientific investigation were carried out simultaneously and doctors could systematically relate diseases' spaces of appearance ("localization") and formation ("configuration"). Only when it became possible to relate the two spaces within the framework of one discourse was it possible to develop discursive practices that enabled and guided the controlled observation and the monitored, planned manipulation of the human body. The clinic allowed constant exchange between a curious gaze and carefully intervening manipulative hands, and an ongoing discourse that recorded, described, and guided the acts of both. Only within the environment created by the clinic could medical phenomena be related to the objects which they signified and at the same time be *parts* of those objects. The signifier, i.e, a pathological symptom, and its signified, e.g., a hidden organic process, presupposed an ontological continuity between the body's inner depth and its surface. This type of signification[7] was made possible only after the two separate surfaces were integrated into a three-dimensional space, an integration made possible by the emergence of the clinic as a relatively segregated, enclosed, and designated region of social space.[8]

II. Places of Knowledge

The reconstruction of Foucault's argument from the *Birth of the Clinic* in these spatial terms can be generalized, taking the archaeology of medical discourse as a special, paradigmatic case. Every discourse constitutes its own, unique "space of localization" for the phenomenal field it studies, a "surface of emergence" (*AK*, 41). Alongside the phenomenal space, each discourse has its own "space of configuration" or, according to Foucault, "a grid of specification" (*AK*, 42), where phenomena are related to objects and objects are differentiated according to their related phenomena. The constitution of these two spaces and of the interrelations between them is part of ongoing discursive practices, but there is no discourse from which it is lacking. The discursive activity takes place within relatively well demarcated places in social space. In the *Archaeology of Knowledge,* Foucault calls such places "institutional sites," e.g., the hospital, the monastery, the laboratory, or the library. The site of discourse, the institutionalized space from and within which one is allowed to speak and claim knowledge as of right, is one of several "modalities of enunciation," i.e., those discursive functions that define the position of the *authorized subject* of a discourse, such as an authorized physician, lawyer, or physicist. Foucault mentions three such modalities: the institutional status, role, or position of the speaking subject (a practicing pediatrician), the institutional site (a children's hospital), and the possible relations of the speaking subjects to various groups of objects that the speech situation allows (to nurses, patients, senior staff, experts in other sites/disciplines, etc.) (*AK,* ch. 4). The spatial dimension is here subsumed under the analysis of discourse and presented as one of its dependent variables. But as the examples of medical discourse clearly demonstrate, the production and reproduction of knowledge through discursive practices cannot be confined to the designated site of knowledge. They are rather entangled in a double spatial interplay: between the site itself, the architectonic of the place of knowledge which constrains and enables the interplay between the phenomenal field and the space of configuration, and the site as a designated place of discursive activity, entangled in a web of inter-relations with other sites of its kind and with the rest of social space.

In order to understand the first interplay one has to study modes of signification, practices of representation, techniques employed for the production of phenomena, and their observation and manipulation, conceptual "grid of specification," and so forth. In order to understand the latter one has to study issues such as the mechanisms of demarcation, the constitution, activation, and reactivation of spatial networks, and the coordination of encounters in space. At least three important links between the two types of spatial interplay should be made explicit. The first is the architectonic organization of the site of knowledge itself: access into and out of demarcated places, control over movement of social agents, and distribution and encounters constrained by the spatial syntax of a site.[9] The same spatial syntax constrains and enables the construction of a site as a place of observation with access to privileged observational posts, the condition of being under the gaze of others. The clinic is a perfect example, but also panoptic institutions, archaeological sites, and laboratories of the natural sciences are caught within a similar web of interrelations. A different link is established when the objects of knowledge as well as actions guided by knowledge claims cannot be confined to a privileged place of power/knowledge. This link, exemplified in cases of epidemics from plagues to AIDS, means that privileged places of knowledge involve special access to social space at large in accordance with the dispersion of objects of knowledge within it. Another example of this link is the "network of collection" any museum tries to weave around itself, placing itself at the center where the rarefaction of objects and their accumulation occurs. The third link is established through the distribution of knowledge and its exchange within and over the entire social space or some of its privileged regions. The revolutionizing effects of printing on the networks of knowledge distribution and exchange in the fifteenth and sixteenth century have been widely acknowledged and extensively studied. The precise effects of the information revolution in this century (including the computer, electronic mail, etc.) can only be guessed at, but they have already transformed the ways knowledge is deployed and exchanged throughout social space.[10]

In order to make this general claim somewhat more concrete and to demonstrate its fruitfulness beyond Foucault's particular genealogical studies, I will now consider the notion of heterotopia.

III. Heterotopia[11]

In *The Order of Things* and again in a posthumously published 1967 lecture[12] Foucault introduced the concept of *heterotopia*. In his usage, "heterotopia" is a relatively segregated site in which several *heterogenic* spatial settings coexist simultaneously. The heterotopic site is clearly demarcated from its surrounding by fixed and controlled boundaries, entrances and exits. Activities in the site are coordinated along special "time slices," and although they may change over time, this occurs without affecting the mechanism that "doubles" the space at the site. At least two spatial grids are at work at the site at the same time: one that governs social space in general and the "other[s]" peculiar to the site. The doubling-effect on space allows agents to relate to objects and to each other in ways otherwise impossible *outside* in social space at large, thus creating a gap between the site and its surrounding. The "other" space at the site always stands in some significant relation to the rest of the ordinary social spaces, designating or marking them as illusionary or real, corrupted, normal, healthy, commonsensical, serious, dignified . . . "as ours."

Foucault argues in his lecture that every culture has its own heterotopic sites and its own way to use them: theaters and cemeteries, places for *rites de passage*, shelters and refuges, and places to take a holiday. In the modern West, the sciences have been especially linked to heterotopic sites. At least since Plato's Academy, institutional production of knowledge has been *emplaced*—set apart both socially and physically. Places of knowledge have changed through the ages with respect to both their inner architectonics and their cultural emplacement. Only toward the turn of the sixteenth century have some of these places become heterotopic in Foucault's sense, and by the mid-seventeenth century several types of heterotopic sites of knowledge have been already institutionalized, for example, the chemical laboratory and mechanical operatory, the early observatories, the botanical garden, and the room of curiosities as institutionalized heterotopic sites.[13] In those early scientific heterotopias, a "space of appearances" was delineated. Its systematic observation was made possible and was interpreted in terms of a coordinated "space of configuration." The revolutionary aspect was not the coexistence of two separate spatial settings in discourse, but *that* and *how* the two resided within the confine of the same site. Phenomena "localized" in the site were observed, recorded, and carefully correlated with that which remained invisible. The seventeenth century's emphasis on observation and experimentation may have drawn attention away from a major function of these segregated places' forcing the invisible to manifest itself, to leave traces, to betray a hidden presence. Yet the invisible appears only to the eyes of those authorized to observe it and only when caught in the grid of that "other space." Two people looking at the same spot on the ground or at the same content of a glass receiver might construe two different objects and might use two different spatial grids through which to pose and relate such objects. One object is an authorized and competent inhabitant of the site and the other is a visitor or a support worker. Like fish in water, the objects construed by the competent inhabitant cannot live outside their special space. Hence the question of their relocation, or, if that is impossible, their representation, becomes crucial.[14] A network of communication and exchange is gradually formed among heterotopic sites. Only privileged residents of already institutionalized sites can use it legitimately. The heterotopic site is therefore at one and the same time a mechanism of social exclusion and a set of conditions of visibility. Together they constitute the double spatial grid at the site and create that gap between it and the social space that surrounds it.

A second wave of heterotopic sites emerged during the nineteenth century with the consolidation of the "disciplines." This second wave is the locus of Foucault's genealogical studies. The institutional frameworks—where men and women who were sick or dangerous and needed education or support were kept—became sites in which Man was "localized" as a cluster of human phenomena and "configurated" through the systematic interpretation of these phenomena. According to Foucault, since the end of the eighteenth century, institutions of care became more and more associated with some discourses of the "human sciences." These discourses, in turn, were more and more concerned with observation and manipulation. But the second wave expanded beyond the disciplines; it included zoological gardens, a rapidly growing network of museums of natural history, anthropology, and national and local history,[15] as well as archaeological and geological sites. Today almost all empirical sciences are emplaced within heterotopic sites or have special branches in such sites. When they are not thus emplaced, as in economics, their status as empirical or scientific or both is constantly challenged. No doubt, the specific location, the levels and modes of segregation and interconnection with social space, the inner spatial layout and the patterns of correlation between the visible and the invisible in the heterotopic scientific site, have all been continuously contested. At least since the mid-nineteenth century the fundamental heterotopic nature of those sites appears as a pervasive, constitutive feature of scientific activity.

The traditional, all too problematic distinction between the human and natural sciences (*Geisteswissenschaften* and *Naturwis-*

senschaften) can be partially reformulated on the basis of the distinction between heterotopic and non-heterotopic sites of knowledge. It might be argued that some intellectual practices, such as history, interpretative sociology, theoretical physics, or geography are indeed culturally placed. Located in culturally demarcated places, such as university campuses or research institutes, those sites serve as regular work places, like the post office or the car factory.[16] The objects of those sciences appear elsewhere in places that are only contingently linked to the sites of the discourses that articulate them. By contrast, experimental physics and molecular biology, but also philology,[17] archaeology, and some branches of linguistics are largely set in heterotopias that constitute spaces in which their objects appear, are observed, and are manipulated. The networks of exchange and transmission of knowledge among non-heterotopic sites would radically differ from the one deployed among heterotopic ones. In heterotopic sites, phenomena and their objects are so much dependent on the site itself that exchange among heterotopic sites must include "chunks" of place or precise instruction for their reproduction or accurate representation. In non-heterotopic sites, the objects of discourse always lie elsewhere, for only "representations" are about to be exchanged. With modern, sophisticated means of communication, they could be exchanged rapidly and efficiently, eliminating the last traces of site-dependent features of discourse. But this site-independence is itself an effect of a certain spatial play in and among sites of knowledge. Furthermore, systematic and constitutive passages link heterotopic and non-heterotopic sites of knowledge. This may be clearly witnessed in interrelation between different zones of activity in theoretical and experimental physics, for example,[18] but also in interrelation between site and office in geology, archaeology, history, and anthropology.

Several provisional conclusions may be drawn from this historical digression, speculative as it may be. First of all, the clinic appears now not as an exception but as a paradigmatic example of the rule: the emergence of heterotopic sites of knowledge as a permanent feature of modern sciences. This suggests that at least in the empirical sciences, and at least for the period of their institutionalization in culture, the site of intellectual activity was crucial in two respects: (1) as a spatial expression of the cultural demarcation of the new kind of discourse; and (2) as a spatially anchored and articulated set of constraints to the site and to conditions of visibility and manipulation of objects within it. Finally, the comparison with non-heterotopic sites of knowledge suggests that heterotopic sites of knowledge are linked to each other and related to their surrounding social space in radically different ways than non-heterotopic sites and this fact may have far reaching consequences. The spatial analysis of discourse cannot be exhausted at the level of the site; it must include an account of relationship between particular sites and the social space. A site is but a privileged intersection of barriers, restriction, and demarcation in social space. No site, not just a discursive one, can be understood only in terms of the world encompassed within it because the differentiation from, intersection within, and commerce across the boundaries are all modes of relation in social space.

IV. The Three Dimensions of Social Space

Foucault's interest with problems related to social space was never systematic but it was continuous. It goes back to *Madness and Civilization*, to the story of the "great confinement," the imprisonment of the poor, the unemployed, prostitutes, and mad people in a rapidly growing network of "general hospitals" that spread all over Europe within a few years. Later, in *The Birth of the Clinic*, Foucault describes the transformation of medical discourse and practice in and around the new clinic in terms of the reorganization of spatial relations. Given the centrality of re-spatialization for the institutionalization of modern medicine, it is not surprising that toward the end of the eighteenth century physicians became "specialists of space"; "along with the military [they] were the first managers of collective space" as Foucault later observed (P/K, 150). When reflecting on those physician's special interest in space, Foucault made, quite provisionally, some new distinctions. Spatial interests, he told Michelle Perrot in a 1977 interview, were directed toward four different aspects of social space: (1) local, environmental conditions; (2) relations and conditions of co-existences—with others, with objects, with animals, and with the dead; (3) residences; and (4) displacement, or movement across social space (P/K, 150–1).

These distinctions are fuzzy and too narrowly linked to the case in point—medicine at the turn of the eighteenth century; we should not take them as more than a starting point.[19] Here too we should suspend the particular case in point in favor of a generalization. Local conditions and the vague notion of "residences"—"the environment, urban problems"—are part of what I would like to call *emplacement*. Co-existences are clearly one possible effect of the *organization of sites* (and of entire regions) and displacement is one of the forms in which a *spatial network* may function.[20] In the discussion of places of knowledge, I have already made a tacit use of these distinctions, distinguishing among the cultural demarcation of a designated place for a type of intellectual activity, the architectonics of the site itself, and the network of relations among sites of different sorts.

Spatial networks are (1) the ever changing patterns of dispersion and dissemination of bodies, objects, and relations over space; (2) their transmission, distribution, exchange, or communication; and; (3) in general, all regular forms of transaction between sites and across space. Networks, and particular regions within them, vary according to their medium, objects, density, effectiveness, or social function, but they are all anchored in physical space, constituting it as a meaningful social space. A power/knowledge complex is always already "networked," so to speak.

Emplacement has to do with the cultural demarcation of a privileged place for a particular set of practices, interactions, or functions of a power/knowledge complex. A place is a demarcated space in which political, social, cultural, or more strictly discursive practices assume a relatively high degree of regularity and in relation to which positions in cultural and political systems are defined (according to access to, freedom of movement within, and control over the demarcated place).[21] Emplacement refers to a social, cultural, or political set of practices that resides somewhere in particular, not to the particular way its residency is arranged. Some, but not all, privileged places may be constituted in well-organized sites in which spatial arrangements embody—or rather *emplace*—some of the regularities that govern the power/knowledge complex. They apply to all heterotopias but also to non-heterotopic sites such as an army camp, a legal court, or a high-tech plant. Some clearly demarcated places, for instance, a modern university campus, may be more or less indifferent to their inner spatial organization, or they may constitute a category that includes many different site-patterns. Thus, the private sphere, for example, is spatially localized, but not necessarily organized according to any particular spatial pattern.[22] And there may well be metaphorical places, i.e., places on a cultural, not necessarily geographical map, like tables, texts, or photographs, in which some cultural function may be said to reside.[23]

The *organization of a site* refers to the physical—symbolically loaded—arrangement of the inner space of a privileged place.[24] In an organized site more or less fixed values are ascribed to outer boundaries, points of access both into the site itself and into particular regions within it. These are more or less fixed conditions of visibility and an overall spatial system of constraints over sporadic and spontaneous encounters. The organization of the site differentiates positions and types of social agents, or perhaps inscribes such a differentiation into space. However, the differentiating scheme can exist apart from its spatial inscription.

Culture works and functions through complex combinations of sites, emplacements, and networks, though the nature of those combinations and the relative weight each of the spatial factors assumes change among spheres of culture, societies, and historical periods. Taxation, for example, has always required developed networks and clear sites in control, but it did not always involve clear emplacement of economic or political activity. Religious authority is usually emplaced and networked, but its reliance on particular architectonics of sites varies. The site was highly important in ancient Greece but is hardly of any relevance in a modern university campus or among modern protestant denominations. Commercialized sport is highly networked, emplaced and linked to a definite and sophisticated architectonic of sites; in ancient Greece, however, the Olympic games were very clearly emplaced and linked to a planned site, although only randomly networked through a larger social space. Modern theater is clearly linked to a planned site, more vaguely emplaced (as in street theater and country theater festivals), and hardly networked at all. When one of the spatial factors sinks to the background or diminishes altogether, the two other are likely to emerge as more dominant as long as a cultural sphere maintains its integrity. The dissolution of a cultural sphere may be described in terms of processes of spatial disintegration—there are no more sites dedicated to a particular cultural activity (as when there were no more sites for teaching Hebrew in Soviet Russia) or no more networks for exchange of cultural products of a certain kind (as in the ban on Hebrew books and presses) and cultural activity is no longer symbolically emplaced. Artisanship in America, for example, is still emplaced in the countryside today but will soon lose even this backyard as new "mall-towns" take the place of villages. The opposite is true for the institutionalization of a culture sphere—as we have seen with regard to scientific heterotopia—which involves a new spatial integration. The understanding of a culture must include understanding the way it is emplaced, networked, and linked to sites with defined spatial syntax. This includes the production of knowledge, but as Foucault used to say, it goes much better when said. It also includes that special web of power/knowledge/pleasure, namely sexuality.

V. The Spatial Deployment of Sexuality

Foucault was usually reluctant to engage in an abstract methodological discussion that would explicate or justify distinctions of that kind, and one does not expect him to justify this type of grid over others—and there are, of course, some others, employed, for example, by social geographers like Henri Lefebvre (1970, 1972) or a social theorist like David Harvey (1982, 1985, 1989). My aim is not to prove that this grid is "valid" or to derive it from a more "fundamental" theoretical layer. My claim is rather that Foucault actually employed them in his genealogical work. The deployment of discourses of sexuality since the second half of the eighteenth century as described in the first volume of *History of Sexuality* may serve as an example both for each of the separate spatial dimensions and for their interrelations. Let me outline briefly the spatial interplay in that complex of power/knowledge/pleasure.

Spatial Networks—The emergence of a plethora of discourses of sexuality was closely related to a growing interest in populations. The attempts to gain demographic knowledge of and control over populations' growth and distribution entailed growing interest in knowledge of and control over patterns of reproduction and hence of sexual behavior. Demographic knowledge and management of population presupposed declaring an area as a territory and delineating its boundaries, coming to know its minutes details,[25] and deploying over that territory overlapping networks of communications, transportation of forces, transfer of money and goods, and transmission of knowledge. Several sexual discourses were woven into various such demographic and territorial networks. Somewhat more vaguely and without specification, Foucault claims that the sites of power/knowledge/pleasure, in which sexuality was shaped and reproduced, served as knots in a network of power relations, anchors for acts of reproduction, and extension of power/knowledge regimes. These sites are "where the intensity of pleasure and the persistency of power catch hold, only to spread elsewhere" (*HS*, 49).

Emplacement—The discourse of sexuality had privileged places, e.g., the bourgeois house, the church, the boarding schools, and then gradually, and especially in the second half of the nineteenth century, medical and psychiatric clinics, police stations, and prisons ("sexual crime"). These were spaces haunted by manifold sexualities (*HS*, 47), "sites [that] radiated discourses [that] aimed at sex" (*HS*, 31), in which scattered sexualities rigidified, became stuck to an age, *a place*, a type of practice" (*HS*, 48). These were the places to which normal and (different types of) abnormal sexual behaviors were assigned particular places. To these concrete places one may add the special space opened for sexuality. By the nineteenth century, the canonic novel on the one hand (cf. Miller 1988) and the scandalous, confessional novel on the other hand (*HS*, 21–4) emerged.

Organization of the site—Some places of sexuality came with their specific architectonic, which, in the case of the boarding school, for example, explicitly took into account the sexuality of children (*HS*, 27–8). New spatial relations among individuals (as both subjects and objects in the emerging sexual discourses) were physically arranged and socially coded: new arrangements of rooms in the house, new plans for schools, and clinics, etc. (*HS*, 44; cf. P/K, 150). All these sites were radically different from an earlier organized site of sexual discourse, the confessional. The location of this cell within the church and its specific layout constituted an irreversibility of gaze and speech, nonreciprocal relations of listening and seeing, and a partial discreetness for the confessing person (not seen when he/she is confessing but may always be observed when going into or out of a confessional).

VI. The Spatialization of the Subject

The spatialization of sexuality may provide us with a privileged perspective upon Foucault's work as a whole. Looking backward from the vantage point of the *History of Sexuality* one may clearly see how Foucault deals, repeatedly and from different perspectives, with questions of self and subjectivity in a way that unifies his work *malgré lui*.[26] This unifying interest in subjectivity has been widely acknowledged by Foucault's readers, following his own self-description. In one of his last interviews Foucault described his project as consisting of three domains of genealogical investigation, three axes of "historical ontology" of the self: in relation to knowledge, power, and ethics.[27] The historical ontology of the self may be interpreted as an elaboration of an ongoing attempt to disseminate the modern subject.[28] Such an attempt was already alluded to in Foucault's first explicit, systematic reflection upon the course of his work and its dazzling itinerary, i.e., the *Archeology of Knowledge*. Referring to his three previous books (*The Order of Things, The Birth of the Clinic, Madness and Civilization* [the omission of the book on Roussel is significant]) he describes his project as "an enterprise by which one tries to throw off *the last anthropological constraints*; an enterprise that wishes, in return, to reveal how these constraints could come about" (*AK*, 15). He has gradually realized that his "studies of madness and the beginning of psychology, of illness and the beginning of clinical medicine, of the sciences of life, language and economics" were attempts to discover the "historical possibility" of the debate on humanism and anthropology (*AK*, 15). Understood in its proper context, this debate occurred between structuralism and humanistic or "anthropologized" marxism, between Sartre of *The Critique of Dialectical Reason*[29] and Lévi-Strauss of *The Savage Mind*,[30] and it concerned the possibility and limits of subjectivity and of history as motivated and carried forward by the agency of free subjects.

For Foucault, that debate itself was still caught within the metaphysical framework of "traditional," "total" history, the kind of history that turns monuments into documents. Against this history he presents a "new," "general" history, one that turns documents into monuments (*AK*, Introduction). "Traditional" (modern) history in its various forms is associated with continuity, "the sovereignty of consciousness," and the idea of "the founding subject" (*AK*, 12). Its rival (postmodern) archaeology, is characterized by attention to disruptions, disparity, and discontinuities. But the postmodern *episteme* is also engaged in a constant act of "sacrifice," the sacrifice of the modern subject of knowledge ("Nietzsche, Genealogy, History," in *LCMP*, 162–64). The metaphysical, founding subject, whose presence in the realm of historical phenomena is always hidden, yet whose reign over it is total and continuous, is now abandoned. Instead, one turns to a series of archaeological, then genealogical studies that try to disperse this subject (cf. *AK*, 54). They draw it back to the minute series of actions and reactions, exercising forces over bodies, which constantly try to sanctify temporary relations of domination and inscribe them into bodies, institutions, and scriptures. The new kind of history pronounced in the *Archaeology* and which Foucault practices from *Madness and Civilization* at least until the first volume of the *History of Sexuality* is constantly and inextricably linked to this historical ontology of the modern self. The deconstructive enterprise was carried indeed along three axes: as a subject of knowledge the modern self was disseminated in *Madness and Civilization, The Birth of the Clinic*, and *The Order of Things*; as an agent of power it was taken apart in both *Madness and Civilization* and *Discipline and Punish*, and as a moral agent that shapes its own identity through action on itself and others, the self was deconstructed in both *Madness and Civilization* and *History of Sexuality* (*BSH*, 37).

This view of the Foucaultian enterprise as centered around the dissemination of the modern subject may be broadened and refined by the spatial analysis. It is my claim that the ongoing destructive genealogy of the subject can be read as the genealogical reconstruction of the changing patterns and the different, interrelated dimensions of spatialization of subjectivity.[31]

From the relatively narrow perspective of a single discourse or group of discourses, a spatialized subject is a function of discourse that associates a position and authority with specific spatial settings. The position and authority of the spatialized subject (the structured fields in which her words, gaze, and hands are enabled and constrained) are, at least in part, effects of the privileged place with which an individual is associated, the architectonic of the site from and in which she speaks and acts, and the various networks that allow her authority to transcend those privileged spaces which guarantee her subjectivity. From a broader perspective that does not tie subjectivity to a particular discourse, a spatialized subject is an individual whose various fields of possibilities—for action, production, reproduction, and discourse—are structured, at least in part, by the complex interrelations between sites, places, and networks. In his genealogical studies Foucault has given evidence for four such domains of structuration:

1. **Rationality**. The confinement of the mad to mental hospitals, the observation of their behavior and its manipulation within the shelter of the asylum, relate one's rationality to the spatialization of madness in a triple link: Rationality is related: (a) to those *sites* in which the irrational is defined, classified, and controlled, (b) to the very *emplacement* of the division between the rational and the irrational, and (c) to the various mechanisms that deploy networks of demarcation between the sane and the mad throughout social space.

2. **Body**. The exposure of the body in the space of the hospital relates one's own body to the place where the deterioration of that body and its coming death is objectified, diagnosed, and prognosticated. One's well-being is an effect of one's position in a medical and para-medical network. Parts of that network rely on the hospital as a special knot, being a source of knowledge and a legitimator of control;[32] other knots, to which Foucault alluded when talking about the Greek care of the self, rely on the "health centers," "nutrition centers," "athletic centers," and the like.

3. **Citizen**. The institutionalization of the carceral penal system relates one's civility and political being (as well as the specific part one takes in civic-space) to the place in which illegality is demarcated, objectified, the place where its classifications are materialized and predictions verified. Like the hospital, prison too is hooked to various networks and sites of political, legal, and therapeutic discourses and power-relations, and is a necessary condition for their functioning.

4. **Desire**. Sexuality, as we have seen, traverses the entire social space; it is emplaced in asylums, clinics, and prisons, and in their (seemingly) perfect counter-place, the decent bourgeois house, and through them spatialized in details. In these four domains subjectivity is spatialized both as an object of various discourses *as well as* a function and effect of discourses, a pole of specific set of relations to statements and a constraint on their production (*AK*,

92–6).[33] In all four domains the three spatial interplays are at work, and none of them is self-evident. As far as the organization of the site is concerned, Foucault argues that the spatialization of the subject is a reason for and result of the heterotopic nature of disciplinary sites and a condition for the possibility of the constitution of the modern subject *qua* "Man." However, the role of the two other spatial interplays, hardly discussed by Foucault, needs further explication.

It is neither self-evident nor necessary that a cultural division between, for example, madness and sanity would be emplaced; it has not always been, and not all divisions that resemble it are. It is also worth remembering that alongside those cultural demarcations which are spatially embodied, there have always been others to which no spatial value has been assigned, sometimes despite repeated efforts by the state, and others that have lost the spatial designation they had. Thus, to give a counter-example, the division between poor and rich has never been quite successfully emplaced, despite repeated efforts of different regimes to do so: e.g., by the Ancien Regime, in confining the poor together with the mad and by postmodern capitalist regimes, in throwing the poor to the streets or confining them to ghettos. The case is similar for ethnic or religious divisions in society, which are often, but not always, emplaced. Societies differ, it is important to note here, in the degree to which they tend to inscribe in space their main divisions (of gender, race, creed, etc.). It is often argued that ancient and primitive societies tend to do that more rigidly, systematically, and significantly than modern ones. But the examples above show that the difference is not in degree, but in kind and in formation (see *SocSpace*, ch. 6).

Lack of clear emplacement means deficient means of objectification and acquisition of knowledge, and limited mechanisms of control. Societies would tend to emplace those they have interest to differentiate in order to know and control, and they would tend to differentiate and know better those they are capable of emplacing. But the poor, one may argue, are not differentiated and controlled by spatial mechanisms but by economic relations of production which are responsible for spatial differentiation. Yet the generation and reproduction of economic differences require, among other things, differential control over means of spatial allocations of men and goods and their spatial deployment. Economic differences necessitate emplacement and reproduce it.[34] A mobile working class is less easy to control than a strictly emplaced one, unless one can ship working hands wherever one wants, or manipulate demand and salaries over an entire social space. Generally speaking, the more efficient the networking of social space, and the more that networked space is accessible to a dominating class, the less one needs to fall back on strategies of particular emplacement. At the opposite end, dominated groups would tend to develop strategies of alternative spatial emplacement and differentiation. On the other hand, when a dominating class rests much of its power on strategies of spatial emplacement and differentiation, dominated groups tend to use alternative, subversive networking, trespassing and infiltration. In short, social conflict may always be mapped according to struggles over, within, and through all three dimensions of spatialization and their interrelations.

From this general, cultural perspective the emplacement of modern subjectivity and its deployment through spatial networks should appear all the more striking. Cultures have always spatialized the self-identity of their members. Examples may be piled here.[35] Foucault's implied claim goes further. It is not self-identity of an individual as a member of a culture, an ethnic group, or a religious community which is at stake in the spatialization of modern subjectivity, but the very boundaries of a universal humanity, of the universally human in man. Modern, Western "Man" could not have come into being without these boundaries being first culturally emplaced, deployed over social space, and objectified in heterotopic sites of knowledge.

In *Being and Time*, Heidegger wrote the following about the spatiality of *Dasein* and its relation to temporality: "*Dasein* can be spatial only as care in the sense of existing as factically falling.... Negatively this means that *Dasein* is never present at hand in space, not even proximally. *Dasein* does not fill up a bit of space as a real thing or item of equipment would ... only on the basis of its ecstatico-horizontal temporality it is possible for *Dasein* to break into space."[36] We can now turn this understanding on its head. Man came into being only when spatialized, and he was spatialized at the historical moment when care was institutionalized through the disciplines and articulated through the discourses of the "human sciences." Positively this means that in the space prepared for him, man has become present at hand in different degrees of proximity and that he does fill up bits of space of different sorts. And finally, it may be that only on the basis of specific forms of modern spatialization has it become possible for man to recognize his peculiar historicity.

VII. Spatialization Is Transcendental

Now, however, after "the death of Man," the paradoxical nature of "man as a double" has been resolved into the three different axes through which the human self is constituted as a subject: knowledge (self as object, as a thing among things), power (self as a freedom among other free agents), and ethics (self as reflexive, capable of posing itself as the object of its own intention). In all three dimensions of relations both time and space lose their transcendental character, and different forms of temporality and spatiality are constructed, changing from one discursive formation to another and from one historical context to another.[37] But there is another sense in which *spatialization*, (and not only temporalization),[38] remains transcendental: the spatialization of discourse, both within (spaces of appearance and object-formation) and without (social space) is a condition for the possibility of discourse, of discourse-power relations, and hence of the constitution of *both* subjects and objects. That subjectivity has been historicized means that spatialization grounds the very possibility of subjectification.

To have reached this somewhat surprising conclusion from the vantage point of the (postmodern) deconstruction of the (modern) subject should not mislead us. The deconstruction of the subject does not mean its elimination but its systematic historicization (witnessed most clearly by the last two volumes of *History of Sexuality*) and its reconstruction as a function, an effect, or a nucleus of resistance to this or that regime of discourse and power. This historicization obeys, however, a transcendental scheme, never to be articulated by Foucault, let alone justified (for grounding was never part of his job).[39] I am not able to spell out the entire layout of that scheme, for it is beyond the scope of this paper.[40] But the above reconstruction of the spatial dimension in Foucault's archaeological and genealogical analysis may support a more limited, yet by no means more modest claim regarding the transcendental role of spatialization.

Spatialization, not space. Spatialization cannot be reduced to space as a "container" in which things exist, and in which they relate to each other in relations of proximity, direction, and containment. To reduce spatial relations to a Euclidian or a Kantian grid is but one of the possible materializations of spatiality in discourse. Spatialization is a dynamic, multidimensional operation of interrelations anywhere words relate to objects and power to freedom (or actions to other actions). Saying this is also not simply reiterating the trivial, i.e, that humans are creatures that exist in (a Kantian) space and therefore that everything human can be described *sub specie geometrica*. My claim—or rather the claim implied by the Foucaultian project—is that an active, ongoing, and ever changing constitution of spatial relations of different types is a condition for the possibility for human experience, both the experience of "things" and the experience of the self.

Foucault is often said to be a Kantian of a sort.[41] It is therefore worth noting what happens to Kant's space and its constitutive role as a form of intuition at the basis of the transcendental subject. Most striking is that the relation between space and subject has been inverted: the former is not part of the transcendental structure of the latter but a transcendental condition for the possibility of the subject's always *historical* constitution. Space remains, however, a transcendental form of experience, a condition of possibility for the constitution and recognition of objects. But in what sense precisely? Words and objects are mediated through discourse, in which both the gaze and the statement (*enoncé*) have necessary spatial correlatives, and those cannot be reduced to each other but are inseparably linked (*AK*, ch. 10; *F*, ch. 3). Discourse delineates a space of appearances, in which phenomena are spatially differentiated and related, as well as interpreted through specific spatial *and* conceptual grids.[42] However, thought through the order of discourse, space is always already a result of spatialization. Space is not merely the *a priori*, *passive* form of external experience which is given always already "in space," but neither is it a "container" in which every object must "have a place," nor a set of relations that must exist between material objects, although it may be all these as well. Discourse always consists of an *active* moment of *spatialization*, of setting objects in a network of spatial relation, of constituting the *specific* spatial grids through and in which objects are experienced, spoken of, observed, and manipulated. For no mute, single, transcendental, form of spatialization is pre-given as a condition for the possibility of discourse; rather, specific, ever changing forms of spatialization are historically constituted in and through discourse.[43] As an aspect of discourse, spatialization is indeed a transcendental, but a transcendental always already historicized, always already embodied within the specific complex of a power/knowledge regime.

This embodiment itself, however, presupposes another form of spatialization: the spatialization of discourse itself in social space. Above I have suggested three distinct, yet linked, spatial operations that relate discourse to social space: organization of a site, demarcation of a place, and deployment of a network. I propose that what may appear as a contingent or provisional result of an interpretive analysis is really a transcendental claim. My claim is that these three spatial mechanisms are always at work in the production and reproduction of discourse, that the specific forms of their constellation constitute the limit, hence the possibility of, discursive practices, and of spatialization *within* discourse. No doubt, in different regimes of power/knowledge, each of these spatial settings may assume a different importance relative to the two others, for the transcendental is always already historicized. Hence, the deployment of a network was much more important in eighteenth-century medical discourse than in contemporary biological discourse. In theological discourse, then and now, the demarcation of a place has been more significant than the two other factors. Or, to take once again the example of sexuality, various sexual discourses have witnessed, since the end of the eighteenth century, the growing weight of the architectonics of the site of discourse. Sometimes, the significance of one of the spatial moments may seem reduced to nothing, e.g., site organization for modern philosophy or a deployment of a network for an esoteric cult. But these changing modes of interface among the three spatial mechanisms should not prevent us from seeing that a temporary annihilation of a spatial factor is one possibility of its materialization, and that in one form or another spatialization is always materialized along these three "axes." Moreover, the examples of Foucaultian genealogies of the mental hospital, the clinic, the prison, and sexuality suggest that the specific form of the interface among the three "axes" accounts, in part, for various aspects of the discursive activity itself, its intellectual products as well as its cultural survival. Spatialization constitutes a set of enabling/restraining limitations on discursive activity, whose reconstruction is crucial for understanding what a discourse has produced and how it was reproduced, transformed, or extinguished from the cultural sphere.

From this point of view, both the heterotopic nature of modern sites of knowledge and the spatialization of modern subjectivity are specific historical configurations of the dynamic structure of the transcendental spatialization of experience. In the modern West, the organization of knowledge and the constitution of subjectivity are made possible by, and in their turn reproduce, a very special, intensive, and quite revolutionary arrangement of social space. The syntax of that space—for both sites and networks—is more important than its symbolic contents, yet it is so effective precisely because its syntax is loaded with social meanings (cf. *SocSpace*, 9–18). Due to the sophisticated interfaces between site and network, control in that space can be highly decentered, diffused, and widespread over huge territories while highly centered in relatively few well-demarcated sites. The most fundamental cultural divisions are so well inscribed into those interfaces of sites and networks, and so well concealed through their vast spatial dissemination that the effects of power relations—with regard to the production of both knowledge and subjectivity—can be intensified and prolonged almost indefinitely. With it, possibilities of resistance are disseminated and intensified. This form of spatialization of power/knowledge makes possible, I believe, what Foucault calls "bio-power," the power formation that characterizes modernity more than any other (*HS*, part V).

The precise features of this spatial arrangement are very difficult to grasp. Those who analyze social space in terms drawn from architecture tend to stop at the level of the site. Anthropologists tend to overemphasize sites and emplacements. And geographers are typically interested in the networks that cross social space and give it a unity and various degrees of density. But from the point of view of one interested in discourse, in power/knowledge complexes, all three spatial dimensions have to be considered at once, both with regard to each other and to their peculiar interrelation. Only when such a comprehensive picture is attempted can one start delineating the peculiar presence of spatialization in modern institutions of power and knowledge. One can do this, however, only to the extent that one realizes the structure of what I have called "transcendental spatialization" and uses it as a guide in the process of thinking.

What is the status of this claim? Not unlike the Kantian transcendental mind, concrete forms of spatialization are claimed to be possibility conditions for the existence of (concrete forms of) discursive (and non-discursive) practices. The thematization of these forms, however, their formulation and justification, is not transcendentally derived. The thematization of spatialization implies the genealogical reconstruction of historical forms of spatialization and their transformations. These empirical-historicist reconstructions are necessary to keep the transcendental argument alive and well or to refute it in due course. The extraction of a transcendental structure is a product of hermeneutic activity.[44] The transcendental argument is hermeneutically reconstructed, not transcendentally derived; it can exist only in and through historicization, in the archaeological studies that decipher regularities (orders or structures) of spatialization, and in the genealogical studies that follow the details of these structures' crystallization and deformations. From this point of view, spatialization constitutes a partial outline of the horizon for research in the history of discourse, social history, and social theory. Some social theorists, like Giddens,[45] Hillier, and Hanson have realized this for social theory; a few others have taken first steps in the history and sociology of science (see *PKMS*). These historical and sociological studies are not only given their "spatial" horizon, modest as they are. They are already capable of giving some support to the transcendental claim and are necessary in order to further refine and corroborate it.

However, in the context of geography and other sciences interested in social space, space itself becomes the object that inhabits the "inner" spaces of a particular discourse and the proposed distinction between three spatial mechanisms is no more than the grid used—or one that might be used—in a particular discourse. After all that has been said and written about the historicity of discourse, how can such a grid claim a transcendental status? The spatial grid is a product of an "archaeology," or a "genealogy," of discourses on other discourses, not particularly of the analysis of social or geographical space. Geography and social theory—to the extent that they are attuned at all to Foucaultian discourse—may borrow this grid from a discourse, which from their point of view is a kind of meta-discourse, a critical reflection on their own practices.[46] That Foucault's discourse claims the status of a meta-discourse is an inevitable result of the discourse itself, discourse in general having become the object of Foucault's thought. Foucault, or at least his philosophically minded readers, cannot escape the predicament of the philosopher, i.e., the one who tries "to think." Even if the spatial distinctions I have proposed above express no more than the shadow of an ephemeral grid employed by a current geographical discourse, they cannot be reduced to such a grid. They are not only an effect of a certain discursive regime (though they are this as well), but a means to describe discursive regimes as such, that particular one included. If those distinctions fail, refuted or rejected due to the empirical results of a contemporary geographical discourse, or of one that will replace it in the future, it is not because they have been but part of a grid of a dying discourse soon to be trashed into the archive, but because they have been inadequate generalizations of the way *discourses* are.[47]

This may seem in direct opposition to Foucault's understanding of thinking as a form of critique. This may appear to be stuck at the time of Foucault's *Archaeology*, taking no account of his later, explicit rejection of criticism as a "search for formal structure with universal value" ("What is Enlightenment?" in *FR*, 45–6), thus betraying all postmodern sensibilities. Thinking, according to this later position, is "a critique of what we are," of the way we are part of a contingent present, and this always includes "the historical analysis of the limits that are imposed on us and an experiment with the possibility of going beyond them" (*FR*, 50). Thinking involves an inescapable effort to think "from the outside," to place oneself in the "interstice" of a regime of power/knowledge, and to introduce a critical gap between whatever discursive (and non-discursive) practices are available at a certain point and one's own activity, philosophical and otherwise. Foucault thinks that this kind of philosophical attitude, especially in its archaeological and genealogical forms, is an alternative to and a negation of Kantian transcendentalism which consistently avoids seeking "to identify the universal structures of all knowledge and of all possible moral action" (*FR*, 46). But, as witnessed in many places in his writing, these anti-transcendentalist attempts "to think" are constantly engaged in transcendental implications. Even in the text quoted above he mentions a scheme, which, if not loaded with a transcendental claim, is useless: "Practical systems," that determine what people do and how "stem from three broad areas: relations of control over things, relations of actions upon others, relations with oneself" (*FR*, 48).[48] Such a conceptual scheme sets the horizon for Foucault's project, or at least this is what he claims. If such a scheme is important, it is not useless to try to amend it, complement it, or replace it altogether. This may call for more transcendental claims. Thinking, even in Foucault's sense, is not opposed to transcendental *working hypotheses*, only to transcendental *points of view*. The critique of the present is inextricably linked to historical research not only in order to introduce contingencies into what we have come to think as natural and necessary. Critique draws its transcendental horizon and guidelines from critique. And through more work in the archive, these horizons may come to shift and to escape the burden of a dominating present. Historicization of the spatiality of discourse and of power/knowledge regimes is one crucial form that a critique of discursive regimes may take. This critique becomes dogmatic if it does not thematize its transcendental horizon, if it refrains from problematizing it, if it hesitates to call it into question, or, in short, if it does not explicate its implied transcendental claims and does not take them as hypotheses.

NOTES

INTRODUCTION

1. Jacques Derrida, *Of Grammatology*, trans. Gayatri Chakravorty Spivak (Baltimore: The Johns Hopkins University Press, 1976), p. 7
2. Umberto Eco, *The Limits of Interpretation* (Bloomington: Indiana University Press, 1990), p. 8. Henceforth cited as *LI*.
3. See Hugh J. Silverman, *Inscriptions: Between Phenomenology and Structuralism* (London and New York: Routledge, 1987) for more detail on Merleau-Ponty's interest in bringing semiology and structuralism into connection with his understanding of phenomenology.

CHAPTER 1   THE REASONS OF THE CODE: READING ECO'S *A THEORY OF SEMIOTICS*

1. Umberto Eco, *A Theory of Semiotics* (Bloomington: Indiana University Press, 1975). Henceforth cited as *TS*. References to materials which appear only in Italian will be made throughout these notes, with the adopted abbreviations. English editions of Eco's books are not always straightforward translations from the Italian, as sections and paragraphs are often added or deleted; as a result, occasionally reference is made to both versions.
2. See some of the early reviews, in particular John Deely, "The Doctrine of Sign: Taking Form at Last," *Semiotica*, 18:2 (1976), pp. 171–93; John Walker, "Comments on Umberto Eco's Book 'A Theory of Semiotics,' " *Leonardo*, 10 (1977), pp. 131–32; Gregory Colomb, "Semiotics since Eco (I) & (II)," *Papers on Language and Literature*, 15:4&5 (Summer and Fall 1980), pp. 442–59; Maria Corti, "Fatta di segni la dea di Eco," *Il Giorno*, 2 (April 1975); Robert E. Innis's review in *International Philosophical Quarterly*, 20:6 (1980): 221–32.

3. In a career that spans now nearly forty years, *The Theory of Semiotics* comes at midpoint. It is not difficult to distinguish an "early" stage in Eco's thought, basically from the mid-fifties to the mid-sixties, a "second" or "mature" stage which covers the years 1968–1980, characterized by the emergence and consolidation of his semiotics (and of which the *Theory* is the high point), and a still ongoing stage of study which appears evenly divided between the philosophy of language and cultural criticism. Of course, the actual picture is much more complex. Eco has always been engaged on several fronts at the same time, something which is still looked upon with suspicion in American academic circles. However, as he explicitly states in the Introduction to *Sette anni di desiderio* (Milano: Bompiani, 1983), p. 5: "Every so often I collect into a volume articles, occasional writings, polemical pieces, the *nugae* or observations that once used to be confined to personal journals or diaries. But in an age that not only allows but encourages circulating in public one's own immediate reactions to problems and events, the pages from a diary come out serially, in the print media. They have the advantage of not being written for posterity, but rather for one's contemporaries, often running into contradictions and risking imprecise judgments. But for the professional writer, this is the most appropriate (and at any rate the most responsible) way of committing oneself politically." A similar remark appears in his preface to *Travels in Hyper Reality* (Bloomington: Indiana University Press, 1989), p. x: "It is true that many American professors write for cultural reviews or for the book page of the daily papers. But many Italian scholars and literary critics also write columns where they take a stand on political questions, and they do this not only as a natural part of their work, but also as their duty. There is, then, a difference in 'patterns of culture.' " Finally, we cannot discount (though we will not take it up here) the influence the writing and success of his two major novels had on his thinking and research through the eighties.

4. For a critical and bibliographical overview, see Gianfranco Bettetini and Francesco Casetti, "Semiotics in Italy," chapter 13, in *The Semiotic Sphere*, eds. Thomas Sebeok and Jean Umiker-Sebeok (New York: Plenum Press, 1986), pp. 293–21. For a comprehensive view of semiotics in Italy up to the appearance of the Italian version of *A Theory of Semiotics* [namely, *Trattato di semiotica generale* (Milano: Bompiani, 1975), henceforth cited as *TSG*], see Augusto Ponzio, *La semiotica in Italia* (Bari: Dedalo Libri, 1976). On Eco's reception in Italy, see the recent book by Margherita Ganeri, *Il "Caso" Eco* (Palermo: Palumbo, 1991), which contains, besides an extensive bibliography, excerpts from articles on and reviews of all of Eco's works from 1956 to the present.

NOTES TO CHAPTER 1

The following collection of critical essays dedicated to the whole of Umberto Eco's work, including *A Theory of Semiotics*, is entitled *Semiotica: storia teoria interpretazione*, eds. P. Magli, G. Manetti, and P. Violi (Milano: Bompiani, 1992).

5. See Peter Carravetta, *Il fantasma di Hermes; saggio su metodo, retorica, interpretare* (Lecce: Milella, 1994), and the article "Repositioning Interpretive Discourse: From 'The Crisis of Reason' to 'Weak Thought,' " in *Differentia*, 2 (1987): 83–126.

6. As late as 1970, Eco is still working within the horizon of a structuralist "semiology"; see for example "La critica semiologica," in *I metodi attuali della critica in Italia*, eds. Cesare Segre and Maria Corti (Torino: ERI, 1970), pp. 371–404. There are however many clear signs here and elsewhere in the writings of these years, that he is preparing the terminological, philosophical, and in part cultural-ideological "shift" toward the notion of "semiotics." See Eco's treatment of Saussure in *TS*, 14–15. In the chapter on "Semiotics in Italy," contained in the aformentioned *The Semiotic Sphere* (p. 302), Bettetini and Casetti write: "In *La struttura assente* (Milano: Bompiani, 1968), Eco breaks away from the extremisms of French structuralism (too biased by ontologism) and makes his way toward a theory of signification that will be further elaborated in [his] *Segno* (Milano: ISEDI, 1973) [henceforth cited as *S*], thus resorting to Peirce's neopragmaticism and Morris's behaviorism and aiming at the unification of the structuralist dimension and Anglo-Saxon philosophy of language, without however neglecting the European logicians."

7. See *S*, 18–19, where Eco cites a 1938 passage by Charles Morris [from Charles Morris, "Foundations of the Theory of Signs," in *Foundations of the Unity of Science*, 2 vols., eds. Otto Neurath, Rudolf Carnap, and Charles Morris (Chicago & London: University of Chicago Press, 1971), vol. 1, pp. 77–137] whereby semiotics will henceforth replace philosophical reflection (on itself and its own language), ultimately becoming a metamethodology; this will be taken up later in this article. See also Thomas A. Sebeok, *American Signatures; Semiotic Inquiry and Method* (Norman: University of Oklahoma Press, 1991), p. 152 ff.

8. Actually *TSG*, the Italian version which, by Eco's own account, was written *after* the English text, says the following: "la semiotica studia tutti i processi culturali come processi di comunicazione. E tuttavia ciascuno di tali processi . . . etc.": The "Therefore" [for "tuttavia"] has actually the sense of a "Yet" in the Italian, so one may conjecture a less causal and necessary relationship between processes of communication and systems of signification.

9. As we will see, Eco's conception of communication is often ambiguous, and will manifest some aporias. For an early critique, see Augusto Ponzio, *La semiotica in Italia*, pp. 41–49.

10. See Gianfranco Bettetini *Produzione del senso e messa in scena* (Milano: Bompiani, 1975), and Eco's own note in *TS*, 30; it is interesting to note that in the body of the text, early on in his exposition (pp. 9–10), Eco defines the "political boundaries of semiotics," in this way also "assigning" to the other dominant schools their own legitimized cultural-ideological working space.
11. Nowhere is this more dramatically demonstrated than in Sebeok's zoosemiotics. See "'Vital Signs' and 'Animal' in Biological and Semiotic Perspective," in Sebeok, *American Signatures*, pp. 107–32 and 159–73.
12. In the background we can clearly hear Peirce's texts, such as "Logic as Semiotic: The Theory of Signs," "Abduction and Induction," and "The General Theory of Probable Inference," which can now be read in *Philosophical Writings of Peirce*, ed. Justus Buchler (New York: Dover, 1955), pp. 98–119, 150–56, 190–217 respectively.
13. We must bear in mind the influence of his teacher Luigi Pareyson (1918–1991), which is everywhere present in the early Eco, at a time when he most willingly responded to the new theories on the horizon and seemed to "try them out" one by one as he focused ever more closely on questions of communication and signification; see, for example, Luigi Pareyson, *Apocalittici e integrati: comunicazioni di massa e teorie della cultura di massa* (Milano: Bompiani, 1964 & 1978), *La definizione dell'arte* (Milano: Mursia, 1968 [1955–63]), and *Opera aperta* (Milano: Bompiani, 1962 & 1972), which collect studies and essays on mass culture, aesthetic theory, and the poetics of the avant-garde respectively. The first essay in *Opera aperta*, "The Poetics of the Open Work" [from the American Edition, *The Open Work*, trans. A. Cancogni (Cambridge: Harvard University Press, 1989), henceforth cited as *OW*], takes up and develops notions fundamental to Luigi Pareyson's *Estetica, teoria della formatività* (Firenze: Sansoni, 1954 & 1960; now Milano: Bompiani, 1990). See also Eco's own essay on the theory of formation and the phenomenology of the work of art, corresponding to ch. 7 of *OW*, pp. 158–66. For a non-semiotic exposition of Pareyson's theory of interpretation, see Peter Carravetta, "An Introduction to the Hermeneutics of Luigi Pareyson," *Differentia, review of Italian thought*, 3:4 (Spring/Autumn 1989): 217–41.
14. Consider the attention given to "non-textual" or "cultural" referents and their possible "effects" not only on code formation and sign-production, but also on meaning-reception and strategies of decoding, in the later *Semiotics and the Philosophy of Language* (Bloomington: Indiana University Press, 1984), henceforth cited as *SPL*, and *The Limits of Interpretation* (Bloomington: Indiana University Press, 1990), henceforth cited as *LI*.

NOTES TO CHAPTER 1

15. But at this stage Eco has left Pareyson behind and is staking out his own territory, strong in the various schools of linguistics and the history of logic, but also subject to the metaphysical contradictions of the latter.
16. Many critics have remarked on how Eco's semiotics tends toward the all-encompassing, the totalizing, and therefore the imperialistic. See sample responses in Ganeri, *Il "Caso" Eco*.
17. See for instance *TS*, 4, where he explicitly mentions Aristotle's distinction between power and act, as parallel to his distinction between rules and process.
18. Let us recall that Eco's first book is on medieval aesthetics and logic, and that he was to return to these areas again and again, from the early *Il Problema estetica in Tommaso D'Aquino* (Milano: Bompiani, 1970 [1956]), to the later *Art and Beauty in the Middle Ages* (New Haven: Yale University Press, 1987), as well as in chapters in *SPL*.
19. See *TS*, 166–67; *SPL*, 19. Locke is also touted as the great forerunner (and maybe "grandfather") of Modern semiotics by John Deely and Thomas Sebeok in *Frontiers in Semiotics*, eds. John Deely, Brooke Williams, and Felicia Kruse (Bloomington: Indiana University Press, 1986), pp. 3–42. See also Sebeok, *American Signatures*, p. 151.
20. In Italy at least, work in this direction has been done by Carlo Sini, in *Semiotica e filosofia* (Bologna: Il Mulino, 1978), and *Passare il segno* (Milano: Il Saggiatore, 1981).
21. Charles Morris was practically first introduced in Italy by Ferruccio Rossi-Landi, with his book *Charles Morris* (Milano: Bocca, 1953 [repr. 1975]), and his translation, the following year, of Morris's *Foundations of a Theory of Signs* (Torino: Paravia 1954).
22. Recall that Morris was, together with Otto Neurath and Rudolf Carnap, one of the theoretical leaders behind the International Encyclopedia of Unified Science project of the mid-thirties to late-thirties. The original nineteen monographs (which include pathbreaking and influential papers by Bloomfield, Kuhn, and Dewey) have been gathered and reissued in a two-volume edition: *Foundations of the Unity of the Science* (Chicago: University of Chicago Press, 1971).
23. Eco's analysis of the KF model (and of all American linguistics), and particularly of the flexible and fruitful model Q (from Quillian's semantics) would require separate and detailed study. He returns to these in *Lector in Fabula* (Milano: Bompiani, 1983) and especially in the modified English version, *The Role of the Reader* (Bloomington: Indiana University Press, 1979), henceforth cited as *RR*. The Q model was to furnish the theoretical underpinnings of his later notion of encyclopedia; cf. *SPL*, 68 ff.
24. Peirce, *Collected Papers* (Cambridge: Harvard University Press, 1965), 2.300.

NOTES TO CHAPTER 1

25. See for instance the different though equally compelling positions of W. V. Quine, "The Inscrutability of Reference," in *Semantics*, eds. Danny Steinberg and Leon Jakobovits (Cambridge: Cambridge University Press, 1970), pp. 142–54, and Donald Davidson, "Reality without Reference," in *Reference, Truth and Reality*, ed. Mark Platts (London: Routledge and Kegan Paul, 1980), pp. 131–40.
26. Aspects and possibilities of this path have been explored by Hans Hörmann, *Meaning and Context; An Introduction to the Psychology of Language*, ed. Robert Innis (New York: Plenum Press, 1986), and by Giuseppe Minnini, *Psicosemiotica* (Bari: Adriatica, 1982).
27. See for instance L. Bloomfield, "Language or Ideas," in *The Philosophy of Linguistics*, ed. Jerrold Katz (Oxford: Oxford University Press, 1985), pp. 19–25: "Non-linguists (unless they happen to be physicalists) constantly forget that a speaker is making noise, and credit him, instead, with the possession of impalpable 'ideas.' It remains for linguists to show, in detail, that the speaker has no 'ideas,' and that the noise is sufficient—for the speaker's words act with trigger-like effect upon the nervous systems of his speech-fellows." See also, in the same anthology, the chapter by J. A. Fodor, "Some Notes On What Linguistics Is About," pp. 146–60.
28. I have dealt in part with the relationship between rhetorical structures of language and the methodological assumptions of scientific discourse in my forthcoming *Il fantasma di Hermes* (see note 5), of which an English version is in progress.
29. One might make the same emblematic claim in the parallel situation of Heidegger's *Being and Time*, which can conceivably represent the culmination of a particular way of doing philosophy, after which the recess or descent or decline of Modern metaphysical thought begins.
30. We must defer to another place and time a study of Eco's notion of the rhetorical, as well as of his own "creative" writing, the novels *The Name of the Rose*, *Foucault's Pendulum*, and *The Island of the Day Before*.
31. See especially "Semantics, Pragmatics, and Text Semiotics" in *LI*, 203–21.
32. See the reconstruction along this axis by John Deely, *Introducing Semiotics; Its History and Doctrine* (Bloomington: Indiana University Press, 1982), especially pp. 2–3.
33. In this direction, which points to juridical semiotics, see Roberta Kevelson, *Inlaws/Outlaws; A Semiotics of Systemic Interaction* (Bloomington: Indiana University Press, 1977).
34. But the tautology is not exploded, or explored, as we find for instance in Heidegger's analyses of the Aristotelian identity principle, or even more so with "things [that] thing," "space spaces," or "thinking

thinks," in some of the essays in *On the Way to Language*, trans. Peter Hertz (New York: Harper and Row, 1971) and *Poetry, Language, Thought*, trans. Albert Hofstadter (New York: Harper and Row, 1971).

35. Hermeneutics, also, "mentions" things, and is circular, as it can begin anywhere on the discursive chain (along the circumference of its "circle," so to speak), but the reference is rehabilitated through diverse modalities of being and existence, of diachronic language transmission, and though it does not exclude the rational-geometric dimension of systems and typologies, it is far from limiting itself to this ordering principle alone.

36. But these claims have been and continue to be challenged. For the sciences, see Paul Feyerabend, *Against Method* (London: NSB, 1975); for the relationship between scientific legitimation and power, see the different positions of Jean-François Lyotard and Michel Foucault. As for the question of scientific epistemology and gender, see *Feminism and Methodology*, ed. Sandra Harding (Bloomington: Indiana University Press, 1987; and *Beyond Methodology*, eds. Mary Fonow and Judith Cook (Bloomington: Indiana University Press, 1991).

37. This area has been studied most profitably by Ferruccio Rossi-Landi, beginning with his early *Significato, comunicazione e parlare comune* (Padova: Marsilio, 1961), and on through *Linguistics and Economics* (The Hague: Mouton, 1975) and *Language as Work & Trade* (South Hadley: Bergin & Garvey, 1983 [Italian edition 1968]). For a critical monograph on Rossi-Landi's entire career, see Augusto Ponzio, *Rossi-Landi e la filosofia del linguaggio* (Bari: Adriatica, 1988).

38. This was *de rigeur* in the late fifties and through the seventies in Italy. Idealism (with its connotations of immanentism, historicism, actualism, aristocratic liberalism, history as freedom, and so on) was the primary polemical target of such different books (and therefore of such different philosophies) as the already mentioned Luigi Pareyson's *Estetica* (1954) and *Verità e interpretazione* (1972); Luciano Anceschi's earlier *Autonomia ed eteronomia dell'arte* (1936, repr. 1976) and his *Da Bacone a Kant* (1972) as well as *Le poetiche del novecento in Italia* (1972); Galvano Della Volpe's *Critica del gusto* (1960, Eng. trans. 1976); Renato Barilli's *Per una estetica mondana* (1964); Enzo Paci's *La filosofia contemporanea* (1957 & 1974); and others. On Anceschi's phenomenological critique, see "Luciano Anceschi," in *Critical Survey of Literary Theory* (Pasadena: Salem Press, 1988), vol. I: 29–35.

39. During this period (early seventies), the question of the foundation of knowledge, and its necessary though always excluded reference to a "real" community, was being explored also by Aldo Gargani in his *Il sapere senza fondamenti* (Torino: Einaudi, 1972), whose position inci-

dentally was not far from that of Rorty just before his *Philosophy and the Mirror of Nature* came out.
40. See the slightly different explication in the Italian text (*TSG*, 319). Vico is given a more generous treatment in *SPL*, 107–08, where his thought is associated with a "cultural anthropology" which effaces the chronological or sequential development of cultures, focusing rather on their cyclical activity, in a sense creating a simultaneity of overlapping cultures, ergo of codes.
41. Vico also had said something to this effect, that each culture is evolved from a prior one, and naturally claims older or more prestigious ancestry vis-à-vis their neighbors or contemporaries; cf. *The New Science of Giambattista Vico* (Ithaca: Cornell University Press, 1985), ¶ 125, 126, 361, etc.
42. Peirce is once again invoked as the inspiring *auctoritas* behind this position, and we have explicit references to paragraphs 5.480, 5.287, 5.283, and 5.284 of his *Collected Papers*.
43. What an opportunity for a deconstructionist to attack the whole edifice of semiotics and efface its arbitrary, self-betraying stratagems, and the fictive, indeed "creative," nature behind, its rigorous conceptual apparatus!
44. This reveals an underlying immanentism, present also, though elaborated in quite different terms, in Lyotard's *Le Différend*: the mere instancing (or: coming into being, being "born") of a sentence necessarily displaces all others and negates another possible one which could not come into existence at the same time or place (or spacetime). But whereas Lyotard will develop this in view of the tensional dis/accord between their semantics and power ("phrases in dispute" is the subtitle of the English version), in Eco the appearance, the givenness of sentences are placed within an already existing signic network, adding to the possibilities of communication by its immediate status as the (new) *nth* element in the channels needed by the signifying chain to connect Sender to Receiver. In code semiotics, there cannot be a "dispute" because there are always alternative channels or routes for the message to get through. And if it fails, well, it didn't exist!
45. Eco refers explicitly to Ernst Cassirer's *Der Erkenntnisproblem in der Philosophie und Wissenschaft der neuren Zeit*. For the importance of neokantian philosophy to structuralism and, by extension, to code semiotics, see G. Puglisi, *Che cosa è lo strutturalismo* (Roma: Astrolabio, 1970).
46. See Morton White, "The Analytic and the Synthetic: An Untenable Dualism," in John Dewey, ed. S. Hook (New York: Dial Press, 1950). Also in L. Linsky, *Semantics and the Philosophy of Language* (Urbana: University of Illinois, 1952).

47. For all intents and purposes, these processes translate into "methodological" steps or subcategories or localized zones of inquiry, and their usefulness or "applicability" is undeniable. Eco's "readings" of contemporary cultural phenomena are rich and varied, and always illuminating. See his *Il Superuomo di massa* (Milano: Bompiani, 1978), as well as the already cited *Apocalittici e Integrati*, *Travels in Hyper Reality*, and *OW*.
48. See Roman Jakobson, "Linguistics and Poetics," in *The Structuralists From Marx to Lévi-Strauss*, eds. Richard and Fernande De George (Garden City: Doubleday, 1972). In the present context, Eco says, "we prefer to translate 'poetics' with 'aesthetics.' " This practical (but also: methodological) move is, like the one concerning Kant above, akin to the bringing of a particular set of problems and issues with their own language, history, and referents into the fold of semiotics, an effect of semiotic cooptation which assumes a perfect formal homology among different metalanguages.
49. Eco quite appropriately recalls Spitzer (*TS*, 263), but we could just as well include, in this lineage, Vico, Schleiermacher, Nietzsche, Dilthey, Timpanaro, Pasquali, Terracini, Menendez-Pidal, Benveniste, and even structuralists like Contini.
50. For Croce's early formulation, see his *Aesthetic*, trans. Douglas Ainslie (Boston: Nonpareil Books, 1983 [1901–02]), pp. 15–16 et infra.
51. It becomes ever more clear how the arts and sciences were traveling parallel routes, at least for the past century or so. And it is well known that Jakobson, Sklovskij, Eichenbaum, and Tynjanov frequented the various circles of the (mostly Russian) avant-garde of the post-WWII period. See Victor Erlich, *Russian Formalism* (L'Aja: Mouton, 1964); Tzvetan Todorov, *Théorie de la literature* (Paris: Seuil, 1965; Boris Tomasevskij, *Teoria della letteratura* (Milano: Feltrinelli, 1978); René Wellek and Austin Warren, *Theory of Literature* (New York: Harcourt, 1970 [1942]). We should recall that the Russian Formalists were primarily concerned with the aesthetics of *literary* communication; cf. Erlich, *Russian Formalisim*, chs. X and XV.
52. This critical movement is too well known and recorded to have it cross-referenced bibliographically. It has given us the crucial work of Lacan, Barthes, Derrida, Kristeva, Genette, and others. According to Gianni Vattimo, if we can elect one school of thought among many as the most representative of a given cultural period, we can say that marxism was the cultural *koinē* of the fifties and part of the sixties, structuralism (and deconstruction) the *koinē* of the late sixties and seventies, and hermeneutics that of the eighties; cf. his article, "Hermeneutics as *Koinē*," in *Theory, Culture & Society*, 5: 2–3 (1988), pp. 399–408.

53. See for example the above-mentioned Galvano Della Volpe, *Critique of Taste*.
54. The rhetoric here evokes a cluster of analogous concepts developed in Italy by transcendental phenomenology. See for instance the notions of "sistematica dei sistemi," and system as "idea limite" in the work by Antonio Banfi (1886–1957), and of his disciple Luciano Anceschi. Of course Eco early on distanced himself from this school of thought, as it represented another polemical target of his *Apocalittici e integrati* (1964); a critique of transcendentalism could still be found as late as 1984 in "The sign as identity" in *SPL*, 25.
55. When he found himself "on the other side of the barricade," that is, when he had written an aesthetic work himself, Eco plays upon this notion; cf. *PNR*, 1–2, 4 et infra.
56. See Eco's handling of epistemic triangles in *Segno* 22–27 and 124–26. For interesting developments of the idea that natural language itself is the "primary modelling system," see Sebeok, *American Signatures*, pp. 175–86. Of course both scholars are aware of and often cite the Whorf-Sapir hypothesis, but in reality very little is made of the overall philosophical and rhetorical implications of this understanding of "human" language.
57. There is of course a non-semiotic way of reading Eco's important article, "*Intentio Lectoris*: The State of the Art," (now a chapter in *LI*, 44–63), and that is, *ethically*, as well as broadly philosophically, in the sense that there is a *limit* to how much we can squeeze out of a text (or the interpretation of any phenomenon whatsoever). Moreover, the argument goes, if we cannot agree as to which is the better interpretation of two contending views, we ought to be able to agree as to what constitutes a totally *false* or *irrelevant* interpretation. This particular piece of Eco's was written partly in response to the interpretive free-for-all that was triggered by some overenthusiastic second-generation deconstructionists (or textualists), especially in North America, and partly to exemplify the difference between interpretation proper and the use of texts as instrumental proofs in something quite alien to the making of the text or event per se.
58. Temptations to see processes which "are the same" or at the very least formally homologous in different historical epochs begin with the affinity between Thomism and structuralism discovered early on in *The Aesthetics of Thomas Aquinas* [*Il Problema Estetico in Tommaso d'Aquino*, 243–64], and appear as late as *LI*, 20.
59. See for instance Paul J. Thibault, *Social Semiotics as Praxis* (Minneapolis: University of Minnesota Press, 1991), for a semiotics which responds to and integrates the thought of Bakhtin, Bateson, Gramsci, Foucault, Halliday, and Habermas.

NOTES TO CHAPTER 2

CHAPTER 2 CONSEQUENCES OF UNLIMITED SEMIOSIS: CARLO SINI'S METAPHYSICS OF THE SIGN AND SEMIOLOGICAL HERMENEUTICS

1. Carlo Sini, *La fenomenologia e la filosofia dell'esperienza. Ciclo di lezioni per l'Anno Accademico 1986–1987* (Milano: Edizioni Unicopli, 1987), pp. 225–26. Henceforth cited as *FF*.
2. "Where word breaks off no thing may be." Martin Heidegger, "The Nature of Language," in *On the Way to Language*, trans. Peter Hertz (New York: Harper and Row, 1982), p. 60. Henceforth cited as *NL*.
3. Martin Heidegger, "What Calls for Thinking?" *Basic Writings* (New York: Harper & Row, 1977), p. 351. Henceforth cited as *CT*.
4. Carlo Sini, *Passare il segno. Semiotica, cosmologia, tecnica* (Milano: Il Saggiatore, 1981), p. 34. Henceforth cited as *PS*.
5. *Rimando* is a key word in Sini's philosophy that has proved to be hard to translate. It conveys some subtleties that are lost in the English "reference." The verb *rimandare* means not only "to refer" but also "to remind," "to compel someone to think of something," "to hark back to something."
6. Charles Sanders Peirce, *Collected Papers* (Cambridge: Harvard University Press, 1965), 5.314.
7. Carlo Sini, *Introduzione alla fenomenologia come scienza* (Milano: Lampugnani Nigri, 1965); *La fenomenologia* (Milano: Garzanti, 1965); *Whitehead e la funzione della filosofia* (Padova, Marsilio, 1966). Of course, this interest in the relationship of phenomenology and science came from the problems raised by Husserl's last work, *The Crisis of the European Sciences*.
8. Carlo Sini, *Il pragmatismo americano* (Bari: Laterza, 1972).
9. Carlo Sini, *Semiotica e filosofia. Segno e linguaggio in Peirce, Nietzsche, Heidegger e Foucault* (Bologna: Il Mulino, 1978); *Passare il segno. Semiotica, cosmologia, tecnica* (Milano: Il Saggiatore, 1981); *Kinesis. Saggio di interpretazione* (Milano: Spirali, 1982); and *Immagini di verità. Dal segno al simbolo* (Milano: Spirali, 1985), [English translation by Massimo Verdiechio, *Images of Truth: From Sign to Symbol* (Atlantic Highlands, NJ: Humanities Press, 1993)].
10. Martin Heidegger, "Was heißt Denken?" *Vorträge und Aufsätze* (Pfullingen: Neske, 1954).
11. The analysis of this "exclusion procedure" reminds us of the pages devoted by Foucault to the dialectics of exclusion that created modern reason by excluding folly. In a certain way, one may say that Sini is radicalizing not only Peirce, but also Foucault. The difference is that Sini's method is more semiotical than genealogical, following Peirce's categorization of signs, whereas Foucault's method is to distinguish types of enunciation.

NOTES TO CHAPTER 3

12. "De-prived" and "private" in Italian are the same word: *privato*.
13. Carlo Sini, *Immagini di verita*, p. 140 (author's translation).
14. "Not everything that appears is phenomenon.... Instead, phenomenon is awareness that happens (*Fenomeno invece è il sapere che accade*)" (*FF*, 235). Sini admits that he is "aware of" the Hegelian implication of his statement.
15. Carlo Sini, *Il silenzio e la parola. Luoghi e confini del sapere per un uomo planetario* (Genova: Marietti, 1989); *I segni dell'anima. Saggio sull'immagine* (Bari: Laterza, 1989). The genealogical inquiry has been expanded in Sini's latest works: *Il simbolo e l'uomo* (Milan: Egea, 1991); *Il profondo e l'espressione. Filosofia, psichiatria e psicanalisi* (Milan: Lanfranchi, 1991); *Pensare il progetto* (Milan: Tranchida, 1992); *Filosofia teoretica* (Milan: Jaca Book, 1992); *Etica della scrittura* (Milan: Il Saggiatore, 1992), and *L'incanto del ritmo* (Milan: Tranchida, 1993).
16. Carlo Sini, *Metodo e filosofia. Ciclo di lezioni per l'Anno Accademico 1985–1986* (Milano: Edizioni Unicopli, 1986).
17. Martin Heidegger, "My Way in Phenomenology," *On Time and Being* (New York: Harper & Row, 1972), pp. 74–82.
18. Carlo Sini, "La fenomenologia e la questione del pensiero," *Filosofia '88*, ed. Gianni Vattimo (Bari: Laterza, 1989), pp. 99–123.
19. Carlo Sini, "Che ne è del passato?" *Il silenzio e la parola*, pp. 62–72. I have tried elsewhere to draw some further conclusions from the problems of past, memory, and recalling thinking (*Andenken*). See Alessandro Carrera, "What happened to Being? On Hermeneutics and Unlimited Semiosis in Carlo Sini and Gianni Vattimo," in *RLA: Romance Languages Annual, 1989*, eds. Ben Lawton, Anthony Tamburri (West Lafayette, Indiana: Purdue Research Foundation, 1990), pp. 94–97, and "Alternative alla storia. Un problema per il pensiero italiano contemporaneo," in *Annali d'Italianistica*, vol. 9, ed. Dino Cervigni (Italy: The Modern and the Postmodern, 1991), pp. 106–23.
20. Carlo Sini, *I segni dell'anima*, p. 140 (author's translation).
21. Martin Heidegger, "Logos (Heraklit, Fragment B 50)," in *Early Greek Thinking* (New York: Harper and Row, 1975).
22. *Etica della scrittura*, Sini's most ambitious recent work, addresses precisely the issue of philosophical ethics, that is, the philosopher's awareness of the "threshold of writing" he or she chooses to inhabit.

CHAPTER 3   LACAN AND THE EVENT OF THE SUBJECT

1. See Jacques Derrida's remarks in "The Purveyor of Truth," or in "Positions" (Jacques Derrida, *Positions*, trans. Alan Bass [Chicago: Chicago University Press, 1981], in particular, note 44, pp. 107–13). More recently, Derrida still writes: "Did Lacan 'liquidate' the subject?

No. The decentered 'subject' of which he speaks certainly doesn't have the traits of the classical subject (though even here, we'd have to take a closer look . . .), though it remains indispensable to the economy of the Lacanian theory." " 'Eating Well,' or the Calculation of the Subject," in *Who Comes after the Subject?* eds. Eduardo Cadava, Peter Connor, Jean-Luc Nancy (New York and London: Routledge, 1991), p. 97. Along the same lines, we could add Philippe Lacoue-Labarthe and Jean-Luc Nancy, *The Title of the Letter: a Reading of Lacan*, trans. François Raffoul and David Pettigrew (Albany: State University of New York Press, 1992). Henceforth cited as *TL*. For an investigation into the complex relations of Lacan to philosophy, we refer the reader to the excellent study of Mikhel Borch-Jacobsen, *Lacan: The Absolute Master* (Stanford: Stanford University Press, 1991) and *Interpreting Lacan*, vol. 6, eds. J. Smith and W. Kerrigan (New Haven: Yale University Press, 1983). Henceforth cited as *IL*. See also William J. Richardson, "Lacan and Non-Philosophy," in *Philosophy and Non-philosophy since Merleau-Ponty (Continental Philosophy I)*, ed. Hugh J. Silverman (New York and London: Routledge, 1988). Henceforth cited as *LNP*.
2. Jacques Lacan, *Le Séminaire, Livre XI, Les quatre concepts fondamentaux de la psychanalyse* (Paris: Editions du Seuil, 1973); *Four Fundamental Concepts of Psychoanalysis*, trans. Alan Sheridan (New York: W. W. Norton & Co., 1978), pp. 73/77 (my emphasis). Henceforth cited as *FFCP* (where the first reference is to the pagination in the French text, followed by the English edition).
3. Jacques Lacan, "Sur la théorie du symbolisme d'Ernest Jones," *Écrits* (Paris: Editions du Seuil, 1966), p. 709. Henceforth cited as *E*. When appropriate, the French reference will be followed by the pagination from the English translation: *Ecrits: A Selection*, trans. Alan Sheridan (New York: W. W. Norton & Co., 1977).
4. *Séminaire XX, Encore*, (Paris: Seuil, 1975), p. 34 (my emphasis). Henceforth cited as *Encore*.
5. Lacan writes, "In my own vocabulary, on the other hand, I symbolize the subject by the barred S ($), in so far as it is constituted as secondary in relation to the signifier" (*FFCP*, 129/141).
6. As William Richardson, for example, suggests: "When all is said and done, what is at stake is the hermeneutic circle itself. And there is Lacan, *bon gré mal gré*, right in the middle of it" (*LNP*, 135).
7. As Lacoue-Labarthe and Nancy note, "The locus of the Lacanian signifier is nevertheless the subject. Fundamentally . . . it is in a *theory of the subject* that the logic of the signifier settles" (*TL*, 65).
8. For Lacan, there is no other possible definition of the signifier. In "Subversion of the Subject and Dialectic of Desire," he goes as far as

NOTES TO CHAPTER 3

to claim: "My definition of the signifier (*there is no other*) is as follows: a signifier is that which represents the subject for another signifier" (*E*, 819/316, my emphasis).

9. *FFCP*, 185/203, my emphasis, translation modified from Sheridan.
10. Lacan insists that "if the subject is what I say it is," then the subject is determined by language and speech (*FFCP*, 180/198).
11. William Richardson, "Lacan and the Subject of Psychoanalysis" (*IL*, 54).
12. Antoine Vergote, "From Freud's 'Other Scene' to Lacan's 'Other'" (*IL*, 195, my emphasis).
13. Lacan explains that "one should see in the unconscious the effects of speech on the subject . . ." (*FFCP*, 115/126).
14. *Lettres de l'Ecole freudienne*, 1, p. 45, quoted by Moustapha Safouan in *Qu'est-ce que le structuralisme?* (Paris: Seuil, 1968), pp. 252–53. Henceforth cited as *QS*.
15. In Anika Rifflet-Lemaire, *Jacques Lacan* (Bruxelles: Charles Dessart, 1970), p. 18.
16. In *La science et la vérité*, Lacan emphasizes the "literal characteristic" of the signifier in its causal relation to the signifier, one which Lacan specifies as "*material* cause" (*E*, 875, my emphasis).
17. As Kerrigan would have us believe: "If Lacan would prefer to say not that the unconscious lives us, but that the unconscious speaks us, the implications remain the same—*an unbending determinism and a systematic inversion of Cartesian themes, such that the subject becomes effect rather than cause, structured rather than structuring, and doubtful in its certainty rather than certain of its doubtfulness*" (*IL*, xvii, my emphasis).
18. He writes in "Sur la théorie du symbolisme d'Ernest Jones": "The unconscious as such comes to be articulated in this duplication of the subject of speech" (*E*, 711).
19. *XI*, 181/199, translation modified. Also: *Position de l'inconscient* (*E*, 840).
20. Lacan writes: "It is the subject who is called—there is only he, therefore, who can be chosen" (*FFCP*, 47/47). We note here again the privilege granted to the subject, the "called one," confirming what we had alluded to in our introduction as the subjective horizon of the Lacanian theory.
21. That impossible coincidence of the subject to itself is illustrated in Lacan's treatment of the so-called liar's paradox. (A paradox that one could schematically present as follows: Given the statement, "I lie." If I lie, then I am not lying, and so I speak the truth; or, if I speak the truth, then I am lying, etc.) According to Lacan this paradox rests on a logic which ignores the division of the speaking subject between a level of enunciation and a level of statement, for, as Moustapha

Safouan explains in a recent work: "There is in fact only a paradox in regard to an 'excessively formal' logic, formal in the sense that it abstracts not from the matter of the reasoning, but rather from the division of the subject between a process of statement and a process of enunciation" (Moustapha Safouan, *Le Transfert et le désir de l'analyste* [Paris: Seuil, 1988], p. 203. Henceforth cited as *TD*).

22. And it *must* refer to another signifier, for, as Lacan explains, "in the absence of this signifier, all the other signifiers represent nothing, since nothing is represented only *for* something else" (*E*, 819/316).

23. Manfred Frank writes, in a rather polemical way: ". . . Lacan succeeds at the trick of making us believe that the actual place of the subject (*Sujet*) is precisely where we would least expect it: in the id, in the unconscious" (Manfred Frank, *What is Neostructuralism?* trans. Sabine Wilke and Richard Gray (Minneapolis: University of Minnesota Press, 1989), p. 293. Henceforth cited as *NS*.

24. This paradox is noted by Serge Cottet in his essay *"Je pense où je ne suis pas, je suis où je ne pense pas,"* in *Lacan* (Paris: Bordas, 1987), p. 13.

25. Jacques Lacan, in *Cahiers pour l'analyse* (Paris: Seuil, 3, Mai-Juin 1966), p. 5.

26. Jacques Lacan, *Le Séminaire, Livre II, Le moi dans la théorie de Freud et dans la technique de la psychanalyse* (Paris: Seuil, 1978); *The Ego in Freud's Theory and in the Technique of Psychoanalysis*, trans. Sylvana Tomaselli (New York: W. W. Norton and Co., 1988), p. 200/167, translation modified. Henceforth cited as *Ego*.

27. Lacan writes, borrowing an expression from Freud (*der Kern unseres Wesen*): "The core of our being does not coincide with the ego" (*Ego*, 59/44), indicating thereby that the hierarchy is also distributed in terms of essence, and accident or contingence, as this other passage indicates: ". . . the ego is the sum of the identifications of the subject, with all that implies as to its radical *contingency*" (*Ego*, 187/155, my emphasis).

28. "Literally the ego is an object" (*Ego*, 60).

29. Serge Leclaire, *Démasquer le réel* (Paris: Seuil, 1971), p. 67. Henceforth cited as *DR*. The author continues by specifying the link between the unconscious and the literal order: "I will now make my thought more precise by noting that the letters and their system constitute in themselves what I have called a place, *namely the unconscious*" (*DR*, 67, my emphasis).

30. Lacan writes: "But the synchronic structure is more hidden, and *it is this structure that takes us to the source, namely metaphor in so far as the first attribution is constituted in it*—the attribution that promulgates 'the dog goes "miaow," the cat goes "woof-woof",' by which the child, by disconnecting the animal from its cry, suddenly raises the

sign to the function of the signifier . . ." (*E*, 805/303, my emphasis, translation slightly modified).
31. Borch-Jacobsen explains, for instance, that "the celebrated division of the subject still remains a division *within* the subject. . . . In consideration of this, the identity of the subject itself remains not questioned in its provenance and essence" (Mikhel Borch-Jacobsen, "Impropriétés de l'inconscient," *L'Artichaut, L'Artichaut and Editions du Miroir*, January 1986, p. 51). The author (in reference to Heidegger's inquiry into the being of the *sum*) continues by stressing that the thematic of a split of the subject does not pose the question of the identity of the subject or of its non-subjective *being*. He also writes in another text: "How can one fail to see that this constant presupposition of a subject-of-the-unconscious or an unconscious-subject immediately shuts off any question on the *being*—the *non-subjective* being—of such a 'subject.' " "Ceci n'est pas une thèse," in *Exercices de la patience* (Paris: Obsidiane, 5, Spring 1983), p. 75.
32. Frank writes for instance, "We saw that Lacan, as opposed to his allegedly more radical successors, is not prepared to sacrifice the concept of 'the subject' in his theory. On the contrary, we would not be exaggerating if we said that the problem of the truth of the subject constitutes the nucleus of his deliberations. . . . [T]he fact that the I (*moi*) fails in its attempt to found itself in the 'dual relation of ego to ego' is, for Lacan, not reason enough for henceforth giving up the notion of subjectivity" (*NS*, 309).
33. William Richardson speaks of the "philosophical darkness that abounds in the presuppositions of Lacan's own discourse" (*LNP*, 135).
34. Frank rightly claims this on page 290 in *NS*. He continues by explaining that the symbolic order is to be understood "in the sense of a texture in whose web the subject has disappeared as subject, only to resurface *ex negativo* as the meaning of the signifiers and as meaning by reason of the signifiers" (*NS*, 305). This meaning then becomes the promised truth of a subjectivity alienated in language.
35. On the proximity between Lacan and Sartre, one that is not stressed too often, see Borch-Jacobsen's claim: "Like the ungraspable Sartrean 'for-itself'—with which, in many ways, this subject [the Lacanian subject] is comparable—he is not what he *is* (the 'signifier,' or the statement that claims to fix him in his being 'in-himself'), and he is what he is *not* (a perpetual nihilation, a perpetual overtaking of the signifiers/statements that objectify him.)" (Mikhel Borch-Jacobsen, *Lacan: The Absolute Master*, pp. 190–91). The author then concludes with this striking formula: "Lacanism is an existentialism. . . ." On Lacan's "existentialism," see Philippe van Haute's suggestive article:

"Psychanalyse et existentialisme: A propos de la théorie lacanienne de la subjectivité," in *Man and World*, 23:4 (October 1990), pp. 453–72.
36. The authors—commenting on Lacan's famous saying, "I am not wherever I am the plaything of my thought; I think of what I am where I do not think to think" (*E*, 517–8/166)—also write: "One sees that these formulas are indeed statements that displace or dislodge the subject, but which nevertheless are enunciations of an I, through which this I conserves the mastery of a certainty which, in spite of its contents, yields nothing to that of the 'I think'" (*TL*, 120–21). In the same perspective: *NS*, 304–5.
37. For example, in his *Séminaire IX* on Identification (seminar of May 5, 1962), Lacan explains: "The emergence (*naissance*) of the subject is such that it can only be conceived as *excluded* from the signifier."
38. J. David Nasio, *Les yeux de Laure: le concept d'objet a dans la théorie de Jacques Lacan* (Paris: Aubier, 1987), p. 70. Henceforth cited as *YL*.
39. Serge Leclaire, for example, speaks of the "impossible-articulation which reveals the insurmountable break between the amorphic heterogeneity of the lack and the literal order which indefinitely attempts to grasp it" (*DR*, 97) or, also, of the "ungraspable and irreducible reality of this lack." In short, "the letter has no hold on . . . the lack" (*DR*, 96).
40. For example, Lacan explains how the subject "alternately reveals and conceals itself through the pulsation of the unconscious . . ." (*FFCP*, 172/188); or: "I have constantly stressed in my preceding statements the *pulsating* function, as it were, of the unconscious, the need to disappear that seems to be in some sense inherent in it" (*FFCP*, 44/43, my emphasis, translation slightly modified).
41. Lacan concludes in the following way: "Where is the background (*fond*)? Is it absence? No. Rupture, split, the stroke of the opening makes absence emerge—just as the cry does not stand out against a background of silence, but on the contrary makes the silence emerge as silence (*FFCP*, 28/26, translation modified).

CHAPTER 4   TRACING THE SIGNIFIER BEHIND
THE SCENES OF DESIRE:
KRISTEVA'S CHALLENGE TO LACAN'S ANALYSIS

1. Julia Kristeva, *La Révolution du langage poétique* (Paris: Seuil, 1974); *Revolution in Poetic Language*, trans. Margaret Waller (New York: Columbia University Press, 1984). Henceforth cited as *RP*.

Julia Kristeva, *Pouvoirs de l'horreur* (Paris: Édition du Seuil, 1980); *Powers of Horror*, trans. Leon Roudiez (New York: Columbia University Press, 1982). Henceforth cited as *PH*.

NOTES TO CHAPTER 4

Julia Kristeva, *Histoires d'amour* (Paris: Editions Denöel, 1983); *Tales of Love*, trans. Leon Roudiez (New York: Columbia University Press, 1987). Henceforth cited as *TL*.

Julia Kristeva, *Au commencement était l'amour*; *In the Beginning Was Love: Psychoanalysis and Faith*, trans. Arthur Goldhammer (New York: Columbia University Press, 1988). Henceforth cited as *BL*.

Julia Kristeva, *Soleil Noir: Depression et Melancolie* (Paris: Gallimard, 1987); *Black Sun*, trans. Leon Roudiez (New York: Columbia University Press, 1989). Henceforth cited as *BS*.

Julia Kristeva, *Étrangers à nous-même* (Paris: Fayard, 1989); *Strangers to Ourselves*, trans. Leon Roudiez (New York: Columbia University Press, 1991). Henceforth cited as *SO*.

Julia Kristeva, *Lettre ouverte à Harlem Désir* (Paris: Éditions Rivages, 1990). Henceforth cited as *LO*.

2. The semiotic element within the signifying process is the drives as they discharge within language. This drive discharge is associated with rhythm and tone. Since these sounds and rhythms are primarily associated with the sounds and rhythms of the maternal body, the semiotic element of language is also associated with the maternal. The semiotic is the subterranean element of "meaning" within signification which does not signify. It has "meaning" without referring; rather than referring to the drives, it points to the drive processes.

The symbolic, on the other hand, is the element of meaning within signification which does signify. The symbolic operates through a chain of signifiers which refer to each other. The symbolic is associated with syntax or grammar and the ability to take a position or make a judgment which syntax engenders. The threshold of the symbolic is what Kristeva calls the "thetic phase," which emerges out of Lacan's mirror stage.

These two elements, semiotic and symbolic, operate in an ongoing dialectic. The semiotic gives rise to, and challenges, the symbolic. Without the symbolic we have only delirium or nature, while without the semiotic, language would be completely empty, if not impossible. We would have no reason to speak if it were not for semiotic drive force. So the dialectic oscillation between the semiotic and symbolic is productive and necessary. This oscillation is the movement between rejection and stasis, separation and recuperation, negation and identification.

3. Julia Kristeva, "Place Names," in *Desire in Language*, trans. Thomas Gora, Alice Jardine, and Leon Roudiez, ed. Leon Roudiez (New York: Columbia University Press, 1977), p. 276. Henceforth cited as *PN*.

4. Jacques Lacan, *The Seminar of Jacques Lacan, The Ego in Freud's Theory and in the Technique of Psychoanalysis, 1954–55*, Book II, trans. Sylvana

Tomaselli (Cambridge: Cambridge University Press, 1988), p. 166. Henceforth cited as SII. Also *Écrits: A Selection*, trans. Alan Sheridan (New York: Norton, 1977), pp. 1–7. Henceforth cited as *E*.
5. Julia Kristeva, "How Does One Speak to Literature," in *Desire and Language*, p. 97. Henceforth cited as *SL*.
6. For an account of negation, see my *Reading Kristeva: Unraveling the Double-bind:* (Bloomington: Indiana University Press, 1993).
7. "Julia Kristeva in Conversation with Rosalind Coward," *Desire* (London: ICA Document, 1984), p. 22. Henceforth cited as *RC*.
8. Freud first identifies "narcissism as a homosexual object-choice through which a man loves another man, who resembles him, in the way in which his mother loved him." Sigmund Freud, "A Special Type of Object Choice made by Men," in *The Standard Edition of the Complete Psychological Words of Sigmund Freud,* trans. James Strachey (London: The Hogarth Press, 1953–1974), vol. 11, 1910. Henceforth cited as *SE*. Freud next describes narcissism as a stage in an infant's development which comes between autoeroticism and object-love. In this stage, the infant cathects himself as a whole. This stage is correlative to the onset of the ego. "Contributions to the Psychology of Love," *SE*, 11, 1911; "A Note on the Unconscious in Psycho-analysis," *SE*, 12, 1912. Later Freud argues that narcissism is related to ego cathexis and is inversely proportional to object-cathexis. "On Narcissism," *SE*, 14, 1914. Freud suggests here that narcissism is not just a stage through which the infant passes. Rather, at this point, Freud sees narcissism as an ongoing structure of the ego. This is the hypothesis that Kristeva takes up.

In the end Freud posits two types of narcissism: primary and secondary. Primary narcissism is an objectless stage in which the infant comprises all of its universe. Secondary narcissism, on the other hand, is a withdrawal of the ego from the world of objects even after the ego has been constituted and has taken love objects. While primary narcissism is a developmental stage, secondary narcissism is an "abnormal" regression to this pre-objectal stage. "Group Psychology and the Analysis of the Ego," *SE*, 18, 1921; "The Ego and the Id," *SE*, 19, 1923.
9. Kristeva argues that the negativity necessary in order to initiate human subjectivity is operating at the level of material negativity. As she describes it, eventually bodily excess gives way to a thetic break into the Symbolic. Bodily patterns are taken over within the Symbolic. Bodily rejection can become symbolic rejection because maternal regulation organizes the psyche before the mirror stage and the oedipal situation. Maternal regulation prefigures the paternal prohibition that finally launches the subject into signification through the

oedipal situation. For Kristeva, bodily drive force already includes the logic and prohibition of the Symbolic—the logic of material rejection—and that bodily drive force is never completely repressed within signification. For a more detailed account of negativity, the logic of rejection, and the death drive, see my *Unraveling the Doublebind*.

10. I have slightly modified Roudiez's translation in this quotation. I think that Kristeva's reading of Lacan is problematic here. Lacan suggests a dialectic between the symbolic and imaginary rather than the substitution of one for the other. But, at this time I will not attempt to develop this intuition.
11. Jacques Lacan, *The Seminar of Jacques Lacan, Freud's Papers on Technique, 1953–54*, Book I, trans. John Forrester (Cambridge: Cambridge University Press, 1988), p. 174. Henceforth cited as *SI*.
12. Lacan says that the child wants *to be* the mother's Phallus: "the child, in his relation to the mother . . . by his dependence on her love, that is to say, by the desire for her desire, identifies himself with the imaginary object of this desire in so far as the mother herself symbolizes it in the Phallus" (*E*, 198). For Lacan, the Phallus is a signifier. (See Jacques Lacan, *Feminine Sexuality*, trans. and ed. J Mitchell and J. Rose [London: Macmillan, 1982], p. 79.) The father becomes a concrete representation of the Phallus in the oedipal situation. The Name-of-the-Father is what keeps the child from the mother. The name, the symbol, breaks the unmediated dyad between mother and child. Lacan suggests that the rupture of this dyad is necessary so that society can continue; this intimate bond in which two are one is antisocial. The father intervenes, in the place of the Phallus, to break it up. This function—another central element of Lacan's "paternal metaphor"—is the Law of the Father.
13. "Imagination in Psychoanalysis," a lecture given by Julia Kristeva at Ohio State University, October 1988.
14. I. Lipkowitz and A. Loselle, "An Interview with Julia Kristeva," *Critical Texts* 3:3 (1986). Henceforth cited as *LL*.
15. "With the Microcosm of the *Talking Cure*," trans. T. Gora and M. Waller, in ed. Smith, *Psychiatry and the Humanities*, vol. 6 (New Haven: Yale University Press, 1983), p. 35. Henceforth cited as *TC*.
16. For example, Kristeva criticizes Lacan for presupposing an always already there of language in *RP*, 130–31 and *TL*, 44.
17. For an extended version of this argument, see my "Kristeva's Imaginary Father and the Crisis in the Paternal Function," (July 1991).
18. I have altered the parenthesis in the Roudiez translation. See *Histoires d'amour*, p. 27.

CHAPTER 5 ELIMINATING THE DISTANCE: FROM BARTHES' ECRITURE-LECTURE TO ECRITURE-VUE

1. Roland Barthes, "Is Painting a Language?" in *The Responsibility of Forms*, trans. and ed. Richard Howard (Berkeley and Los Angeles: University of California Press, 1985), p. 152.
2. Mieke Bal and Norman Bryson, "Semiotics and Art History," *Art Bulletin* LXXIII, June 1991, pp. 174–208. Henceforth cited as *SAH*.
3. See Bryson's introduction to *Calligram: Essays in New Art History from France* (Cambridge: Cambridge University Press, 1988). Hereafter, *Calligram*.
4. "Traditional art history" is, admittedly, a sweeping term and requires clarification. I assert that methodologies seeking to produce an interpretation from a singular analytic stance are guilty of robbing the work of its discursive independence. Stylistic, iconographic, and formalist approaches certainly fall under this heading; even Marxist, feminist, and psychoanalytic methods, formerly the critical black sheep of the field, can be implicated here.
5. The phrase is Bal and Bryson's, *SAH*, p. 207. Bryson also discusses the notion of cultural baggage in the *Calligram* introduction: "When people look at representational painting and recognize what they see, their recognition does not unfold in the solitary recess of the sensorium, but through the activation of codes or recognition that are learnt by interaction with others, in the acquisition of human culture" (xxi).
6. Louis Marin, *Études sémiologiques* (Paris: Klmcksieck, 1971), p. 24, as quoted in *Handbook of Semiotics*, trans. and rev. ed. Winfried Nöth (Bloomington and Indianapolis: Indiana University Press, 1988), p. 458.
7. Kate Bush, "The Sensual World," from the album *The Sensual World*, Kate Bush Music Ltd, 1989.
8. Barthes, *Pleasure of the Text* (New York: Noonday Press, 1975), trans. Richard Miller, p. 6.
9. Barthes, *The Grain of the Voice: Interviews 1962–1980*, trans. Linda Coverdale (New York: Hill and Wang, 1985), p. 63. Hereafter, *Grain*.
10. Richard Howard, preface to Barthes' *S/Z*, trans. Richard Miller (New York: Noonday Press, 1974), x. Henceforth cited as *S/Z*.
11. I coin this phrase to suggest that the application of codes to a painting becomes a "writing-looking," or the act of producing a discourse about how we look at the painting. The English translation of *vue* is full of nuances evoking the act of looking sensitively: *sight, view, sur-*

vey, insight. The word *lecture* is in fact implicit in the *écriture-vue* construct, as it is understood that "looking" at a painting includes "reading" its meaning(s).
12. For an alternate view of the intersection of iconography and Barthes' codes, see *SAH*, p. 203.
13. *Classic* and *modern* must not be mistaken here for the terms conventionally used by art historians to designate certain style periods. There is not an automatic connection, for example, between Barthes' classic text and "classical" art as represented by antiquity. Similarly, his modern text should not be assumed to belong chronologically to art history's "modernist" era, or necessarily to share its characteristics.
14. So as not to disrupt the flow of the commentary with the interruption of citations, I will collectively acknowledge the sources from which I drew in this portion of the essay:
    (a) *Renaissance literature and philosophy, botany:*
    Mirella Levi d'Ancono, *Botticelli's Primavera* (Firenze: Leo S. Olschki Editori, 1983);
    (b) *Medici history:*
    Umberto Baldini, *Primavera: the Restoration of a Masterpiece* (New York: Harry N. Abrams, Inc., 1989);
    (c) *Mythology:*
    Arthur Cotterell, *A Dictionary of World Mythology* (Oxford and Melbourne: Oxford University Press, 1986);
    (d) *Iconography:*
    James Hall, *Dictionary of Subjects and Symbols in Art*, rev. ed. (New York: Harper and Row, 1979).
15. The epigraphs in this portion of the essay are extracted from Balzac's *Sarrasine*, as translated and reprinted in *S/Z*.

CHAPTER 6   THE END(S) OF PICTORIAL REPRESENTATION: MERLEAU-PONTY AND LYOTARD

1. The best known works on the psychology of art are Rudolph Arnheim's numerous books and papers, particularly his *Art and Visual Perception* (Berkeley: University of California Press, 1954) and *Toward a Psychology of Art* (Berkeley: University of California Press, 1966). Other authors who have also made major contributions are Gyorgy Kepes, Wolfgang Köhler, and E. H. Gombrich.
2. See Ludwig Wittgenstein (his various writings on aesthetics, collected in a number of editions), Nelson Goodman in *Languages of Art* (Indianapolis: Bobbs-Merrill, 1968; second edition, 1976), and Monroe Beardsley in *Aesthetics from Classical Greece to the Present* (New York: 1966).

3. Maurice Merleau-Ponty, "Eye and Mind," in *The Primacy of Perception* (Evanston: Northwestern University Press, 1964), p. 160. Henceforth cited as *EM*.
4. Merleau-Ponty, "Cézanne's Doubt," in *Sense and Nonsense* (Evanston: Northwestern University Press, 1964), pp. 13–14. Henceforth cited as *CD*.
5. Merleau-Ponty's influence is evident throughout *Discours, figure* (Paris: Editions Klincksieck, 1971). See, for instance, the section entitled "Le Parti pris du figural."
6. Jean-François Lyotard, *Discours, figure*, p. 21.
7. cf. Paul Klee in *Das Bildnerische Denken* and *Pädagogisches Skizzenbuch*.
8. Jean-François Lyotard, "The Connivances of Desire with the Figural," in *Driftworks* (New York: Semiotext(e), 1984), p. 57. Henceforth cited as *Driftworks*.

CHAPTER 7 LACAN'S HAMLET: MOURNING, WOMAN, AND THE PHALLUS: LACAN'S *HAMLET*

1. For a fuller discussion of this issue, see, Debra B. Bergoffen, "Sophocles' *Antigone* and Freud's *Civilization and Its Discontents*," *American Imago*, 43:2 (1986), pp. 151–167.
2. Rebecca Smith, "A Heart Cleft in Twain. The Dilemma of Shakespeare's Gertrude," *The Woman's Part: Feminist Criticism of Shakespeare*, eds. Carolyn Swift Lenz, Gayle Greene, and Carole Neely (Urbana: University of Illinois Press, 1980), pp. 199, 207.
3. Baldwin Maxwell, "Hamlet's Mother," *Shakespeare Quarterly*, 25 (1964), p. 236. Henceforth cited as *HM*.
4. Kay Stockholder, "Sex and Authority in Hamlet, King Lear and Pericles," *Mosaic*, 18:3 (1985), p. 20.
5. Dianne Elizabeth Dreher, *Domination and Defiance: Fathers and Daughters in Shakespeare* (Lexington: University Press of Kentucky, 1986), p. 78.

CHAPTER 8 A METAPHOR OF THE UNSPOKEN: KRISTEVA'S SEMIOTIC *CHORA*

1. Jacques Derrida, "Structure, Sign and Play," in *Writing and Difference*, trans. Alan Bass (Chicago: University of Chicago Press, 1978), pp. 231–32, 245. Henceforth cited as *SSP*.
2. Michel Foucault, "Questions on Geography," in *Power/Knowledge: Selected Interviews and Other Writings, 1972–1977*, ed. C. Gordon (New York: Pantheon, 1980), p. 69.

3. Jacques Lacan, "The Mirror Stage," in *Ecrits*, trans. A. Sheridan (New York: W. W. Norton, 1977), p. 4.
4. Elaine Showalter, "Feminist Criticism in the Wilderness," in *Writing and Sexual Difference* (Chicago: University of Chicago Press, 1982), pp. 262–63.
5. Julia Kristeva, "Women's Time," in *The Kristeva Reader*, ed. Toril Moi (New York: Columbia University Press, 1986), p. 191. Henceforth cited as *WT*.
6. Michel Foucault, "The Eye of Power," in *Power/Knowledge*, p. 149. Henceforth cited as *EP*.
7. As seen in the opening quote, Foucault's investment in space as a philosophical metaphor is great. Thus, his subsequent assault upon this banishment of it from philosophy: "I remember ten years or so ago discussing these problems of the politics of space, and being told that it was reactionary to go on so much about space, and that time and the 'project' were what life and progress are about. I should say that this reproach came from a psychologist—psychology, the truth and shame of nineteenth-century philosophy" (*EP*, 150).
8. Alice Jardine, *Gynesis* (Ithaca: Cornell University Press, 1985), p. 25.
9. Sigmund Freud, "The 'Uncanny,'" p. 245.
10. Recognize here the time/space dichotomy seen earlier in Foucault's characterization of the history of philosophy. Note how Foucault, in his own appropriation of the "feminine" side of this binary pair is, just as Jardine suggests, incorporating the other-than-myself into the master narrative.
11. Julia Kristeva, "About Chinese Women," in *The Kristeva Reader*, p. 191. Henceforth cited as *ACW*.
12. "The child: sole evidence, for the symbolic order, of *jouissance* and pregnancy, thanks to whom the woman will be coded in the chain of production and thus perceived as a temporalized parent" (*ACW*, 154).
13. See Julia Kristeva, "Motherhood According to Bellini," in *Desire in Language: A Semiotic Approach to Literature and Art*, trans T. Gora, A. Jardine, and L. Roudiez (New York: Columbia University Press, 1980), p. 238.
14. Kristeva, "Stabat Mater," in *The Kristeva Reader*, p. 174. Henceforth cited as *SM*.
15. Some changes in spacing were necessary to reconstruct the text here.
16. Kristeva, "Revolution in Poetic Language," in *The Kristeva Reader*, p. 92. Henceforth cited as *RPL*.
17. Plato, "Timaeus," in *Timaeus and Critias*, trans. D. Lee (New York: Penguin Books, 1965), p. 67. Henceforth cited as *T*.
18. Kristeva, "Place Names," in *Desire in Language*, p. 284.

19. Perhaps, as we shall see later, and as we saw in the Kronos myth, the child is still desiring some sort of reunion with her.
20. Richard Kearney, *Poetics of Imagining* (London: Harper Collins, 1991), p. 194.
21. Catherine Marchak, "The Joy of Transgression: Bataille and Kristeva," *Philosophy Today* (Winter 1990), p. 357. Henceforth cited as *JT*.
22. Judith Butler, "The Body Politics of Julia Kristeva," in *Gender Trouble* (New York: Routledge, 1990), p. 82. Henceforth cited as *BPJK*.
23. Marchak, *JT*, p. 358. See also Kristeva, *RPL*, p. 119.
24. See Moi's introduction in *The Kristeva Reader*. This will have major implications when we try to assess the extent of Kristeva's "feminism."
25. Simone deBeauvoir, *The Second Sex*, trans. H. Parshley (New York: Random House, Inc., 1989), p. xxiv.
26. Friedrich Nietzsche, *Thus Spoke Zarathustra*, trans. W. Kaufmann (New York: Penguin Books, 1966), p. 66.
27. Butler asserts that Kristeva has allowed the semiotic to transgress the symbolic at times, while keeping this female mode of signification always subject to the "paternal law." Secondly, she claims that Kristeva's talk of the semiotic and its transgressions through poetic language (for man) and childbirth (for women) serves only to reify motherhood. Thirdly, her conception of female heterosexuality as the impetus toward reproduction, becoming a mother oneself, implies that lesbian sexuality is an incomplete or neurotic expression of this "natural" tendency. See Butler, *BPJK*.
28. Nancy Fraser, "The Uses and Abuses of French Discourse Theories for Feminist Politics," *Boundary*, 2 (Summer 1990), p. 100.

CHAPTER 9 THE SIGN OF THE ROSE: FILMING ECO

1. Umberto Eco, *A Theory of Semiotics* (Bloomington: Indiana University Press, 1976), p. 49.
2. *American Film*, p. 26.
3. See Umberto Eco, "Narrative Structures in Fleming," in *The Role of the Reader* (Bloomington: Indiana University Press, 1979), pp. 144–72. Dating from 1965, Eco could hardly know that he would be able to realize his fantasy and have the 007 character image—or at least one of them—embody the hero of his own film.

    As Eco himself concludes the essay: "Since the decoding of a message cannot be established by its author, but depends on the concrete circumstances of reception, it is difficult to guess what Fleming is or will be for his readers. When an act of communication provokes a response in public opinion, the definitive verification will take place not within the ambit of the book but in that of the society that reads

it" (p. 172). Can one say that the definitive verification of Fleming's Bond takes on new shape as it is turned into something in the interstices of a Perry Mason, a Sherlock Holmes, and a Captain Kirk?
4. Umberto Eco, *Postscript to The Name of the Rose*, trans. William Weaver (San Diego: Harcourt Brace Jovanovich, 1983), p. 2. Henceforth cited as *Postscript*.

CHAPTER 10

1. [This essay was first presented as a lecture at the State University of New York at Stony Brook when Julia Kristeva was Visiting Professor of Philosophy in the Fall 1988. She has graciously permitted us to publish it here.—Ed.]

CHAPTER 11   APPROACHES TO SEMIOETHICS

1. See Thomas Sebeok, Alfred Hayes, and Mary Catherine Bateson, eds. *Approaches to Semiotics*, Transactions of the Indiana University Conference on Paralinguistics and Kinesis (The Hague: Mouton, 1964).

Jean-Luc Marion writes of "*the* call as such." The semioethical call neither is nor has an "as" or a "such" and is not *kath auto* in the essentialist senses of these words. See Jean-Luc Marion, *Réduction et donation. Recherches sur Husserl, Heidegger et la phénoménologie* (Paris: Presses Universitaires de France, 1989), p. 295. See also Jacques Derrida, *Donner le temps*, 1, *La Fausse monnaie* (Paris: Galilée, 1991), pp. 72–4. Henceforth cited as *D*.

I say "in" rather than "at" the moment because we are to discover in a moment that a moment is a spread. Compare "In the moments he is about to sacrifice Isaac," Søren Kierkegaard, *Fear and Trembling*, eds. and trans. Edna and Howard Hong (Princeton: Princeton University Press, 1963), p. 74. I thank Jill Robbins for bringing this phrase to my attention. Compare also "In the same moment with his advent, he stepped aboard the steamer Fidéle, on the point of starting for New Orleans." Herman Melville, *The Confidence Man: His Masquerade* (Evanston: Northwestern University Press and the Newberrry Library, 1984). I thank Peggy Kamuf for bringing this sentence to my attention.

The main questions treated in this essay, the question of the tightness of the intertwining of the traces of Derrida and Levinas, is resumed in John Llewelyn, "En ce moment même. . . : une répétition qui n'en est pas une," forthcoming in the proceedings of the colloquium "Le Passage des Frontiéres (autour du travail de Jacques Derrida)" that took place at Cerisy la Salle in July 1992. For more sustained treatments see Robert Bernasconi, *Between Levinas and Derrida* (Bloomington: Indiana University Press, 1994) and Simon Critchley, *The Ethics of Deconstruction: Derrida and Levinas* (Oxford: Blackwell, 1992).

Section V of this essay owes much to participants in a seminar conducted by Robert Bernasconi and Paul Davies at DePaul University, Chicago, in 1991.

2. Ferdinand de Saussure, *Cours de linguistique générale* (Paris: Payot, 1971).
3. Jacques Derrida, *La voix et le phénomène* (Paris: Presses Universitaires de France, 1967), p. 17–18 ; *Speech and Phenomena*, trans. David B. Allison (Evanston: Northwestern University Press, 1973), p. 17. Henceforth cited as *VP* for the French and *SP* for the English translation.
4. Emmanuel Levinas, *Autrement qu'être ou au-delà de l'essence* (The Hague: Nijhoff, 1978), p. 46; *Otherwise than Being or Beyond Essence*, trans. Alphonso Lingis (The Hague: Nijhoff, 1981), p. 189. Henceforth cited as *AE* for the French and *OB* for the English translation.
5. Jacques Derrida, *Positions* (Paris: Minuit, 1972), p. 32–33; *Positions*, trans. Alan Bass (Chicago: University of Chicago Press, 1981), p. 22. Henceforth cited as *P* for the French and *P-trans* for the English translation.
6. Edmund Husserl, *Ideen zu einer reinen Phänomenologie und phänomenologischen Philosophie, I* (The Hague: Nijhoff, 1950), p. 312; *Ideas*, trans. W. R. Boyce Gibson (London: Allen and Unwin, 1931), p. 355. Henceforth cited as *Ideen* for the German and *Ideas* for the English translation.
7. Emmanuel Levinas, *En découvrant l'existence avec Husserl et Heidegger* (Paris: Vrin, 1982), p. 218 ff; *Collected Philosophical Papers*, trans. Alphonso Lingis (The Hague: Nijhoff, 1987), pp. 110 ff. Henceforth cited as *EDE* for the French and *CPP* for the English translation.
8. Jacques Derrida, *Marges de la philosophie* (Paris: Minuit, 1972), p. 112; *Margins of Philosophy*, trans. Alan Bass (Chicago: University of Chicago Press, 1982), pp. 95–96. Henceforth cited as *M* for the French and *MP* for the English translation.
9. Edmund Husserl, *L'origine de la géométrie*, trans. and introduction by Jacques Derrida (Paris: Presses Universitaires de France, 1962), pp. 44 ff; Jacques Derrida, *Edmund Husserl's Origin of Geometry*, trans. John P. Leavey (New York: Nicholas Hays, 1978), pp. 56 ff. Henceforth cited as *ODG* for the French and *HOG* for the English translation of Derrida's translation.
10. See *AE*, 95; *OB*, 75; as well as Emmanuel Levinas, *Du sacré au saint* (Paris: Minuit, 1977), pp. 132–48, and *Nine Talmudic Readings*, trans. Annette Aronowicz (Bloomington: Indiana University Press, 1990),

pp. 167–77. For further references, see Catherine Chalier, *Figures du féminin: Lecture d'Emmanuel Lévinas* (Paris: La nuit surveillée, 1982); also her "Ethics and the Feminine," and Tina Chanter, "Antigone's Dilemma," in Robert Bernasconi and Simon Critchley, eds., *Rereading Levinas* (Bloomington: Indiana University Press, 1991); Tina Chanter, "Feminism and the Other," in Robert Bernasconi and David Wood eds., *The Provocation of Levinas: Rethinking the Other* (London: Routledge, 1988); John Llewelyn, *The Middle Voice of Ecological Conscience: A Chiasmic Reading of Responsibility in the Neighborhood of Levinas, Heidegger and Others* (New York: St. Martin's Press, 1991), chapter 9.

11. Jacques Derrida, *Limited Inc, Glyph 2 Supplement* (Baltimore: The Johns Hopkins University Press, 1977), p. 81; *Limited Inc*, trans. Samuel Weber and Jeffrey Mehlman (Evanston: Northwestern University Press, 1988), pp. 109–10.

12. See Jacques Derrida and Pierre-Jean Labarrière, *Altérités* (Paris: Osiris, 1986), p. 75. Henceforth cited as *A*. See also Robert Bernasconi, "The Trace of Levinas in Derrida," in *Derrida and Différance*, eds. David Wood and Robert Bernasconi (Evanston: Northwestern University Press, 1988), pp. 13–29.

13. See Emmanuel Levinas, *Totalité et infini* (The Hague: Nijhoff, 1961, 4th ed., 1971), p. xiv; *Totality and Infinity*, trans. Alphonso Lingis (The Hague: Nijhoff, 1969), p. 26. Henceforth cited as *TI* and *TI-trans*. See also *A*, 70–75.

14. See Jacques Derrida, *De la grammatologie* (Paris: Minuit, 1967), p. 70–73; *Of Grammatology*, trans. Gayatri Chakravorty Spivak (Baltimore: The Johns Hopkins University Press, 1974), pp. 48–50. Henceforth cited as *G* for the French and *OG* for the English translation.

15. "Number of the Name shadowed by the Yes I Hear"? Are there also allusions to "the number of his name" of Revelation 13:17; to the Book named Numbers which tells of God addressing Moses in the Tabernacle of the Presence; and to *Nombres* by Philippe Sollers? Derrida writes of Sollers: "*Numbers* begins by putting the signer's name in an umbra. . . . No longer answerable to anyone, unjustifiable . . . *(Ne répond plus devant personne, injustifiable . . .)*" (*D*, 329, 296).

16. See Jacques Derrida, *Psyché: Inventions de l'autre* (Paris: Galilée, 1987), p. 648–49.

17. See Jacques Derrida, *Le Problème de la genèse dans la philosophie de Husserl* (Paris: Presses Universitaires de Paris, 1990). Henceforth cited as *PG*.

18. *Otherwise than Being or Beyond Essence* is dedicated:
To the memory of those who were closest among the six million assassinated by the National Socialists, and of the millions on millions

―――――――― NOTES TO CHAPTER 12 ――――――――

of all confessions and all nations, victims of the same hatred of the other man, the same anti-semitism.

On the same page is written, in Hebrew (I thank Peter Hayman for the translation), a list of the names of those who were closest, followed by the acronym for "May your soul be bound up in the bundle of life" (1 Samuel 25:29).
19. Emmanuel Levinas, *L'au-delà du verset* (Paris: Minuit, 1982), p. 157.
20. Jacques Derrida, *La Carte postale de Socrate à Freud et au-delà* (Paris: Flammarion, 1980), p. 205; *The Post Card: From Socrates to Freud and Beyond*, trans. Alan Bass (Chicago: University of Chicago Press, 1987), p. 190. See also *CPP*, 106 and *M*, 187; *MP*, 157.

CHAPTER 12   STUMPING THE SUN:
TOWARD A POST-METAPHORICS

1. Roland Barthes, *A Lover's Discourse*, translated by Richard Howard (New York: Hill and Wang, 1978), 215.
2. Aristotle, *Physics*, trans. P. H. Wicksteed and F. M. Cornford (Cambridge: Loeb, 1957), II, 193a–b, pp. 111–15.
3. Jacques Derrida, "White Mythology," in *The Margins of Philosophy*, trans. by Alan Bass (Chicago: University of Chicago Press, 1982), p. 209. Henceforth cited as *MP*.
4. cf. Aristotle's *Rhetoric* III, 10, 1410b10–19.
5. Homer, *Odyssey*, translated A. T. Murray (Cambridge: Loeb, 1919), 14.213–215. Henceforth cited as *O*.
6. Jean Starobinski, "The Inside and the Outside," in *The Hudson Review*, trans. Frederick Brown, 28:3 (Autumn 1975), p. 346. My thanks to Joel Shapiro for bringing this article to my attention. Henceforth cited as *I/O*.
7. For example, a "spot [*sema*] of white round like the moon" on a horse (*O*, 23.455).
8. *Iliad* 9.236–237; henceforth cited as *I*; cf. *I*, 2.53, 8.171, 13.244, *O* 21.413, "shewing forth his signs [*semata phainon*]" on the right; brightness can also be a sign of evil—"Brightest of all is he, yet withal is he a sign of evil" (*Iliad*, 22.30). Henceforth cited as *I*; cf.. There is one instance of a human—a woman—giving a sign as the internal reflection of Zeus' external signs (*O* 20.111).
9. Cf. *I* 2.814, 6.419, 7.86, 89, 10.415, 11.166, 21.322 (notice that *teteuxetai* is used here, as in *O*, 21.2341), 23.45, 255, 257, 24.16, 51, 349, 416, 755, 799, 801, *O*, 1.291, 2.222, 11.75.
10. Emmanuel Levinas, "Meaning and Sense," in *Collected Philosophical Papers*, trans. Alphonso Lingis (The Hague: Martinus Nijhoff, 1987), p.105.

293

CHAPTER 13   THE CARTOGRAPHY OF KNOWLEDGE AND
POWER: FOUCAULT RECONSIDERED

1. See, for example, Michel Foucault, "Questions of Geography," and "The Eye of Power," in *Power/Knowledge: Selected Interviews and Other Writings, 1972–1977*, ed. C. Gordon (New York: Pantheon, 1980). Henceforth cited as *P/K*. Also "Space Knowledge and Power," in *The Foucault Reader*, ed. Paul Rabinow (New York: Pantheon, 1984). Henceforth cited as *FR*.
2. See, for example, "The Subject and Power," and "On the Genealogy of Ethics: An Overview of Work in Progress," in *Michel Foucault: Beyond Structuralism and Hermeneutics*, eds. Herbert Dreyfus and Paul Rabinow (Chicago: University of Chicago Press, 1983). Henceforth cited as *BSH*.
3. The distinction between metaphoric and literal language of space is problematic of course, and can be maintained only with regard to a fixed context of use. Spatial metaphors are employed and displayed throughout Foucault's work, but especially in his earlier writings in literary theory. See Michel Foucault, "Preface to Transgression" and "Fantasia in the Library," in *Language, Counter-Memory, Practice: Selected Essays and Interviews*, trans. Donald Bouchard and Sherry Simon (Ithaca: Cornell University Press, 1977). Henceforth cited as *LCMP*. See also *Death and the Labyrinth: The World of Raymond Roussel* (Berkeley: University of California, 1986). Foucault explains his use of spatial metaphors to speak about discourse by the need to bypass "the model of individual consciousness with its intrinsic temporality." Spatial metaphors are "strategic"; they enable "one to grasp precisely the points at which discourses are transformed in, through and on the basis of relations of power" (*P/K*, 69–70).
4. Most notably in the *Birth of the Clinic: An Archeology of Medical Perception*, trans. A. M. Sheridan Smith (New York: Vintage, 1973) with not only its "primary," "secondary," and "tertiary spatialization[s]," but also spaces of "localization" and "configuration"(pp. 3–16). Henceforth cited as *BC*.
5. Alongside *The Birth of The Clinic*, Foucault was writing his book on Raymond Roussel; both books were published in 1963. As Gilles Deleuze has convincingly argued in *Foucault*, trans. and ed. Séan Hand (Minneapolis: University of Minnesota Press, 1986), Foucault's attention to visibility (and its relation to the language of things the space in which they both relate to and differ from each other) pervades both books (which in so many respects are so different). It also links them in a surprising way. Deleuze's *Foucault* is henceforth cited as *F*.

6. Cf., for example, Foucault's description of the deployment of "general hospitals" throughout France in the last hundred years of the *ancien régime*, (Michel Foucault, *Madness and Civilization*, trans. Richard Howard [New York: Pantheon, 1965], ch. 2. Henceforth cited as *MC*). The general hospital was a place that inhabited "a strange power that the king establishes between the police and the courts, at the limits of the law," in which the bourgeoisie mingled with the monarchy to the exclusion of the church. This exclusion pushed the church to reorganize its own network of closed institutions and compete with the court over the right and power to confine and provide aid to those who deserved confinement.
7. I have argued elsewhere, in Ophir, "Michel Foucault and the Semiotics of the Phenomenal," *Dialogue*, 27:3 (Fall 1988), pp. 387–415, that it is possible to reconstruct the fundamental difference between Foucault's three *epistemes* as a difference between three distinct modes of conceiving or arranging the phenomenal domain as a system of signs, and accordingly a difference between three types of relations between signifier and signified. In the Renaissance, signifieds could always appear on the phenomenal surface, becoming signifiers in their turn, but there was no fixed code or necessary ontological relation that linked the two. In the Classic *episteme*, signifiers and signified are related through fixed codes yet they are ontologically separated; the signifieds, whether Platonic Forms or types in a table, remain invisible in principle, never to be perceived (and hence never to become signifiers in their turn). In the modern *episteme*, the signified remains invisible, but it is ontologically related to its signifier. Signification occurs precisely because the signifier is a part or aspect of the signified that "expresses" the signified's hidden nature, and because it is the nature of the signified to be overtly manifested through various, partial expressions.
8. Foucault later summarizes this point in the *Archaeology of Knowledge*, trans. A. M. Sheridan-Smith (New York: Pantheon, 1972). Henceforth cited as *AK*. The constitution of the subject of medical discourse, the position of a doctor, who is at one and the same time the "direct questioner, the observing eye, the touching finger, the organ that decipher signs . . ." involves "a whole group of [spatial] relations." Those included the "relationship between the hospital space as a place of assistance, of purified, systematic observation, and of partially proved, partially experimental therapeutics, and a whole group of perceptual codes of the human body . . . relations between the doctor therapeutic role, his pedagogic role, his role as an intermediary in the diffusion of medical knowledge, and his role as a responsible representative of public health in the social space" (*AK*, 53).

9. Hillier and his colleagues at the University College, London, have been working for more than a decade on a sophisticated methodology for the articulation, formalization, and quantification, but also generation, of spatial relations in social space. Their spatial syntax is based on three simple distinctions: between *closed* and *open* cells; between a space *distributed* among cells that shape its form and structure collectively and a *non-distributed space* enclosed within one cell; and between *symmetrical* and *non-symmetrical* spatial relations. See B. Hillier and J. Hanson, *The Sociology of Space* (Cambridge: Cambridge University Press, 1984). Henceforth cited as *SocSpace*.
10. Classifying these three types of links I have already presupposed a three-dimensional conception of social space which I explicate below.
11. This section is based on my work in S. Shapin and A. Ophir, "The Place of Knowledge: A Methodological Survey," *Science in Context*, 4 (1991). Henceforth cited as *PKMS*.
12. See Foucault's remarks on the heterotopic nature of the Chinese encyclopedia in Borges in *The Order of Things* (New York: Pantheon, 1971), pp. xvi–xx. Henceforth cited as *OT*. See also "Of Other Spaces," *Diacritics* 16 (1986), p. 22. Henceforth cited as *OS*.
13. For a systematic survey of the (up to now not too extensive) literature concerning those early sites of knowledge see *PKMS*. An exemplary analysis of the site of a chemical laboratory is given in O. Hannoway, "Laboratory Design and the Aim of Science: Andreas Libavius versus Tycho Brahe," *Isis*, 77 (1986). The mechanical operatory of Robert Boyle is analyzed in detail, with deep sociological insights, in S. Shapin, "The House of Experiment in Seventeenth-Century England," *Isis*, 79 (1988). To this study and to some fruitful conversations with its author I owe a great debt.
14. On representation of objects as a problem of displacement and transmutation, see B. Latour, *Science in Action: How to Follow Scientists and Engineers through Society* (Milton Keynes: Open University Press, 1987), ch. 2; and, S. Shapin and S. Schaeffer, *Leviathan and the Air-Pump: Hobbes, Boyle and the Experimental Life* (New Jersey: Princeton University Press, 1985).
15. On the emergence of the museum of history see G. Bazin, *Le temps de musées* (Liege/Bruxelles: Desoer, 1967) and O. Impey and A. MacGregor, *The Origins of Museums* (Oxford: Clarendon Press, 1985).
16. It is plausible to expect, I think, that the more sophisticated a production process becomes, i.e., the more it involves the production and transmission of knowledge, the more heterotopic becomes the nature of its site. The high-tech plant may be a good example. See G. Kunda, *Engineering Culture: Control and Commitment in a High-tech Corporation* (Philadelphia: Temple University Press, 1992).

NOTES TO CHAPTER 13

17. At least insofar as philology deals with rare manuscripts. These can hardly be found today outside the archive, in which they are not simply stored but usually classified and arranged in ways that project on space divisions of time and genres, as well as genealogies of transcriptions. The library, according to Foucault, became really heterotopic, a site for the spatialization of history, only in the nineteenth century with the desire "to enclose in one place all times, all epochs, all forms, all tastes, and the idea of constituting a place for all time that is itself outside of time and inaccessible to its ravages" (*OS*, 26).
18. On the exchange between heterotopic and non-heterotopic sites in physics see P. Gallison, "The Trading Zone: Coordination between Experiment and Theory in the Modern Laboratory," (presented at the International Workshop on the Place of Knowledge, Tel Aviv and Jerusalem, May 1988).
19. However, this attempt to differentiate aspects or dimensions of social space may be understood in terms of the two distinct spatial settings *within* discourse. Here Foucault is trying to render social space itself into a "space of localization," the space in which social phenomena take place, and at the same time to understand that very same space as a "space of configuration" for a new group of objects. But whereas the theoretical aspects of social space are worthy of a serious theoretical effort, I am concerned here mainly with its relation to the production of knowledge through discursive practices and complexes of power/knowledge.
20. Residences, so it seems, are but one form of coexistence—with neighbors, animals, and objects, at least (*P/K*, 150). Local environmental conditions are essential only if one believes that objects—of discursive or non-discursive practices—with which one is concerned are directly affected by them. Finally, displacement is but one aspect of one's concern with territory and the social space at large.
21. There are "blocks," like the educational institution, Foucault observes, "in which the adjustment of abilities, the resources of communication, and power relations constitute regulated and concerted systems" (*P/K*, 150). These "blocks" are the disciplines, each of them being a perfect example of my "privileged place." But privileged places do not necessarily inhabit disciplinary institutions (e.g., the court; the temple, the place of the prophet), and unlike the disciplinary institutions, some blocks of power/knowledge are not emplaced in organized sites (e.g., the modern banking system, or the printed and electronic media).
22. Though the particular pattern chosen is significant, the differentiation of rooms in a house is always part of a certain form of power relations among its inhabitants (cf. *P/K*, 148–49).

23. Barthes claims, for example, that photography has become the place of death in modern culture. See Roland Barthes, *Camera Lucida: Reflections on Photography*, trans. Richard Howard (New York: Hill and Wang, 1981). This suggestion should be taken literally, I think, meaning the metaphorization of certain cultural phenomena, the encounter with death in Barthes' case, the fact that direct experience becomes inaccessible, always mediated through its representations. But those metaphorical places would always have a necessary material-spatial component such as the tangible photograph. Cultural agencies, then, distribute reproductions all over the social space.
24. Spatial syntax cannot be reduced to spatial semantics, even when the semantics of social space is utterly intelligible and the meaning of symbols created by spatial formations is obvious and evident. In fact, whenever social meaning is embodied in spatial elements there are more cells designated by a special mark that specifies them and makes them unchangeable vis-à-vis other cells in the same space. In other words, more semantics means more constraints on possible spatial relations, on movement and visibility. See *SocSpace*, pp. 9–18, 207–22.
25. See the work of Jacques Revel, who reconstructs the growth transformations of the "knowledge of the territory" of the French state, from the beginning of the monarchy to the Third Republic (J. Revel, "Knowledge of the Territory," *Science in Context*, 4:1 (1991).
26. See *AK*, p. 17. Also Michel Foucault, *Technologies of the Self: A Seminar with Michel Foucault*, eds. L. Martin, H. Gutman, and P. Hutton (Amherst: University of Massachusetts Press, 1988), p. 15.
27. See *BSH*, p. 237. A somewhat different description of the "modes by which in our culture, human beings are made subjects" is given in another late interview, "The Subject and Power" (also in *BSH*). See also Rabinow's Introduction to *FR*, pp. 7–11.
28. It is usually acknowledged that "the most general theme of Foucault's work has been the problem of the subject" (*FR*, 12). But with the shifting of attention to self and self-formation it may seem that Foucault retrospectively projects a unifying theme on his work. See T. McCarthy, "The Critique of Impure Reason: Foucault and the Frankfurt School," in *Ideals and Illusions* (Cambridge, MA: MIT Press, 1991). Henceforth cited as *II*. This is a mistake that results, I believe, from an overemphasis on Foucault's shift from the formation of the self by others to patterns of self-formation. The theme of the care of the self is not a return to the modern subject or to a modern concept of freedom but an attempt to examine ways the self did in the past and may in the present participate in its own formation and resist the forces of normalization.

NOTES TO CHAPTER 13

29. See Jean-Paul Sartre, *Critique of Dialectical Reason*, trans. Alan Sheridan-Smith (London: New Left Books and Atlantic Highlands, NJ: Humanities Press, 1976).
30. See Claude Lévi-Strauss, *The Savage Mind* (Chicago: University of Chicago Press, 1967).
31. The embodiment of the subject too, of course. However, the body in Foucault has received much attention, whereas the spatialization of embodiment has not. The body of the condemned prisoner, the body of the homosexual who has come out of his closet, or the body of the woman constantly on an ever changing diet, as well as the soul of the authentic self, of the criminal pervert, or of the neurotic mother, are constituted in and through mechanisms of spatialization. Note also that by no means do I claim that Foucauldian genealogies may be reduced to or exhausted by this kind of spatial reconstruction.
32. See the discussion in A. Kirby, *The Politics of Location* (London: Methuen, 1982). Henceforth cited as *PL*.
33. See Michel Foucault, "The Order of Discourse," in *Untying the Text*, ed. R. Young (London: Routledge and Kegan Paul, 1981), pp. 56–64. Henceforth cited as *UT*.
34. The geographers have much to say about this: see *PL* and also D. Harvey, *The Limits to Capital* (Oxford: Blackwell, 1982), chs. 12–13.
35. The ancient Greeks, for example, inscribed in the civic-space of their *polis* the main lines of differentiation between the Greek male and his "others": the barbarian, the slave, woman, and child. See P. Vidal-Naquet, *The Black Hunter: Forms of Thought and Forms of Society in the Greek World* (Baltimore: Johns Hopkins University Press, 1986); A. Ophir, *Plato's Invisible Cities: Discourse and Power in Plato's Republic* (London: Routledge, 1990). In primitive culture, spatial arrangements are said to strictly embody and express social stratification and norms, so strictly indeed, that one effective way to destroy such a culture would be to force it to change its spatial arrangement (see Lévi-Strauss, *Tristes tropiques: An Anthropological Study of Primitive Societies in Brazil* (New York: Athenaeum, 1970), p. 204. In modern societies, the "collective memory" of a culture is supposed to be inscribed in the spatial order within houses and through the entire city's outdoor architecture, carrying with it the horizons of one's identity as a member to that culture (See M. Hallbwachs, *The Collective Memory* (New York: Harper, 1980).
36. Martin Heidegger, *Being and Time*, trans. John Macquarrie and Edward Robinson (New York: Harper and Row, 1962), sec. 70.
37. In *The Order of Things*, Foucault discusses the constitution of the temporality of the objects of a given discourse or *epistemé* (*OT*, 150–57). In his inaugural lecture at the Collège de France, he speaks about the

temporality of discourse itself, but he also exemplifies it in the very form and gesture of his speech act. See *UT*. In both cases temporality does not precede discourse or condition it from without; it is one of the categories of experience which discourse itself makes possible.

38. This was Foucault's position at least until the first volume of the *History of Sexuality*. As Deleuze puts it: "For a long time Foucault thought about the outside [of the self] as complete spatiality which is deeper than time; but in his later works he suggests the possibility of bringing time back to the outside and of thinking the outside as time" (*F*, 108). Hence the late return to Heidegger, exemplified in the introduction to the second volume: Michel Foucault, *The History of Sexuality*, vol. 2, *The Use of Pleasure* (New York: Vintage Books, 1985), pp. 6–7.

39. However, one abandons the grounding, not the transcendental. The search for the transcendental has become a search for the regularity of historical formations, a search for order in the Archive. The formulation of the transcendental is not derived or deduced from anywhere. It is a result of a hermeneutic practice and should be taken as an hypothesis put forward to be tested and refuted. See A. Ophir, "Des Ordres dans l'Archive," *Annales*, 3 (May–June 1990).

40. Many among Foucault's readers and critics have pointed out the implicit transcendental status of the Archaeology. See *BSH*, ch. 3; B. Brown and M. Cousins, "The Linguistic Fault: The Case of Foucault's Archaeology," *Economy and Society*, 9:3 (1980); Manfred Frank, *What is Neostructuralism?* (Minneapolis: University of Minnesota Press, 1989), ch. 11. According to the semiotic interpretation of the notion of the *epistemé*, underlying each *epistemé*, there is a fundamental semiotic relation—between the visible and the invisible, between the signifier and the signified—that constrains and enables experience in a given period. The semiotic relation plays the role of historical *a priori* in each period, but the table of semiotic relation is strictly speaking transcendental.

41. This is true despite the deconstruction of the Kantian subject in the last chapters of *The Order of Things*. In the early sixties Foucault published a French translation of Kant's *Anthropology* to which he wrote an introduction. In the eighties he dealt again with Kantian themes, especially in his famous lecture on Kant's "Was ist die Aufklärung?" (see *FR*). Foucault distinguished between two philosophical traditions that started with Kant, the analytical-transcendental tradition—with the three critiques—and the interpretative-historical tradition—with the lesser, historical writing. He clearly places himself in the second tradition. Against this self-description, I would like

to stress Foucault's affinity to the Kant of the transcendental consciousness, whose timeless structure Foucault tried to bring back to history. On this aspect of Foucault's work, see *F*, pp. 60–69.

42. Phenomena may be related and differentiated according to their positions in a geometrical space, but the geometrical space is only one possibility of spatialization. In painting, geography, anthropology, or medicine, spatial relations are usually conceived through non-geometrical grids, as spatial relations between physical phenomena they were conceived throughout the Middle Ages.

43. From this follows an important difference between spatialization in Foucault and Heidegger's concept of "Worlding" and the spatialization of *Dasein*, or Derrida's notion of the spatiality of any sign system, of *écriture*, and therefore of discourse.

44. Hans-Georg Gadamer, *Truth and Method*, trans. and ed. Garrett Barden and John Cumming (New York: Continuum, 1960), pp. 225–40.

45. See A. Giddens, *The Constitution of Society* (Cambridge: Polity Press, 1984). Henceforth cited as *CS*.

46. Other possible "quasi-transcendental" grids that try to map social space and understand its possible forms of organization were proposed by social theorists and geographers, especially of the school of "human geography." See, for example, *PL* and also T. Hagerstrand, *Innovation Diffusion as a Spatial Process* (Chicago: University of Chicago Press, 1967). A necessary comparative analysis of these different approaches lies beyond the scope of this paper.

47. "Discourse" itself, with the grid that it implies (of enunciative functions, modalities of reproduction, spatialization, materialization, etc.), will no doubt disappear when Foucauldian and Foucauldian-like discourses will be replaced by other theoretical discourses or by whatever will then designate such intellectual processes. This is an inevitable consequence of the historicist position to which Foucault is committed. Does this commitment mean that one cannot try transcendental hypotheses? No, I think it only means that one should never forget that they are but hypotheses and that one can never bootstrap oneself from within the hermeneutic circle in order to ground them.

48. See Habermas's three systems of relations: to the objective world, to the inter-subjective social world, and to the self. In particular, see Jürgen Habermas, *The Theory of Communicative Action*, vol. 1 (Boston: Beacon Press, 1984), chs. 1 and 3, esp. pp. 84 ff. See also *II*, 453–54.

SELECTIVE BIBLIOGRAPHY

CULTURAL SEMIOSIS: TRACING THE SIGNIFIER

Hélène Volat

GENERAL:

Adams, Hazard, and Leroy Searle, eds. *Critical Theory Since 1965*. Tallahassee: University of Florida Press, 1986.

Bannet, Eve Taylor. *Structuralism and the Logic of Dissent: Barthes, Derrida, Foucault, Lacan*. Urbana: University of Illinois Press, 1989.

Berger, Arthur. *Signs in Contemporary Culture: An Introduction to Semiotics*. New York: Longman, 1984.

Bergoffen, Debra B. "'Sophocles' *Antigone* and Freud's *Civilization and Its Discontents*." *American Imago*, 43:2 (1986), 151–167.

Blanchard, Marc Eli. *Description: Sign, Self, Desire. Critical Theory in the Wake of Semiotics*. New York: Mouton, 1980.

Blonsky, Marshall. *On Signs*. Baltimore: Johns Hopkins University Press, 1985.

Brumethe, Peter, and David Wills, eds. *Deconstruction and the Visual Arts: Art, Media, and Architecture*. Cambridge: Cambridge University Press, 1994.

Bryson, Norman, ed. *Calligram: Essays in New Art History from France*. Cambridge: Cambridge University Press, 1988.

Cadavo, Eduardo, Peter Connor, and Jean-Luc Nancy, eds. *Who Comes after the Subject?* New York and London: Routledge, 1991.

Carravetta, Peter. "Repositioning Interpretive Discourse: From 'The Crisis of Reason' to 'Weak Thought.' " *Differentia*, 2 (1987): 83–126.

———. *Prefaces to the Diaphora; Rhetorics, Allegory, and the Interpretation of Postmodernity*. West Lafayette: Purdue University Press, 1991.

———. *Il fantasma di Hermes; saggio su metodo, retorica, interpretare*. Lecce: Milella, 1994.

Carroll, David. *Paraesthetics: Foucault, Lyotard, Derrida*. New York: Methuen, 1987.

Certeau, Michel de. *Heterologies: Discourse on the Other*. Minneapolis: University of Minnesota Press, 1986.

Coward, R., and J. Ellis. *Language and Materialism: Developments in Semiology and the Theory of the Subject*. London and Boston: Routledge, 1977.

Culler, Jonathan. *Framing the Signs: Criticism and its Institutions*. Norman: University of Oklahoma Press, 1988.

———. *The Pursuit of Signs: Semiotics, Literature, Deconstruction*. Ithaca: Cornell University Press, 1981.

Deely, John. *Introducing Semiotics: Its History and Doctrine*. Bloomington: Indiana University Press, 1982.

Deely, John, Brooke Williams, and Patricia E. Kruse, eds. *Frontiers in Semiotics*. Bloomington: Indiana University Press, 1986.

De George, Richard and Fernande, eds. *Structuralism From Marx to Lévi-Strauss*. Garden City: Doubleday, 1972.

Deleuze, Gilles, and Félix Guattari. *On the Line*. New York: Semiotext(e), 1983.

De Man, Paul. *Allegories of Reading: Figural Language in Rousseau, Nietzsche, Rilke and Proust*. New Haven: Yale University Press, 1979.

Descombes, Vincent. *Objects of All Sorts: A Philosophical Grammar*. Baltimore: Johns Hopkins University Press, 1986.

During, Simon, ed. *The Cultural Studies Reader*. London and New York: Routledge, 1993.

Easthope, Anthony. *British Post-Structuralism Since 1968*. New York: Routledge, 1988.

Eco, Umberto, M. Santambrogio, and P. Violi, eds. *Meaning and Mental Representation*. Bloomington: Indiana University Press, 1988.

Frank, Manfred. *What is Neostructuralism?* Trans. Sabine Wilke and Richard Gray. Minneapolis: University of Minnesota Press, 1989.

Gadamer, Hans-Georg. *Truth and Method*. Trans. and ed. Garrett Barden and John Cumming. New York: Continuum, 1975, 1979.

Garvin, Harry, ed. *Phenomenology, Structuralism, Semiology*. Lewisburg: Bucknell University Press, 1976.

Gillan, Garth. *From Sign to Symbol*. Altlantic Highlands: Humanities Press, 1982.

Gozich, Wlad. *The Culture of Literacy*. Cambridge: Harvard University Press, 1994.

Greimas, A. J. *On Meaning: Selected Writings in Semiotic Theory*. Minneapolis: University of Minnesota Press, 1987.

Haley, Michael C. *The Semeiosis of Poetic Metaphor*. Bloomington: Indiana University Press, 1988.

Hart, Kevin. *The Trespass of the Sign: Deconstruction, Theology and Philosophy*. New York: Cambridge University Press, 1989.

Harvey, Robert. "Sartre/Cinema: Spectator/Art Which Is Not One." *Cinema Journal* (Spring 1991).

Harvey, Sander. *Semiotic Perspectives*. London: Allen & Unwin, 1982.

Hawkes, Terence. *Structuralism and Semiotics*. Berkeley: University of California Press, 1977.

Heidegger, Martin. *Being and Time*. Trans. John Macquarrie and John Robinson. New York: Harper and Row, 1962. New translation from Joan Stambaugh. Albany: SUNY Press, 1996.

Husserl, Edmund. *Logical Investigations*. 2 vols. Trans. J. N. Findlay. London: Routledge and Kegan Paul, 1970.

Huyssen, Andreas. *After the Great Divide: Modernism, Mass Culture, Postmodernism*. Bloomington: Indiana University Press, 1987.

Irigaray, Luce. *This Sex Which Is Not One*. Ithaca: Cornell University Press, 1985.

Jameson, Fredric. *The Prison House of Language*. Princeton: Princeton University Press, 1972.

———. *Postmodernism, The Cultural Logic of Late Capitalism*. Durham: Duke University Press, 1991.

Jardine, Alice. *Gynesis*. Ithaca: Cornell University Press, 1985.

Kaplan, Alice Y. *Reproductions of Banality: Fascism, Literature and French Intellectual Life*. Minneapolis: University of Minnesota Press, 1986.

Katz, Jerrold. *The Philosophy of Linguistics*. Oxford: Oxford University Press, 1985.

Kearney, Richard. *Poetics of Imagining*. London: Harper Collins, 1991.

———. *Poetics of Modernity*. Atlantic Highlands: Humanities Press, 1995.

Kevelson, Roberta. *Inlaws/Outlaws; A Semiotics of Systemic Interaction*. Bloomington: Indiana University Press, 1977.

Lanigan, Richard L. *Phenomenology of Communication: Merleau-Ponty's Thematics in Communicology and Semiology*. Pittsburgh: Duquesne University Press, 1988.

Lanigan, Richard L., ed. *Semiotics and Phenomenology*. Amsterdam: Mouton, 1982. Special issue of *Semiotica*, 41:1–4 (1982).

Lindsay, Cecile. "Experiments in Postmodern Dialogue." *Diacritics*, 14:3 (Fall 1984), 53–62.

Lingis, Alphonso. *Sensation: Intelligibility in Sensibility*. Atlantic Highlands: Humanities Press, 1996.

MacCabe, Colin. *Tracing the Signifier: Theoretical Essays, Film, Linguistics, Literature*. Minneapolis: University of Minnesota Press, 1985.

MacCannell, Dean. *The Time of the Sign: A Semiotic Interpretation of Modern Culture*. Bloomington: Indiana University Press, 1982.

Martin, Wallace. *Recent Theories of Narrative*. Ithaca: Cornell University Press, 1986.

Merrell, Floyd. *Semiotic Foundations: Steps Toward an Epistemology of Written Texts*. Bloomington: Indiana University Press, 1982.

Metz, Christian. *The Imaginary Signifier: Psychoanalysis and the Cinema*. Bloomington: Indiana University Press, 1982.

Morris, Charles. "Foundations of the Theory of Signs." In *Foundations of the Unity of Science*. 2 vols. Eds. Otto Neurath, Rudolf Carnap, and Charles Morris. Chicago and London: University of Chicago Press, 1971. Vol. 1: 77–137.

SELECTIVE BIBLIOGRAPHY

Nancy, Jean-Luc. *The Gravity of Thought*. Trans. F. Raffoul and Gregery Recco. Atlantic Highlands: Humanities Press, 1997.

Neuman, Mark, and Michael Payne, eds. *Self, Sign and Symbol*. Lewisburg: Bucknell University Press, 1987.

Nietzsche, Friedrich. *The Gay Science*. Trans. Walter Kaufmann. New York: Vintage, 1974.

Nöth, Winfied, ed. *Handbook of Semiotics*. Bloomington: Indiana University Press, 1990.

Ophir, Adi. *Plato's Invisible Cities: Discourse and Power in Plato's Republic*. London: Routledge, 1991.

Pavel, Thomas G. *The Feud of Language: A History of Structuralist Thought*. Oxford: Blackwell, 1989.

Peirce, Charles S. *Philosophical Writings*. Ed. Justus Buchler. New York: Dover, 1955.

Pinto, Julio. *The Reading of Time: A Semantico-Semiotic Approach*. New York: Mouton, 1989.

Posner, Roland. *Rational Discourse and Poetic Communication: Methods of Linguistic, Literary and Philosophical Analysis*. Berlin: Mouton, 1982.

Rapaport, Herman. *Heidegger and Derrida: Reflections on Time and Language*. Lincoln: University of Nebraska Press, 1989.

Riddel, Joseph. "Coup de Man; Or, the Uses and Abuses of Semiotics." *Cultural Critique*, 4 (Fall 1986), 81–109.

Riffaterre, Michael. *Fictional Truth*. Baltimore: John Hopkins University Press, 1990.

Schleifer, Ronald. *A. J. Greimas and the Nature of Meaning: Linguistics, Semiotics and Discourse Theory*. Lincoln: University of Nebraska Press, 1987.

Scholes, Robert. *Semiotics and Interpretation*. New Haven: Yale University Press, 1982.

Sebeok, Thomas, Alfred Hayes, and Mary Catherine Bateson, eds. *Approaches to Semiotics*, Transactions of the Indiana University Conference on Paralinguistics and Kinesis. The Hague: Mouton, 1964.

Sebeok, Thomas A. *American Signatures: Semiotic Inquiry and Method*. Norman: University of Oklahoma Press, 1992.

Sebeok, Thomas A., and Jean Umiker-Sebeok, eds. *The Semiotic Sphere*. New York: Plenum Press, 1986.

Silverman, Hugh J. *Writing the Politics of Difference*. Albany: SUNY Press, 1991.

———. *Textualities: Between Hermeneutics and Deconstruction*. New York and London: Routledge, 1994.

Silverman, Hugh J. *Inscriptions: Between Phenomenology and Structuralism*. London and New York: Routledge, 1987. Second edition: *Inscriptions: After Phenomenology and Structuralism*. Evanston: Northeastern University Press, 1997.

Silverman, Hugh J., and Gary E. Aylesworth, eds. *The Textual Sublime: Deconstruction and its Differences*. Albany: SUNY Press, 1990.

Silverman, Kaja. *The Subject of Semiotics*. New York: Oxford University Press, 1983.

Sinha, Chris. *Language and Representation: A Socio-naturalistic Approach to Human Development*. New York: New York University Press, 1988.

Solomon, Jack. *The Signs of Our Time: Semiotics, the Hidden Message of Environments, Objects and Cultural Images*. New York: St. Martin's Press, 1988.

Spivak, Gayatri. *In Other Worlds*. New York: Routledge, 1988.

Taylor, Mark C., and Esa Saarinen. *Imagologies: Media Philosophy*. London and New York: Routledge, 1994.

Tejera, Victorino. *Semiotics: From Peirce to Barthes*. Leiden: E. J. Brill, 1988.

Thibault, Paul J. *Social Semiotics as Praxis*. Minneapolis: University of Minnesota Press, 1991.

Tyler, Stephen A. *The Unspeakable: Discourse, Dialogue and Rhetoric in the Postmodern World*. Madison: University of Wisconsin Press, 1987.

Vattimo, Gianni. *The End of Modernity*. Trans. Jon R. Snyder. Baltimore: Johns Hopkins University Press, 1988.

Wurzer, Wilhelm S. *Filming and Judgment: Between Heidegger and Adorno*. New Jersey: Humanities Press International, 1990.

Zima, Peter, ed. *Semiotics and Dialectics. Ideology and the Text*. Amsterdam: Benjamins, 1981.

BARTHES, Roland

Original Texts

Elements of Semiology. Trans. Annette Lavers and Colin Smith. New York: Hill & Wang, 1968.

Critical Essays. Trans. Richard Howard. Evanston: Northwestern University Press, 1972.

Mythologies. Trans. Annette Lavers. New York: Hill & Wang, 1972.

S/Z. Trans. Richard Miller. New York: Noonday, 1974.

Pleasure of the Text. Trans. Richard Miller. New York: Noonday, 1975.

Roland Barthes by Roland Barthes. Trans. Richard Howard. New York: Hall and Wang, 1977.

A Lover's Discourse. Trans. Richard Howard. New York: Hill & Wang, 1978.

New Critical Essays. Trans. Richard Howard. New York: Hill and Wang, 1980.

Camera Lucida: Reflections on Photography. Trans. Richard Howard. New York: Hill and Wang, 1981.
Empire of Signs. Trans. Richard Howard. New York: Hill and Wang, 1982.
A Roland Barthes Reader. Ed. Susan Sontag. New York: Hill and Wang, 1982.
The Grain of the Voice: Interviews 1962–80. Trans. Linda Coverdale. New York: Hill and Wang, 1984.
The Responsibility of Forms: Critical Essays on Music, Art and Representation. Trans. Richard Howard. New York: Hill & Wang, 1985.
The Rustle of Language. Trans. Richard Howard. New York: Hill & Wang, 1986.
Criticism and Truth. Trans. Katrine Pilcher Keuneman. Minneapolis: University of Minnesota Press, 1987.
The Semiotic Challenge. Trans. Richard Howard. New York: Hill & Wang, 1988.

On Barthes

Bryson, Norman, and Mieka Bal. "Semiotics and Art History." *Art Bulletin*, LXXIII, June 1991, 174–208.
Calvet, Louis-Jean. *Roland Barthes: A Biography.* Trans. Sarah Wykes. Bloomington: Indiana University Press, 1995.
Culler, Jonathan. *Roland Barthes.* New York: Oxford University Press, 1983.
Freedman, Sanford, and C. A. Taylor. *Roland Barthes: A Bibliographical Reader's Guide.* New York: Garland, 1983.
Lavers, Annette. *Roland Barthes: Structuralism and After.* Cambridge: Harvard University Press, 1982.
Thody, Philip. *Roland Barthes: A Conservative Estimate.* London: Macmillan, 1977.
Ungar, Steven, *Roland Barthes: The Professor of Desire.* Lincoln: University of Nebraska Press, 1983.
Ungar, Steven, and Betty McGraw, eds. *Signs in Culture: Roland Barthes Today.* Iowa City: University of Iowa Press, 1989.
Wasserman, Georges R. *Roland Barthes.* Boston: Twayne, 1981.
Wiseman, Mary Bittner. *The Ecstasies of Roland Barthes.* London and New York: Routledge, 1989.

DERRIDA, Jacques

Original Texts

Speech and Phenomena and Other Essays on Husserl's Theory of Signs. Trans. David B. Allison. Evanston: Northwestern University Press, 1973, 1979.

─────────── SELECTIVE BIBLIOGRAPHY ───────────

Of Grammatology. Trans. Gayatri Chakravorty Spivak. Baltimore: Johns Hopkins University Press, 1975.
Writing and Difference. Trans. Alan Bass. Chicago: University of Chicago Press, 1978.
Dissemination. Trans. Barbara Johnson. Chicago: University of Chicago Press, 1981.
Positions. Trans. Alan Bass. Chicago: University of Chicago Press, 1981.
Margins of Philosophy. Trans. Alan Bass. Chicago: University of Chicago Press, 1982.
Signéponge/Signsponge. Trans. Richard Rand. New York: Columbia University Press, 1984.
The Post Card: From Socrates to Freud and Beyond. Trans. Alan Bass. Chicago: University of Chicago Press, 1987.
The Truth in Painting. Trans. Geoffrey Bennington and Ian McLeod. Chicago: University of Chicago Press, 1987.
Limited Inc. Ed. Gerald Gaff and trans. Samuel Weber and Jeffrey Mehlman. Evanston: Northwestern University Press, 1988.
A Derrida Reader. Ed. Peggy Kamuf. New York: Columbia, 1990.
The Gift of Death. Trans. David Wills. Chicago: University of Chicago Press, 1990.
Acts of Literature. Ed. Derek Attridge. New York and London: Routledge, 1992.
Jacques Derrida. Trans. Geoffrey Bennington. Chicago: The University of Chicago Press, 1993.

On Derrida

Argyros, Alex. "Narratives of the Future: Heidegger and Derrida on Technology." *New Orleans Review*, 17:2 (Summer 1990), 53–58.
Bernasconi, Robert. *Between Levinas and Derrida*. Bloomington: Indiana University Press, 1994.
Carlshamre, Staffan. *Language and Time: An Attempt to Arrest the Thought of Jacques Derrida*. Goteborg: Acta Universitatis Gothoburgensis, 1986.
Casey, Edward S. "Origin(s) In (Of) Heidegger/Derrida." *Journal of Philosophy*, 81 (1984), 601–10.
Critchley, Simon. *The Ethics of Deconstruction: Derrida and Levinas*. Oxford: Blackwell, 1992.
Culler, Jonathan. "Jacques Derrida." In *Structuralism and Since: From Levi-Strauss to Derrida*. Ed. John Sturrock. London: Oxford University Press, 1979, 154–80.
Cumming, Robert D. "The Odd Couple: Heidegger and Derrida." *Review of Metaphysics*, 34 (1981), 487–521.
Gasché, Rodolphe. *The Faces of the Manor: Derrida and the Philosophy of Reflection*. Cambridge: Harvard University Press, 1986.

SELECTIVE BIBLIOGRAPHY

Hartman, Geoffrey. *Saving the Text: Philosophy/Derrida/Literature*. Baltimore: Johns Hopkins University Press, 1982.

Harvey, Irene. *Derrida and the Economy of Différance*. Bloomington: Indiana University Press, 1986.

Holland, Nancy. "Heidegger and Derrida Redux: A Close Reading." In *Hermeneutics and Deconstruction*. Eds. Hugh J. Silverman and Don Ihde. Albany: SUNY Press, 1985, 24–32.

Hoy, David Couzens. "Deciding Derrida: On the Work (and Play) of the French Philosopher." *London Review of Books*, 4:3 (1982), 3–5.

Krupnick, Mark, ed. *Displacement: Derrida and After*. Bloomington: Indiana University Press, 1983.

Lawlor, Leonard R. *Imagination and Chance: The Difference between Paul Ricoeur and Jacques Derrida*. Albany: SUNY Press, 1993.

Liszka, James J. "Derrida: Philosophy of the Liminal." *Man and World*, 16 (1983), 233–50.

Llewelyn, John. *Derrida on the Threshold of Sense*. London: Macmillan, 1986.

Magliola, Robert. *Derrida on the Mend*. West Lafayette: Purdue University Press, 1985.

Melville, Stephen. *Philosophy Beside Itself: On Deconstruction and Modernism*. Minneapolis: University of Minnesota Press, 1986.

Norris, Christopher. *Deconstruction: Theory and Practice*. New York and London: Methuen, 1982.

———. *Derrida*. London: Fontana Modern Masters, 1987.

Sallis, John. "Heidegger/Derrida—Presence." *Journal of Philosophy*, 81 (1984), 594–601.

Sallis, John, ed. *Deconstruction and Philosophy: The Texts of Jacques Derrida*. Chicago: University of Chicago Press, 1987.

Sheehan, Thomas J. "Derrida and Heidegger." In *Hermeneutics and Deconstruction*. Eds. Hugh J. Silveman and Don Ihde. Albany: SUNY Press, 1985, 201–18.

Silverman, Hugh J. "Self-Decentering: Derrida Incorporated." *Research in Phenomenology*, 8 (1978), pp. 45–65.

Silverman, Hugh J., ed. *Derrida and Deconstruction*. London and New York: Routledge, 1989.

Staten, Henry. *Wittgenstein and Derrida*. Lincoln: University of Nebraska Press, 1985.

Stewart, Garrett. "Lit et rature: 'An Earsignted View.' " *Lit: Literature Interpretation Theory*, 1:1–2 (Dec. 1989), 1–18.

Wood, David. "Derrida and the Paradoxes of Reflection." *Journal of British Society for Phenomenology*, 11:3 (1980), 225–38.

———. "Heidegger and Derrida." *Research in Phenomenology*, 17 (1987), 132–49.

———. *The Deconstruction of Time*. Atlantic Highlands: Humanities Press, 1989.
Wood, David, ed. *Derrida: A Critical Reader*. Oxford: Blackwell, 1992.
Wood, David, and Robert Bernasconi, eds. *Derrida and 'Différance.'* Evanston: Northwestern University Press, 1988.

ECO, Umberto

Original Texts

A Theory of Semiotics. Bloomington: Indiana University Press, 1976.
The Role of the Reader: Explorations in the Semiotics of Texts. Bloomington: Indiana University Press, 1979.
The Name of the Rose. Trans. William Weaver. San Diego: Harcourt, Brace, Jovanovich, 1983.
Postscript to the Name of the Rose. Trans. William Weaver. New York: Harcourt, 1984.
Semiotics and the Philosophy of Language. Bloomington: Indiana University Press, 1984.
Art and Beauty in the Middle Ages. Trans. Hugh Bredin. New Haven: Yale University Press, 1986.
On the Medieval Theory of Signs. Eds. Umberto Eco and C. Marmo. Philadelphia: Benjamins, 1989.
The Open Work. Trans. Anna Concogni. Cambridge: Harvard University Press, 1989.
The Poetics of Chaosmos. Trans. Ellen Esnock. Cambridge: Harvard University Press, 1989.
Travels in Hyperreality. Trans. William Weaver. Bloomington: Indiana University Press, 1989.
The Limits of Interpretation. Bloomington: Indiana University Press, 1990.

On Eco

Bettetini, Gianfranco, and Francesco Casetti, "Semiotics in Italy." In *The Semiotic Sphere*. Eds. Thomas Sebeok and Jean Umiker-Sebeok. New York: Plenum Press, 1986, 293–321.
Capozzi, Rocco. "Palimpsests and Laughter: The Dialogical Pleasure of Unlimited Intertextuality in *The Name of the Rose*." *Italica,* 66:4 (Winter 1989), 412–428.
Collette, Carolyn. "Umberto Eco, Semiotics and the Merchant's Tale." *The Chaucer Review*, 24:2 (1989), 132–138.

Colomb, Gregory. "Semiotics since Eco (I) & (II)." *Papers on Language and Literature*, 15:4&5 (Summer and Fall 1980), 442–59.
Corti, Maria, "Fatta di segni la dea di Eco." *Il Giorno*, 2 (April 1975)
De Lauretis, Teresa. *Umberto Eco*. Firenze: La Nuova Italia, 1981.
Deely, John. "The Doctrine of Sign: Taking Form at Last." *Semiotica*, 18:2 (1976), 171–193.
Innis, Robert. "Review" in *International Philosophical Quarterly*, 20:6 (1980), 221–232.
Luke, Allan. "Open and Closed Texts: The Ideological/Semantic Analysis of Textbook Narratives," *Journal of Pragmatics*. 13:1 (Feb. 1989), 53–80.
John Walker. "Comments on Umberto Eco's Book 'A Theory of Semiotics.'" *Leonardo*, 10 (1977), 131–32.

FOUCAULT, Michel

Original Texts

Madness and Civilization: History of Insanity in the Age of Reason. Trans. Richard Howard. New York: Pantheon, 1965.
The Order of Things: An Archeology of the Human Sciences. Trans. anon. New York: Pantheon, 1970, 1971.
The Archaeology of Knowledge. Trans. A. M. Sheridan-Smith. New York: Pantheon, 1972, 1976.
The Birth of the Clinic. Trans. A. M. Sheridan-Smith. New York: Vintage Books, 1973.
The History of Sexuality. Vol. 1. Trans. Robert Hurley. New York: Vintage Books, 1976.
Discipline and Punish: The Birth of the Prison. Trans. Alan Sheridan. New York: Pantheon, 1977.
Language, Counter-memory, Practice: Selected Essays and Interviews. Ed. (with an introduction by) D. F. Bouchard. Trans. D. F. Bouchard and Sherry Simon. Ithaca: Cornell University Press, 1977.
Power/Knowledge. Selected Interviews and Other Writings (1972–1977). Ed. and trans. C. Gordon. New York: Pantheon Books, 1980.
"The Order of Discourse." In *Untying the Text: A Post Structuralist Reader*. Ed. Robert Young. Boston: Routledge & Kegan Paul, 1981.
The Foucault Reader. Ed. Paul Rabinow. New York: Pantheon Books, 1984.
The History of Sexuality. Vol. 2. *The Use of Pleasure*. Trans. Robert Hurley. New York: Vintage Books, 1985.
Death and the Labyrinth: The World of Raymond Roussel. Trans. Charles Ruas. Berkeley: University of California, 1986.
The History of Sexuality. Vol. 3. *The Care of the Self*. Trans. Robert Hurley. New York: Vintage Books, 1986.

Politics, Philosophy, Culture: Interviews and Other Writings (1977–1984). Ed. (with introduction by) Lawrence Kritzman. Trans. Alan Sheridan and others. New York: Routledge, 1988.

Technologies of the Self: A Seminar with Michel Foucault. Eds. L. Martin, H. Gutman, and P. Hutton. Amherst: University of Massachusetts Press, 1988.

On Foucault

Bernauer, James. *Foucault's Force of Flight.* Atlantic Highlands: Humanities Press, 1990.

Boyne, Roy. *Foucault and Derrida: The Other Side of Reason.* Boston: Unwin & Hyman, 1990.

Deleuze, Gilles. *Foucault.* Minneapolis: University of Minnesota Press, 1986.

Dreyfus, Hubert, and Paul Rabinow, eds. *Michel Foucault: Beyond Structuralism and Hermeneutics.* Chicago: University of Chicago Press, 1983.

Gane, Mike, ed. *Towards a Critique of Foucault.* New York: Routledge, 1986.

Hoy, David, ed. *Foucault: A Critical Reader.* New York: Blackwell, 1986.

Mahon, Michael. *Foucault's Nietzschean Genealogy: Truth, Power and the Subject.* Albany: SUNY Press, 1992.

Ophir, Adi. "Michel Foucault and the Semiotics of the Phenomenal." *Dialogue,* 27:3 (Fall 1988), 387–15.

Pheby, Keith. *Intervention: Displacing the Metaphysical Subject.* Washington: Maisonneuve Press, 1988.

Poster, Mark. *Critical Theory and Post-structuralism: In Search of a Context.* Ithaca: Cornell University Press, 1989.

Racevskis, Karlis. *Michel Foucault and the Subversion of the Intellect.* Ithaca: Cornell University Press, 1983.

Shapin, S., and Adi Ophir. "The Place of Knowledge: A Methodological Survey." *Science in Context,* 4 (1991).

KRISTEVA, Julia

Original Texts

Essays in Semiotics/Essais de sémiotique. Eds. Julia Kristeva, Josette Rey-Debove, Donna Jean Umiker. The Hague: Mouton, 1971.

"The Semiotic Activity." *Screen,* 14:1–2 (Spring-Summer 1973), 25–39.

"Four Types of Signifying Practice." *Semiotext(e),* 1 (Winter 1974), 65–74.

"Semiology and Grammatology." Interview of Jacques Derrida by Julia Kristeva. In Jacques Derrida, *Positions.* Trans. and annotated Alan Bass. Chicago: University of Chicago Press, 1975, 15–26.

"The Subject in Signifying Practice." *Semiotext(e),* 1:3, (1975), 19–26.

Desire in Language: A Semiotic Approach to Literature and Art. Ed. Leon S. Roudiez. Trans. Thomas Gora, Alice Jardine, and Leon S. Roudiez. New York: Columbia University Press, 1980.
Powers of Horror. Trans. Leon S. Roudiez. New York: Columbia University Press, 1982.
Revolution in Poetic Language. Trans. Margaret Waller. New York: Columbia University Press, 1984.
The Kristeva Reader. Ed. Toril Moi. New York: Columbia University Press, 1986.
Tales of Love. Trans. Leon S. Roudiez. New York: Columbia University Press, 1987.
In the Beginning Was Love: Psychoanalysis and Faith. Trans. Arthur Goldhammer. New York: Columbia University Press, 1988.
Black Sun. Trans. Leon S. Roudiez. New York: Columbia University Press, 1989.
Language, the Unknown. An Initiation into Linguistics. Trans. Anne M. Menke. New York: Columbia University Press, 1989.
Strangers to Ourselves. Trans. Leon S. Roudiez. New York: Columbia University Press, 1991.
Nations without Nationalism. Trans. Leon S. Roudiez. New York: Columbia University Press, 1993.

On Kristeva

Brandt, Joan. "The Systematics of a Non-System: Julia Kristeva's Revisionary Semiotics." *The American Journal of Semiotics*, 5:1 (1987), 133–50.
Butler, Judith. *Gender Trouble*. New York: Routledge, 1990.
Coward, Rosalind. "Julia Kristeva in Conversation with Rosalind Coward." *Desire, ICA Documents*. London: Institute for Contemporary Arts, 1984.
Crownfield, David, ed. *Body/Text in Julia Kristeva*. Albany: State University of New York Press, 1992.
Fletcher, John, and Andrew Benjamin, eds. *Abjection, Melancholia and Love: The Work of Julia Kristeva*. London and New York: Routledge, 1990.
Fraser, Nancy, and Sandra Lee Bauthy, eds. *Revaluing French Femmism*. Bloomington: Indiana University Press, 1992.
Jones, Ann Rosalind. "Writing the Body: Towards an Understanding of l'Écriture féminine." *Feminist Studies*, 7:2 (Summer 1981), 247–63.
Lechte, John. *Julia Kristeva*. London and New York: Routledge, 1990.
Lewis, Philip. "Revolutionary Semiotics." *Diacritics*, 4:2 (Fall 1974), 28–32.
Lipkowitz, I., and A. Loselle. "An Interview with Julia Kristeva." *Critical Texts*, 3:3 (1986).

Marchak, Catherine. "The Joy of Transgression: Bataille and Kristeva." *Philosophy Today* (Winter 1990), 354–63.
Oliver, Kelly, ed. *Ethics, Politics, and Difference in Julia Kristeva's Writing.* New York: Routledge, 1993.
Oliver, Kelly. *Reading Kristeva: Unraveling the Double-bind.* Bloomington: Indiana University Press, 1993.
Richman, Michelle. "Sex and Signs: The Language of French Feminist Criticism." *Language and Style,* 13 (Fall 1980), 62–80.
Salleh, Kay. "On the Dialectics of Signifying Practice." *Thesis Eleven,* 5/6 (1982), 72–84.
Wason, Peter, and Ormond Uren. "The Semantics of Semiotics." *The New Society,* 30 (Dec. 26, 1974), 812–14.

LACAN, Jacques

Original Texts

The Language of the Self: Speech and Language in Psychoanalysis. Trans. Anthony Wilden. Baltimore: Johns Hopkins University Press, 1968, 1981.
"Desire and the Interpretation of Desire in Hamlet." In *Literature and Psychoanalyses.* Ed. Shoshana Felman. Baltimore: Johns Hopkins University Press, 1982, 11–52.
Écrits: A Selection. Trans. Alan Sheridan. New York: Norton, 1977.
Four Fundamental Concepts of Psychoanalysis. Trans. Alan Sheridan. New York: W. W. Norton & Co., 1978.
The Ego in Freud's Theory and in the Technique of Psychoanalysis. Trans. Sylvana Tomaselli. New York: W. W. Norton and Co., 1988.
The Seminar of Jacques Lacan: Freud's Papers on Technique, 1953–54. Book I. Trans. John Forrester. Cambridge: Cambridge University Press, 1988.

On Lacan

Borch-Jacobsen, Mikhel. *Lacan: The Absolute Master.* Stanford: Stanford University Press, 1991.
Clark, Michael. *Jacques Lacan. An Annotated Bibliography.* New York: Garland, 1988.
Davis, Robert Con, ed. *The Fictional Father: Lacanian Readings of the Text.* Amherst: University of Massachusetts Press, 1981.
———. *Lacan and Narration: The Psychological Difference in Narrative Theory.* Baltimore: Johns Hopkins University Press, 1984.
Gallop, Jane. *Reading Lacan.* Ithaca: Cornell University Press, 1985.

Glogowski, James. "The Psychoanalytic Textuality of Jacques Lacan." *Prose Studies*, 11:3 (Dec. 1988), 13–20.
Hogan, P. C., and L. Pandit, eds. *Criticism and Lacan: Essays and Dialogue on Language, Structure and the Unconscious*. Athens: University of Georgia Press, 1990.
Lacoue-Labarthe, Philippe, and Jean-Luc Nancy. *The Title of the Letter: A Reading of Lacan*. Trans. François Raffoul and David Pettigrew. Albany: State University of New York Press, 1992.
Lang, Hermann. *Language and the Unconscious: Jacques Lacan's Humanities of Psychoanalysis*. Trans. Thomas P. Buchalman. Atlantic Highlands: Humanities Press, 1997.
MacCannell, Juliet Flower. *Figuring Lacan: Criticism and the Cultural Unconscious*. Lincoln: University of Nebraska Press, 1986.
Muller, John P., and William J. Richardson. *Lacan and Language: A Reader's Guide to Écrits*. New York: International University, 1982.
Raffoul, François, and David Pettigrew, eds. *Disseminating Lacan*. Albany: SUNY Press, 1996.
Richardson, William J. "Lacan and Non-Philosophy." In *Philosophy and Non-Philosophy since Merleau-Ponty, Continental Philosophy I*. Ed. Hugh J. Silverman. New York and London: Routledge, 1988, 120–135.
Smith, Joseph, and W. Kerrigan. *Interpreting Lacan*. New Haven: Yale University Press, 1983.

LYOTARD, Jean-François

Original Texts

"The Differend, the Referent and the Proper Name." Trans. George Van Den Abbeele. *Diacritics*, 14:3 (Fall 1984), 4–14.
The Postmodern Condition: A Report on Knowledge. Trans. Geoff Bennington and Brian Massumi. Minneapolis: University of Minnesota Press, 1984.
Just Gaming. Trans. Wlad Gozich. Minneapolis: University of Minnesota Press, 1985.
Toward the Postmodern. Eds. Robert Harvey and Mark Roberts. Atlantic Highlands: Humanities Press, 1993.

On Lyotard

Bennington, Geoff. "Lyotard: From Discourse and Figure to Experimentation and Event." *Paragraph*, 6 (Oct. 1985), 19–27.
Dews, Peter. *Logics of Disintegration: Post-Structuralist Thought and the Claims of Critical Theory*. New York: Verso, 1987.
Diacritics, 14:3 (Fall 1984). Special issue. *Jean-François Lyotard*.

Leo, John R., "Postmodernity, Narratives, Sexual Politics: Reflections on Jean-François Lyotard." *The Centennial Review*, 32:4 (Fall 1988), 336–350.

Lindsay, Cecile. "Experiments in Postmodern Dialogue." *Diacritics*, 14:3 (Fall 1984), 52–62.

Silverman, Hugh J. "Trances of the Sublime: Visibility, Expressivity, and the Unconscious." In Veronique Foti, ed. *Merleau-Ponty: Materiality Painting*. Atlantic Highlands: Humanities Press, 1996.

MERLEAU-PONTY, Maurice

Original Texts

Phenomenology of Perception. Trans. Colin Smith. New York: Routledge, 1962.

The Primacy of Perception. Ed. James M. Edie. Evanston: Northwestern University Press, 1964.

Sense and Nonsense. Trans. Hubert L. Dreyfus and Patricia A. Dreyfus. Evanston: Northwestern University Press, 1964.

Signs. Trans. (with an introduction by) Richard C. McCleary. Evanston: Northwestern University Press, 1964.

The Visible and the Invisible. Trans. Alphonso Lingis. Evanston: Northwestern University Press, 1968.

Consciousness and the Acquisition of Language. Trans. Hugh J. Silverman. Evanston: Northwestern University Press, 1973.

The Prose of the World. Trans. John O'Neill. Evanston: Northwestern University Press, 1973.

Texts and Dialogues: On Philosophy, Politics, and Cultural Understanding. Eds. Hugh J. Silverman and James Barry Jr. Atlantic Highlands: Humanities Press, 1992.

On Merleau-Ponty

Busch, Thomas W., and Shaun Gallagher, eds. *Merleau-Ponty: Humanities and Postmodernism*. Albany: SUNY Press, 1992.

Dillon, M. C. *Merleau-Ponty's Ontology*. Bloomington: Indiana University Press, 1988.

———. *Merleau-Ponty Vivant*. Albany: SUNY Press, 1991.

———. *Écart and Différance: Merleau-Ponty and Derrida on Seeing and Writing*. Atlantic Highlands: Humanities Press, 1996.

Fóti, Véronique, ed. *Merleau-Ponty: Difference, Materiality, Painting*. Atlantic Highlands: Humanities Press, 1996.

Hoeller, Keith, ed. *Merleau-Ponty and Psychology*. Atlantic Highlands: Humanities Press, 1993.

Johnson, Galen A. *The Merleau-Ponty Aesthetics Reader*. Evanston: Northwestern University Press, 1993.
Johnson, Galen A., and Michael B. Smith, eds. *Ontology and Alterity in Merleau-Ponty*. Evanston: Northwestern University Press, 1987.
Lanigan, Richard L. *Speaking and Semiology: Maurice Merleau-Ponty's Theory of Existential Communication*. The Hague: Mouton, 1972.
Silverman, Hugh J. *Inscriptions: After Phenomonology and Structuralism*. Evanston: Northwestern University Press, 1997.
Silverman, Hugh J., ed. *Philosophy and Non-Philosophy since Merleau-Ponty*. London and New York: Routledge, 1988. New Edition: Evanston: Northwestern University Press, 1997.
Silverman, Hugh J., Algis Mickumas, Theodore Kisiel, and Alphonso Lingis, eds. *The Horizons of Continental Philosophy: Essays on Husserl, Heidegger, and Merleau-Ponty*. Dordrecht: Kluwer, 1988.
Silverman, Hugh J., John Sallis, and Thomas Seebohm, eds. *Continental Philosophy in America*. Pittsburgh: Duquesne University Press, 1983.

SAUSSURE, Ferdinand de

Original Texts

Course in General Linguistics. Trans. W. Baskin. New York: McGraw-Hill, 1959.
Course in General Linguistics. Eds. C. Bally and A. Sechelaye, in collaboration with A. Reidlinger. Trans. Roy Harris. London: Duckworth, 1983.

On Saussure

Culler, Jonathan. *Ferdinand de Saussure*. New York: Penguin, 1976.
Gadet, Françoise. *Saussure and Contemporary Culture*. London: Radius/Century Hutchinson, 1989.
Harris, Roy. *Reading Saussure: A Critical Commentary on the Cours de Linguistique Générale*. La Salle: Open Court, 1987.
Koerner, E. F. K. *Bibliographia Saussureana, 1870–1970. An Annotated, Classified Bibliography on the Background, Development, and Actual Relevance of Ferdinand de Saussure's General Theory of Language*. Metuchen: Scarecrow, 1972.
Silverman, Hugh J. "French Structuralism and After: de Saussure, Lévi-Strauss, Barthes, Lacan, Foucault." In *Continental Philosophy in the 20th Century*, ed. Richard Kearney. London and New York: Routledge, 1994, 390–408.

Starobinski, Jean. *Words upon Words. The Anagrams of Ferdinand de Saussure*. New Haven: Yale University Press, 1979.

Strozier, Robert. *Saussure, Derrida and the Metaphysics of Subjectivity*. New York: Mouton, 1988.

SINI, Carlo

Original Text

Images of Truth: From Sign to Symbol. Trans. Massimo Verdicchio. Atlantic Highlands: Humanities Press, 1993.

On Sini

Carrera, Alessandro. "What Happened to Being? On Hermeneutics and Unlimited Semiosis in Carlo Sini and Gianni Vattimo." In *RLA: Romance Languages Annual, 1989*. Eds. Ben Lawton and Anthony Tamburri. West Lafayette, Indiana: Purdue Research Foundation, 1990, 94–97.

NOTES ON CONTRIBUTORS

M. ALISON ARNETT

M. Alison Arnett is completing a doctorate in Philosophy at Boston College. She is writing specifically on Hannah Arendt and her role as a philosopher and thinker in America.

DEBORAH B. BERGOFFEN

Deborah B. Bergoffen is Professor of Philosophy and Women's Studies at George Mason University where she chaired the Department of Philosophy and Religion from 1980 to 1987 and received the university's Distinguished Faculty Award in 1989. She was Executive Co-Director of the Society for Phenomenology and Existential Philosophy from 1993–96. Recent publications include "Casting Shadows: The Body in Descartes, Sartre, de Beauvoir and Lacan," "Posthumous Popularity: Reading, Privileging, Politicizing Nietzsche," and "The Body Politic: Democratic Metaphors, Totalitarian Practices, Erotic Rebellions." Her new book is entitled *The Philosophy of Simone de Beauvoir: Gendered Phenomenologies, Erotic Generosities* (SUNY Press, 1996).

PETER CARRAVETTA

Peter Carravetta is Professor of Italian at Queens College, CUNY. He is editor of *Differentia: Journal of Italian Thought* and has edited with P. Spedicato *Postmoderno e letteratura: Percorsi e visioni della critica in America* (Bompiani, 1984). He is author of *Prefaces to the Diaphora: Rhetorics, Allegory, and the Interpretation of Postmodernity* (Purdue University Press, 1991).

ALESSANDRO CARRERA

Alessandro Carrera teaches Italian Literature at New York University and collaborates with the Italian Cultural Institute in New York. He taught previously at the University of Houston and McMaster University in Hamilton, Ontario. Carrera has published a number of books, two on music: *Musica e pubblico giovanile* (Feltrinelli, 1980) and *La musica e la psiche* (Riza, 1984); one in philosophy: *L'esperienza dell'istante. Metafisica, tempo, scrittura* (Lanfranchi, 1995); one novel *La torre e la pianura* (Udine, 1994); and three collections of poems: *La resurrezione delle cose* (Milan, 1988); *La ricerca della maturità* (Udine, 1992); and *The Perfect Bride/La sposa perfetta* (1992).

JULIA KRISTEVA

Julia Kristeva is professor of Linguistics at the University of Paris–VII. She also teaches regularly as a Visiting Professor at Columbia University and has been Visiting Professor at the State University of New York at Stony Brook. *The Kristeva Reader,* edited by Toril Moi, is published by Blackwell (1986). Her many books published by Columbia University Press in English include *Revolution in Poetic Language* (1984), *Desire in Language* (1984), *Powers of Horror* (1982), *Tales of Love* (1987), *In the Beginning was Love: Psychoanalysis and Faith* (1988), *Language: The Unknown* (1989), *Black Sun: Depression and Melancholia* (1989), *Strangers to Ourselves* (1991), *Nations without Nationalism* (1993), *The Old Man and the Wolves* (1994), *Time and Senses: Proust and the Experience of Literature* (1996), and *New Maladies of the Soul* (1996). Her novels include *Samurai* (1992).

JOHN LLEWELYN

John Llewelyn has held teaching positions as Reader in Philosophy at the University of Edinburgh (Scotland), Arthur J. Schmitt Visiting Professor of Philosophy at Loyola University of Chicago and Visiting Professor at the University of Memphis. He is the author of a number of books including *Beyond Metaphysics?: The Hermeneutic Circle in Contemporary Continental Philosophy* (Humanities Press, 1985), *Derrida and the Thresholds of Sense* (Macmillan, 1986), *The Middle Voice of Ecological Conscience: A Chiasmic Reading of Responsibility in the Neighborhood of Levinas, Heidegger and Others* (Macmillan/St. Martin's Press, 1991), and *Emmanuel Levinas: The Genealogy of Ethics* (Routledge, 1996).

MICHAEL NAAS

Michael Naas is Associate Professor of Philosophy at DePaul University. He has written articles on ancient Greek literature and philosophy and on contemporary French thought. He is the author of *Turning: From Persuasion to Philosophy* (Humanities Press, 1994) and is the co-translator of Jacques Derrida's *The Other Heading* (Indiana University Press, 1992), *Memoirs of the Blind* (University of Chicago Press, 1993), and *The Hyphen—the Judeo-Christian Connection* (Humanities Press, forthcoming 1997) by Jean-François Lyotard and Eberhard Gruber.

KELLY OLIVER

Kelly Oliver is Associate Professor of Philosophy at the University of Texas at Austin. She is author of *Reading Kristeva: Unraveling the Double-bind* (Indiana University Press, 1993) and *Womanizing Nietzsche: French Readings of the Figure of Woman* (Routledge, 1995). She edited *Ethics, Politics, and Difference in Julia Kristeva's Writing* (Routledge, 1993) and co-edited an issue of *Hypatia* (Spring, 1992) on philosophy and language.

ADI OPHIR

Adi Ophir teaches in the Institute for History and Philosophy of Science and Ideas in the School of History at Tel Aviv University in Israel. He is author of *Plato's Invisible Cities: Discourse and Power*

―――――― CONTRIBUTORS ――――――

in Plato's Republic (Routledge, 1990), and of articles such as "Michel Foucault and the Semiotics of the Phenomenal," *Dialogue* (1988); "The Semiotics of Power: Reading Michel Foucault's Discipline and Punish," *Manuscrito* (1989); "Des Ordres dans l'archive," *Annales* (1990); and "A Place of Knowledge Recreated: The Library of Michel de Montaigne," *Science In Context* (1991).

FRANÇOIS RAFFOUL

François Raffoul is an *ancien élève* of the École Normal Superieure (St. Cloud). He holds a doctorate in Philosophy from the École des Hautes Études en Sciences Sociales from Paris and has taught French at Yale University and Philosophy at the State University of New York at Stony Brook. He is author of *Heidegger and the Subject* (Humanities Press, 1997) and has translated (with David Pettigrew) J-L. Nancy and P. Lacoue-Labarthe, *The Title of the Letter* (SUNY Press, 1992) and Francoise Dastur, *Heidegger and the Question of Time*, and (with Greg Recco), J-L. Nancy, *The Gravity of Thought* (Humanities Press, 1997). He also edited (with D. Pettigrew) *Disseminating Lacan* (SUNY Press, 1996).

MARK ROBERTS

Mark Roberts teaches Philosophy at Suffolk Community College, at Dowling College, and at the State University of New York at Stony Brook. He co-translated and co-edited Mikel Dufrenne's *In the Presence of the Sensuous: Essays in Aesthetics* (Humanities Press, 1987) and Jean-François Lyotard's *Toward the Postmodern* (Humanities Press, 1993).

STEPHANIE JOHN SAGE

Stephanie John Sage holds a master's degree in Art History and Criticism from the State University of New York at Stony Brook.

CONTRIBUTORS

About the Editor
HUGH J. SILVERMAN

Hugh J. Silverman is Professor of Philosophy and Comparative Literature at the State University of New York at Stony Brook. He has held visiting teaching positions at the Universities of Warwick and Leeds (England), the Université de Nice (France), the Università di Torino (Italy), the Universität-Wien (Austria), the University of Helsinki (Finland), and at Stanford University, Duquesne University, and New York University in the United States. He is Executive Director of the International Association for Philosophy and Literature and previously served for six years as Executive Co-Director of the Society for Phenomenology and Existential Philosophy (1980–86). Author of *Inscriptions: Between Phenomenology and Structuralism* (Routledge, 1987), *Textualities: Between Hermeneutics and Deconstruction* (Routledge, 1994), and numerous book chapters and articles in continental philosophy, aesthetics, philosophical psychology, and literary/cultural theory, he has lectured widely in North America, Britain, and Continental Europe. He is editor of *Writing the Politics of Difference* (SUNY Press, 1991) and *Piaget, Philosophy and the Human Sciences* (Humanities/Harvester, 1980; Northwestern University Press, 1997), and co-editor of *Jean-Paul Sartre: Contemporary Approaches to his Philosophy* (Duquesne/Harvester, 1980), *Continental Philosophy in America* (Duquesne, 1983), *Descriptions* (SUNY Press, 1985), *Hermeneutics and Deconstruction* (SUNY Press, 1985), *Critical and Dialectical Phenomenology* (SUNY Press, 1987), *The Horizons of Continental Philosophy: Essays on Husserl, Heidegger, and Merleau-Ponty* (Nijhoff/Kluwer, 1988), *Postmodernism and Continental Philosophy* (SUNY Press, 1988), *The Textual Sublime: Deconstruction and its Differences* (SUNY Press, 1990), Merleau-Ponty's *Texts and Dialogues: On Philosophy, Politics, and Cultural Understanding* (Humanities Press, 1992, 1996), and *Textualität der Philosophie—Philosophie und Literatur* (Oldenbourg, 1994), as well as the first five volumes in the *Continental Philosophy* series: *Philosophy and Non-Philosophy since Merleau-Ponty* (Routledge, 1988; Northwestern University Press, 1997), *Derrida and Deconstruction* (Routledge, 1989), *Postmodernism—Philosophy and the Arts* (Routledge, 1990), *Gadamer and Hermeneutics* (Routledge, 1991), *Questioning Foundations: Truth/ Subjectivity/ Culture* (Routledge, 1993).